Racism
Postrace

ROOPALI MUKHERJEE | SARAH BANET-WEISER | HERMAN GRAY, EDITORS

Racism
Postrace

DUKE UNIVERSITY PRESS

Durham and London

2019

© 2019 Duke University Press
Printed and bound by CPI Group (UK) Ltd, Croydon, CR0 4YY
Designed by Julienne Alexander
Typeset in Garamond Premier Pro and Helvetica LT Std
by Westchester Publishing Services

Library of Congress Cataloging-in-Publication Data
Names: Mukherjee, Roopali, editor. | Banet-Weiser, Sarah,
[date] editor. | Gray, Herman, [date] editor.
Title: Racism Postrace / Roopali Mukherjee, Sarah Banet-Weiser,
and Herman Gray, editors.
Description: Durham : Duke University Press, 2019. |
Includes bibliographical references and index.
Identifiers: LCCN 2018044275 (print)
LCCN 2019000354 (ebook)
ISBN 9781478003250 (ebook)
ISBN 9781478001386 (hardcover : alk. paper)
ISBN 9781478001805 (pbk. : alk. paper)
Subjects: LCSH: Post-racialism—United States. | Race
awareness—United States. | Racism—United States.
| Ethnicity—United States—Psychological aspects.
| United States—Race relations—Psychological aspects. |
Ethnicity—United States—Philosophy.
| United States—Race relations—Philosophy.
Classification: LCC E184.A1 (ebook) | LCC E184.A1 R334 2019
(print) | DDC 305.800973—dc23
LC record available at https://lccn.loc.gov/2018044275

Cover art: *Notes for a Poem on the Third World (chapter one).*
2018. © Glenn Ligon, Courtesy Regen Projects, Los Angeles.

Contents

PART TWO Performances

Introduction

Postrace Racial Projects

SARAH BANET-WEISER, ROOPALI MUKHERJEE,
AND HERMAN GRAY

As objects of study go, the concept of postrace has proved at once sticky and slippery—sticky in terms of its adhesive and adaptive grasp on public consciousness (Bobo 2014) and slippery in its ambivalence on race and difference, and unsettling of paradigmatic struggles for racial justice and equality. By most accounts, the term entered the US popular lexicon over the course of raucous electoral campaigns in 2008, which culminated in the election of the first African American to the US presidency. Received meanings of the term generally signify a repudiation of racial discrimination and racism, indeed, of racial categories themselves as meaningful. Ushered in by complex shifts in demographics, marriage and immigration trends, and youth attitudes set in contrast with the racial sentiments of older generations, postrace articulated rosy views of racial assimilation and an alacritous stance on diversity and difference. Circulating with enthusiasm across the political and ideological spectrum, including in the Left and liberal press, through viral circuits of social media, among public figures, and within the performative repertoires of the 2008 campaign itself, Barack Obama's unprecedented victory emerged as nothing short of "epochal," cleaving time itself, as filmmaker Spike Lee put it, "from B.B., Before Barack to A.B., After Barack" (quoted in Colapinto 2008).[1] As news reports, op-ed columns, popular media, and book-length commentaries indulged celebrations of "Americans as they might wish to be seen: fair-minded, freedom loving, and racially harmonious" (C. A. Young and Song 2014, 1071), the 2008 election took shape as "trailblazing" and "historic" (Herbert 2008), promising a "particularly American achievement, an affirmation of American ideals and a celebration of American circumstances" (Wallace-Wells 2006, B1). As "the last of the republic's old barriers to entry come tumbling down" (Alter 2006), putting "a period on the sorriest chapter in American history" (Morris 2007), news headlines heralded, at long last, "the end of race as we know it" (Early 2008), speculating on "the end of black politics" (Bai 2008) and "the end of white America" (Hsu 2009). A sign of its currency in popular culture, the term found its way into the *Urban Dictionary*, defined, in plain terms, as "a society or time period in which discussions around race and racism have been deemed no longer relevant within current social dynamics." Making a familiar temporal link, the dictionary added, "Popularized after the election of Barack Obama to the presidency of the United States of America in 2008." On November 4, 2008, in the giddy euphoria of election night celebrations, perfectly on cue, a black voter from California proclaimed, "Color has no meaning and Obama has proved it" (quoted in Feldmann 2008, 25). Likewise, paraphrasing a jubilant white voter, the *Atlantic*'s Twitter feed summed things up, announcing: "Glad the battle btwn black & white, slave & slave owner finally over."[2]

Obviously, the battle was far from over, for the concept of postrace also mobilized a different, far less rosy response. If Obama's 2008 victory worked to shore up postracialism's vaunted status within the cultural imaginary, the historic campaign and presidency witnessed, with equal fervor, the emergence of new "born-again" racisms (Goldberg, 2009, 21; Kelley 2011) shaped in their continuities with older cultural logics of white racial grievance but also articulating new and distinct formations of whiteness, racial discrimination, and antiblack racisms. If postracialism spurred breathless proclamations about the end of racism in 2008, the moment also shored up support for populist formations of the Tea Party and birtherism, and vigilant strains of anti-immigrant, Islamophobic, and xenophobic sentiments with open calls to hunt "terrorists," "criminals," and "illegals" (Enck-Wanzer 2011; Joseph 2011). By 2016, strident proclamations about the "forgotten" white working class had helped to recalibrate forms of racist license, recuperating and reopening

US political discourse to regressive pre–civil rights–era racial appeals and delivering stunning electoral dividends a mere eight years later.

In turn, these reactionary strains of racism spurred and energized a vast array of social movements, including in support of the Obama administration's 2012 Deferred Action for Childhood Arrivals (DACA) policies; mass mobilizations in support of undocumented workers and opposing state violence in "antiterror" and border detention camps; academic boycotts opposing the occupation of Palestine; the Black Lives Matter movement, which drew attention to and organized against spectacular and deadly encounters of militarized police against unarmed black men and women; and city, municipal, and campus sanctuary resolutions in the wake of the Trump administration's repeal of DACA and new policies like the "travel ban" and "extreme vetting" to limit US entry for immigrants and refugees from predominantly Muslim countries. These mobilizations, which are linked in their resistance to deeply racialized forms of state violence, repression, and surveillance, work variously to loosen the sticky resonance of postracialism and its euphoric promise of racial justice, equality, and progress. Likewise, puncturing what Catherine Squires (2014) terms the "post-racial mystique," research reports, analyses, and studies prior to, during, and since the 2008 election present a staggering dossier of counterevidence, underscoring a brutal range of abiding and, indeed, deepening inequalities tracking familiar axes of ethnoracial difference. Thus, for example, as these studies show, public schools across the United States have grown more, not less, racially segregated since the landmark *Brown v. Board of Education* Supreme Court decision in 1954 (Hannah-Jones 2017; Reardon et al. 2012; US General Accounting Office 2016). Only 67 percent of Latino/as have access to affordable health care (US Department of Health and Human Services 2011). Black children still attend consistently underfunded schools (Yin 2017) and are 61 percent more at risk of being conscripted into the school-to-prison pipeline (Amurao 2013; McMillan Cottom 2017). Latinos were nearly twice as likely—and African Americans a staggering five times more likely—to be incarcerated than whites (Sakala 2014), and the imprisonment rate for black women was twice that of white women (Alexander 2011; Haney López 2010, 2011; Wilson Gilmore 2007). Black family income, on average, remains at little more than half that of white families nationwide (Black Demographics 2012; DeNavas-Walt et al. 2013; DeSilver 2013; Heckman 2011; Oliver and Shapiro 2006). In 2015, despite some improvements, Latinos still earned only 69 percent of white men's earnings, and Latinas remained lowest in income comparisons with white men, earning 58 cents on every white man's dollar (compared with 65 cents for black women, and 82 cents for white women) (Patten 2016).

Against these findings, proclamations of a postracial society, instead, work to obscure the relations of structural racisms, concocting a heady palliative against the continuing resonance and necessity of progressive antiracist struggle (E. R. Edwards 2011; Roediger 2006). Open to the lash of ridicule and scorn and, at the same time, celebrated within national scripts of racial transcendence and progress, the discursive career of postrace emerges, thus, ambivalent and unsettled but also productive and generative, profound in its affective grasp on the cultural imaginary and dangerous in its capacities to confound and stymie struggles for racial justice and equality. Indeed, in the context of rising white nationalisms across the world (Da Costa 2016), manifesting in, among other things, the visible recurrence of white nationalist rallies in the United States and the Trump administration's lenient response to them, renewed efforts to criminalize public protest and mass demonstrations, and continued attempts to redraw voting districts as a means to disenfranchise nonwhite voters, postracial promises of "freedom" clearly do not mean freedom for all people.

It is this halting and tendentious career, the quality of its influence on contemporary racial formations as well as its power to structure—as well as trouble—modes of racism and antiracism that this book explores. We trace rich expressions of postracialism over and through a wide cultural terrain—in public policy debates, academic disputes, popular cultural performances, media expressions, sport cultures, technology industries, music, and fashion spectacles. At once absurd and alluring, these fragmentary, and often contradictory, meanings of postrace reveal the subtle but pervasive exigencies of power and powerlessness, and the range of social, political, and economic interests at stake in both the articulations and the structuring silences that postrace coheres. Enshrining specific orderings of racial experience and circumstance as rational and normal, while marginalizing others as laughable, odd, or dangerous, the range of cultural meanings associated with postrace offers us a point of entry for critical interrogation into the discursive, affective, and material problem of the color line in the current moment. Among its core contributions, then, this book is dedicated, first and foremost, to parsing the meanings and mythic orders of postrace, unpacking in careful detail the dynamics and consequences of social power as they designate, authorize, and normalize specific connotations of race and racism.

Additionally, this book recognizes the real and deadly effects of postrace, taking stock of the historical, politico-economic, and cultural implications of its emergence as the "racial common sense" in the United States. Our concern here is with the ways that media representations and affective resonances bear critically on their capacities to make the world. As such, we approach post-race as a construct with real political and material consequences, and the cases we showcase in the book grapple with the links between the structural and cultural productivities of the postracial, unpacking the mythic registers and relationships of postrace as key to understanding public policies and practices geared to state repression and violence, the material impacts of populist white anger, as well as those of social movements and alliances geared to racial and social justice. The collection's second core contribution, then, is to present careful analyses of the assumptions and implications of postrace, emphasizing its organizing force in shaping and articulating identities as well as social structures. Engaging with the spatiotemporal configurations of W. E. B. Du Bois's famous admonition that the problem of the twentieth—and now, twenty-first—century remains the problem of the color line, the project's third and final contribution is to parse how discourses of the postracial mark and moderate Du Boisian prognoses about racial justice, equality, and progress.

Defining Postrace

We approach postrace as *the* racial project of our time. We focus on unpacking how postracialism shores up fresh instantiations of structural racisms, distributing resources and value and assigning privilege and stigma. In other words, we take account of both the material and the discursive consequences of postrace. Part of what we are trying to capture here are the various ways in which the cultural production, consumption, and circulation of the postracial mediates—both illuminating and obscuring—the ways in which racial formations continue to produce the material conditions and constraints for a range of cultural practices and dynamics. The postracial manifests not in electoral politics alone but equally in popular cultural realms, including sports, social media, fashion, reality TV, and music. It shapes media productions and offers ready alibis to rationalize increasing rates of inequality across a range of social arenas, from education to incarceration, housing to health care. Presenting a series of case studies, each focused on specific cultural practices, state apparatuses, media texts, and/or performative regimes, the contributors to this volume variously interrogate the implications of postracialism vis-à-vis postracism and, in particular, the conjuring tricks by which "race disappears but whiteness persists" (Roediger 2008). That is, we seek to understand how postrace intervenes within discourses of color blindness, diversity, and multiculturalism to manage, adjudicate, and redistribute advantages, handicaps, vulnerabilities, and risks based on racial differences.

Using postrace as an optic to better understand both historical and contemporary practices of racial formation and racial projects, the essays in this collection look forward toward the anticipatory influences of postrace, informed by scholarship on a range of developing regimes and cultural practices—the continuing commodification and fetishization of branded authenticity (Banet-Weiser 2012) and the hypervisibility of branded difference (H. Gray 2013b); the proliferation of data-lives and digital selves shaping, and shaped by, online spaces that remain structured by race and difference (Nakamura and Chow-White 2012); increased race-based surveillance and targeted health outcomes made possible by advances in genomics and biotech research (Nelson 2016; D. Roberts 2011); political and intellectual crises, still on the horizon, embroiled within fresh dilemmas of transgendered and transracial formations (Draz 2017; Tuvel 2017).

Finally, the essays in this collection explore the dynamics of social, cultural, and economic power that have decisively configured the neoliberal governmentalities of official antiracisms, in the current moment most often expressed as "multiculturalism" (S. Ahmed 2012; Duggan 2004; Ferguson 2012; Melamed 2011). This volume seeks to understand postrace as part of a *longue durée* of racial containment, adaptation, and absorption geared to foreclosing other more progressive paradigms for antiracist reform (Winant 2002). Parsing issues of discursive power and myth, of material structures and lived circumstance, and of histories of resistance and voice, the essays gathered in this anthology engage with a range of urgent and important questions: What lessons should we glean from the meteoric rise of the concept, its broad coalescence in the triumphalist euphoria of the Obama moment, and, indeed, its anticlimactic palling over the course of, and in the wake of, his historic presidency? What measure of its power as a political game changer might we take? How does it track the material conditions and shifting governmentalities of US race relations; the afterlives of enslavement, segregation, and white supremacy? And, as a powerful iteration of enduring national scripts, what prognoses does postrace make about continuing struggles over racial equality and autonomy, and the long-deferred promise of racial transcendence and freedom?

Historicizing Postrace

While Obama's 2008 election is commonly signaled as the inaugural moment of postrace, there is a longer, more complicated history that precedes this moment. The essays in this collection problematize received histories of postrace that link the concept to the singular 2008 Obama moment. Engaging with a range of transformations associated with the civil rights and post–civil rights era, such as assaults on affirmative action and social justice more broadly, the rise of reactionary misogynies and a return to virulent masculinities as an organizing logic of populist movements, culture wars emanating out of social panics over queer organizing and feminist movements, and so on, our work in this volume historicizes postrace in its relations with hegemonic orders of color blindness and the economic, political, and cultural nostrums of neoliberalism.

Discourses of color blindness, as Kimberlé Williams Crenshaw and others have shown (Cho 2009; Crenshaw 1995), are premised centrally on strategic erasures within which the "white norm" and silent operations of white privilege do not disappear but, rather, become "submerged" within racial consciousness (Crenshaw 1995, 115). Setting the scene with plotlines pitting "self-made" heroes against "state-made" villains (Lubiano 1992, 354), such color-blind erasures turn on the technical fiction of "nonrecognition" in which individuals are asked to not consider race, gender, and other kinds of difference even though, as Neil Gotanda reminds us, "it is impossible to not think about a subject without having at first thought about it at least a little" (2000, 36). Crucially, these modes of "e-racing" make room for strategic "re-racings," especially in the context of workplace tokenism, criminality, and national security. Like the relations between "old money" and "new money," those e-raced by the "crossover" logics of color blindness are granted access to selective dividends of racial privilege even though, as Crenshaw points out, everyone still understands the "difference between the truly privileged and the newly entitled" (1997, 107). These mutually reinforcing amalgams of wishful thinking, studied denials, scripted declarations, and tortured performances gradually but unmistakably reenvisioned the domain of racism, yielding sticky new modalities of "racism without racists" (Bonilla-Silva 2014), adaptive in their grasp on long-deferred dreams of racial progress and transcendence. The notion of postrace, then, emerges not so much as an epochal game changer, cleaving time itself, as Spike Lee would have it, but instead, as this anthology underscores, as an iteration, albeit a powerful one, of formidable and enduring national scripts.

The affective allure of postrace as proof of long-promised progressive change tracks larger formations of what historians identify as a two-phased "racial break" within the history of racial modernity. As Howard Winant (2002) explains, the first phase, starting after World War II and culminating in the 1960s, initiated a shift or break in a worldwide racial system that had endured for centuries. Converging in and across a range of progressive antiracist movements—anticolonialism, antiapartheid, the worldwide rejection of fascism, and the US civil rights movement—the racial break called white supremacy into question to an extent unparalleled in modern history, bringing an unprecedented slate of progressive antiracist demands to state and civic attention. But by the 1970s, notes Winant, a second phase emerged facilitating "adaptations" of centuries-old and deeply entrenched systems of racial injustice toward the "containment" of recent antiracist challenges (2002, 145–46). In this crucial second phase, the racial break consolidated a new racial common sense, which conceded to some of the demands of antiracist movements but, equally, served to adapt modes of racial power and absorb conceptual paradigms for racial reform. Repackaging the ideological structures of white supremacy away from earlier modes of violent and overt racisms, the racial break incorporated civil rights reforms into the agenda of the political center, developing a comprehensive program of racial democracy that simultaneously reinforced key dimensions of US nationalist ideology (173).

Starting in the 1970s, massive transformations in the American economy spurred by global forces of deindustrialization, foreign competition, and rising unemployment consolidated in the potent and visceral politics of white backlash. The liberal retreat from racial justice (S. Steinberg 1995), forged in the social contexts of rising opposition to busing as a means to desegregate public schools in the mid-1970s (Delmont 2016) and the 1978 Supreme Court decision in *Regents v. Bakke*, which ruled affirmative action legal but invalidated the use of racial quotas, helped to recruit new patrons of color blindness from among the ranks of besieged white masculinities and proponents of claims of "reverse racism" and antiwhite discrimination. Over the 1980s and into the 1990s, these shifts paved the way for support from political constituencies firmly committed to defending white supremacy as ex-Klansman David Duke and other vocal white supremacists joined campaigns against affirmative action, claiming color blindness and the language and legacies of the black civil rights movement for politically regressive ends. As ballot initiatives from California to Michigan ran their course, bludgeoning affirmative action with racist precision, the divisive bent of these campaigns entangled the racial projects of color blindness with the transparent racial-subordination agendas of the radical Right, injuring the brand for moderate-to-liberal voters (Cho 2009). A new concept like postrace would effectively rearticulate the "liberal embrace of colorblindness" (Haney López 2011, 808) but without so much of its retro-regressive baggage. Crucially, postrace would reach key constituencies of youth and moderate-to-liberal voters whom the tainted brand of color blindness had turned off and away.

Unfettered by regressive political baggage, thus, postrace produced powerfully integrative and cohering effects targeting the state and demanding the dismantling of administrative protocols of indexing, auditing, indeed even seeing race (Flores, Moon, and Nakayama 2006; Goldberg 2002; HoSang 2010). Synchronized with the 2008 Obama election, the arrival of postrace, then, is marked crucially by the corroborating synergies between color blindness and postrace but, equally, by strategic differences between these concepts. Yoking antiracist discourses to color-blind denials of racial privilege and stigma, the postracial break ushered in a new racial common sense that achieved twin ends that remain, to the present, key to foreclosing alternative and more democratic paradigms for antiracist reform (Melamed 2011). Concealing the intersectional links between race and material inequality, and working to disconnect the legacies of white supremacy from enduring mythic and material inequalities, postrace works, like color blindness before it, as an alibi for versions of racial capitalism—creating and stigmatizing redundant labor, organizing and exposing the most vulnerable consumers to financial insecurity, and exploiting differential access to economic risk on the basis of race.

Far from disrupting the ongoing march of the "neoliberalization of race" (Goldberg 2007), postrace embeds and eases a bundle of neoliberal beliefs: the naturalness of the market, the primacy of the competitive individual, the superiority of the private over the public, and so on (Hall, Massey, and Rustin 2013). Enrolling whole populations materially and imaginatively into a financialized and marketized view of the world, postrace renders racial grievances by people of color an anachronism while amplifying white grievance, the former surviving as little more than tedious investments in long-ago crimes and fetishizing a victimhood that no longer exists. Corraling black and other people of color into neoliberal regimes of "enterprise culture" (N. Rose 1996, 57–58), these beliefs re-race these "dangerous individuals," demanding that they abdicate their "reverse racisms" as the "provenance of an unjust, irrational ascription and prejudice" (Singh 2004, 11). Shoring up resonant mythologies of progress and advancement in which twin bad habits of state dependence and racial grievance are censured with fresh vigor, postrace authorizes antiracist projects from which "the threat of racial protest is banished, or its promise magically fulfilled" (E. R. Edwards 2011, 33). Embodied by Obama, together with a fresh cohort of telegenic black and brown political stars (Antonio Villaraigosa, then mayor of Los Angeles; Cory Booker, then mayor of Newark, New Jersey; Deval Patrick, then governor of Massachusetts; Nikki Haley, the former governor of South Carolina; and so on), the semiotic and mythic schema of postrace substantiates new modes of "racism without race, racism gone private, racism without the categories to name it as such" (Goldberg 2009), drawing vast numbers of people to the "common sense" of race as the difference that makes, or should make, no difference at all.

The foregoing series of shifts suggest neither an epochal transformation nor a coherent trajectory to the discursive career of postrace. Indeed, our work in this collection explores the terms of a critical historiography of postrace, instead probing the halting and circuitous perambulations of the racial projects of postrace, tracking fragmentary, and often contradictory, expressions of the postracial across a range of cultural artifacts from fashion to music, public policy to social media.

Mediating Postrace

The shifts and transitions between color-blind racism and postracialism are maintained and normalized within the broad reach of the media industries. The concept of postrace, in other words, has gained in discursive legitimacy in part through its mediations in culture and, specifically, via ideological consolidations of the analytic gaze it engenders.

One of the ways that postrace has been visualized in the media is through the identity category of the "ethnically ambiguous," a malleable representation that fits with ease within a neoliberal multicultural framework.[3] Well before Obama's 2008 election, the commercial and for-profit media-industrial complex was taking full advantage of these manifestations of racial ambiguity, and television casting, advertising, branding, social media, and fashion became newly invested in versions of the racially flexible. Thus, Hollywood unveiled a "revolutionary, colorblind approach to casting" that featured people of various ethnicities "without much attention to the actors' ethnoracial identities" (Medved 2003, 13A; see also Beltrán 2005; La Ferla 2003; Warner 2015). Mattell introduced "Madison, Chelsea and Kayla, a new line of ethnically ambiguous dolls" in step with the advent of "mosaic marketing," which sought to develop advertisements not targeted to specific ethnoracial groups but, rather, "to grab all the diversity" by being as ethnically "indistinct" as possible (R. Walker 2003, D1). Black filmmakers like John Singleton and

Spike Lee who, twenty years earlier, had brought gut-wrenching race dramas to the screen, now produced features in which "differences in skin color [were] no big deal" and where "ethnicity never [became] an issue" (Medved 2003, 13A).[4] And culture columnists took note of the crossover appeal of "ethnically vague" actors like Vin Diesel and Halle Berry and star athletes like Tiger Woods and Derek Jeter who signaled the "disappearance of whiteness as synonym for American-ness" (R. Walker 2003, D1).[5]

The identity category of the ethnically ambiguous is, like other racial identities, a technology of race, and one that has been profitable for the media industries. As a technology of race, the mediatization of the concept of postrace *produces* race and, in particular, produces the conditions that make possible aggressive claims of whiteness and white grievance. That is, if we take the ethnically ambiguous as a quintessential media sign of the postracial, and as such as neutral and desirable, we find postrace at the core of authorizations of lifestyle commodification, multiculturalism, and biogenetics as conditions for the possibilities in which whiteness can both mark and reassert its hegemony in a racial capitalism without stigma. If, as Omi and Winant (1994) argue, race and racial identities are "unstable, flexible, and subject to constant conflict and reinvention," the media industries' use and commodification of this flexibility reveal not just the political and cultural but also the economic stakes of postrace.

Rewarding ethnically ambiguous faces, bodies, and personae, now perceived as good, desirable, and successful, meant not only that bodies and biographies that insist on older forms of ethnoracial identity and difference could be read as undesirable and/or dangerous but also that only some versions of diversity and difference would survive within the emerging mediascape where postrace was fast taking shape as a hip cultural trend. Recognizing and rewarding some versions of difference, race postrace eases, indeed, as Herman Gray argues, it demands specific forms of racial and ethnic visibility in order to be recognized in an attention economy. Depoliticizing racial categories in line with the "fashionable argument that race itself is a fiction" (La Ferla 2003), media celebrations of mixed race ambiguity work to shore up key adjustments in the racial privilege/stigma divide and, as Ralina Joseph (2012) reminds us, are keenly aligned with neoliberal assaults on black and poor populations—adjudicating risk, asset stripping, financializing and imperiling life—based on contemporary understandings of racial identity and difference now delinked from racism.

The media work of postrace, then, is to maintain that the raced body (blackness and otherness) is no longer aligned with abjection, subordination, and suspicion; rather, we should simply celebrate the "remix" identity, which is at once marked by race but also "ethnically neutral." The postracial work of race relies on the obduracy of race in the face of the desire for, if not the end or absence of race, then, the ambivalence and ambiguity of race as the basis for the social arrangement of advantage. The "proliferation of difference" (H. Gray 2013b) that populates the commercial media context relies on a conception of racial capitalism that, like other capitalisms, promises a level playing field through the positioning of race in general and whiteness in particular as the neutral, unmarked, defining starting point. That is, in the context of racial capitalism, it is through the discourse of the postracial that the collective, public, and historical understanding of race as the basis of economic, social, and cultural disadvantage is relegated to the realm of private, personal, and individual. In turn, the notion of a collective commitment to the common good, and the role of the state in protecting the common good, is racialized and thus degraded through the work of culture and mediations that rely on the desire for and representation of racial ambivalence and ambiguity.

These operations in the realms of law and public policy, financial incentives and policy protections for corporations, and attacks on the unemployed and working poor captured by the term "racial capitalism" stress the alliance between capitalism as a racial project and racism as a foundational component of capitalism (Robinson 2000). This alliance requires that blackness anchors and signifies as a site of social excess, value extraction, and threat that forms the discursive ground on which postracial ambiguity can operate. Indeed, this alliance is evident, for instance, in ongoing attacks on the state and the rhetoric of dependency versus entitlement, or in what Clyde Woods (2009) describes as asset stripping in the case of New Orleans, where, in the aftermath of Hurricane Katrina, we witnessed the transfer of public goods to the private sector in the name of rebuilding and revitalization; or in the case of the most recent financial crisis where African Americans were systematically targeted as sites of financial risk to be bundled and sold on the stock market. In other words, mainstream mediations of hip and fashionable racial ambiguity move apace with racialized antiblack and anti-immigrant sentiments. Both provide social traction and political legibility to articulations of postracial white grievance while shoring up the ways that racial capitalism both marks and exploits racialized bodies and circumstances at the same time that it uses racial ambiguity as an alibi for doing so.

Indeed, through media, cultural, and political discourses, the postracial end of race produces and enshrines a profound *incapacity* to see race as a social and economic basis of social and cultural dis/advantage. In this motivated discursive incapacity, race is either belittled as identity politics by liberals and political conservatives or relegated to the realm of anachronistic grievance on the part of blacks and other people of color. And collective social commitments to public goods like education, citizenship, and health care emerge particularly vexed and acrimonious where the public is allied with specifically raced identities and linked explicitly with racial histories, traditions, and memories. Thus, the work of the postracial within racial capitalism is to critique, demonize, and resist, as an instance of race and racial thinking, the notion of a collective commitment to the common good and the role of the state in protecting the common good against rapacious privatized incentives of the market. If the critical link here is the role of dominant media and culture in the active production of the discursive incapacity to see the links between the contours of racial capitalism and the postracial operations of race, the monumental task that confronts social organizations like Black Lives Matter and the sanctuary movement in the United States is the struggle to productively link race, racialization, and capitalism, that is, to render visible, and enable ways of seeing, race as foundational to capitalism and as a crucial site of subjugated knowledges fueling critical resistances to racial injustice, state violence, mass incarceration, and economic exploitation.

On the one hand, the essays collected here attend precisely to these dappled operations of power and powerlessness, unpacking the ways that postrace has become authorized as a cultural signifier of extraordinary affective resonance and tactical appeal. On the other hand, the chapters in this volume grapple with a whole range of counterknowledges premised on disbelief, skepticism, and refusal that seek tenaciously to show up the conceits and specious allure of the significations of postrace. Through a series of case studies, the chapters explore specific media events and performances as well as embattled cultural episodes—some historical and others playing out in the current moment—that render the terms of juxtapositions between proliferations, resonances, and critiques within discourses of postracialism as well as the implications of these battles.

Drawing the most ardent of proselytizers and detractors, opposing views on postrace divide into warring camps—on one side, the full-throated certainty of voices, both elite and nonelite, celebrating the arrival, at long last, of a postracial America and, on the other, somber warnings of postracialism's repulsive dissimulations and denials, emphasizing the cruel joke it plays on people's lives and life chances, brutally adjudicated, now as in the past, by the material power of race and its intersectional orders of difference. Grappling with polarized and irreconcilable contests over the idea of postrace, the collection underscores the importance of careful analyses of the term as it enshrines specific orderings of racial experience and circumstance as rational and normal while relegating others as absurd and impossible.

Organization of the Chapters

The collection includes new works by scholars, both established and emerging, working in a range of disciplines, including film, media, visual, and cultural studies; critical race, gender, and ethnic studies; American studies; critical legal and policy studies; and communication, journalism, and information studies. Methodologically diverse and including a mix of historical and contemporary analyses, the chapters collectively advance our larger project of critically unpacking agglomerations of articulation, silence, and cultural practice, which variously enshrine as well as trouble postrace as the "truth" of race in the twenty-first century. These works are organized in two parts, "Assumptions" and "Performances."

The essays collected in the first part, "Assumptions," explore a range of conceptual assumptions about racial history and "progress" that are linked to the allure of the postracial. They consider key assertions and silences ushered in by the postracial closure, erasure, and disappearance of race as a recognized axis of inequality, a legitimate circumstance, and a meaningful object of study and intervention. Attending to the paradoxes inherent in pursuing historical, cultural, media, and policy analyses on something that, allegedly, no longer has a name, these chapters take note of the embedded logics of visibility, recognition, and discipline that cohere in the term, as well as key assumptions about resistance and its urgency (or lack thereof), which the term telegraphs, raises, or reconciles.

These works are linked in their emphasis on how postrace embeds veiled strategies for attacking state-sanctioned guarantors of basic protections for people of color, including security, safety, and reduced risk of exposure to vulnerabilities in health, housing, social justice, and hunger. Unpacking postrace within the long history of racial formations, the contributors in this part contextualize postrace within broader sociolegal policy responses to race (e.g., color blindness, diversity, multiculturalism) and trace some of the ways that race and difference take new form, keeping pace with shifts in contemporary material and discursive conditions.

Our emphasis in this part is on thinking through the range of ways that the postracial articulates with linked modalities of social, political, and ideological power. How, for example, are contemporary reinscriptions of misogyny and antifeminism shaped and impacted by dilemmas raised by postrace? How do current struggles over colorism, ethnophobia, and racism, proliferating at various registers across and beyond the United States, temper and amplify the discursive labors of postracialism in the service of the global and raced projects of neoliberal racial capitalism? And, further, in what ways are contemporary inscriptions of postracialism linked to currently unfolding epistemic tensions over fact and falsehood, articulating with profound epistemological anxieties over evidence and rumor, truth and propaganda?

Attending to the modalities of racial power, in terms of both the unseen structures of social and economic forces and the practices, meanings, and modalities through which racism functions, these works urge us to consider the ways that postrace empowers ongoing challenges by political conservatives and members of the extreme Right to question and denounce the nature of evidence and the veracity of social institutions, organizations, and professionals like journalists, scientists, and policy makers in the knowledge industry whose job it is to identify, research, and analyze the evidence on which we make decisions and reach new understandings of the social world. Culturally these disputes and critical challenges are evident in the long battle over climate science, claims to racial neutrality in legal and public policy decisions, and more recently the veneration of Confederate monuments by new strains of old white supremacy. These circumstances shape the field of force in which the discourse of postracial race operates—the nature of the discourse, its effects, and the language and symbolic forms through which the truth of race is known. Postracial race is conditioned too by progressive struggles and antiracist movements, including Black Lives Matter, DACA and sanctuary mobilizations in support of immigrant rights, and LGBTQ rights movements, against the work of postracialism in the United States. Contextualized within a series of familiar and ongoing struggles, the chapters collected in the first part of the book variously challenge the assumptions of postrace, clearing important paths for critically evaluating the dangerous discursive and structural racial projects of postrace.

In the second part, "Performances," the collection features chapters examining specific practices—celebrity and spectacle, media artifacts and events—that showcase specific difficulties, and illegitimacies, each in ways that advance the larger political and cultural projects of postrace. Attending to shifts in television programs and film genres, social media platforms and other DIY practices, politico-economic or policy shifts, and performances of racial identity or difference that appear increasingly nonsensical, anachronistic, or untranslatable within the logics of postrace, the chapters in this part show how subtle and seemingly unrelated cultural shifts cohere dangerous new instantiations of structural racisms and vitiate an urgent politics of progressive antiracist struggle.

These chapters explore the racial break between color-blind racism and postrace and demonstrate the various ways that this transition is both maintained and normalized within media cultures. If the first part of the book theorized and historicized the assumptions that undergird postrace, the second part takes up particular case studies as a way to show how the conditions of postrace manifest in specific ways within varied media industries. These analyses draw from the mainstream of popular culture as well as more marginal but nevertheless rich media proliferations, including those operating through affective registers of ridicule, scorn, and irony as well as more frontal modalities of defiance and dissent. These chapters explore a range of efforts aimed at destabilizing the discursive potency of postrace as well as cultural moments that reveal the enshrining of postrace as the dominant discourse of our time.

The media industries explored in this part offer various arguments and theorizations about the dynamics of social, cultural, and economic power that consolidate official antiracisms of neoliberalism, often expressed as "multiculturalism." For example, the global fashion industry, governed by neoliberal economies and this multiculturalism, marks racial otherness through visibility as evidence of racial progress and even racial transcendence. Indeed, the fashion industry allows designers, editors, photographers, and stylists to articulate a multicultural racial identity even when nonwhite bodies are not represented. Popular music capitalizes on a postracial concept of racial progress and insistently, relentlessly, declares that we should be "happy," and that postrace is a platform for emotional uplift in a moment of widespread social inequality and uncertainty. Reality television programs about popular music, such as *The Voice*, position singers as a medium for a variety of "posts"—postrace, postgender, postclass—where ostensibly unmarked expressions of talent transcend racial and gender specificity. Reality television uses postracial ideals to reinscribe racial boundaries and offers an opportunity to explore how race is woven into the highly stylized fabric of daily life represented on TV. Professional sports in the United States celebrate the ambivalence of the postracial moment, vaunting sports as an "equal playing field" for all while also supporting audience engagement with the explicit race politics that structure these professions. In other words, tracking how the commercial and for-profit media-industrial complex takes advantage of postracial performances of racial ambiguity and multiculturalism, these essays consider how television casting, popular music, advertising, branding, social media, and fashion have become invested in the racially flexible.

Some of these performances highlight spontaneous eruptions of epistemic refusal; others enact highly strategic grassroots interventions geared to the constitution and circulation of counterknowledges. Independent web-distributed producers of media programs, for example, offer an opportunity to critique corporate efforts to embrace postracial representations of race as a marketing tactic. Indeed, a queer perspective on representation allows for moving beyond the marketing tactics of postrace in order to seek out spaces that encourage intersectional specificity. Circulating within economies of racial affect, the sentiments and sensations they express, their expressions of desire, trauma, melancholy, and haunting, the actions they motivate and the effects they produce are deeply cultural and social and therefore a central province of our contemplation in this collection. The "deconstructive jolt" of these performances, and their capacities to demystify and denaturalize the allure of postrace facilitate interrogations of a range of cultural voices, spaces, and practices struggling to organize alternative "truths" about the continuing violence of the color line.

Notes

Portions of this chapter revise and restate work previously published in Roopali Mukherjee, "Antiracism Limited: A Pre-history of Post-race," *Cultural Studies* 30, no. 1 (January 2016): 47–77.

1 Certainly, postracial rhetoric has been deployed with force by right-wing politicians as well as right-leaning news outlets, and conservatives and neoconservatives alike from early cultural events like Clarence Thomas's appointment to the US Supreme Court in 1991 to General Colin Powell's service on George W. Bush's cabinet as US secretary of state from 2001 to 2005, and Condoleezza Rice after Powell from 2005 to 2009. But, as David Roediger (2006) and others have pointed out, the concept of postrace is not reducible merely to the right-wing politics of backlash and reaction. Rather, the term coheres a wider heteronomous racial project reaching across the ideological spectrum, and articulated not just by conservatives but also by left liberal voices, including, for example, David Remnick, editor in chief of the *New Yorker*, the popular-culture critic Touré, and New Jersey senator and ex-mayor of Newark, Cory Booker.
2 The line appeared on *Atlantic* magazine's Twitter feed after Obama's victory had been announced at the close of polls on November 4, 2008. It paraphrases a quote from a white woman from Virginia who was in the jubilant crowd that gathered in Grant Park in Chicago.
3 The 2000 US census marked the first time that respondents were able to check off more than one racial/ethnic category. By the 2010 census, the total US population had increased

by 9.7 percent, and the number of people who chose the "multiple race" option had grown by 32 percent (N. A. Jones and Bullock 2012).

4 Examples include John Singleton's *2 Fast 2 Furious* and F. Gary Gray's *The Italian Job*, both released in 2003, and Spike Lee's *25th Hour* in 2002 and *Inside Man*, which opened in 2006.

5 In the wake of a sex scandal that rocked golf star Tiger Woods's pristine postracial image in late 2009, *Vanity Fair* reverted, as if by default, to well-established racial markers of "black brute" masculinities, using as the cover for its February 2010 issue a "blackened" and shirtless portrait of the athlete (www.vanityfair.com/culture/features/2010/02/tiger-woods-201002).

PART ONE

Assumptions

The chapters collected in this first part of the book take note of the shifting modalities of the postracial race, particularly the assumptions that underlie and animate its discursive and material power. The chapters take different approaches to underscoring how race and its intersectional orders of difference have neither moved off nor been replaced so much as they now emerge rearticulated into new forms. The contributors posit key ways that postrace embeds a series of contradictions—giving license to overt expressions of antiblack grievance and older strains of white supremacy but also new national scripts that translate race as a multicultural lifestyle choice at the same time that they give rise to progressive antiracist movements like Black Lives Matter. Likewise, postrace sharpens and substantiates the enduring nexus between anti-immigration and racial nationalism, and between US empire and globalization as a range of social media and networking platforms in their links to legacy media amplify but also deny intersectional linkages across contemporary racial, gendered, and classed inequalities.

The essays in this part variously unpack how the postracial articulates with linked modalities of social, political, and ideological power. Thus, the authors ask how, for example, the dilemmas raised by postrace might shape and impact contemporary reinscriptions of misogyny and antifeminism. How do current struggles over colorism, ethnophobia, and racism, proliferating at various registers across and beyond the United States, temper and acclimate the discursive labors of postracialism to the global and raced projects of neoliberal racial capitalism? And, further, in what ways are contemporary inscriptions of postracialism linked to currently unfolding epistemic tensions over fact and falsehood, articulating with profound epistemological anxieties over evidence and rumor, truth and propaganda?

We regard postracial sociolegal policy responses to race (e.g., color blindness, diversity, multiculturalism) as veiled strategies to attack state-sanctioned guarantors of protections for people of color, including ongoing struggles for physical and financial security; environmental, labor, and electoral rights; the fight for access to decent food, housing, health care, and education; and the means to organize for progressive social justice. We suggest that these practices, meanings, circulations and modalities of race must be conceptualized in the *longue durée*, acknowledging how long and shifting histories of race embed unseen but powerful social and economic forces, and how they modulate but also empower feelings of desire, trauma, melancholy, and haunting expressed collectively and publicly. These economies of racial affect, the sentiments and sensations they express, the actions they motivate, and the effects they produce are deeply cultural and social and therefore a central province of our contemplation in this part of the book.

We find, equally, that the links between economic conditions of exchange and profit and the contradictions of postracial race have enabled dangerous alliances across technological, cultural, and scientific discourses where belonging and identity, organized by whiteness and white grievance, circulate and find traction within echo chambers organized by digital media platforms and social networks. Insulating and intensifying identities as well as differences, these echo chambers have fed and fueled an increasingly audacious range of challenges by political conservatives and members of the extreme Right. These challenges have yielded a steady drumbeat of attacks on the nature of evidence and the credibility of facts and empirical veracity, evident in the long battle over climate science, claims to racial neutrality in legal and public policy decisions, and, more recently, the redefinition and renewed veneration of Confederate monuments and war heroes. Confronting the work of knowledge industry institutions, organizations, and professionals like journalists, scientists, scholars, and policy makers whose job it is to identify, research, and analyze evidence on which we make decisions and reach new understandings of our social world, these challenges are linked to—and allied with—inscriptions of postracialism and their challenge to the truth of racial inequalities and the continuing significance of the color line.

Challenges to the assumptions of postrace require that this baseline of suspicion and false consensus be critically evaluated and denounced. Indeed, our work is directed precisely to unpacking the discursive work of postrace in clearing ground and shoring up support for a range of new challenges shaping the terrain on which the discourse of postracial race operates—the nature of the discourse, its effects, and the linguistic and symbolic forms through which the truth of race is known. Indeed, our work must understand how postrace is conditioned too by antiracist movements like Black Lives Matter, support for immigrant rights, LGBTQ rights movements, and the emergent promise of the student-led gun control movement, which work against the power and allure of postracial race in the United States. As postracial narratives set about erasing race as a recognized axis of inequality, as a legitimate circumstance, and a meaningful object of study and intervention, the chapters in this part of the book consider key assertions and silences ushered in by the postracial closure, erasure, and disappearance, grappling with paradoxes inherent in pursuing historical, cultural, media, and policy analyses on something that, allegedly, no longer has a name.

1

Race after Race

HERMAN GRAY

Let's face it, the idea of postrace in the midst of one of the most racially charged and turbulent moments of the new century so far is oxymoronic—in the United States we are experiencing an epidemic loss of black life at the hands of police violence; since the 2016 presidential election cycle we have state-sanctioned voter suppression of black voters; race is at the center of intense racial suspicion, division, and resentment; no longer a fringe element in the national discourse, white racial nationalism aimed at demonizing black and LGBTQ people and at restricting Muslim, Latino, and Arab immigration with the expressed aim of mobilizing and stoking white solidarity, resentment, and identity emanates from the White House. The postracial alibi for race, that postrace signals the diminution of the impact of race in modern American civic and public life, does not hold. Against the force of race in shaping the history, imagination, social relations, and psychic life of the United States, the concept of postracial is empirically mute and analytically incapable of telling us much about the continuing and powerful role of race in the contemporary life of the republic. The "post" so readily available to journalists, politicians, and scholars from various political perspectives that sought to tame the unruliness of race instead has been overtaken, indeed overwhelmed, by "race." Race has made trouble for the post with its stubborn refusal to be transformed into a more acceptable, polite, and equitable claim on social difference, which in the postracial lingua franca the words "multicultural," "diversity," and "color blindness" came to describe. With race's unwieldy and unruly eruptions in the form of virulent white supremacy, the racial basis of mass black and brown incarceration, the concentration of wealth at the top, the magnitude of loss incurred by the financial and housing crisis, we are reminded once again of the centrality of race to the foundation of the American project. Despite the postracial claims to the contrary, we are reminded of the powerful role of race in the nature of our social relations, the assignment of value, and the distribution of rewards and vulnerability.

In this chapter, I dwell on the discursive production and capacity of the post, the conditions of possibility that produced it, and the conditions that it in turn makes possible—including the trouble race makes for the postracial. Taking into account the long historical legacy that produced the concept of race in the first place, I treat the claim to the postracial "in this time," especially the disavowal of race in the form of the commitment to color blindness and the aggressive avowal of white nationalism, as a signal about the importance of race. Built as it is around a narrative of teleological movement toward a notion of progress, the postracial narrates a future in which race is benign, if not inert. In other words, the claim to postrace is not innocent. Rather, it is an operation of power knowledge, whose arrangement produces the very racial order of things, which it claims to diminish if not eliminate. Moreover, I shall suggest that in this time of race, postrace operates through knowledge, practices, and technologies—*codes* and algorithms—that take hold of genomes, zip codes, and credit scores in addition to bodies, morals, manners, and norms.

Rather than attempt to settle the dispute over the postracial, I am more interested in identifying the elements that a postracial conception of the present make possible in the first place. That is, whether or not we are in a moment of history and social life in the United States that we would describe as postracial, the fact is that the term is discursively productive and as such begs to be taken seriously in terms of *what makes it* possible as well as *what it makes* possible. Do we gain analytic confidence and empirical accuracy when the term "postracial" is used to refer to something in the world? To what are we referring—a political condition, a structure of feeling, a historical period, an arrangement of time that we recognize as distinct from some other, or merely a shift from previous arrangements of resources and their social distribution based on race? Perhaps postrace is a triumph of the widely held view in scholarly communities and progressive political circles that race is a fiction, a social construction, which in effect signals the end of disputes about race.

I am not convinced that this business of race, or more likely postrace, settles the matter or that the analytic and empirical salience of race in the condition of the postracial is itself a settled matter. That said, I am interested in the role of time, temporality, and progress in relation to the condition of "the post" that marks and qualifies race in the formulation "postracial." I want to trouble the post's implicit periodization of race by replacing a singularly temporal notion of time with the concept of space-time and emphasizing the incommensurable, conflicted, incomplete ways that race continues to organize social life and to matter in many aspects of our quotidian world. That is to say, the claim to the postracial implies a temporal sense of movement from one (unfair and unequal) condition to another (fair and equal). This temporality takes on board a cultural judgment and political stake in interpreting this movement as progress, as signs that things are better racially. The idea of the postracial establishes a breach in the fabric of social history and cultural memory into which have stepped some of the most virulent forms and expressions of racism and white supremacy. That is, the postracial provides cover for cultural styles of racism where quotidian ideas of racial tolerance and inclusion thrive, where racism does not need racists and is communicated in the form of codes (Bonilla-Silva 2014; Haney Lopez 2014; S. Holland 2012; Joseph 2017). Adding the idea of space-time and emphasizing the distribution, circulation, doubling back, and simultaneity of race and its operation across time underscore the vexed, salient, and contested nature of race.

If not postrace, what then: The postracial condition? The time after race? The afterlife of race? With alternate conceptions of the space-time of race, writers like Saidiya Hartman (2007) use the idea of the *afterlife* of slavery to focus on the continuing impact of racial slavery in the twentieth century. Kara Keeling (2019) uses the term "queer times" to describe race and its relationship to related attachments based on location, sexuality, gender history and the conjuncture of space-time shifts, digital technologies, and mediated identities. David T. Goldberg's spatial account of the *threat* of race also exemplifies what a spatial analysis stands to bring to conceptions of race that complicate simple narratives of progress (Goldberg 2009; see also Wright 2015). In different ways but with careful attention to shifting and multiple conceptions of space-time conjunctures and an appreciation for simultaneity of identity, attachment, and belonging, these writers reject the easy periodization of a given time and history of race that conceives of it as bounded, temporal, finished. These writers reject both the singularity and temporal sense of race time and the artificial unities of nation time, homogeneous identities, and smooth affinities that postrace purports to organize.

Stressing the space-time dimension of race rather than the purported temporality that organizes and propels the postracial as a narrative of progress marking an end of race transfers attention to the proliferation and transformation of race as a technology of power. Rather than mark the absolute, even provisional, end of race, I read the language of the postracial for what it gathers and covers—the negotiations, disputes, conflicts, resentments, and dis-ease that race produces and the postracial reli(e)ves. Accordingly, the space-time conception of the postrace is productive—that is, it helps us see how the claim to postracial makes race, produces material effects, structures sentiment, and organizes meaning. So, with the space and time of race, I mean to call up the cultural practices and technologies (including the genome, the digital, and the code) through which race in the postrace operates and the effect it produces in the way we see, know, and feel race in our everyday experience of racial capitalism, social inequality, environmental racism, the carceral state, and the (white) cultures of resentment and grievance.

Thinking the postracial in terms of the space-time of race lines up with the shift in the nature of power knowledge that produces race and on which its practices depend and the nature of the society—in this case society of control—in which it operates. In the disciplinary society the norm, the body, the intellect, and morality are the locus for the circulation of racial meaning and racial practices in the media, public policy, interpersonal experience, and the law. According to Foucault (1977, 1990, 2007), the nature of power that operates in the society of discipline takes hold of the body and exercises discipline through subjection of the body and by way of cultural and social practices aimed to produce conformity in compliance with norms and in the name of the normal. Notions of the ideal apply as much to race as to gender, morality as to souls, sex as to sexuality. With the widely accepted liberal (in the American university at least) idea of race as a social construction, in the narrative of postrace, race exists in matters of the heart, in psychological makeup, in the market, and in our DNA.[1] Culturally, race is expressed affectively in the form of identification and attachment and secured through policing the boundaries of difference, virtue, desire, belonging, and attachment.

In the society of control, race—its signification, practice, and effect—is embedded in the code, the metric, and the algorithm. In everything from creditworthiness to investments and assets, vulnerability to disease, and life expectancy, the population organized by race experiences the world through the differential exposure to risk, disease, life, and death. With the credit score, driver's license number, Social Security number, or online purchases in the society of control, citizen-consumers are arrayed on a grid of risk and calculation where geographic histories and tastes are calculated according to predictive models that assess, arrange, and deliver our capacities and decisions to a host of business and financial interests in our risk and purchasing power. That is to say, racial subjects are arrayed on a grid of risk and calculation where everything from genealogy to online purchases is calculated according to algorithms that assess and distribute access to life (Deleuze and Guattari 1987; Foucault 2004). This is a racial logic that targets and organizes the distribution of risk according to the calculus of what you buy, who you love, how you drive, and your gene pool. In the control society, both the materiality and the meaning of race take refuge in genetics, genomics, statistical regularities, and distributions of certain genetic markers. Race also organizes and fuels the intensities of in-group belonging and out-group resentment expressed as white nationalism and nurtured in social media networks and platforms. Having abandoned its lineage to racial science (e.g., the bell curve, IQ testing, craniology), the new science of race, like capitalism, is now coded, and codified in algorithms, DNA sequencing, and statistical regularities (Nelson 2016; D. Roberts 2011).

Thinking about the postrace as a specific instantiation of the space-time of race captures what Kara Keeling (2019), Saidiya Hartman (2007), and Cedric Robinson (2000) stress about the link between race and capitalism. They suggest that the very foundation on which racial slavery was built involved, and continues to involve, metrics of risk, investment, calculation to assess profit and loss, risk and investment in human labor, the production and extraction of value, and the organization of the plantation system and its affiliated social forms of policing, capture, financialization, and banking. Thinking race through space-time enables us to see these relationships not as past (as postrace might suggest) but simultaneously, multiply, relationally in the afterlife of slavery, including the postracial.

Conditions of Possibility

What are the conditions that produced the discourse of postracial as an expression and modality of race? The space-time of the postracial includes a complex of cultural, economic, political, psychic, and social elements that taken together enable the postracial condition. So let us treat postrace as a contested site and expression of power knowledge where race is produced as a feature of disciplinary control, where the truth of the race that it produces is not *the* truth of race but *a* truth about race.

The discourse of postrace avows race (a truth of race exists at the genomic level) and disavows race (race is a social construction and remains largely a feature of the past). This truth of race appears regularly in popular culture, political discourse, and academic studies. Subjection to this truth of race (as past) appears as an acknowledgment and celebration of effective struggle for media visibility, state recognition, and the affirmation of cultural significance embodied in the great struggles for racial and ethnic equality, the hallmark of which is the passage of the civil rights acts of the 1960s (and their subsequent revisions in the 1970s and challenges to them in the first decade of the twenty-first century). These victories both condition and serve as evidence of the postracial condition. The pervasive language of multiculturalism and diversity celebrates social and cultural differences (that include but are not limited to race) as desirable social goals in government, colleges and universities, and corporations (Joseph 2017). The language of diversity and multiculturalism as descriptions of the postracial order of things also opened the way for powerful affective identity claims on whiteness (rather than merely white ethnicity) as a political category and white grievance as the basis from which to make claims on the state for redress for (reverse) discrimination (Mukherjee 2006b; Perlman 2016).

Not to be forgotten in the space-time of the postracial is the pivotal role of postracial race in fueling moral panics about crime, violence, Mexican and Arab immigration, and the surveillance and mass prison warehousing of black and brown bodies in the name of security and safety. These panics and the carceral state and industrial complexes they fueled also mapped onto American deindustrialization, globalization, and neoliberal forms of governance in Western liberal democracies. This commitment to neoliberalism and globalization was commandeered by the financial sector, corporations, and political conservatives aiming to minimize the state's reach in corporate financial regulation, public policies extending and protecting social entitlements, and regulatory oversight in areas like consumer and worker protections in the environment and employment. Today, this American version of neoliberalism extends the calculus of the market to all aspects of public and private life (Foucault 2004). Normative citizenship and effective governance are increasingly measured by the calculation and practice of efficiency among corporations, the state, and individuals. Self-sufficiency in private life means assuming more individual burden for shared civic and public responsibilities, including the allocation of taxes for public goods like health care, public education, and infrastructure improvements and the insulation of corporations and the wealthy from social and financial risks. Race in the space-time of the postracial also figures in the intensification of a state of permanent war, in a voluntary military staffed by people of color where US empire and military strength are projected throughout the world's hot zones.

These postracial political and cultural economies and the racialized social practices they produce, organize, and signify were amplified with the election and reelection of Barack Obama and intensified with the election of Donald Trump. The truth of race deployed by postrace is the locus of intense disputes on the very meaning of the nation, who belongs, the very meaning of human life, fairness, and equality. As a signifier, postracial race brings into sharp focus the affective impact and social articulation of psychic, social, and cultural economies where racial knowledge, racial resentment, and racial recognition serve as optics through which we experience race, including the postrace disavowal of race.

We might think of postrace as the discursive bid on a coherent account of racial disavowal—an amalgam and arrangement of social, cultural, political, economic, and geographic sensory and material circumstances that animate the idea that we are done with race (especially in the face of so much that indicates that we are far from done with race). In the face of so much evidence that race continues to matter, for race not to matter at the level of public policy, economic distribution of resources, and social relations, *other* things must surely matter. What things have to matter for the claim to the postracial as a condition of race to have coherence, to yield up its truth? What categories of perception and habituation are mobilized, what frames of reference and meaning are operating to make sense of postrace in the midst of the proliferation and intensification of race? What feelings give form, intuition, and a lived sense of race in the space-time of postrace, where race is disavowed?

I want to illustrate how paying attention to the conjuncture of events and histories that postrace seeks to define as truth can be productive. To do so I turn to a classic essay titled, simply, "1968" (Mercer 1994). The cultural critic and art historian Kobena Mercer argued that the year 1968 was historically significant and resonant globally for political movements that challenged social injustice and oppression around the world. The year 1968 signifies and holds together world historical events—the acceleration of the final stages of decolonial struggles in Africa and Asia, the escalation of the Vietnam War, and the role of the United States in prosecuting that war. That year marked the zenith of the global opposition to the Vietnam War and support for social change by students and young people especially in the United States, Latin America, and Europe, who joined national liberation movements. Feminist and queer movements for gender and sexual equality found traction, while the civil rights movement shifted its critical organizing campaign north (and west), focusing attention on urban poverty and inequality. Meanwhile, the Black Panther Party, black cultural and political nationalism, and various strains of internationalism drove the radicalization of the black and brown liberation movements in the United States. Martin Luther King Jr. forcefully critiqued US imperialism in general and the Vietnam War in particular. For many, his assassination was a direct consequence of these more radical and expansive shifts in his political priorities. At the same time, 1968 saw ever more aggressive domestic campaigns by the FBI and other federal agencies against the Black Panther Party and other black radical organizations. Urban protest and mass mobilizations provoked and radicalized white backlash that demonized and criminalized black and brown people while appearing ever more extreme in their opposition to racial justice. For Mercer this amalgam of historical events came to signify a critical cultural moment of global social pressure, political challenges to the status quo, and critical calls to action. As a cultural signifier, 1968 makes legible the mutually influential impact of these events on each other and on world history.

Like 1968 as the cultural and political signifier of a conjuncture, the postracial too brings together different strains of identity, attraction, attachment, affect, and political anxiety, as well as shifts in the political economy of globalization and the neoliberal United States. The postracial discourse relies on a conception of social progress in which race is rendered less and less salient in legal, public policy, and political discourse; in explanations of social inequality and exposure to premature death, incarceration, and risk, race is less and less salient in accounting for the social and economic (mis)fortunes of individual citizens. The language of postracial race that frames the terms of white grievance about gender, ethnic, and racial group advantage at the hands of the state is also *more* salient. Indeed, as a proxy for postracial race, this white grievance has only intensified with the election of Donald Trump. The narrative of postrace race emerged from the conservative and neoconservative consensus that insists that the passage of major civil rights legislation in the 1960s (and the election of the nation's first black president almost a half century later) marked the end of a role for race in the public and civil life of the United States. This consensus and its consolidation in public policy, legislation, and the cultural common sense generated a new popular consensus of disavowal of race in the civic life of the nation. This turning away took the form of legal, legislative, economic, and cultural attacks on affirmative action, racial quotas, targets and timetables, and hiring and admission goals as a way to redress historic, economic, political, and social inequalities and disadvantages organized by race. These policy proscriptions were secured by fidelity to individual merit, proof of intentional discrimination, commitment to color-blind public policy, and culture and ethnicity as the basis for inclusion (and, occasionally, redress for historic wrongs based on race). The postracial narrative in legal, social, and economic areas is institutionally sanctioned and deployed at the state and local levels in the courts, media, and popular discourse. By shifting responsibility for making, documenting, and adjudicating racial claims for discrimination and redress (in the areas of housing, voting rights, social safety nets, health, and criminal justice) to the state and local municipalities, the conjuncture which the postracial expressed effectively set the terms within which to dispute race in the space-time of postrace. The social, legal, and cultural attacks on the state for race-based claims and the protection of racialized sectors of the nation effectively aligned the state with liberalism, wasteful government, and (questionable) members of society. Accordingly, the discourse of the postracial disavows the salience of race by aligning the financial excess and wasteful domestic spending by the state with dependency, insecurity, and entitlements as against self-sufficiency, color blindness, and a severely limited but efficient state allow the free market to reign.

In the aftermath of the civil rights bills (and subsequent attacks on them), meanwhile, postracial disavowal of race as a social factor in the organization of society and the distribution of inequality is an example of the continuing salience of race. Indeed, in this play of race, race is the driving force in the moral panics about family decline, black criminality, and welfare dependency. Through cultural stories and associations in media, popular culture, and political discourse, black poor and working-class populations are both the expression and the causes of these social ills. Although these disputes, avowals, and disavowals were largely discursive, they produced material effects in the body politic in the form of social policy, legislation, the allocation (and withholding) of social services, the growth of the prison system, and the organization of racial sentiment and moral panics. This discourse of race also conditioned the terms and practice of race as a technology of power that, in the case of disavowal, is expressed as postrace. The postracial is possible because of the conjuncture of these events and the transformation of disavowal into a discourse of color-blind public policy and multiculturalism as cultural diversity and difference. So the postracial is the site of discursive disputes over the conception and salience of race where, on the one hand, race is disavowed in the present and confined to the past, and, on the other, the very confinement to the past is itself an expression of race. This is the postracial as one modality of race.

I end by focusing on another modality, one particular scene of race—science, media, and knowledge—to consider how a truth of race actually is produced as postracial. I turn briefly to the logic of control and the digitalization of information, the use of coding, and algorithms and related digital technologies and social networking platforms that disappear race at the same time as the amplification and intensification of race, where the materiality of the individual and collective body remains the primary cultural and social site where race as a technology of power is performed.

With the emphasis on codes of race operating in the time of the postracial and the social organization of identity around lifestyle and choice, on the one hand, and the codes of the science of genomics and population, on the other, we can see the forms and contours of this technology of power with postrace at the center. To appreciate this technology of power with racial knowledge at the center, I look to the digital media and genomic science.

Technologies of the Postracial

Because of transformations in digital media, public policy, and diversity discourse, the postracial terrain of racial projects is somewhat distinct from its twentieth-century antecedents. With the knowledge of new racial science and digital media capacities, the stake in gaining cultural representation, visibility, and meaning has expanded beyond the primacy of Frantz Fanon's epidermal schema as a site of knowledge and truth. As I noted earlier, the materiality of the racial body remains a crucial site for the workings of postracial race, and to be sure, while culturally, racial differences are actually celebrated in certain countries in the global North, politically and socially, racial groups are the targets of regulation, violence, and abjection. In the United States, to take one example, cultural practices in public and private institutions celebrate multiculturalism, while legal and juridical rulings outlaw race as a basis for allocation of resources or claims to grievance in public life. In this new condition of race making, racial projects produce visibility *and* regulation, celebration *and* exploitation, including the intensification and amplification of whiteness as the basis for grievance and the loss of authority.

The post–civil rights conjuncture in the United States that produced the first black American president is not one where there is a paucity of images of racial difference or the incapacity to decipher the significance of race. In the internet age, social media, streaming services, broadcast, and cable all are vibrant and robust sites of racial engagement, significance, and belonging for racial and ethnic identifications, thanks in part to the digital technologies that make distinct media ecologies possible, the political struggles that make the conception of multiculturalism and diversity available, and the genomics research that makes the new science of race possible. The United States may be described as a condition of racial excess and abundance (Fleetwood 2011). (This excess of racial difference and significance—Arab, Muslim, black, Latina, anything non-Western—appears to be linked to heightened moral panics and xenophobia among conservative and right-wing political constituencies in Western Europe and the United States about globalization, migration, and terrorism.)

We come to the heart of my query about the status of race and media in the digital, postracial, and genomic context. As the truth of race moves quickly to the level of the genomic, cultural celebrations and white political grievance and social suspicions of the other based on race and ethnicity intensify. In its deployment, circulation, and effect, race organizes, sorts, and informs social life even as claims in science, media, politics, and popular culture insist on the flagging salience of race. So racial projects produce racial knowledge and racial subjects within a condition of abundance and excess where the production of race and the search for evidence of its scientific truth have gone digital and genomic, where accounts of population variations based on race (among other factors) confirm the importance of racial difference. The market logic of multicultural difference as commodity lifestyle based on race (gender, age, and disposable income) arranges popular knowledge in the media, popular culture, and public discourse as the foundation for identification and belonging.

Over its resilient history in the United States, various iterations of racial science, including eugenics, craniology, IQ testing, and genomics, helped to install and authorize the intellectual, cultural, and social firmament necessary to produce race as a purported social fact. With appeals variously to religion, science, philology, and the state, racial science endeavored to show that, like the world of nature, the social world of history and culture could be described and apprehended by classifying, ordering, assigning value, and searching for variation (Robinson 2007).

Thinking of the relationship among race, science, and media as dynamic and a technique of power (each part or component of the alignment moving independently and with different temporalities and logic) is a productive way to view the articulation among genomic racial science, biotechnology, digital media, and postracial discourses of diversity, multiculturalism, and color blindness (Nakamura and Chow-White 2012). While similar relationships organized accounts of race from the nineteenth and twentieth centuries, the emphasis on the constitutive elements of new racial projects permits researchers to track race and the shifting forms they take into new zones of knowledge, authority, and expression.

In the United States the cultural visibility of race and the legal rejection of racial policies by twenty-first-century practices of science, media, and postracial diversity provide an alibi to disavow race and for white conservative, right-wing, ultranationalists to aggressively claim and deploy race (certainly in the nineteenth- and twentieth-century sense) and to recognize, even celebrate, multicultural identities and traditions. Similarly, in the case of media platforms that include social media networks, gaming, entertainment, and streaming content, race is avowed in the form of racially based niche markets, racially organized alliances, and networks of white supremacists and simultaneously disavowed based on economic capacity and resources, market variation, and consumer needs. In other words, as the political arm of the alliance of racial knowledge would have it, race is no longer the most salient impediment to access, participation, and representation in commercial democratic media by communities of color. Rather, marketable distinctions, especially those organized around racial and ethnic differences (but marketed as cultural distinctions), drive access and representation in media. In the case of social media platforms, participation by racial groups is not precluded on racial grounds but operates on the basis of revised twentieth-century racial models of identity politics for whites and separate but equal media content, platforms, and representation (e.g., black social media networks or ethnic language media).

In genomic racial science, racial difference operates in the search for statistically significant genomic variation and genealogical clustering by populations. In other words, scientists attempt to identify and measure human variation according to group classification on the basis of statistical estimates of gene frequencies that differ among geographic populations. This form of racial knowledge allows for the proliferation of population variation, geographic distribution, the search for original and authentic bloodlines, and genealogical recuperation in the name not so much of an explicit racial science underwritten by racism and racial projects but by scientific authority staked in rigorous and disinterested scientific techniques and methods and a liberal humanism that enlists the participation of members of diverse population groups (Joseph 2017). This concern with rigor and recognition of difference operates through the optic and epistemology of racial distinction. In the case of the discourse of diversity and multiculturalism, both of whose legal and economic counterparts disavow the salience of race, race is made on the basis of racial knowledge and social meaning tempered by science, media, and culture. This strategy can be seen, for instance, in the use of DNA to track bloodlines of Native people in North America to authenticate legal and genealogical membership both to protect legal claims to property and to ensure heritage, or with the use of DNA from African Americans as the means of expanding the database for scientific research, targeted medical therapies tailored for blacks, and building police databases for criminal investigations (D. Roberts 2011; Tallbear 2013). Finally, consider the use of genomic research and data for genetic ancestry testing as the basis for African American claims about black heritage and for seeking black redress and reparations for centuries of injustice (Duster 2012; Nelson 2016).

Making race by disavowing racial difference I read as a bid to parse the truth of race as still a fundamental feature of the social order and not just seeing race as a matter of targeting a specific group, identity, or location. In this sense we could say that with the intensification of race making in biogenetic technologies, race is an effect of projects that produce racial understandings and racial truths that are no less pernicious in their effects than their nineteenth- and twentieth-century predecessors.

The story that I have been trying to tell is about the changing nature of race, the truth of which is a product of the alliance of racial science, mediated technologies, cultural recognition of racial difference, and political disavowal of those same differences. The deployment of race takes on different forms, mobilizes different discursive and material resources, and produces different effects in the *longue durée*. Race continues to work through multiple and dispersed forms of subjection to the effects of its truth as freedom from and subjection to regulation, vulnerability, risk, and security.

I have been suggesting that we have entered a different period of scientific and technological race making, one that has produced yet another round of disputes, contestations, and attempts to deploy the alibi of human variation as the justification for ordering, classifying, and managing human populations in the name of the truth of race rooted in the science of racial knowledge. It is tempting to render this latest round of race making as innocent and disinterested, driven only by the quest of impartial science to know and to take advantage of the latest technological innovation.

Yet with every new instantiation of this very old story we have yet another opportunity to make race and the social worlds that it aims to build matter less to manage, regulate, and exploit populations. While we may elect to make race matter more or less in other ways, we need not proceed on this terrain uncritically and without the essential insights learned from fictions of nineteenth-, twentieth-, and now twenty-first-century racial knowledge that claim for themselves the truth of race. We are once again in the position to decide how to make race matter less in shaping human history, what the truth of race is, and how it is deployed in the service of human sociality. That is to say, with the questions we ask and the truths we seek from our science and our politics, we are once again in the position to decide what difference race makes for our understanding of human potential and social relations.

Note

1 In conservative political discourse and public policy the fiction of race even extends to the disavowal of a role for race in the production of social structures, racist histories, and economic inequality.

2

Theorizing Race in the Age of Inequality

DANIEL MARTINEZ HOSANG AND JOSEPH LOWNDES

Malcolm X famously noted that "racism is like a Cadillac, they bring out a new model every year" (Lipsitz 1998, 183). Malcolm's insight is readily understandable yet easily forgotten. While racial subordination is an enduring feature of US political history, it continually changes in response to shifting social and political conditions, interests, and structures. Race performs dynamic and often contradictory work, continuing to produce hierarchy and exclusion while also articulating new forms of mobility and incorporation. Like all forms of popular common sense, racism is a composite, bearing vestiges of bygone forces as well as traces of emerging developments and thought (Gramsci 1971; Hall 1980).

In this chapter we examine the changing labor of race in the present moment of "postrace," in which, as Roopali Mukherjee explains, "recognition and, indeed, explicit avowal of some racial differences [are] deployed as evidence of the declining significance of race in the life chances and experiences of whites as well as non-whites" (Mukherjee 2016, 50). To theorize the labor of race in the time of postrace, we must consider the ways that a specific set of economic, political, and social conditions require and make visible new modes of racial meaning and power. How is race imbricated in the current reorganization of the dominant settlements of the postwar United States, such as the restructuring of the economy and the demobilization of mass-based social movements? How have these processes transformed racial meaning, power, and logic? How might scholars and activists alike identify the political opportunities and breaks created by these new conditions?

We begin to consider these questions through a brief review of the dominant analytic frameworks used to conceptualize the relationship between race and class in the United States. We then examine two contemporary cases—involving transformations in the racialization of the economy and within electoral politics—to consider the labor of race in the time of post-race. We conclude with a discussion of the new opportunities for political organizing and social movements presented by these transformations.

Theorizing Race and Class

While there are important nuances and distinctions in the extant scholarship, two important theoretical lineaments are worth exploring in brief. For many political historians and social scientists who study race, the prevailing framework used to interpret US racial politics in the post–World War II era has been predicated on an understanding of antagonistic racial orders, traditions, or nationalisms competing for political authority. In this view, there is an objective racial antagonism—often metonymically represented as W. E. B. Du Bois's "problem of the color-line"—that structures political conflict. As the sociologists Michael Omi and Howard Winant argue, race must be treated as "an autonomous field of social conflict, political organization, and cultural/ideological meaning" (1994, 48). These accounts vary in their particular renderings and detail, but this framework often maps a conflict between an egalitarian, liberal, and inclusive antiracist political bloc, on the one hand, and a hierarchical and conservative racist bloc, on the other. Contemporary accounts of racial disparities—in wealth, income, incarceration rates, health outcomes, and education—further index this opposition. The "new Jim Crow" of the prison system or the racialized "achievement gap" in education, for example, can ultimately be traced back to the antagonism of the color line. This work is rooted in claims about the micropolitics of racial antagonism (including recent attention to unconscious bias and microaggression), as well as systemic analyses of institutional and structural racism. Such analyses include much of the mainstream scholarship in ethnic studies, the race subfields of the social sciences, and many activist formations (A. Reed and Chowkwanyun 2012).

By contrast, an alternative analysis interprets racial conflict and disparity as fundamentally rooted in divergent and antagonistic class interests. From this perspective, the overrepresentation of African Americans and Latino/as among the nation's working poor and economically abandoned is not primarily a manifestation of the antagonism of the color line, but speaks instead to the imperatives of capital in an era of financialization, continued deindustrialization, and widening inequality. While this analysis has long held currency in Marxist-inflected studies of slavery and US industrialization, it has received renewed attention in several new works by an influential group of scholars grounded in African American history and politics, who point to the ways in which race now operates primarily to mask or mystify class antagonisms. Karen E. Fields and Barbara J. Fields have referred to this process as "racecraft"—a "mental terrain" and "persuasive belief" that function as a folk ideology and more closely parallel the epistemology of seventeenth-century witchcraft than any contemporary social scientific inquiry (2014, 18). Adolph Reed and Merlin Chowkwanyun (2012) similarly argue that contemporary antiracist formations have largely been emptied of their oppositional politics, as likely to abet the upward redistribution of wealth as to resist it. The historian Jacqueline Jones positions race itself as a national "creation myth" that legitimates contemporary forms of economic inequality: "Today, certain groups of people are impoverished, exploited in the workplace, or incarcerated in large numbers. This is not the case because of their 'race,' however, but rather because at a particular point in US history certain other groups began to invoke the myth of race in a bid for economic and political power" (J. Jones 2013, x). From this perspective, it is economic inequality and the imbalance in power it demands that produce the race concept as ideologically salient and socially useful.

In a generative essay titled "Race, Articulation, and Societies Structured in Dominance," the cultural and social theorist Stuart Hall helps to adjudicate this analytic row. Hall calls for "an analysis of the specific forms which racism assumes in its ideological functioning" in relation to "the dominant class relations." He argues for an attention to the specific ways in which racism "secures a whole social formation under a dominant class" within particular historic conditions (Hall 1980, 342). Like Reed and Chowkwanyun, Fields and Fields, and Jones, Hall insists that an analysis of race can never be abstracted from the antagonisms produced by class conflict and exploitation. But for Hall, race plays a critical and historically specific ideological role in this process, often becoming the "modality in which class is 'lived,' the medium through which class relations are experienced, the form in which it is appropriated and 'fought through'" (1980, 341). Hall notes the particular ideological labor that race often performs within a society "structured in dominance." He explains that "racism discovers what other ideologies have to construct: an apparently 'natural' and universal basis in nature itself. . . . it articulates securely with an us/them structure of corporate class consciousness. . . . racisms also dehistoricize—translating historically-specific structures into the timeless language of nature" (342). Race plays a critical role in constituting the political subjects of a capitalist economy, making legible the range of political roles—tied to capacities for autonomy, self-regulation, and ownership on the one hand and dependence, indolence, and subservience on the other—necessary to reproduce capitalism itself.

Hall's insights laid much of the groundwork for contemporary scholars attempting to theorize the particular ideological labor of race in the context of widening economic inequalities. Jodi Melamed, for example, has argued that neoliberal policy itself "engenders new racial subjects, as it creates and distinguishes between newly privileged and stigmatized collectivities, yet multiculturalism codes the wealth, mobility, and political power of neoliberalism's beneficiaries to be the just desserts of 'multicultural world citizens,' while representing those neoliberalism dispossesses to be handicapped by their own 'monoculturalism' or other historico-cultural deficiencies" (Melamed 2006, 1). Neoliberal multiculturalism performs historically specific work by "breaking with an older racism's reliance on phenotype to innovate new ways of fixing human capacities to naturalize inequality. The new racism deploys economic, ideological, cultural, and religious distinctions to produce lesser personhoods, laying these new categories of privilege and stigma across conventional racial categories, fracturing them into differential status groups" (14).

An analysis of the contemporary political and ideological labor of race requires an analysis of the constellation of forces that constitute the present conjuncture. An important body of scholarship and political activism in the twentieth century popularized the contention that racial groupings, boundaries, and meanings are socially constructed rather than expressive of group-based biological or genetic difference. Race is indeed properly understood as a social construction. But it is also (or more particularly) a political construction, created by and through historically specific structures of power. Any society "structured in dominance" requires a shared basis of comprehending and reproducing distinctions of merit and stigma, autonomy and dependency, and authority and dispossession; within the United States, conceptualizations of race have always provided a central legitimating vocabulary and grammar. As Barbara Fields (1990, 102–4) argues, it is not simply that plantation economies worked through white and black populations; it is that these economies were productive of the very ideas of whiteness and blackness as legitimate and meaningful political distinctions. The value afforded to various categories of labor (honorable or degraded), the status of capital (heroic or parasitic), and the relationship forged between state and market all depend on such distinctions.

These new conditions pose important challenges to the dominant traditions of antiracist political action in the United States. Since the end of World War II, both the main scholarly work on race within the United States and the major political projects committed to civil rights and racial justice have generally been premised upon a set of assumptions about the nature of the US state and economy and the possibilities of inclusion within both: an expanding economy that could produce enough surplus and employment to secure the inclusion of people of color, as well as the stability and strength of key institutional formations (including education, criminal justice, health care, environmental management, the military, and elections) capable of incorporating new racialized subjects.

In this context, racial justice political strategies, scholarship, and analysis have generally been centered on eradicating racial antagonisms, bias, and exclusion in order to win access to institutions and resources for racially subordinated groups. In a period when the overall US economy continued to grow, promising higher wages and standards of living to each new generation, and as US institutions were regarded as exemplars of a well-functioning civil society, those assumptions seemed fully warranted. Thus, struggles over affirmative action, housing desegregation, employment discrimination, voting rights, and access to resources and services were all premised on both the effectiveness of the relevant institutions and access to a surplus, especially in the form of public budgets, capable of financing these efforts.

There is increasing evidence, however, that these conditions can no longer be presumed. For example, when the University of California's affirmative action programs were first challenged in the late 1970s by Allan Bakke, the institution itself was well financed and prosperous—providing an affordable and accessible education to students and secure employment to many thousands of people. While the struggle over affirmative action continues today in that state, the institution itself has experienced dramatic change, characterized by steep increases in tuition and student debt, the rise of the contingent workforce, and continual disinvestment from the state.

The accelerating wealth and income gap, along with four decades of privatization, deregulation, and regressive tax policy, has essentially removed a large proportion of surplus from the authority of the state and thus from the demands of racially subordinated groups. The institutions and sectors that have historically been the subject of racial justice activism—schools, representative government, public and private sector employment—are themselves in deep crisis. And in the age of permanent war, global migration and displacement, and ecological crisis, the question posed by James Baldwin more than fifty years ago, "Do I really want to be integrated into a burning house?" (1985, 334), takes on new urgency and meaning. A racial justice analysis focused on institutional inclusion and incorporation can no longer ignore these conditions.

In the sections that follow, we consider two contemporary cases that demonstrate the shifting grounds of racialization in the age of inequality. On first blush, these cases might suggest the political salience of racism is declining. Following Hall and Melamed, however, we demonstrate the ways that racial logic and domination continue to perform important political labor, even in the time of postrace.

"Parasites of Government" and the Transformation of White Racial Subsidies

In early 2010, amid the mounting job losses and growing budget deficits of the Great Recession, the conservative radio commentator Rush Limbaugh (2010) took to the air to warn his listeners of an odious group of "freeloaders ... [who] live off of your tax payments and they want more.... They don't produce anything. They live solely off the output of the private sector." They were, he explained on another show, "parasites of government" (Limbaugh 2011). Wisconsin governor Scott Walker described members of the same group as the "haves" and "taxpayers who foot the bills" as the "have-nots" (Greenhouse 2011). Governor Mitch Daniels of Indiana labeled the group's members "a new privileged class in America" (B. Smith and Haberman 2010; see also McCartin 2011).

The charges rehearsed by Limbaugh and others draw from an enduring discourse of "producerism" within US political culture, in which the virtuous, striving, and browbeaten producer struggles to fend off the parasite, a dependent subject who consumes tax dollars and productive labor to subsidize a profligate and excessive lifestyle (Berlet and Lyons 2000; Gordon and Fraser 1994). These representations have long been racialized and gendered; "welfare queens" and "illegal aliens" alike have been similarly condemned as freeloaders and parasites who exploit the largesse of hardworking (white) taxpayers (Gutiérrez 2008; Hancock 2004; Quadagno 1994).

The focus of Limbaugh's scorn, however, was a group of wage earners who had rarely been represented on the latter side of the producerist/parasite divide: public sector workers and their unions. While women and people of color constitute a larger proportion of state and municipal workers in comparison to the private sector in some states, in 2011, 70 percent of this workforce nationally still identified as white, and nearly a third were white men (Cooper, Gable, and Austin 2012). Indeed, in Wisconsin, whites are slightly overrepresented in the public sector workforce compared with the overall population of the state, while black and Latino/a workers are slightly underrepresented (Walker and Bennett 2015, 191). Yet their whiteness did not indemnify significant numbers of public sector workers from these antistatist attacks. Emergency workers, lifeguards, city and county employees, teachers, and other school employees were increasingly criticized as parasitic—excessive, indulgent, dependent, and a threat to the body politic. As Minnesota governor Tim Pawlenty explained soon after the election, "Unionized public employees are making more money, receiving more generous benefits, and enjoying greater job security than the working families forced to pay for it with ever-higher taxes, deficits and debt" (2010). These charges came from across the political spectrum, as Democratic governors including California's Jerry Brown and New York's Andrew Cuomo and Republicans such as New Jersey's Chris Christie and Ohio's John Kasich all maintained that taxpayers could no longer meet the allegedly insatiable demands of public sector unions. Proposals to renegotiate or eliminate union contracts and to retract collective bargaining rights suddenly moved to the center of political debate in many states.[1]

As several commentators observed at the time, public sector workers found themselves increasingly represented in these claims as "the new welfare queens"—slothful, gluttonous, and parasitic—buttressed by outrageous tales of a class of people living beyond the rules that apply to others. These allegations draw on resonant themes in the US political culture of antistatism, market-based individualism, and right-wing populism. But as Chip Berlet and Matthew Lyons (2000) and others have demonstrated, the subject of "lazy parasites" threatening the producerist ethic has almost always been imagined in white supremacist terms, in which white workers guard against the claims of a racialized class that has variously included mothers on welfare, immigrants, the undeserving poor, and other people of color. Producerism, long associated with whiteness and masculinity, has stood in contrast to parasitism, expressed most visibly through representations of people of color as indulgent, dependent, and excessive. These constructions and distinctions have constituted a central strain of antistatism since the New Deal.

White workers, especially in public sector jobs such as firefighters, teachers, and transit workers, have not historically been represented in these terms; the antistatist logic of racialization has never stigmatized them as parasitic and unfit. Yet in this discourse, they emerge as among the primary culprits of the Great Recession: failed subjects who hijack the state in order to live off the labor of others and escape the rules of competition that apply to everyone else. Opponents of public sector workers have attempted to transpose the script of parasitism onto workers who have historically been exempt from such charges, essentially constructing a more racially inclusive antistatism.[2] Claims that public sector unions and workers are parasitic on the body politic are only cognizable because of this history of racialized populism.

To be clear, the opprobrium now visited on some white workers does not augur a new mode of postracial class conflict in which capital preys upon labor on a color-blind basis. White public sector workers are not losing their whiteness in any social or embodied sense, and white privilege and white supremacy continue to be powerful, dynamic forces in US political culture, structuring life opportunities, vulnerability to violence and death, and differential access to power.

We posit instead that the continued upward redistribution of wealth and state power that has accelerated since the Great Recession has lessened the economic guarantees and privileges that many white workers once took for granted as what Du Bois famously described as the "wages of whiteness." This period marks the first time since the New Deal that large sections of the white working and middle classes have experienced sustained economic abandonment—facing levels of debt, impoverishment, and vulnerability that historically existed only in particular regions or economic sectors. Whiteness no longer grants the same economic entitlements and political authority as it did throughout much of the postwar era.

Before the New Deal, for many white workers, particularly immigrants from southern and Eastern Europe and agricultural laborers in the US South, whiteness secured some social and political privileges but few economic guarantees. The social insurance programs originating from the New

Deal in the 1930s and 1940s changed that dynamic (Katznelson 2005). Legislation and policy implementation concerning agriculture, industrial labor, pensions, housing, and education excluded African Americans and most other people of color even as whites were lifted out of poverty.

The economically stable white working and middle classes created by the New Deal political order became open to Republican appeals in the 1960s as the Democratic Party became more closely associated with black civil rights. The courting of white voters on the basis of antiblack racism was attempted by Barry Goldwater in 1964 and was key to Richard Nixon's electoral success in 1968. White working- and middle-class voters were hailed as the "silent majority," "middle America," "forgotten Americans," and "Reagan Democrats" by Republicans and as anything from "angry white men" to "soccer moms" by centrist Democrats. In all these cases, the parties successfully appealed to white Americans across classes in opposition to both government elites and those constructed as the dependent poor.

This strategy was effective as long as enough white voters were relatively economically secure to make the discourse work. Neoliberal economic reorganization has slowly chipped away at both the political standing and the economic security of an increasing percentage of white middle- and low-wage workers. At the height of the postwar period, a condemnation of white workers as dependent and parasitic would not have received broad bipartisan support. Today, those prohibitions are being transformed.

The economic guarantees for white workers within the New Deal order have faced pressures since the 1970s, evident in political attacks on unions, income redistribution programs, and employment standards that lifted millions of white workers during the postwar period. Since the 1990s, these confrontations have only accelerated. Today, the wealth gap between the richest 20 percent and the rest of the country is now the widest it has been since the late nineteenth century, with the top one-tenth of 1 percent of Americans worth as much as the bottom 90 percent. More than forty-five million people in the United States live below the official poverty line; nineteen million live in extreme poverty. Race unmistakably structures these dispossessions; historic and contemporary patterns of segregation, land appropriation, and discrimination render people of color much more vulnerable to economic inequalities. But in the hollowing out of the broad middle class, whiteness no longer guarantees the same form of material security and even social identity as it once did, rendering its future far less stable than its past. The economic policies and practices of neoliberalism—valorizing the market, reorganizing the state, ending downward redistribution, removing protections—are made legible and inhabited through cultural and racial constructs of autonomy, dependency, and worthiness (Hall and O'Shea 2013). In this context, the scripts of parasitism that have long justified the subordination of people of color become available to stigmatize and represent some white workers in order to justify their exclusion from the social wage.

If elites have abandoned their commitment to sustaining the white middle class, how will they describe and explain those who fall out of it? The stigmatization facing some white workers has also been paralleled by a growing tendency to advance cultural and even biological explanations for the increase in white precarity and vulnerability, placing increasing numbers of whites in categories once reserved for people of color. White poverty is increasingly framed through explanations of dependence, criminality, family disorganization, and genetic deficiency. The antiblack tropes of cultural and familial degradation proposed by Daniel Patrick Moynihan in his report *The Negro Family* (1965) now circulate in explanations of white poverty, as do caricatures of genetic degradation pressed by Richard Herrnstein and Charles Murray's book *The Bell Curve* (1994).

In *The Bell Curve*, Herrnstein and Murray argued that a "cognitive elite" emerged in the twentieth century that was disconnected from a much larger population with lower average IQ. The authors contended that intelligence resulted from a mixture of environment and genetic inheritance that could be mapped through racial categories; in their schema, whites and East Asians were concentrated in larger proportions at the higher end of the cognitive ability spectrum, while African Americans were concentrated at the bottom.

Writing nearly two decades later, Charles Murray, in his book *Coming Apart: The State of White America 1960–2010* (2012), continues to argue that a cognitive hierarchy in the United States explains social inequality, but he no longer exempts whites from charges of intellectual inferiority. He proposes instead what is for all intents and purposes a new racial category made up of the white poor.

Why has Murray expanded his focus from traditional racial categorizations to elaborate new differentiations among whites? He argues that for decades, sociological research on "trends in American life" has used racial categories with whites as the reference point. "But," he writes, "this strategy has distracted our attention from the way that the reference point itself is changing" (12). He argues that the white poor have become behaviorally similar to the black poor he had described in previous work in terms of declining marriage rates, out-of-wedlock births, aversion to work, and increased criminality, and cognitively similar to them in terms of genetic inheritance. Under the chapter titles "Marriage," "Industriousness," "Honesty," and "Religiosity," Murray portrays a socially disorganized, lazy, dependent, morally deficient, and genetically debased population. Murray's shifting racialization parallels the economic, political, and social changes that have disorganized the assurances many white Americans took for granted during the postwar era.

The flagship US conservative weekly *National Review* has also taken to pathologizing white poverty. In an article titled "The White Ghetto" (2014), Kevin Williamson offered a vivid portrait of Appalachia, employing descriptions of cultural dysfunction that a generation ago were almost exclusively used against people of color: "You have the pills and the dope, the morning beers . . . the federally funded ritual of trading cases of food-stamp Pepsi for packs of Kentucky's Best cigarettes and good old hard currency . . . the occasional blast of meth . . . petty crime, the draw (welfare) . . . recreational making and surgical unmaking of teenaged mothers, and death. . . . If the people here weren't 98.5 percent white, we'd call it a reservation."

Again, these descriptions do not supplant or displace enduring accounts of racialized poverty but instead reply upon and reproduce them. In the following passage, for example, Williamson uses antiblack narratives as a touchstone to explain how white poverty and social disorganization have similar roots: "Like its black urban counterparts, the Big White Ghetto suffers from a whole trainload of social problems, but the most significant among them may be adverse selection: Those who have the required work skills, the academic ability, or the simple desperate native enterprising grit to do so get the hell out as fast as they can, and they have been doing that for decades" (2014).[3]

Following a familiar conservative script, Williamson attributes the crisis in Appalachia to a culture of dependency enabled by the antipoverty programs of Lyndon Johnson's Great Society. When Johnson originally proposed an "unconditional war on poverty" as he toured eastern Kentucky, he emphasized that what would become the Great Society was not just meant for urban black America. It makes sense, then, that as the white poor become new targets of pathology in conservative arguments for austerity, Appalachia is a tactically useful entry point.

Liberals too have taken up describing the white poor in terms once used for African Americans. In his book *Our Kids: The American Dream in Crisis* (2015), the political scientist Robert Putnam also tries to make sense of the yawning economic gap that has produced a significant white lumpenproletariat. Yet instead of focusing on structural explanations, he links economic phenomena with culture and behavior, much as Moynihan did in 1965. "The collapse of the traditional family hit the black community earliest and hardest," he writes, "in part because that community was already clustered at the bottom of the economic hierarchy. That led observers to frame the initial discussion of the phenomenon in racial terms, as Daniel Patrick Moynihan did in his controversial 1965 report, *The Negro Family: The Case for National Action*. But it would turn out that white families were not immune to the changes, and with the benefit of hindsight it's clear that from about 1965 to 1980, American family life underwent a massive transformation" (62).

While Putnam sees economic disparity as a causal factor in the radically reduced prospects for the poor, he, like Murray, makes family central as well. "The collapse of the working-class family," he writes, "is a central contributor to the growing opportunity gap" (244). Thus, just as the Moynihan Report sought to explain black poverty through the lens of moral decay, heteropatriarchal family breakdown, and social deviance, so now do explanations of white poverty from figures like Murray and Putnam. In foregrounding cultural, genetic, and familial traits that make some white workers unfit to succeed in the market, they reproduce a long history of racist explanations for inequality that disregarded the forces of economic exploitation and abandonment.

On the one hand, then, the condemnations of white public sector workers and the explanations for inequality proffered by Murray, Putnam, and others demonstrate that some of the central racialized conditions in the postwar economic, political, and social settlement have changed. The (economic) wages of whiteness are no longer guaranteed. On the other hand, these new conditions are premised upon an enduring racialized logic and domination that has long naturalized white supremacy. They are rooted in a social vision based on categories of worthiness and unworthiness that ignores structural explanations of inequality and invites scrutiny into the failures or successes of the individual body and family.

The reorganization of white economic and social privilege in the age of inequality is not totalizing. The legacy of many generations of investment in whiteness as a form of property and value endures and continues to structure life opportunities (C. Harris 1993). The trillions of public and private dollars that white households retain in retirement and investment accounts, Social Security, home values, and employment and educational opportunities made possible by this long history of white racial preference continue to provide economic security for many white families. Conversely, the disinvestment, abandonment, and asset stripping that prevented the accumulation of wealth in many communities of color make those households much more vulnerable and economically, politically, and socially insecure. In the time of postrace, race continues to perform critical political labor (Lipsitz 2006). And to the degree that whiteness fails to afford such privilege, we can expect many white subjects to resist a decline in status. Indeed, as we discuss later in the chapter, the 2016 presidential campaign of Donald Trump is an expression of such resistance to changes in the GOP and in the United States more generally.

"One of Our Own" and the Transformation of Herrenvolk Democracy

The reorganization of whiteness and its curtailed economic guarantees have been accompanied by a parallel transformation in electoral politics, where a new set of conditions has reordered a postwar settlement. While the consolidation of a white majoritarian electoral bloc from the New Deal through the Reagan era was constituted in large measure *against* blackness, across that same time period an increasingly visible black freedom movement sharpened critiques of white supremacy, militarism, and class domination and made broad, substantive demands on the political system. These movements were only partially successful in programmatic terms. And, indeed, just as New Deal Democrats embraced the power of the federal government to move whites into economic security, the modern Republican Party from the 1960s through the 1980s extended a critique of state power as a way of constructing white opposition to black freedom.

In the 1990s, both parties sought to expand their base of white votes through racial demonization on positions related to welfare and crime, and the rollback of affirmative action and antidiscrimination law and policy. Precisely because of the success of these efforts, in the current moment, racial politics can no longer be harnessed in the same way to mobilize white voters. By the time of Barack Obama's election in 2008, the bipartisan project to dismantle welfare, abolish affirmative action and school desegregation, weaken antidiscrimination protections, militarize immigration policy, and fully realize the prison-industrial complex was largely complete. With the demobilization of antiracist social movements from below, these developments shifted the terrain of contemporary racial politics.

One consequence of these conditions has been to free political actors to appropriate the rhetoric and symbolism of civil rights to advance agendas alien to those of the black freedom movement of the twentieth century. Certainly, the social bases and policy positions of the contemporary GOP bear the unmistakable stamp of the "Goldwater-to-Atwater" period of high racism in that party, witnessed in current voter suppression campaigns and hostility toward federal assistance, affirmative action, and antidiscrimination law, and more recently denunciations of the Black Lives Matter movement (Lowndes 2008). Yet Republican political figures and conservative pundits and activists have embraced a version of multiculturalism that interprets the chief aims of the civil rights movement as neoliberal freedom and has sought to emphasize this identity through the inclusion of people of color at the elite level. The presidential administrations of George W. Bush included far more people of color in key cabinet positions, including Colin Powell as secretary of state, Alberto Gonzales as attorney general, and Condoleezza Rice as national security adviser and then secretary of state, than any prior administration of either party.

Bush himself contended that black freedom was equitable to market freedom. Speaking at the national convention of the National Association for the Advancement of Colored People (NAACP) in 2006, he celebrated the organization's commitment to the "blessings of liberty and opportunity" and framed a market-based notion of freedom. "Most of your forefathers," he said, "came in chains as property of other people. Today their children and grandchildren have the opportunity to own their own property" (Bush 2006).

The Republican embrace of neoliberal multiculturalism continued to develop after the Bush years, moving from its prior association with "compassionate conservatism" to mainstream conservatism itself. In 2011, the American Conservative Union announced that Florida congressman Allen West would deliver the coveted closing keynote address at the annual Conservative Political Action Conference (CPAC). A few months earlier, West became the first African American Republican elected to represent the state since the end of Reconstruction, backed by an outpouring of Tea Party support. West caught the attention of conservatives nationally after delivering a fiery address to a 2009 Tea Party rally in Ft. Lauderdale, Florida, telling the audience, "We have a class warfare that's going on. You've got a producing class, and you've got an entitlement class." West narrated his own story, of his rising from "the inner city of Atlanta" to serving for twenty-two years in the military and "leading men and women into combat," as a tale not just of racial striving but of US exceptionalism rooted in antistatism. West never suggested this "entitlement class" was black or relegated to the inner city. He explained, "These people [the entitlement class] are living in and amongst us," and they were poised, like the wayward public sector workers, to bring down the nation. West concluded, "If you are ready to stand up, to get your musket, to fix your bayonet and to charge into the ranks, then you are my brother or sister in this fight" (Taylor 2011; "Allen West The Revolution" 2009). The overwhelmingly white audience gave West a wild ovation, and a video of the speech soon went viral in conservative circles, garnering millions of views on YouTube.

In announcing that West would deliver the keynote address, David Keene, CPAC organizer and chair, declared that Congressman West was "one of our own" who "epitomizes the core conservative values CPAC attendees treasure: a basic belief in human freedom, traditional values, and a love of country based on an appreciation of the nation's founding documents" ("Allen West CPAC Speech" 2011). West's address did not disappoint. Indeed, he anticipated and delivered many of the policy positions that five years later would come to mark Trumpism: a valorization of the free market, tax cuts for the private sector, and limited government; a hostility to same sex-marriage and reproductive rights; a robust militarism and fortified national borders; and an unapologetic critique of "radical Islamist belligerents who transport the seventh century ideologies that is [sic] anathema to the values of American and Western Civilization." And as in his Tea Party rally address, he narrated his conservatism from within his personal life and trajectory, linking his roots as a working-class black southerner to his family's tradition of militarism and patriotism. He concluded his speech, "This son of America stands before you on this grand stage committing himself to his country, to its national character, to its fiscal and national security, to the preservation of the life, liberty, and pursuit of happiness of every American. . . . I do it for the men and women in uniform. I do it for the little boy and little girl wearing a high school junior ROTC uniform just like I did. I do it for the unborn American child" (West 2011).

While West's single term in Congress was marked by controversy and hyperbole, his ascension within the GOP is far from aberrant. Since 2010, some of the most popular figures among the conservative rank and file have been people of color: Louisiana governor Bobby Jindal, South Carolina governor Nikki Haley, Senators Ted Cruz of Texas, Tim Scott of South Carolina, Mia Love of Utah, and Marco Rubio of Florida, and Dr. Ben Carson. To be sure, their rise does not mark the abandonment of racialized appeals and alignments within the GOP, as continued debates over immigration, police violence, voter registration, and affirmative action demonstrate. But as claims to whiteness no longer indemnify many white people against charges of parasitism or dependence, it is instructive that a growing number of people of color become valorized as the standard-bearers for a producerist, militarized, and patriotic antistatism. Here, we see the possibilities of civil rights narratives of uplift and transformation becoming increasingly mobilized toward defending and naturalizing market logics, defining neoliberalism as a form of antiracist freedom.

The Democratic Party has similarly embraced civil rights universalism even as it has pursued policies detrimental to people of color. Bill Clinton built his national career on the Democratic Leadership Council strategy of appealing to white reaction. In a moment of violent spectacle early in his 1992 bid for the Democratic nomination for president, Clinton flew to Little Rock, Arkansas, on the eve of the New Hampshire primary to personally oversee the death row execution of Ricky Ray Rector, a mentally disabled black man. That same election year he scolded rapper Sister Souljah and snubbed Jesse Jackson at the Rainbow Coalition annual convention. Clinton signed historic national anticrime legislation, contributing greatly to the rise of the modern carceral state in the United States, and furthered the dismantling of the US welfare system. These legislative acts, like his campaign actions, were meant to stanch the hemorrhaging of white voters to the GOP.

Yet Clinton evinced another, seemingly opposite political strategy throughout, which was to demonstrate an ease and facility with black America. This Clinton was often seen on the golf course with his friend and Revlon executive Vernon Jordan. He spoke frankly about racism. On a historic trip to Africa, he apologized for slavery. And, famously, during his impeachment for lying about an extramarital affair with a White House intern, Toni Morrison (1998) called him "our first black president."

While seemingly in contradiction, these two sides to Clinton evince a deeper shift in the main currents of elite US politics that can be seen at work in both parties: a cultural celebration of black America offers moral authority, a narrative of overcoming, and a commitment to individual freedom that is increasingly delinked from the historic imperatives of racial justice; and an antistatist, pro-market, anti-egalitarianism that produces profound racial inequality.

The Obama presidential campaign in 2008 exemplified these two sides even more so than had been the case with Bill Clinton. Obama's campaign in 2008 traded continually on the cultural significance of his blackness as a symbol of civil rights achievement specifically, and American exceptionalism more generally. From his victory speech following the Iowa caucuses where he insisted, "They said this day would never come" to the Democratic National Committee's declaration of "I Have a Dream Day" on the day of his nomination at the Democratic National Convention in Denver, the Obama campaign suggestively associated the candidate with civil rights achievements in powerful ways without making substantive links to policy prescriptions aimed at the advancement of the black freedom struggle.

These contradictions are expressed politically, for example, not only in the cases of Bush, Clinton, Obama, figures like Cory Booker, or the growing roster of conservative leaders of color but also in the corporate entanglements of groups like the Congressional Black Caucus, the NAACP, the National Council of La Raza, and leaders of color in the education privatization movement such as Michelle Rhee. Leading multinational corporations, the US military, top universities, and other elite institutions all have unmistakable investments in neoliberal multiculturalism. Far from an insistence on color blindness, they explicitly seek to incorporate some people of color in ways that naturalize their authority. Moreover, representations of antiracism perform diverse ideological labor, used to authorize the ethical and moral authority of many actors—Glenn Beck, Condoleezza Rice, George W. Bush, Barack Obama, and the hundreds of multinational corporations that use Black History Month and similar events to market their products. New fault lines of stigmatization are being generated and regenerated within nonwhite communities—privileging some subjects while stigmatizing others.

In addition, the new incorporation of leaders of color and antiracist rhetoric still reproduces regimes of racial hierarchy and domination. Figures like West, Obama, and Booker are only valorized and embraced to the extent that they frame their claims in the same terms of American exceptionalism, market freedoms, and antistatism that animated an explicitly racist political discourse in the mid-twentieth century, for example, around education, employment, and housing desegregation. In addition, blackness still often embodies and expresses excess and danger in this discourse. Consider, for example, Michelle Obama's speech to the graduating class of Martin Luther King Jr. Preparatory High School in Chicago in 2015 in which she describes "the story of that quiet majority of good folks—families like mine and young people like all of you who face real challenges but make good choices every single day" (White House, Office of the First Lady, 2015). Like the silent majority, this "quiet majority of good folks" defined by their cultural attributes, upright decisions, and moral values are implicitly constructed in contrast to a violent and lawless racially coded other, whose poor choices and diminished values make them culpable in their own degradation. Black incorporation here offers a reformulation and modest desegregation in the membership of the herrenvolk while retaining its core elements: long-standing articulations of American cultural superiority, valorization of individual freedoms, and the denigration of bad subjects. In the moment of postrace symbolized by Obama's ascent, race still operates powerfully, shaped by the long legacy of herrenvolk democracy.

Precarious White Rage

While these shifts in the racial order are meaningful, two conditions must be stressed: First, like all political shifts, they are partial, incomplete, and unrealized. Second, the economic and social changes underfoot have also produced countervailing political movements, efforts that seek to resuscitate the economic, political, and social guarantees of whiteness that characterized much of the postwar period. This white racial revolt was most explicit during the 2016 presidential election and the candidacy of Donald Trump, which linked anxious racial standing to economic precarity and fears of political abandonment.

As he announced his candidacy for the Republican nomination in June 2015, Trump insisted that many Mexicans in the United States were "rapists" and "killers"; his exhortations to "build a wall" on the border with Mexico drew wild applause at campaign rallies across the country (Moreno 2015). He continued to expand the dimensions of his racist platform by calling for the tracking of Muslims within the United States and a ban on those who seek to enter the country. The unabashed language of white supremacy and misogyny, rage, and even violence at Trump rallies was like nothing seen in decades. It was a rage also undergirded with references to permanent loss and mourning. While Trump's campaign slogan was "Make America Great Again," he foregrounded themes of a fully realized and even irreversible loss, defeat, and abandonment. Throughout his campaign, Trump told crowds: "We don't win any more." "We don't make anything." "We are losing so much." Unlike the leaders of past populist revolts, Trump seemed less a champion of working people than a figure who confirmed their debased status, reveling in such terms as "disgust," "weakness," "losing," and "pathetic."

Thus, Trump's candidacy and his mobilization of white rage can rightly be read as reactions to the declining guarantees that whiteness has provided. But the campaign can also be understood as an affirmation and mourning of this loss. Like the champions of the 2016 Brexit vote in the United Kingdom and similar anti-immigrant parties and movements in Europe, Trump summons a racial populism to sustain the fantasy that economic inequality and the vulnerability it produces can be defeated through attacks on immigrants and people of color. But Trump's unanticipated rise also serves as confirmation that the white producerist order of the twentieth century is no longer dominant in US politics.

In many ways, then, the silent majority has become unmoored. Unlike in an earlier period, it no longer can constitute an electoral majority in US politics. Republican strategists who long tied the party's fortunes to this bloc are rethinking these commitments, witnessed in growing (if still bungled) efforts to appeal to more voters of color. As narrated by Trump, the silent majority now invokes an increasingly unstable political identity, one that is unapologetic about using violence and intimidation as ordinary practices of politics. As national GOP elites attempt to expand the base of the party by making multicultural appeals while also pursuing economic policies that further widen the gap between the very rich and everyone else, opportunities for the growth of powerfully racist and nativist politics abound. As the Trump movement has already demonstrated, dangerous forms of white populism will likely develop both inside and outside the party system.

Conclusion

The present conjuncture requires us to think about race and postrace simultaneously, and to develop analytic frameworks and projects capable of conceptualizing both together. The scholarship and political activism that have foregrounded race as a central dividing line help us to recognize the many ways that the structural, institutional, and discursive settlements of the postwar era continue to have profound effects on political culture and life possibilities in the United States. The recurrent crisis of racist police and vigilante violence across the nation, the persistent use of racist invective by some political candidates, and the racialized disparities in health, education, housing, and many other realms of social and political life demand an analysis that attends to the historic continuities of racial domination. At the same time, undeniable shifts in material conditions and discursive frameworks require equally thorough attention. Trying to understand contemporary forms of racial domination and hierarchy through historical comparisons and metaphors alone (such as Jim Crow and slavery) can diminish our ability to comprehend and engage the specificity of these new developments.

It is not merely that racialized domination is historically produced and continually reinforced by capitalism. Capitalism has historically *required* racialization to produce class rule and stymie the promise of democracy. With this in mind, we can also imagine white subjects choosing to align with progressive political projects led by and from communities of color because it is in these locations that the political analysis, organization, and legacies of opposition are most capable of producing resistance to privatization and abandonment. From this perspective, white efforts to promote racial justice are not realized through bland forms of "allyship" to support people of color around "their issues," but would be forged through a recognition of the interdependence between communities of color fighting their abandonment and heightened forms of white precarity. On the other hand, increased economic abandonment has pushed many whites toward a reactionary politics that links race to economic status—a politics that seeks to make racial standing a bulwark against neoliberal domination.

Resisting state violence, reversing privatization, reclaiming the public realm, and advancing democratic control of public institutions will require the articulation of a political vision that seeks the simultaneous end of white supremacy and class rule. Failure to do so may well enable new forms of both.

Notes

The section titled "'Parasites of Government' and the Transformation of White Racial Subsidies" incorporates material previously published in Daniel Martinez HoSang and Joseph Lowndes, "'Parasites of Government': Racial Antistatism and Representations of Public Employees amid the Great Recession," *American Quarterly* 68, no. 4 (December 2016): 931–54.

1 Following the 2010 elections, the National Conference of State Legislatures reported a significant increase in legislative proposals at the state level seeking to restrict collective bargaining rights and weaken unions. See Freeman and Han 2012, 393; Rachleff 2012.

2 Our use of the term "script" here borrows from Molina 2014.

3 For a broader history of this discourse, see K. Taylor 2015.

"Jamming" the Color Line

Comedy, Carnival, and Contestations of Commodity Colorism

RADHIKA PARAMESWARAN

U.S. CONSULATE IN INDIA APOLOGIZES FOR DIPLOMAT'S GAFFE

An American diplomat is under fire in India after making reference to the "dirty and dark" skin of the Tamilian ethnic group there. U.S. Vice Consul Maureen Chao told Indian students that her skin became "dirty and dark like the Tamilians" after a long train journey. The American consulate in Chennai on Saturday apologized for Chao's comments.
—REED EPSTEIN, *Politico.com*, August 15, 2011

American diplomat Maureen Chao's impolitic blunder in India—committed in the midst of a hegemonic crafting of a postracial era in her own nation—narrates a story of her skin's temporal degradation, an ethnic and national border-crossing tale of its journey from an unmarked, normative first world lightness toward the abject third world destination of "Tamil" darkness (Epstein 2011). Chao's portable racism, expressed casually on distant shores that appear to be insulated from her homeland's racial politics, lays bare the hollow promises of a postracial America in which skin color differences no longer matter and racial hierarchies have withered away. Compounding Chao's racism even while purporting to expose it, the online news site Politico.com's prominently displayed photograph accompanying this report showcases a visual exhibit of the anonymous, dark-skinned *Homo sapien* species, "Tamilian family." Joining colonial projects of scientific racism, the image verifies empirically the precise qualities of the epidermal dirtiness and darkness that are referenced in the diplomat's remarks. Politico.com's randomly chosen Associated Press wire image regurgitates a stock representation of rural South Asian poverty replete with visual signifiers of dark skin, emaciated bodies, and silent suffering. The camera freezes a man dressed in a *lungi* (traditional garment wrapped around the waist) and three young girls in shabby clothing, their faces devoid of smiles, walking on a dirt road; the brief caption "A Tamilian Family Is Pictured" reduces the family to an epidermal prototype, a generalized third world diorama standing in for "Wretched Dark-Skinned Oppression." Embedded in the realist genre of photojournalism, this illustration's racist skin pedagogy, which runs counter to postrace's euphoric disavowal of the color line, teaches online audiences that any poor Tamilian family could embody the abject darkness that Chao feared.

Yet, the members of this very same "Tamilian family," subject to the racist and classist discourses of traveling first world elites, cannot claim immunity from similar penalties of exclusion that may be levied upon them within the boundaries of their own national, regional, and ethnic communities. I would predict (based on years of fieldwork and research in India) that if we could thaw the frozen Associated Press image featured in Politico.com's story and walk with this family down the unpaved road, they would soon encounter a billboard for a skin-lightening product that promises Indian (and Tamilian) consumers the luxury of changing their skin color—of wiping away dirt, pollution, fatigue, *and* melanin—and, hence, altering their destinies in an upwardly mobile neoliberal India where *all* citizens are being told they can aspire to first world prosperity. In globalizing India, the primary site for my research, global, national, and regional skin-lightening cosmetics constitute the largest and the most rapidly growing sector of the beauty industry (Grabham 2009; Parameswaran 2011; Parameswaran and Cardoza 2009). Peddling and legitimizing ontologies of racism and colorism—discrimination based in skin color and tone—in India and elsewhere, the global skin-lightening industry's commercial stories of skin makeovers *regenerate* the color line in the midst of postrace's pronouncements that the hegemony of whiteness and racial divisions (brown, black, white, or the favored multiracial) has become inconsequential. These global makeover stories of an industry that has witnessed dramatic expansion in the midst of a postrace climate claim to reverse the effects of time, weather, age, sunlight, and stress and eliminate the constraints that culture, race, ethnicity, caste, and class impose on the body (Ashikari 2005; Grabham 2009; Kenway and Bullen 2011; Leong 2006; Mire 2005; Rondilla 2009; Saraswati 2010). Advertisements for skin-lightening cosmetics sold in India capture the paradox of market-driven ideologies of freedom (Parameswaran 2011). These commodity tales bolster colorism, casteism, racism, classism, and sexism even as they seek to reassure consumers that these products can liberate them from the "semantics of abjection" scripted by these very same structures of oppression (Kenway and Bullen 2011, 285). Commercial beauty discourses promoting skin codes of social distinction in postcolonial India sustain a pigmentocracy that earns its legitimacy from casteism and classism, racism and colonial history, and disputed hegemonic mythologies of a superior light-skinned Aryan race's conquest of dark-skinned Dravidians.

While advertising representations of skin-lightening beauty products have garnered the most attention from cultural studies critics, this chapter shifts our attention to the lesser-heard voices of critique and dissent that are challenging colorism and racism in everyday life and in promotional discourses of consumer culture. Resistance to the color line in Indian communities emerges from the dissenting opinions and actions of ordinary individuals, activist organizations, and celebrities *and* from voices in popular culture, digital media, and journalistic avenues (Parameswaran 2013). I zoom my critical lenses here onto amateur citizen-authored digital parodies and spoofs of skin-lightening commercials that are posted in cyberspace, comedic narratives whose meanings interact with and flow into a larger field of growing opposition to colorism in India. The participants crafting these mediated critiques of colorism range from anonymous individuals using pseudonyms to modest and makeshift production companies, and revealing the transnational scope of dissent in cyberspace, members of the South Asian diaspora are also part of this virtual grassroots community centered on exposing the malignancy of colorism and the shortsightedness of postrace.

The following broad question drives my scrutiny of these texts: How do these amateur cultural productions that parody mainstream advertising make "strange" the global hegemonic grip of light/white skin and the normality of pervasive colorism, sexism, and racism in India? Joining a global community of digital activists, the producers of these spoofs and parodies of colorism in promotional discourse participate in the dissident politics of "culture jamming," which refers to activist multimedia productions and performances that draw on varied technological, representational, and corporeal forms and genres. Culture jamming, as Sandlin notes, includes "such cultural activities as producing and disseminating 'subvertisements,' hosting and participating in virtual protests using the Internet, enacting 'placejamming' projects (in which public spaces are reclaimed), and participating in do-it-yourself (DIY) political theater and 'shopping interventions'" (2007, 77). While a great deal of existing work on comedic culture jamming concentrates on the United States, some recent work has begun to address the rising popularity of parodies and satirical productions—targeting news, electoral and state politics, and public affairs—that are giving rise to new assemblages of contentious, comedic, and argumentative culture in non-Western parts of the world (El Marzouki 2015; Kumar 2015; Semati 2012).

Enacting their creative mode of argumentation, producers of online videos that are jamming the color line tackle a cocktail of intersecting oppressions—racism, sexism, and classism—that live and breathe within the confines of commodity colorism and that shape skin color's fluctuating ideological contours in different cultures, nations, and communities. Colorism's pervasive influences on institutional and everyday life, as Kimberly Norwood's (2014) recently edited volume on skin tone bias demonstrates, challenges any easy assumptions that the United States has entered a much awaited postracial epoch of progress in which skin color has ceased to matter. Norwood and Foreman (2014) write that colorism perpetuates the influences and legacies of slavery's skin color hierarchies; lighter-skinned blacks in the United States are more likely to hold professional middle-class jobs, occupy positions of power in state and corporate institutions, dodge prison and other penalties in the criminal justice system, and gain coveted visibility in mainstream culture.

Global articulations of colorism, including its variations in the vast rising superpower nations of India and China, cannot be conflated easily with the operations of white racism or colorism in black communities in the United States, yet the logics and premises that inflate the currency of colorism's dispersed global avatars in Asia share the same hierarchical territory of racial pigmentocracies as in the global North. Building on Norwood's critical project of questioning the end of racism, I argue that proclamations of a postracial society in the United States are both premature *and* provincial, failing to see the winds of globalization that bring with it immigrants who cross regional and national borders (and who import their cultural brands of racism/colorism into new homelands) and conceiving of race and skin color as germane only within the territorial space of America. This chapter thus attempts to disentangle discussions of skin color and race from the "boundaries of the nation state" and, more specifically, to challenge the dominant paradigm in scholarship that often "ends up shoring and maintaining a U.S. centered ethos in our understanding of race" (Shome 2010, 149). Shome urges scholars to disturb the provincial US-centered nationalism that polices research on race to the point where "international" or "global" conditions are almost absent: "We show little interest in racial politics in other parts of the world and in doing so, reinforce a U.S. centered introversion, insularity, and arrogance that plagues everyday living in the U.S." (152).

Given the urgency of tackling postrace and its global mutations, how can we understand the significance of modest popular interventions that partake in voicing protest against the politics of pigmentocracy but may not resemble a coherent or recognizable social movement? Taking advantage of the emergence of the internet as a participatory medium, producers of carnivalesque parodies of skin-lightening advertisements are enacting dimensions of cultural citizenship that exceed the boundaries of traditional ideas of state-sponsored citizenship, that is, the classic roles that citizens are assumed to play in electoral politics and in relation to the operation of the nation-state (i.e., voting, participating in formal politics, etc.). Toby Miller (2007) refers to the classic model of citizenship (i.e., the right to vote) as political citizenship and differentiates it from "the right to work," or economic citizenship, and the "right to produce and consume information," which he terms "cultural citizenship." John Hartley takes this one step further to make the case for DIY and do-it-with-others (DIWO) online entertainment and comedic productions as embodying practices of "silly citizenship" that scholars must take very seriously: "This kind of silly citizenship has become part of the mediated political landscape, with both professional and amateur creativity expended in the cause of political agency" (2010, 241). Studying formulations of silly citizenship—the comedic, entertaining, and festive aspects of "purposeful play" in DIY projects—requires us to recognize that civic participation need not always be "reducible to Habermasian rationality" (244).

Mocking Lightened Femininity in the Marketplace

Hindustan Lever, the leader in India's skin-lightening cosmetics market, exports the modestly priced and widely distributed domestic Fair & Lovely brand to more than thirty-eight countries in Asia and Africa, and translated versions of television commercials originally produced for Indian consumers are beamed to audiences in other nations, including Bangladesh, Tanzania, Saudi Arabia, and Malaysia. Lever's skin-lightening products are widely available in the global South and within the commercial circuits of ethnic non-Western and South Asian retail and grocery store outlets that cater to diasporic communities in the global North. Until recently, a majority of Lever's products and product advertising almost exclusively targeted young Indian women consumers (not men) and understandably so because the pressure to have light, even, and wrinkle-free skin, along with the weight of other beauty norms, affects women in India to a much greater degree than men. With rare exceptions, a diverse gallery of media and cultural representations (women's magazine covers, film and television programs, images of models and Bollywood celebrities, and advertising texts) and cultural practices on the ground (the arranged marriage system and associated matrimonial ads and websites) have consistently promoted light skin as a compulsory norm of feminine beauty (Parameswaran and Cardoza 2009). In that sense, the upward mobility that light skin, a symbol of purity and upper caste and class status, promises Indian women is not all that different from what it has meant for black women in the United States, although the histories of pigmentocracies may be quite different in these two contexts. Drawing on Bourdieu's concept of cultural capital, Hunter (2002) contends that light skin operates as a form of social capital for black women because women who possess this coveted attribute of beauty can mobilize it to change their economic and cultural status. Her analysis of national survey data shows that light-skinned black women had higher education, higher incomes, and spouses of higher economic status. Thompson and Keith (2001), who also conducted a national survey, write that black women experience "quadruple" oppression due to their multiple marginalities along the axes of gender, class, race, and skin color. Skin color discrimination in India operates in a similar gendered fashion, although the histories of caste formation and European colonialism along other vectors of identity, including religious background and ethnic affiliation, play different roles in shaping Indian women's lives.

Some producers of advertising parodies take on Lever's makeover rhetoric in television and print advertising to mock story lines that seek to convince women consumers that skin-lightening cosmetics can induce a measurable and visible difference in skin color, which can then be harnessed to achieve success in securing either an ideal husband (educated, lives in the West, and has a white-collar job) or professional employment in India's burgeoning service and corporate sectors. Fawzia Mirza's Hindi-language video production "Fair and Lovely Commercial Spoof" (2010; subtitled in English) restages a Fair & Lovely television commercial that narrates a dramatic story of corporeal transformation that brings instant celebrity and professional success. In the original Lever commercial, a father and daughter, dressed in traditional Indian clothing and coded as unsophisticated travelers from the village, wander randomly into an upscale modern beauty company in the city and ask the receptionist if they can perform *puja* (Hindu worship rituals) in the lobby only to be ridiculed for their ignorance and, in particular, for the dark-skinned daughter's unattractive appearance. The indignant father seeks out a remedy for skin lightening based in ancient Indian herbal and ayurvedic ingredients, which first rain down from the sky and are then blended together in a carved bowl to produce Fair & Lovely's authentic ayurvedic cream. After she uses the cream, the formerly sad young protagonist now looks lighter and happier, basking in a luminous glow that surrounds her as she faces the stunned receptionist who rebuked her earlier, and then she descends from a plane like a celebrity to greet paparazzi waiting to receive her.

Fawzia Mirza, a Canadian-born American lesbian Muslim woman actor, activist, and filmmaker, who traces her family origins to Pakistan and India, scripts a short theatrical production that mocks Fair & Lovely's original story of coming to the rescue of abject dark-skinned South Asian women. Situated within progressive formations of antiracist and antihomophobic activism that question postrace discourses of racial equality as a finished project, this particular satire on colorism fits into Mirza's broader repertoire of plays and video performances that dismantle stereotypes of race, religion, sexual orientation, and class. In Mirza's video satire, which reproduces the original quasi-religious, nationalist story line of Lever's commercial, she herself plays the abject dark-skinned South Asian woman, except, in a strange twist of affairs, after her humiliation at the hands of the snobbish receptionist, the protagonist uses the ayurvedic cream her father concocts to find her face transformed into that of a white unicorn. One scene in Mirza's video displays a series of faces—similar to the changing faces in Fair & Lovely's print advertisements—becoming progressively lighter, with the last white unicorn face representing complete metamorphosis and erasure of all dark skin. This transformed half-human, half-beast creature receives the prestige of being appointed the official representative of the modern beauty company when the CEO invites the braying white unicorn to stand by his side onstage at a press conference. Mirza's video, which critiques commodity colorism in the South Asian context from a diasporic location, reveals the potential of the internet to create "liminal spaces from which migrants can resist, challenge, and speak against regimes of truth imposed on them by their homeland and the host society" (Chan 2005, 336).

Offering a more pointed critique of colorism and gender in the Indian cultural context, another video ridicules the arranged marriage system in South Asia in which light skin color is quite often openly acknowledged as an asset and a bargaining chip for women seeking to advance their class status (Jha and Adelman 2009). One familiar story line in Fair & Lovely's television commercials mines the bride-viewing/inspection rituals of the traditional arranged marriage system to foreground the abject body and distraught emotional state of the dark-skinned Indian woman, who is rejected repeatedly by prospective grooms and their families, until she uses skin-lightening creams, acquires the right kind of beauty, and then ensnares a successful and handsome husband. A Bengali-language video's homespun parody of such commercials re-creates these original arranged-marriage skin stories of abjection followed by redemption, but it exaggerates the bride's emotional reactions to her rejection and then subsequent acceptance at the hands of the prospective husband ("Fair and Lovely Spoof" 2010). When the young South Asian groom tells the modest young woman (her covered head bowed submissively) standing in front of him during the bride inspection ritual that she is too dark-skinned to marry him, this repurposed bride, unlike the passive brides on television commercials who gaze sadly at their reflections in mirrors, screams hysterically and runs into the bedroom to sob. Her mother hands her a large plastic bottle labeled "Bleach" while assuring her that this product is guaranteed to change her into a beautiful woman. When the young bride opens the bathroom door with her face covered in white paste, the overwhelmed groom rushes toward her as if overcome with desire. The video ends with the bride and her female friend, with white paste on their faces, giggling and chanting the words "Fair and lovely, be fair not ugly."

Going in another direction to critique the promotion of light-skinned feminine beauty, Humara TV's "Fair and Lowly" video ("Fair and Lowly" 2012) satirizes the medicalized and pharmaceutical rhetoric in advertising that invests skin-lightening products for women with the credible aura of scientific modernity. Market vocabularies of science aimed at popularizing packaged and fast food and kitchen appliances for upwardly mobile middle-class and lower-class Indian women saturated Indian television advertising in the late nineties (Munshi 1998), and soon global and national skin-lightening advertising also followed the same trend. In advertising, images of doctors in white coats, pharmaceutical jargon, diagrams and pictures of the dermis and epidermis, and recommended daily skin regimens work to code dark skin as a disease that cannot be cured permanently but that can be managed with the help of cosmetics (Mire 2000; Parameswaran and Cardoza 2009).

Delhi-based Nick Kharkongor, a playwright and creative media producer, deploys exaggerated caricature in his Humara TV video spoof to drive home his critique of the lightness fetish that pervades popular culture in India. In this oppositional comedic story, a very dark-skinned, overweight woman with a thick Indian accent consults with her doctor to solve the insurmountable problem of the skin she is stuck in: "I hate my dark skin. It is because of my dark skin that I suffer from a deep inferiority complex, low self esteem, and domestic violence." This doctor's prescription for a cure, a can of paint labeled "South Asian Paints Fairness Cream, Ideal for South Asian Skin," mocks a new wave of local skin-lightening cosmetics whose essentialist advertising brags about the perfect match between ayurvedic science using herbal ingredients and Indian skin. The doctor's discussion of different choices in South Asian bleaching paints—Virgin White for purity and chastity, Paneer White for vegetarians (paneer is a fresh cheese used in Indian cuisine), Deepika White for film star whiteness, Kareena White for 50 percent whiter than Deepika White (Kareena Kapoor is a light-skinned Bollywood actress), and Anna White for preventing corruption of skin (Anna Hazare is a well-known anticorruption activist)—for his dark-skinned patients in the next few scenes indexes in a comical and intertextual fashion familiar objects and icons of Indian culinary and popular culture. Following the doctor's advice, the dark-skinned woman, her husband, and her son apply thick coats of white paint to their faces, and in an instant they morph into a Caucasian white family, with the racist doctor pronouncing, "The white family is a happy family." The use of the word "white" in this parody (and others in the next section) and images of whitened consumers in a selection of other spoofs—where dark brown Indian faces turn into white faces with blue eyes and blond hair—that demonstrate the outcomes of skin lightening signal the cosmopolitan opening up of a readily accessible pan–South Asian cultural imagination to the lexicon of race, signaling a nascent public racial consciousness that casts a collective South Asian identity as marginal in relation to a privileged Euro-American white identity, and it acknowledges a global racial order that structures local articulations of colorism.

Comedy and New Consumer Formations:
Skin Lightening for Men

Although women have been the primary global target market for skin-lightening cosmetics, advertising's discourses of colorism in India have recently moved into new demographic terrain by taking on the project of training men to desire and acquire light skin. Skin-lightening advertising for such newer products as Emami's Fair & Handsome cream and Hindustan Lever's Fair & Lovely Menz Active cream performs a "tutelary function" when it coaches Indian men to embrace "particular technologies of the self and specific modes of comportment" that were formerly the preserve of women (Rajagopal 1998, 16). Capitalist modes of subjectification in a changing India, an emerging market nation that is in the midst of banishing its socialist past, spare very few citizens who are undergoing their aggressive interpellation as consumers of branded lifestyles.

Several parodies featuring male protagonists execute a double-edged critical task: on the one hand, they lampoon skin-lightening advertising targeted at Indian male consumers, but, on the other hand, by enacting role reversals, they also throw into sharp relief the cultural pressures exerted on women to transform their skin color. A video produced in Malayalam ("Fair and Lovely" 2007) follows a young South Indian man's quest to shed his melanin after two beautiful women reject him for being too dark-skinned. After listening to his parents' lament about his prospects for marriage, the young man retreats to the bathroom and gazes at his reflection in the mirror. Within seconds, emulating the omniscient and disembodied voice-over of advertising, a moment of enlightenment and redemption unfolds when a golden glow first surrounds the dejected protagonist, and then a hand holding out a tube of skin-lightening cream commands him to use the cream so he can become a "light boy." When he displays his triumphant lightened face to his mother, the image on the screen turns into a somber warning: "Fair&lovely is not responsible for white spots, burning sensation or missing teeth. Use as directed."

Two English-language parodies set in the United States, one in an Indian grocery store and the other on a college campus, make similar comedic arguments about the foolishness of seeking escape from the scourge of dark skin. On "Make Me White" (2010), a short comedic skit of Samosa TV, a multiethnic South Asian YouTube comedy channel located in Los Angeles, a South Asian man donning the aesthetics of blackface is wandering the aisles of a grocery store when he spots a beautiful light-skinned South Asian woman shopping in the company of her Sikh boyfriend. When he corners the woman and asks her out on a date, she scoffs at his request and says, "You are way too dark for me." The dejected young man finds "Make Me White" bleach cream in the store, and when he walks by the same couple outside on the street wearing his new face, now stripped of blackface, the beautiful woman abandons her boyfriend for him. In a more subtle way, this over-the-top parody also echoes criticism of blackface practices enacted in the Indian entertainment and advertising industries that has been expressed elsewhere. In the post "Bollywood Blackface" (Hades 2012) hosted on the satirical website *The Times of Bullshit*, the author sutures the history of racism in the United States with the colorism of skin-lightening advertisements' rhetoric in India, arguing that models who darken their faces for before (dark)/after (light) narratives are perpetuating blackface, "a form of theatrical makeup used in minstrel shows, and later vaudeville, in which performers create a stereotyped caricature of a black person."

A potpourri of oppressions, identities, and languages—racism, colorism, East Asian women, South Asian women, African American man, South Asian man, whitish/lightish man (ambiguous racial identity), English, and Bengali—defy racial and national boundaries in the next parody, which appears to be set on a bucolic college campus in the United States. A young, dark-skinned black man approaches a group of young Asian women sitting on a bench outside a big brick building ("Fair and Lovely" 2012). After these women chase him away for not meeting their standards of attractiveness, the young man seeks advice from a light-skinned South Asian man who lends him a tube of Fair & Lovely cream. Viewers then see the black male protagonist standing in front of a bathroom mirror and applying the cream to his face as a voice in Bengali, with English subtitles, announces: "Fun and easy to apply! Made with thousands of chemicals (but mostly bleach). You'll see results in no time!" The image of the black man dissolves gradually into a very light-skinned man with European features, and the same shallow Asian women who reacted to him with disgust in his earlier dark-skinned incarnation now throw themselves at him to signal their approval.

Picking up on this theme of stretching the epidermis across different racial communities and juxtaposing blackness with commodity colorism, an intriguing midshot spoof photograph of a light-skinned Barack Obama sporting straight brown hair, blue eyes, and lightened skin positioned next to a tube of Fair & Lovely cream went viral in cyberspace, appearing on numerous websites with such titles as "White OBAMA . . . FAIR & LOVELY KA ASAR" (*ka asar* means "effect"). Similarly, a fake news report titled "Fair and Lovely Disappointed with Obama Win" (Hades 2008), published on *The Times of Bullshit,* speculates that Fair & Lovely, India, was a major contributor to John McCain's presidential campaign in 2008 because an Obama victory would undercut the company's premise that dark-skinned people are always doomed to fail. This satirical report quotes a fake spokesperson of the company expressing concern over the outcome of the 2008 US presidential race: "A blacker man with a wheatish complexion becoming the most powerful man in the world is disastrous for our brand." Continuing with its comedic spin on Fair & Lovely's crisis of legitimacy brought on by Obama's victory and popularity, the report also shares fake information on the company's future ambition to "introduce a skin-darkening cream in the U.S. to capitalize on the Obama win."

In addition to creating solidarity across racial and ethnic boundaries, such satirical texts featuring black men also grapple with intersections of colorism and racism *within* communities of color, namely, South Asians' perceptions and treatment of black people in India and elsewhere among the global Indian diaspora living in the global North. The proliferation of commodity colorism in conjunction with other events has brought discussion of South Asians' racism toward black communities into public media and digital spaces, a first crucial step toward addressing these toxic racial hostilities that have long been swept under the carpet. Following the racist attacks against Indian university students in 2008 and 2009 in Australia, *Outlook* magazine in India carried a pioneering introspective cover story on racism in India that asked, "Aren't we racist too? Even as we point fingers at Australia, we forget how we are prejudiced against dark skin" (Dasgupta 2009). In a searing column in the same issue, Diepiriye Kuku (2009), a gay black activist and academic who spent some time in India, indicts colorism for perpetuating racism: "Racism in India is systematic and independent of the presence of foreigners of any hue. This climate permits and promotes this lawlessness and disdain for dark skin. Most Indian pop-icons have light-damn-near-white skin. Several stars even promote skin-bleaching creams that promise to improve one's popularity and career success." Kim Barrington Narisetti (2014), who is married to an Indian man, recounts vividly her experiences with racism in India as "a dark-skinned African-American woman who lived in New Delhi for nearly four years." Describing numerous painful encounters with racism in India in public spaces, from metropolitan airports to upscale hotel lobbies, she finds a clear link between racism and colorism: "Dark skin has a lot of negative connotations attached to it whether you're Indian or of African descent, hence the bustling skin lightening market."

Finally, another Hindi-language video parody, "Gore Gote: India's Number 1 Testicular Fairness Cream" (2014), produced by Culture Machine and SnG Comedy, pushes the boundaries of taste and sexual norms in public discourse to call attention to a wave of new skin-lightening cosmetic products that have been introduced in the Indian marketplace in the last decade. Comedian Varun Thakur scripted this parody following the increased targeting of Indian men as consumers of skin-lightening creams *and* the launch of a whitening shower gel for women called Clean & Dry Intimate Wash: "We have a vagina bleaching product. We have a fairness cream for every body part except testicles" (Payne 2014). At the beginning of the Gore Gote video, Mukesh (played by Thakur), an abject young man who laments his virginity and is longing for sex, confesses to viewers, with shame and sadness lacing his voice, that he has had no success in dating women. As Mukesh speaks, the camera invites us to witness his humiliating rejection in the intimate space of a bedroom: when Mukesh removes his clothes, we see a young woman, her face signifying repulsion and horror, as she looks pointedly at his genitals to communicate the clear message that she will not have sex with him. When Thakur's parents take pity on him and try to arrange his marriage, we see a young bride turning Thakur down for not matching her own light skin color. Soon after, an actor dressed up to look like the Bollywood star Shahrukh Khan, who is the celebrity brand ambassador of Fair & Handsome cream, advises the young man to use Gore Gote Fairness Cream for the Balls. A male voice-over accompanying a split-screen image of the cream and the lower half of a male body encased in white underwear promises that this new product will remove dark scars and blemishes, dirt and pollution, and semen stains to restore testicles to lightened purity and cleanliness. Mukesh faithfully applies the cream to his groin, and on his wedding night, we see him winning the prize of sex when his smiling bride, overwhelmed with joy, gazes upon his lightened private parts.

Colorism, Postracialism, and Carnival: Confronting Global Pigmentocracies

How can we make sense of the progressive potential of the "silly citizenship" dramatized by the spoofs and parodies of commodity colorism, sexism, and racism analyzed in this chapter? Poaching from and hijacking advertising narratives, these culture-jamming videos perform the aesthetics of "repetition with a difference" (Hutcheon 1985) to germinate subversive speech; they mimic the form of corporate advertising but trouble these texts' seemingly normative content and exclusionary logic by deconstructing their "argument from within" (Kumar 2015). Amateur video critiques of colorism also insert ordinary citizens' oppositional "production and community-building practices" into the crevices of public culture (A. Harris 2004, 164), and they speak back to hegemonic Western discourses of postrace and postfeminism (and postcaste in India) that exceed territorial boundaries via global flows of popular culture. Rossing (2012) has argued in the context of the United States that progressive racial humor can be an effective tool to confront ideologies of postracialism, create affirmative spaces for race consciousness, and expose the continued resilience of white privilege. Although not explicitly targeted at dismantling postrace per se, these digital productions that deploy humor to deliver critiques of the color line remind us that we are still far from a postracial era in which concerns about bodily difference—race and skin color—have evaporated. While advertisements for skin-lightening products mask their blended racism, casteism, and sexism by claiming to level the playing field for marginalized consumers, culture-jamming videos expose the corrosive ways in which these texts uphold light/white supremacy and cast dark skin as deviant and diseased. Certainly, as Harold (2004) has cautioned in her essay on the political effects of pranking rhetoric, we cannot overestimate the capacity of comedic and satirical cultural forms to produce the kinds of policy or legal interventions that activist social movements have facilitated. Nevertheless, when positioned against the resounding historical silence on colorism and racism in South Asia, these funny viral archives of contestation, working alongside other modes of opposition (Parameswaran 2013), do contribute to constituting a public culture of resistance (Hariman 2008) that generates productive cacophony and opens up spaces for reflection on the resilience of the global color line.

This chapter's scrutiny of colorism also points to the outdated provinciality of US-based postracialism as a historical, sociological, and spatial concept. Insisting on the importance of finding ways to insert race into the vocabularies and terminologies of globalization, Thomas and Clarke note that "race and processes of racialization are not usually considered central issues in academic discussions of global economic and political transformations" (2006, 1). John Jackson argues that "theories of globalizing 'flows' and transnational scapes" are limited in how much they can "account for the entrenched and institutionalized non-*flow*ingness and ine-*scap*ability of race in contemporary American society—and all around the world" (2006, 193). The boom in the global and domestic skin-lightening industry in India, the consumption of these commodities elsewhere in the global South and the global North, the widespread promotion of colorism and pigmentocracy in advertising texts, *and* the pungent counterdiscourses of the spoofs and parodies explored here converge to produce a textured global racio-scape of hegemony and dissent, one whose ideological contours cannot be reducible to assertions of white supremacy or black inferiority but nevertheless share the same epistemological ground of racialized difference and hierarchy based in the epidermis.

Hence, racism, colorism, classism, and casteism can converge simultaneously, despite postrace's willful wishing away of difference, on the bodies of the dark-skinned "Tamilian family" discussed at the beginning of this chapter.

When taken together, these modest comedic artistic productions, which circulate anticommercial skin stories of caricature and satire, produce ethical pedagogies of popular culture that are part of the everyday politics and aesthetics of a global civil society centered on challenging postrace, postcaste, and postfeminist rhetoric. Urging scholars to think about dissent in ways beyond heroic rebellions and demonstrating masses, de Goede (2005) argues that anticorporate humor, drawing inspiration from the histories of folk theater and carnival, engages in the politics of "making strange" or denaturalizing hegemonic norms and cultural practices. Literary critic Mikhail Bakhtin writes, "Laughter demolishes fear and piety before an object, before a world, making of it an object of familiar contact and thus clearing the ground for an absolutely free investigation of it" (1981, 23). From a Bakhtinian perspective, the dramatic techniques of parody and irony—including exaggerations of oppression, reversals of the social order, exhibitions of vulgarity, and amplifications of authority—challenge the rationality of powerful institutions and call attention to their contingency and vulnerability. Furthermore, as James Scott has argued about quotidian forms of resistance, "They play an important imaginative function. . . . They . . . create an imaginative breathing space in which the normal categories of order and hierarchy seem less than completely inevitable" (1990, 168). Dark-skinned women turning into unicorns, South Asian actors painting their faces white, South Asian and African American faces dissolving into white faces, crude portrayals of excessive emotion, tasteless transgressions of sexual norms, and cross-cultural juxtapositions of Barack Obama with Fair & Lovely cream call out global commodity colorism, interrupt postrace's premature denial of racism, and invite alternative imaginations of the stigmatized body.

4

On the Postracial Question

RODERICK A. FERGUSON

On what grounds do we assume that we live in a postracial society? And isn't this presumption another way of saying that we have been emancipated socially, politically, and economically from the "prior" restrictions of state and capital within the United States? After all, there's the election of Barack Obama, the first African American president. There's also the fact that niche markets exist for virtually every social group out there. Moreover, millennials—if we believe the statistics—are more tolerant on matters of race than previous generations. In general, doesn't this postracial presumption imagine that the combined might of liberal tolerance, legal advances, and market interests has vanquished a racist past and ushered in an unprecedented harmony between various sectors within our society? This reverie not only recounts the general fantasy of postracial discourses but also points to the claims that this delusion makes about state and capital—that they have been perfected not simply through but also because of race. Indeed, it would seem that postracial discourses have advanced the notion that we have entered a historic moment in which state and capital—by virtue of their inclusiveness—have ushered in the dawn of social emancipation, making the question of postracial society into a referendum not only about race but also about state and capital's abilities to fulfill antiracist ideals.

The postracial question, therefore, is a statement about the capacities of liberal capitalism, but it is also more than that. Having developed in the wake of antiracist social movements of the fifties, sixties, and seventies, postracial discourses are also implicit referenda about those movements. More specifically, postracial discourses are as much tallies of the presumed futility of anticapitalist and socialist modes of achieving antiracism. In this way, postracial discourses are actually "civilizational" ones that posit political, economic, and historiographical theses about US society in the post–civil rights moment. At the same time that postracial discourses posit liberal capitalism as the most likely candidate for producing an antiracist social world, they also shape our understandings of how practical anticapitalist and redistributive efforts are in realizing the same aim. In other words, the postracial question is not only about the fantastical abilities of liberal capitalism; it is also a way of imagining the end of a radical vision of antiracism. Postracial society connotes an improvement upon and alternative to anticapitalist revolution, the formation that—in the post–World War II moment—contended that it, rather than liberal capitalism, could produce antiracist redistribution. Postracialism has thus emerged as both the executioner of and the cemetery for the memory of antiracist movements that demanded the abolition of capital as one of the conditions for racial justice. Inasmuch as it subjugates that history, the discourse of postracialism keeps the nature of liberal capitalism as a racial project bound to racial inequality unasked and unexplored.

This chapter attempts to analyze the politico-economic and historiographical contours of postracial discourse. The chapter first considers antiracist formations as alternative to the ones recommended and imagined by liberal capitalism, focusing on antiracist socialist formations in the late sixties and seventies. It does so as an attempt to show that liberal capitalist social formations were not the only contenders for how to imagine antiracist societies. The chapter then traces the genealogy of postracialist discourses to the emergence of multiculturalist formations within civil society, in general, and capital, in particular. From corporations like Coca-Cola, Pepsi, Hertz, Burger King, McDonald's, McCann-Erickson Worldwide, and NBC to affirmative action programs that provided many young people of color access to elite colleges and universities, civil society and capitalist economic formations have selectively promoted forms of minority difference and minoritized subjects for representation and institutional access. This selective promotion provides the material conditions for asserting postracialism at the levels of both state and capital. Again, these procedures not only assert the superiority of liberal capitalism but also help to occlude the memory and history of anticapitalist engagements with and alternatives to structural racism, particularly the structural racism produced by the very state and economic formations that would later claim moral superiority.

As I hope to show, anticapitalist formations tried to demonstrate the linkages between racial exploitation and capitalism. In response, corporations attempted to reform their own racial contradictions, giving the impression that capital was not essentially given to racial exclusion.[1] This was a way of contending that racism and capitalism were contingent rather than necessary associations. In doing so, corporations could assert that liberal capitalism was the end of history and that anticapitalist formations could never be the basis of a social or political imagination where antiracism is concerned. In a rebuttal to the connections that were made between capitalist exploitation and racial inequality, state and capital would assert themselves as the primary and most appropriate appreciators of racial difference and thereby construct socialism as an unnecessary way to reimagine the social world. State and capital's "care" for racial difference would then be perceived as a sign of their own ethical revolution in relation to race, a revolution that proposed liberal capitalism as the more developed and mature solution to racial inequality.

Reperiodizing Postracial Discourses

In her article "Post-racialism," critical race theorist Sumi Cho writes, "Post-racialism is a twenty-first century ideology that reflects a belief that due to the significant racial progress that has been made, the state need not engage in race-based decision making or adopt race-based remedies" (2009, 1594). Because of this progress, she goes on to state, "civil society should eschew race as a central organizing principle of social action" (1589). One of the aims of postracialism as a discourse is the way in which it affects how we remember the state in its past and how we think of the state in its present. In addition, the discourse of postracialism produces a narrative of the politics that were necessary in the past versus the kinds of political interventions that are warranted in the present. As Cho states, "Post-racialism also represents a political retreat from race by redefining the terms of racial politics. Not only are racial remedies and racial discourse off the table, but so are acts of collective political organization and resistance by racialized individuals" (1596).

Cho's definition points to the historiographical qualities of postracial discourse—that is, that it is a way of writing the racial state and antiracist movements. If postracialism asserts that "civil society should eschew race as a central organizing principle of social action" and argues that the "state need not engage in race-based decision-making or adopt race-based remedies," then postracialism is also a comment on the social movements that attempted to make race a central component of social redress. Cho's definition thus points to the social interests of postracialism—that is, its attempts to regulate racial redress and thereby prescribe what social formations are fit for antiracist transformation and what formations are not. In an effort to illustrate this historiographical aspect of postracial discourse, this chapter adjusts the periodization of postracialism, moving its "origins" from the twenty-first century to the sixties and seventies, that moment in which the United States witnessed the rise of antiracist and redistributive social movements and saw the ascendancy of antiracist maneuvers among US corporations and the US government. While postracialism has emerged as an explicit discourse because of the 2008 election of Barack Obama, giving it power at the levels of common sense and politics, its origins lie in the decades before 2008, as responses to specifically redistributive modes of antiracist organizing. By engaging postracialism as a hegemonic response to the redistributive imaginations and actions of more radical movements, I am extending arguments that I made in *The Reorder of Things: The University and Its Pedagogies of Minority Difference* (2012). In that book, I argued that state, capital, and the academy began to affirm minority difference in ways that seemed to resemble the social movements but actually stripped those movements of their goals of redistribution. This chapter takes that argument and applies it to the discourse of postracialism, demonstrating how the assertion of racial progress was a way of promoting visions of antiracism that cohered with liberal capitalism. One of the effects of the discourse of postracialism is the consigning of anticapitalist articulations of antiracism to the dustbin of history. In other words, the seeds of postracialism were planted in the twentieth century, emerging contemporaneously with the very forms of organizing and politics that postracialism would go on to polemicize.

Capitalism and the Articulations of Race

In order to understand the political and economic stakes of postracialism, we must visit the political struggles that rebutted US liberal capitalism's argument that it was best positioned to address racial inequality. To begin with, it is important to note that radical antiracist formations emerged in the twentieth century to contest the racial exclusions that were part of capital's operations. Indeed, antiracist and anticapitalist organizing among US people of color in the 1960s and 1970s helped to encourage analyses that would tie a vision of an antiracist future to efforts to abolish capitalist forms of inequality. We might, in fact, understand the latter part of the sixties and the beginning of the seventies as periods in which various social actors were attempting to observe and theorize racism as one of the irresolvable contradictions of capitalism. For instance, in 1969 Huey Newton would argue, "The Black Panther Party is a revolutionary Nationalist group and we see a major contradiction between capitalism in this country and our interests. We realize that this country became very rich upon slavery and that slavery is capitalism in the extreme. We have two evils to fight, capitalism and racism. We must destroy both racism and capitalism" (Newton 1995, 51). As a political organization, the Black Panther Party encouraged analyses that sought to illuminate the links between the histories of capitalism and the histories of racial exploitation.

We might also think of Angela Davis's 1972 article "Reflections on the Black Woman's Role in the Community of Slaves" as an example of analysis that emerged within that period as well as analysis that attempted to connect racial inequality with capitalist protocols. In that text, Davis uses the figure of the enslaved black woman in the United States to observe the contradictory existence of slave labor within a national economy ostensibly devoted to the ideals of free labor. According to Davis, the black woman became a symbol of "some of the many contradictions unloosed by the effort to forcibly inject slavery into the early stages of American capitalism" (1972, 85). Davis's analysis marked the ways in which racially gendered nonwhite labor had constituted US capital as an enterprise structured by race, class, and gender. The examples from Newton and Davis represent collective efforts to rearticulate the relationship between race and capital by attending to their links rather than seeing them as discrete and separate social formations.

The sense that race was constitutive of capital's character rather than eccentric to it could be seen in other contexts as well. For instance, it was also in that moment that the racial contradictions of capitalism were perceived as ways to understand the workings of US empire. The Puerto Rican Young Lords would argue, "Amerikkkan racist influence has really succeeded in dividing Puerto Rico along color lines especially within the last ten years. . . . On top of all this is u.s. capitalism controlling the economy of the island and making bundles of money in alliance with the Puerto Rican capitalist class" (Enck-Wanzer 2010, 138). In terms of wars in Asia, Lisa Lowe has argued,

"The foreign policy that framed wars in Korea and Vietnam and neocolonial domination in the Philippines was a liberal hybrid that combined economic internationalism and anti-communism, responding equally to the need to take economic supremacy and to contain the Soviet Union diplomatically" (1996, 18). As the social movements and protests of the time demonstrate, capitalism—in that moment—was seen as an explicit sign of a thoroughly racialized political economy that had both domestic and global reaches.

This theorization of capital as a racial project is best captured in the category "racial capitalism," a concept that first appeared in Cedric Robinson's classic text *Black Marxism: The Making of the Black Radical Tradition*. The book was monumental for historicizing the links between capitalism and racial exploitation, for illustrating that the "very foundations of capitalism had never been ... a closed system" (Robinson 2000, 4). In his foreword to the text, Robin D. G. Kelley argues, "Robinson not only finds racialism firmly rooted in premodern European civilization but locates the origins of capitalism there as well. Building on the work of the Black radical sociologist Oliver Cromwell Cox, Robinson directly challenges the Marxist idea that capitalism was a revolutionary negation of feudalism" (2000, xiii). This notion that capital was the "revolutionary negation of feudalism" fostered a developmental argument that positioned capitalism as the "beyond" of feudalism. Rebutting that argument, *Black Marxism* intervened to show that capitalism was not an absolute departure from feudalism since it extended feudalism's racialized elements. As Kelley states, "Instead, Robinson explains, capitalism emerged within the feudal order and grew in fits and starts, flowering in the cultural soil of the West—most notably in the racialism that has come to characterize European society" (xiii). In Robinson's formulations, capital's contradictions—its production of unfreedom in the guise of free labor—partly emanate from capital's racialized roots in feudalism. As Kelley goes on to say, "Capitalism and racism, in other words, did not break from the old order but rather evolved from it to produce a modern world system of 'racial capitalism' dependent on slavery, violence, imperialism, and genocide" (xiii).

In her own engagement with *Black Marxism*, Jodi Melamed emphasizes how the book originates within a social movement tradition that addressed capitalism as a site for antiracist activation. As she observes, "The black radical tradition for Robinson has been an explicitly materialist antiracism because it has sought to make comprehensible and occupiable intellectual, ethical, and political positions antagonistic to contemporaneous configurations of racial capitalism" (Melamed 2011, 48). One outcome of the discourse of postracialism has been to make materialist forms of antiracism intellectually, politically, and ethically incomprehensible and uninhabitable. As Sumi Cho (2009) argues, rendering those forms uninhabitable was undermined by both liberals and leftists. More specifically, in their commitment to the universalism of class analysis, liberals and leftists suppressed the legitimacy and memory of materialist articulations of antiracism. As David Roediger argued in his essay "The Retreat from Race and Class," "As the twenty-first century starts, the idea of a colorless struggle for human progress is unfortunately back with a vengeance" (2006). Contrast this with the activist and intellectual formations of the 1960s when race was popularly understood as a constitutive contradiction of capitalism, a moment in which anticapitalism was regarded as the necessary precondition for an antiracist society. Suppressing this history of activists and intellectual formations of the 1960s and the links between race and capital have become effects of postracial discourses.

The Ethics of Black Capitalism

From the late 1960s onward, state and capital would attempt to provide the discursive conditions for what we now consider postracial discourses. As I have detailed in *The Reorder of Things* (2012), Richard Nixon would promote "black capitalism" as a way of arguing that state and capital could work hand in hand to usher in the ethical promises of democracy and a democratically informed capitalism as well. In the maneuvers of capital, we actually see how postracialism is not limited to discourses of color blindness but can be born through an explicit engagement with difference as well, a version of difference that has been thoroughly adapted to the needs of capitalist valorization.

In such a context, capital's engagement with race and minority difference would be both an instance of capitalist valorization and capital's ethical transformation. For example, in a 1968 editorial for the *New York Amsterdam News*, Floyd McKissick, a lawyer, Nixon supporter, and former director of the Congress of Racial Equality, conditioned the ethical possibilities of capitalism on its engagement with racial inequality and difference. He wrote, "There is a great difference between Black Capitalism and white Capitalism. It is a difference that every Black man must understand. White capitalism has been a destructive, violent force. It has been used to subjugate the colored people of the world. It has been used to oppress Black people in America" (McKissick 1968, 7). In this passage, McKissick presents black capitalism as the more progressive and ethical version of capitalism. Black capitalism's presumably progressive and ethical nature comes from the notion that it can learn from the racial exploitations produced by capitalism and launch a version of capitalism that can overcome the history of racial and economic subjugation. As McKissick states, "The movement for Black capitalism is designed to alleviate much of the poverty and powerlessness of the Black population of America" (7).

As an ethical proposition, black capitalism would in a sense "become" the ethical subject of liberal government. In his discussion of that subject, the political theorist John Stuart Mill argued that representative government would educate its citizenry in the "unselfish sentiment of identification with the public," an identification that—as David Lloyd argues—is part of the citizen-subject's "ethical training." In the context of black capitalism, capital would become the subject that identified with a presumably ascendant black public. Capital would also be the context for educating others to identify with that public. For McKissick the political and ethical agenda of black capitalism is explicit. As he states, "Any Black Man who exploits his black brother or who resorts to the white man's methods of deceit, treachery or chicanery, is as much a danger to the interests of the Black Masses as his white counterpart" (McKissick 1968, 7). Black capitalism would ostensibly retain the ethical and political ideals of the Black Power movement—ideals around unity and collective development—but extend them to the workings of capital. As he goes on to say, "Black Capitalism, if it is to be worth the effort, will be a means, not an end, and its goal will be to benefit every Black American and to give hope for the future" (7).

In this sense black capitalism would be a discourse that would extend and revise what Karl Marx and Friedrich Engels addressed in *The Communist Manifesto* as the "revolutionary" aspect of bourgeois social formations. In their discussion of the bourgeois revolution, they wrote, "The bourgeoisie, wherever it has got the upper hand, has put an end to all feudal, patriarchal, idyllic relations. It has pitilessly torn asunder the motley feudal ties that bound man to his 'natural superiors,' and has left remaining no other bond between man and man than naked self-interest and callous 'cash payment'" (Marx and Engels 1964, 61). Black capitalism would extend the bourgeois tradition of attempting to put an end to the social relations wrought by racist systems of exploitation and institute new sets of relations in which race would not be the basis of exploitation but of self and communal affirmation.

As an "ethical" formation, black capitalism promised to even surpass the bourgeois revolution by producing bonds that were deeper than those characterized by "naked self-interest and callous 'cash payment.'" As McKissick states, "The idea of Black Capitalism is not to create a few more Black millionaires who will remain isolated from their people and indifferent to the needs of other Black Americans" (1968, 7). Indeed, black capitalism would supposedly be a means of deepening connections to the needs of black people and black communities. It would cease to "resolve personal worth into exchange value"; it would overcome "egotistical calculation" and "brutal exploitation." It would enable a postracialist discourse by presuming that capital—assisted by a benevolently antiracist state—could become the most appropriate vehicle for racial liberation and antiracist transcendence.

As a discourse, black capitalism had broad significance. It helped to revise presumptions about state and capital's relationships with race, suggesting that state and capital were capable of reform where racism was concerned and that liberal capitalism could offer the most developed forms of emancipation. Black capitalism would help to foster the idea that state and capital could be emancipated from the historical burden of racial exploitation. In doing so, it would promise a new ethical order for citizens, businesses, and state institutions, an ethical order that would purportedly relieve citizens, businesses, and the state of the racialized contradictions that organized life in the United States under slavery and Jim Crow.

The dream of black capitalism was one in which capital would produce something other than and, indeed, antithetical to the egoistic individual. In "On the Jewish Question," Marx addresses property-owning civil society as the location of that egoism, writing, "The perfected political state is, by its nature, the *species-life* of man as opposed to his material life. All the presuppositions of this egoistic life continue to exist in civil society outside the political sphere, as qualities of civil society" (1978, 33). Marx here describes a split between the collective identity promoted by the state's emphasis on citizenship and the acquisitive individualism necessitated by the private sphere of property ownership. As he puts it, "[Man] lives in the political community where he regards himself as a communal being, and in civil society where he acts simply as a private individual, treats other men as means, and becomes the plaything of alien powers" (34). Marx was describing a world in which the sense of community promoted by the state seemingly contradicted the self-interested requirements of property.

As far as McKissick was concerned however, black capitalism held out the promise of a society that could reconcile the sense of community with the need for property ownership. This could be a society that would offer something other than the den of the private individual, the place where humans are treated as means to an end, and the sphere in which human beings could transcend their history as the "plaything of alien powers." The egoistic realm of civil society could change precisely because a revolution had—through an interpretation of Black Power—made property ownership into a means of communal development and identification, had made it into a force for antiracism rather than racial exploitation. Black capitalism was thus a crucial juncture in the transformation of capital into a presumed force for racial progress and the herald of a new phase of American civilization, a phase that would apparently reject its recently racist past.

As a sign of capital's ethical progress, black capitalism would help to sow the seeds of a discourse of American civilization, one in which capitalism would be the promised transcendence of a racist past and present. Discussing this ideological component of capitalism, Raymond Williams wrote in *Marxism and Literature*, "[Civilization] expressed two states which were historically linked: an achieved state, which could be contrasted with 'barbarism,' but now also an achieved state of development, which implied historical process and progress" (1977, 13). In Williams's sense, civilization functions as the measurement and the end point of historical and social development. Black capitalism held out the possibility of a mode of capital that would function in a similar way, as an "achieved state of development" that "implied historical process and progress." That process and progress would yield a postracial future denoted through the incorporation of minoritized subjects to fill the ranks of capital's bourgeois managerial stratum.

Postracial discourse, via black capitalism, would also put to new uses civilization's exercise of reason. Discussing the function of reason in civilizational discourses, Williams argues, "In the perspective of the Universal Histories the characteristic central property and agency was reason—an enlightened comprehension of ourselves and the world, which allows us to create higher forms of social and natural order, overcoming ignorance and superstition and the social and political forms to which they have led and which they support" (1977, 16). As the intellectual and ethical component of civilization, reason—for Williams—is a way of imagining and promoting a rational institutional life. For him, this promotion captures the historiographical implications of civilization as a social process. Put simply, rational beings make rational institutions in and for Western civilization. As he argues, "History, in this sense, was the progressive establishment of more rational and therefore more civilized systems" (16).

Black capitalism would plant the seeds of a more rational version of capitalism that would yield the political and economic world of postracialism. As such, postracial discourse would offer itself as a mode of reason that had overcome the ugliness of slavery, racial segregation, and the institutions that they supported. Interestingly, reason here is understood as the property that allows humans to create "higher forms of social and natural order, overcoming ignorance and superstition and the social and political forms to which they have led and which they support." As a discourse and expression of civilization, the post-racial would claim to have created "higher forms of social and natural order," forms not based on the irrational institutional worlds that characterized racial subjugation.

In contrast to the period in which Marx was writing, the weight of state and capital's ethical development would shift from a suspicion of difference and particularity toward a qualified retooling of those elements. Under this new schema of emancipation, minority difference could be taken as evidence that state and capital could overcome their contradictions, making minority difference an alibi for state and capital's claims of ethical growth and evolution rather than signs of their irresolvable limits and failures. The forms of minority difference and particularity could go from defects to benefits and thereby deepen the character of capital. A whole new chapter in the history and architecture of emancipation under liberal capitalism was being written, one in which racial progress and dreams of postracialism could be ushered in—as we will see—by the glad tidings of corporations.

Capital and the Rebuke of Materialist Antiracism

In the seventies, various corporations would make public efforts to demonstrate that they could overcome their own histories of racial exclusion and exploitation. One of the primary ways in which they did so was by mounting a variety of diversity programs. Rather than discrete signs of capital's benevolence, those programs signal the economic revolution inspired by parts of the civil rights and Black Power movements, a revolution in US capitalism itself. As I argued in the previous section, capital's response to the antiracist movements would inaugurate its ethical transformation. By demonstrating that it could respond to social movement demands of access and representation, capital would also rebuke movement claims that antiracist emancipation required alternatives to capitalism.

For instance, a *New York Amsterdam News* article from 1970 highlighted efforts by the Coca-Cola Bottling Company of New York to bolster its program for supporting minority businesses and recruiting minority employees "at all levels."[2] The article states, "Long before many other corporations had decided on which minority business enterprise to support, the New York Bottling Company already had its first minority support efforts underway" ("Coca-Cola Acts" 1970). The bottling company contracted with minority businesses that were able to provide supplies and services that it needed. It also hired a black advertising agency, Zebra, to produce a commercial featuring "minority performers." In addition, the company used its advertising dollars in Black and Puerto Rican radio stations, magazines, and newspapers and also contracted with minority businesses to underwrite its insurance plans. By initiating programs of minority business support, recruiting people of color, and contracting with minority-owned businesses, the company attempted to use diversity initiatives around race to shape its ethical and antiracist reinvention.

The Coca-Cola Company was not the only corporation to engage in such a transformation. A 1977 *Chicago Tribune* article entitled "McDonald's Does It All to Help Minorities" frames the advances that the McDonald's Corporation made regarding racial exclusion against the antiracist and materialist analyses of progressive critics. As the article states, "Social critics often point to the fast food franchise as one of the prime ways the rich [almost always white] get richer and the poor [almost always black] keep profit on the rise with every hamburger, chicken leg, and fish fillet they consume" (Gaspar 1977, E8). But these social critics, the article goes on to state, are misguided where a company like McDonald's is concerned: "That might be a tidy theory somewhere. But talk with any of the black owner-operators of McDonald's hamburger outlets in Chicago, and you'll get a different story" (E8). To support its argument, the article states that in 1977, 27 percent of the McDonald's estalishments in Chicago were black-owned. In addition, Denis Detzel, then head of McDonald's affirmative action department, asserted the company's commitment to racial redress by arguing, "Basically, we get new black ownership through our current black owners, and McDonald's tries to make an active attempt in our licensing department to attract qualified Black and Latino operators" (E8). Licensing minority-owned McDonald's restaurants was a primary way for the corporation to claim it was overcoming the racial exclusions of American business. In fact, the article suggests that corporate licensing was a means of achieving real-world change versus the "theories" that could only be offered by "social critics."

Another way that capital demonstrated its responsiveness to antiracist transformation was by partnering with antiracist organizations. In 1974, for instance, the Quaker Oats Company partnered with the Chicago-based social justice organization Operation Push to boost its number of minority employees "'in the shortest time possible'" ("Quaker, McDonald's" 1975, 16). The company's foundation donated "$200,000 to minority agencies in 1974 and established a special $100,000 corporate fund to encourage contractors to use minority suppliers" (16). The company also advocated for fair housing, "school lunch programs, welfare reform, and increased loans to minority banks" (16).

The ethical revolution that began in the seventies extended into the eighties as well. Early in that decade, the Coca-Cola Company, for example, would develop its programs for supporting minority businesses and employees. Through the company's agreement with Operation Push, Coca-Cola involved blacks and Latinos in "the company's economic opportunities and benefits" ("Coca Cola Opening Up" 1984, n.p.). Such partnerships would allow Brian Dyson, then president of Coca-Cola U.S.A., to proclaim, "We were the leader and not just in the soft-drink business" (n.p.). It would seem that corporations were finally rising to the antiracist occasion initially set by the movements of the fifties and sixties.

But the ethical transformation that was inspired by the antiracist movements did not end the historic contradictions that have constituted capital. Perhaps the clearest example of that was a lawsuit that more than two thousand employees of Coca-Cola brought against the company for discrimination. In 1999, twenty-two hundred plaintiffs charged the company with discrimination in pay and promotion. The lawsuit stated, "Not only do barriers exist for African American employees seeking upward advancement within the company, but similar barriers virtually segregate the company into divisions where African American leadership is acceptable and divisions where it is not" ("Coke Faces Mass Race Bias Lawsuit" 1999). Contrary to the presumption that capital was better suited to resolve historic forms of racism, the lawsuit implied that Coca-Cola was producing familiar and new hierarchies of race within the corporation itself.

Postracial Discourse and the Drama of Emancipation

The lawsuit against Coca-Cola and other companies points to the fiction of capital's postracial emancipation, the one that posits capital as the guarantor of antiracist progress. In part, the roots of such a notion can be located in the founding ideology of capitalist economic formations. As Marx intimates in "On the Jewish Question," the liberal property-owning state promotes the illusion of emancipation by establishing itself and property expansion as the horizons of emancipation. Indeed, we might read Marx's critique of political emancipation as an analysis of how the liberal capitalist state works to arrogate the conditions of emancipation unto itself. As a social formation that works to appropriate the terms of emancipation for itself, liberal capitalism must necessarily wage a hegemonic struggle with rival political and social formations.

Marx and Engels imply as much in *The Communist Manifesto*, which states, "By freedom is meant, under the present bourgeois conditions of production, free trade, free selling, and buying" (1964, 84). They go on to point that controlling the definition of freedom constitutes bourgeois subjectivity: "From the moment when individual property can no longer be transformed into bourgeois property, into capital, from that moment, you say, individuality vanishes" (85). The bourgeois thesis about the liberal individual and free trade is, thus, a thesis about the ethical development of the human and citizen, that full maturity is an identification with liberal capitalism.

In the case of capital as it was transformed by the antiracist movements, postracial emancipation has come to mean that the fully developed citizen would identify with capital as the vehicle for antiracist progress. Such a formulation—capital as the model for ethical identification with a world free of racism—would both naturalize capitalism as the end of history and prevent an interrogation of capital as the perfection of antiracist emancipation. In doing so, it would reaffirm one of the strategies of liberal capitalism—to protect its models of freedom from critique and interrogation. Marx and Engels get at this in *The Holy Family*, which asserts, "[Absolute Criticism] distorted the Jewish question in such a way that it did not need to investigate political emancipation, which that question deals with[,] but could be satisfied with a criticism of the Jewish religion and a description of the Christian-German state" (1956, 121). Liberal capitalism, therefore, tries to shield its privileged narrative—political emancipation—from critique. We find ourselves in a similar position as the discourse of postracialism has convinced us that we do not need to investigate liberal capitalism as the purportedly sole route to antiracist freedom.

Notes

1 For work in this area, see Weems 1998, particularly the chapter "The Revolution Will Be Marketed: American Corporations and Black Consumers during the 1960s"; B. Wilson 2000, particularly the chapter "The Southern Shift to Fordism: Leverage for Civil Rights"; Austin 2004; Mayes 2009, especially the chapter "Holiday Marketing, Multiculturalism, and the Mainstreaming of Kwanzaa"; Chambers 2011, particularly the chapter "Civil Rights and the Advertising Industry."

2 It is important to note that the Coca-Cola Bottling Company was an independently owned operation, so its programming was not necessarily representative of the parent body.

5

Becked Up

Glenn Beck, White Supremacy, and
the Hijacking of the Civil Rights Legacy

CYNTHIA A. YOUNG

It was August 2010, and Glenn Beck was on a roll. With a popular Fox News show, a syndicated radio show, and multiple *New York Times* best-selling books, Beck was riding a high tide of right-wing conservatism. For months Beck had been hyping his "Restoring Honor" rally, which was to be held at the Lincoln Memorial on the forty-seventh anniversary of Martin Luther King Jr.'s "I Have a Dream" speech. Initially, Beck denied that he had chosen the date to correspond to the famous March on Washington, explicitly pitching the rally as political. As the date approached, however, Beck switched tack, embracing the alleged coincidence. He began to speak of the event in general terms as a rally to reaffirm faith, hope, and charity, the values that "made America great." As the event drew closer, Beck warmed to his theme, describing the rally as a product of "divine providence," with exalted goals. "We are the people of the civil rights movement," he said in one radio monologue, "We are the ones that must stand for civil and equal rights, justice, equal justice.... We are the inheritors and protectors of the civil rights movement." The same man who a year earlier had accused President Obama of being a "racist" with a "deep-seated hatred for white people" (Schwen n.d.) was now claiming the mantle of civil rights. The same commentator who was the public face of the Tea Party, a group condemned by the National Association for the Advancement of Colored People in a July 2010 resolution for having "racist elements," was now positioning himself as the protector and inheritor of civil rights.

Given Beck's reputation, it is easy to dismiss such statements as the attention-seeking behavior of a man trying to stay in the spotlight, and they undoubtedly are. But Beck's defiant claiming of Martin Luther King Jr.'s civil rights mantle reflects a larger appropriation of King by the Right. It represents a defensive, aggressively nativist, and often racist form of whiteness that expresses itself through discourse and symbols most commonly associated with the 1960s movement for racial equality. The suturing together of perceived white victimhood, vehement Islamophobia, extreme nativism, and civil rights–era rhetoric is the subject of this essay. On one level, the union of anti-immigrant politics and perceived white victimhood is nothing new; nativist fear-mongering has historically fueled white workers' sense that cheap, foreign labor is endangering their real or imagined jobs. What is new, however, is the civil rights–era gloss over patently racist and nativist interests, the product of an odd conjuncture in our allegedly postracial United States. In what follows, I explore the contours of a postracial whiteness that uses Martin Luther King Jr. and civil rights symbolism to advance positions and policies that are, either implicitly or explicitly, antiblack and anti-immigrant. The use of King points to a bizarre symbolic inversion of historical and contemporary reality in which the civil rights leader is made to speak for white dispossession. He is made to produce, if not reflect, the idea that in this postracial age, it is actually white people who are most disadvantaged precisely because they allegedly do not make identity-based claims on the state in the way that racial and ethnic minorities do. While, in theory, postraciality is supposed to signify the end of race-thinking, in practice it means the rise of an explicitly white racial consciousness, one that sometimes skirts and other times leans quite hard into earlier, violently racist forms of whiteness. In unpacking the logic by which the civil rights struggle has been repurposed for a predominantly white, middle-class, and conservative constituency, I want to understand how black civil rights has become an avenue for expressing retrograde white identity politics. I am interested in how civil rights rhetoric helps express a form of whiteness that is both racist and avowedly antiracist, a form of whiteness that simultaneously claims to be disempowered and uniquely empowered to "take the country back."

The articulation of a reactionary white identity to Martin Luther King Jr. and the civil rights movement he has come to embody has emerged in a unique historical conjuncture. In the first decades of the twenty-first century, the 9/11 attacks, wars in Iraq and Afghanistan, the global financial crisis of 2007–8, and the election of the first black US president have accompanied, or in some instances occasioned, ever-widening racial, economic, political, health, and educational gaps. Those gaps combined with significant cultural shifts have contributed to the remaking of white identity as uniquely vulnerable and victimized in the contemporary moment.[1]

In particular, the September 11, 2001, attacks on the Pentagon and the World Trade Center *and* the media's coverage of that event set the foundation for the myth of a uniquely imperiled white identity to emerge. In the United States, the attacks were depicted at the time and are now remembered as a traumatic nation- and world-redefining event.[2] The spectacularly telegenic nature of the World Trade Center attacks combined with the twenty-four-hour news cycle burned images of the collapsing towers and an ash-filled Ground Zero into a generation's collective consciousness. The narrativizing of the 9/11 dead as blameless victims and heroic first responders and the terrorists as fanatical Muslims who hate America "because of its freedoms" enabled the reframing of the United States as a homeland rather than a nation. The trauma was at once personal—a home invasion—and collective: "we" were all targets now. The popular media's failure to locate the attacks within the global context of US imperialism obscured the fact that populations in the Middle East and elsewhere are more vulnerable to sudden death and violent displacement because of US foreign policy than US residents have ever been. What set in among many was a collective disavowal of US culpability for creating the conditions in which Al Qaeda could emerge, making it nearly impossible (and unpatriotic) to implicate the United States in a global structure of violence and exploitation. Instead, a new take on an old American exceptionalism presented 9/11 as a unique collective wound, one that required a "therapeutic patriotism" and a "war on terror" to preserve the United States as the preeminent symbol of democracy and freedom in the world.[3] The idea that radical Islamic terrorism targeted US culture, not US policies, enabled the surface invocation of the United States as tolerant of multiculturalism—recall President Bush's praise for Muslim Americans in the wake of 9/11—while also allowing white people to believe that they were being targeted for who they were: quintessential Americans. Where the civil rights movement demonstrated that white rights and privileges came at the expense of black people, 9/11 allowed white Americans to reimagine themselves as collective victims of global terror. It became a powerful way for whites to lay claim to victimhood-by-proxy.

This imagined victimhood coincided with an emerging demographic context that will render whites of European descent a statistical minority by the middle of this century. Faced with their impending minority status, whites across the political spectrum have shown themselves to be susceptible to a defensive white racism. A study published by social psychologists Maureen Craig and Jennifer Richeson (2014) found that a nationally representative sample of white Americans exhibited "pro-White" and racially biased attitudes when made aware of the nation's shifting racial demographics. The greater the perceived threat to white privilege and power, the larger the spike in racist sentiment toward all racial minorities, even toward those groups, such as Asians and black Americans, that do not primarily contribute to this demographic shift.

One measure of this spike is the historic rise in hate groups. A Southern Poverty Law Center (SPLC) report estimated that the number of active hate groups had risen from 602 in 2000 to more than 1,000 in 2011 (Potok 2012). Though the intervening years saw a small decline, 2014 was a boom year for hate groups, which now stand at just under 900 (Southern Poverty Law Center n.d.). The SPLC attributed that historic increase to the growing presence of a radical right dominated by the patriot movement. Inspired by Timothy McVeigh's bombing of a federal building in Oklahoma City, the number of militia and patriot groups peaked in the mid-1990s at 858 before falling to 143 in 2002. The election of President Obama, however, revived the dying movement, with the number of groups skyrocketing from 149 in 2008 to 512 in 2009. By the year 2011, the number of patriot and militia groups had more than doubled, to 1,274 (Potok 2012). Though this is responsible for an increasing number of terrorist attacks on US soil, the real story here is not so much the expansion of the radical Right as it is the mainstreaming of it. President Donald Trump is just the latest, most sensational tip of this iceberg. Proliferating nativist and xenophobic beliefs and rhetoric over the last decade laid the foundation for Trump's candidacy and presidency.[4]

One vehicle for this mainstreaming has been the Tea Party itself. Founded in the Bush era to protest tax policy and bailout programs put in place after the 2008 economic crash, the Tea Party really only gained momentum after President Obama's inauguration. The Tea Party movement consists of six primary organizations—FreedomWorks Tea Party, Resistnet, Tea Party Nation, 1776 Tea Party, Tea Party Patriots, and Tea Party Express— and a host of grassroots organizers who bring their Tea Party perspective to local issues. In 2010, all but FreedomWorks, the most mainstream and least grassroots group within this network, had so-called Birthers in prominent leadership positions. "In [Birther] ranks," one Tea Party analysis rightly insists, "an abiding obsession with President Obama's birth certificate is often a stand-in for the belief that the first black president is not a 'real American'" (Burghardt and Zeskin 2010, 7). To one degree or another, the Tea Party has been a haven for racists and nativists, forging ties with various right-wing entities. Resistnet has been a hub for Islamophobes and Birthers, 1776 Tea Party is linked to the Minuteman project and the anti-immigrant movement, while the Tea Party Patriots are closely aligned with militias and Christian nationalists. The Tea Party Express has fought numerous charges of racism in part based on the actions and deeds of avowed anti-Semite and white supremacist Mark Williams, who was the group's first chairperson (Burghardt and Zeskin 2010, 49). Tea Party Nation, a Tennessee-based group, has also made alliances with Birthers, Christian nationalists (white separatists, if not supremacists), and nativists, though it has also publicly opposed abortion, gay life, and anything that allegedly opposes Christian teachings. It is a diffuse and varied network, split between Tea Partiers prepared to challenge mainstream Republicans and those who want to remain outside of the political mainstream altogether. With the success of Donald Trump's campaign, however, it is difficult to say that even this distinction holds. His candidacy was popular with so-called mainstream Republicans and white nationalists, as reported by Evan Osnos (2015) in the *New Yorker*.

Since 2008, the Tea Party's primary target has been the first black president. During his presidency, Obama was the Tea Party's target, reflecting the fact that his election was "a transformative moment for white people" (Sanneh 2010, 2), contributing to a feeling of white disenfranchisement. Researchers Christopher Parker and Matt Barreto (2014) contend that Tea Partiers fervently believed that President Obama was out to destroy "their country" and undermine the values upon which the country was allegedly founded. The president's blackness upended some white people's sense of what racialized body could properly represent US power, even as it fueled a postracial rhetoric that substituted Obama's political success for group racial success. So focused, irrational, and intense was the Tea Party's Obamaphobia that disapproval of Obama was the strongest independent variable driving Tea Party identification in a 2012 study. Despite their talk of the federal debt and fiscal responsibility, respondents demonstrated more vehement anti-Obama sentiment than they did fiscally conservative sentiment (Maxwell and Parent 2012). If the Tea Party was motivated by a particular dislike of President Obama, that feeling was bolstered by an abiding racial animus; an inability, in Baratunde Thurston's words, to allow black people "to be that which they are," that is, fully enfranchised citizens.[5] The respondents in Parker and Barretto's (2014) longitudinal study of the Tea Party expressed significant, if coded, antiblack racism and antipathy toward immigrants, though they carefully avoided using overtly racist language. Opposition to immigrants from Central and South America or antipathy toward African Americans was not about race, Tea Partiers claimed, but rather stemmed from their belief, sometimes implied, sometimes directly stated, that both groups eschewed hard work and loyalty to an imagined national community. However, a 2013 study by Knowles and colleagues indicated that along with social conservatism, antiminority attitudes were the most reliable predictor of Tea Party affiliation. Though antiblack racism provided the symbolic repertoire for the monkey and witch doctor caricatures of President Obama seen at Tea Party rallies, this racism more often found indirect articulation.[6] Tea Party supporters opposed welfare and other social programs that they identified with minorities because they undercut so-called American values of thrift and hard work. Echoing familiar culturally racist tropes, Tea Partiers in one study disguised their "racial resentment" in "terms of more symbolic, philosophical complaints about Black culture" as lacking in industriousness and ambition. Black Americans, these respondents contended, have developed a dependency on the federal government (Knowles et al. 2013, 6).

This denial of structural inequality and the emergence of cultural, rather than biological, racism are hallmarks of our neoliberal era. When privatization, market deregulation, and entrepreneurship are imagined to be the only effective social levelers, then economic inequality is imagined to stem only from individual (poor) choices or inaction, and racism is only a matter of individual prejudice. These neoliberal shibboleths have a double-edged nature, for if black and brown people are to blame for their own impoverished plight, then perhaps so are white people. Or as one widely read and reviled piece by Kevin Williamson (2016) in the *National Review* argued, then perhaps poor white people are the problem. "If you spend time in hardscrabble, white upstate New York, or eastern Kentucky, or my own native West Texas," Williamson wrote, "and you take an honest look at the welfare dependency, the drug and alcohol addiction, the family anarchy—that is to say the whelping of human children with all the respect and wisdom of a stray dog . . . you will come to a realization." You will discover, Williamson concludes, that "the white American underclass is in thrall to a vicious, selfish culture whose main products are misery and used heroin needles" and "deserve[s] to die." This discourse of cultural racism honed on black and brown bodies is now being wielded against white ones.

While white elites may see the problem of white poverty as proof of inherent dysfunction, others see it as proof that white fortunes are declining in the face of a new multicultural reality. Researchers Christopher Parker and Matt Barreto write, "We believe that people are driven to support the Tea Party from the anxiety they feel as they perceive the America they know, the country they love, slipping away, threatened by the rapidly changing face of what they believe is the 'real' America: a heterosexual, Christian, middle-class, (mostly) male, white country" (2014, 3). A main indicator of this shift is the alleged rise in antiwhite bias. Taking the color-blind racism described in Bonilla-Silva's classic *Racism without Racists* (2014) to a new level, many Tea Partiers not only deny the existence of structural racism but also see a "playing field tilted away from them" (Burke 2015, 38). That is, the rise of racial and ethnic minorities means the fall of the white majority. It is a zero-sum game for many white people. A 2011 study found that white respondents were "more likely to see decreases in bias against Blacks as related to increases in bias against Whites," while black respondents saw no correlation between the two. Another feature of the study was the mismatch between black and white perceptions of declining antiblack bias. Both groups saw a decline, but white respondents saw bias vanishing to the point of insignificance, while black respondents saw a much more gradual decrease, with bias still substantially impacting black life chances (Norton and Sommers 2011, 215–18).

Claims to a postracial reality, a prevalent theme at Tea Party events, not only facilitate claims of white structural disadvantage but also increasingly fuel articulations of antiblack racism and nativism. For Tea Party supporters, race and religion are inextricably bound up in US nationhood. The "real American" is a flexible signifier that can seem to include nonwhite citizens even as the very definition of what constitutes the "real America" is racially and religiously coded. While color-blind racists are drawn to the Tea Party, participation in Tea Party events bolsters white identification through "assertions of national decline and the embrace of libertarian ideology" (Knowles et al. 2013, 8). Tea Partiers present themselves as untainted by racism even as their sense of whiteness and civic belonging is imagined to be the ideal form of, indeed identical to, US identity and citizenship.

While it may be the case that the Tea Party draws a white race-conscious, if not always overtly racist, contingent, it also represents broader trends in our political and cultural formation. Based on membership numbers, most people view the Tea Party as a fringe group, but several opinion polls from 2010 showed that between 14 and 16 percent of the adult population supported the Tea Party (Burghardt and Zeskin 2010, 8). Four years later, a Gallup poll showed that roughly one in four Republicans supported the Tea Party, and nearly forty-five million Americans considered themselves sympathizers (Newport n.d.). As the recent Republican presidential candidate race shows, the Tea Party represents a significant and increasingly vocal white, male and middle-class constituency even if its official membership numbers do not reflect that. It also serves as a fertile recruitment ground for more extreme anti-immigrant and white supremacist groups who attend Tea Party rallies. While what the Institute for Research and Education on Human Rights calls the Nativist Establishment, organizations like Federation for American Immigration Reform and NumbersUSA, has exercised less political influence since 2008, the Tea Party has increasingly launched anti-immigrant campaigns, even as anti-immigrant leaders are increasingly taking on leadership roles within the Tea Party itself (Burghardt and Zeskind 2012, 1). The Tea Party has been a vocal supporter of Arizona's S.B. 1070 and Alabama's H.B. 56, which made it illegal to be undocumented. It was also instrumental in defeating the Border Security, Economic Opportunity, and Immigration Modernization Act of 2013, which provided some immigrants with a pathway to citizenship. The bill narrowly passed in the Senate only to languish in the Republican-controlled House. The Development, Relief and Education for Minors Act, otherwise known as the DREAM Act, has also been a frequent target, as has birthright citizenship provided for by the Fourteenth Amendment. In other words, anti-immigrant activism has been a primary way through which Tea Partiers express a sense of white entitlement, an identity that hinges on connecting immigrants to symbols historically reserved for black people. A 2011 study of white attitudes toward immigrants revealed that "just under 70 percent of whites view Latinos as particularly prone to be on welfare[,] suggest[ing] that the connection between Latinos and welfare is now firmly in place." The discourse of undeserving welfare recipients, long a coded way of referring to black people, has extended to cover immigrants, particularly those from Latin and Central America. Though respondents reserve their harshest criticisms for illegal immigrants, Abrajano and Hajnal suggest that when respondents were asked simply about Mexican or Central American immigrants generally "the answers tend not to differ all that much" (2015, 52). Evidence of what they describe as a "white backlash," such negative "reactions to larger immigrant populations are analogous to past white responses to larger black populations" (12). This has led to efforts in many states to restrict immigrant access to public services such as education and health care.

I have been arguing thus far that the attacks of 9/11, the impending minoritization of white people, and the election of the first black president have provided the building blocks for a conservative white identity that sees itself as traumatized and uniquely under siege. If this identity sees itself as already or in danger of becoming disenfranchised, it sees the nation as similarly imperiled: subject to terrorism, besieged by undocumented immigrants, and experiencing a precipitous moral decline brought on by the decentering of so-called European American values and mores. In one sense, these claims are nothing new. Conservative social movements have long perpetuated the belief that their constituents were in danger of losing status and privileges if certain threats to the body politic—Communists, Socialists, immigrants, freed slaves—were not effectively contained. The policy positions endorsed by Tea Party conservatives are also nothing new. During the Reagan era, barely fifteen years after the passage of the 1964 Civil Rights Act and the 1965 Voting Rights Act, the Right was already arguing that federal oversight and enforcement of civil rights law was no longer necessary. The addition of postrace rhetoric to the already toxic narrative cocktail of undeserving black people and an imperiled (white) nation has, however, facilitated the articulation of a particular white racial identity. A postracial era, for this group, does not mean we are beyond racism and inequality; rather, it indicates that the boot is on the other foot. Put another way, "postracial" signifies that the United States is post-(antiblack) racism, though not necessarily postracism altogether. Instead, from this perspective it is white people who are disadvantaged, white people who are in danger of being (or are already in fact) discriminated against because their identity does not fit a multicultural, "politically correct" paradigm enforced by racial minorities, undocumented immigrants, and their supporters on the left. A 2014 Public Policy Research Institute survey on American values found that 52 percent of white Americans "believe that discrimination against whites has become as big a problem as discrimination against minorities." Among Republicans the percentage rose to 61 percent, while among Tea Partiers it peaked at 73 percent (Piacenza 2014).

The increasing use of postracial discourse has paralleled, if not produced, an intensifying investment in white privilege and power that has white nationalist, often white supremacist, undertones and overtones. It is worth noting here that a possessive investment in whiteness, to use George Lipsitz's phrase, is signaled by this discourse, but, in fact, its use by members of the white working and middle classes speaks to the relative decline in their economic, social, and political fortunes. As some white people face their increasing obsolescence, as wages decline, jobs disappear, and their interests become marginal to this late neoliberal order, postracial rhetoric has facilitated a retrospective acknowledgment of white privilege *only* and in the wake of its alleged loss. Rather than its invisibility fueling a continued investment in whiteness and white privilege, as Lipsitz argues, postracial whiteness requires that a past and historically distant white privilege be made visible through the mourning of its alleged loss. That is, postracialism's possessive investment in whiteness is defined by three elements. It reflects the devaluation of some forms of whiteness, calls for an equalizing or revaluing of whiteness across class sectors, and denies the legacy and ongoing devastation wrought by white privilege. The primary affective registers through which postracial rhetoric operates in this articulation are anger and fear. If whites are angry, it is because they are fearful targets of discrimination. Their perceived vulnerability animates a self-righteousness that denies white racism, even as it depends on that racism to stake a claim to privileges that have been allegedly eviscerated.

The deployment of an (ironically) racialized postracial discourse has made the turn to civil rights rhetoric simultaneously unfortunate and utterly predictable. Though left-wing groups around the world have long adopted civil rights rhetoric to advance their own social justice fights, it is increasingly common for right-wing groups to use the same language to advance nativist, racially coded agendas of their own. Analyzing websites, fund-raising letters, speeches, advertisements, and editorials, researchers Lio, Melzer, and Reese (2008, 5) found that U.S. English, the largest English-only organization in the United States, has utilized civil rights rhetoric highlighting "model" versus "nightmare" citizens for over a decade. Spanish-speaking immigrants, according to U.S. English, seek to tear down the shared cultural fabric of the United States. U.S. English, in its view, is waging a defensive campaign to stop those who would rid the United States of its model (read: white, male, conservative) citizens. Rather than seeing this move as wholly disingenuous, it is perhaps more productive to see it as a reflection of the fact that the civil rights movement has provided the primary lingua franca for most US social and political issues since the 1960s. The language of equality, freedom, and justice so compellingly articulated by civil rights activists has been adapted by everyone from pro-life activists to animal rights groups to convey the purportedly unassailable rightness of their positions. Central to this appropriation is Martin Luther King Jr., who is easily the most recognizable symbol of the civil rights movement even by those born decades after the movement's decline. His politics have been reduced to that of nonviolent protest and desegregation, while more radical aspects of his legacy, such as the Poor People's Campaign and King's opposition to the war in Vietnam, have been shunted aside. Latching onto King's legacy can also be extremely profitable. The National Basketball Association and corporations like Alcatel Communications, Nike, and Apple have utilized either symbolism evoking King or his actual words and voice to advance their commercial interests. Whether the cause is in line with civil rights goals, opposed to them, or completely unrelated seems to matter little in the race to link one's cause or company to what is perceived to be one of the few morally unassailable movements in US history. The linking of Dr. King's legacy to a postracial discourse that masks a nativist and often racist political agenda not only runs counter to the principles and values espoused by King but in fact works in the interest of white domination, if not outright supremacy. In focusing on Glenn Beck's deployment of 9/11 and Martin Luther King Jr., I am interested in examining the contours of a reactionary form of whiteness that is both defensive, that is, premised upon a sense of profound injury, *and* offensive, based on a sense of postracial white entitlement that fuses antiblack racism, Islamophobia, and nativism into a toxic political mix.

By the time Glenn Beck framed his 2010 "Restoring Honor" rally as a civil rights rally, he had established himself as a prominent spokesperson for the Tea Party and the religious Right. Beck's ability to forge a media empire around his persona as a man with homespun, "real American" values was aided by impeccable timing, huckster instincts, and canny showmanship. Beck was a drive-time FM radio DJ in several small markets before he landed at Tampa's WFLA-970 in the waning days of 1999. A few months after Beck arrived at Clear Channel's WFLA, the 2000 presidential election crisis happened, and Beck had ringside seats, narrating the ins and outs of the recount from his Tampa perch. Though earlier in his career Beck had been a libertarian who supported abortion rights and drug decriminalization, with the election crisis he emerged as a religious conservative—he had recently converted to Mormonism—and right-wing commentator. So successful was his rightward turn that Clear Channel decided to take Beck national in September 2001. His first day on XM satellite radio was September 10, when Beck did riffs on Johnnie Cochran and frequent target "race warlord" Jesse Jackson, using one of his dialect-inflected black voices, a feature of his shtick since his earliest days in radio. In another bit, Beck pretended to claim responsibility for the lynching of African American James Byrd, who had been chained to a pickup truck and dragged to his death by white supremacists in Jasper, Texas (Zaitchik 2010, 73). In other words, it was just another day for Beck, another opportunity for him to showcase his antiblack racism in the guise of humor.

And then planes hit the Pentagon and the Twin Towers, a once-in-a-lifetime opportunity for Beck. On September 11, Beck opened every hour of his show with the playing of "The Star-Spangled Banner," punctuating listener calls with his own copious tears (Zaitchik 2010, 74). Working the phones like a radio televangelist, Beck filled the airwaves with frequent references to "god and country" and angry diatribes against various nations. "The man in me," Beck declared, "would love to drop a nuke on Pakistan if they had anything to do with it." Another caller prompted this: "Let them see the fury of the United States when it is fully unleashed. You think we have enemies now? Wait until we take out Libya, Afghanistan, Palestine." Upping the ante even further, Beck finally landed on this: "Any [country] with ties to Bin Laden I wouldn't mind turning into a giant glowing parking lot" (74–75). The on-air crying lasted for months, as did the tough talk, with Beck shuttling back and forth between the two for dramatic effect. When Dr. Laura Schlesinger refused to alter her personal advice format to satisfy the public's desire for terrorism talk, Clear Channel offered its stations Beck as an alternative. As he had with the 2000 election recount, Beck used the attacks and the subsequent war on terror to reinvent himself yet again, this time as a spokesperson for the Bush administration. He staged a series of pro-war "Rallies for America" from March through May 2003. Featuring traditional country music, appearances by veterans and their families, and Jumbotron video messages from President Bush himself, the rallies concluded with Beck taking the stage to deliver a mash-up of his greatest hits.

On the heels of those rallies, Beck published his first nonfiction book, *The Real America: Messages from the Heart and Heartland*, which was pitched as a paean to a time when god, country, and small-town values reigned supreme. The book's introduction describes "the real America" as a "place in the heart," a "home" to which we all need to return (Beck 2003, loc. 56, 81). In that fictive world—Beck admits it is aspirational—neighbors care about and protect one another. Into this Middle American utopia, Beck inserts King not to decry racism but to argue that "political correctness" threatens to destroy King's legacy. Beck writes: "Martin Luther King's dream will come true in the Real America: a colorblind society—but without political correctness. Unfortunately, King's dream has been perverted and twisted by so many, white and black alike, that it is barely recognizable today. In the Real America, we will know that white men aren't racist; one *man* can be racist. Black men aren't lazy; one *man* can be lazy and racism is not an American problem, it's a human problem" (loc. 88). Individual prejudice exists, but structural racism does not. This contention is exactly why Beck and so many white conservatives frequently invoke the famous "content of our character" line from King's "I Have a Dream" speech. Isolated from the rest of King's March on Washington speech, the line "I have a dream that my four little children will one day live in a nation where they will not be judged by the color of their skin, but by the content of their character" can be contorted to suggest that society should judge only on an individual, ahistorical basis. Contexts and disparities, be they historical, political, economic, or racial, need not be taken into consideration, and to do so is to commit the sin against which King allegedly warned. This deployment of King produces a cardboard cutout version of him as a figure concerned with individual, not group, progress, as a man concerned with changing hearts and minds rather than structures of white supremacy.

Immediately after invoking King in the name of political incorrectness, Beck harkens back to a fictive "evening of September 11," one "without violence, without sorrow, without mourning" (2003, loc. 90). Just as Beck would contend when he launched his September 9/12 Movement at the end of the decade, here he asserted that in the days after 9/11, Americans were united in their care and concern for one another. This mythic unity is bolstered by the image of the ideal citizen—white, American, conservative, and middle-aged. It also depends upon its other, that is to say: nonwhite, foreign, anti-Christian, and young. To point out that hate crimes against those presumed to be Muslim proliferated in the days after the attacks or that the US state detained hundreds of immigrants from Arab and Muslim countries in the wake of 9/11 is irrelevant to Beck because they are not part of his imagined community. This image of individual black moral rectitude and white unity is cemented, paradoxically, through a critique of black and Middle Eastern communities. What Beck is really endorsing is an imaginary moment of white unification produced on the one hand by a sense of profound injury and on the other by a belief in US military might and imperial destiny. In the "real America," we are supposedly governed by care and concern for our neighbors and the homespun wisdom of a Mayberry-style middle America. What makes Beck's vision resonate is this image of domestic harmony paired with an unabashed vision of U.S. global domination. Beck's "real America" is Janus-faced: warm and (selectively) welcoming on the domestic front, but harsh and unrelenting on the international one. If King is a morally unassailable symbol of nonviolent antiracism, then linking King to 9/11 allows

Beck to associate the injuries of 9/11 with those of antiblack racism. Paradoxically and counter to King's legacy, the attendant psychic and moral injury inflicted by 9/11 justifies violent, imperial responses in other countries in order to secure the peace and nonviolence of this one. This insistence that military violence outside US borders secures domestic peace inside them is precisely the logic that the 9/11 attacks were designed to refute. It is also the logic necessary for Beck's formulation to work. Writing of Israel, David Theo Goldberg describes a "bifurcated condition" produced by a state of "a permanent war elsewhere—its horrors hidden from view, complaint or criticism cordoned off behind the Wall (or across the ocean), while the spectre of peace and prosperity is maintained at home" (2008, 37). It is the nonviolence of Dr. King that bolsters the image of peace and prosperity on which the endorsement of military violence depends. This, it bears noting, distorts King and the larger civil rights movement for which he stands by writing out the overwhelming racial and state violence with which nonviolent protests were routinely met. Peaceful protests were not entirely peaceful because police and ordinary citizens wielded dogs, batons, fire hoses, and fists to secure the racial order. In invoking a mythical post-9/11 moment where "we" were all united behind the righteous force of US power, coded as productive (of national community) rather than destructive (of other communities and nations), Beck ignores and actively writes out this racist past and present. Beck's national community, like his narration of civil rights history, is highly selective. It does not include Hollywood, political correctness, Communism (disguised, according to Beck, as liberalism), or the tolerance of sexuality-related but unspecified, un-Godly practices, all of which *The Real America* decries. The "we" about which Beck waxes poetic turns out to be a "we" defined by exclusion; it is riven with simultaneously acknowledged and unacknowledged conflicts over race, gender, sexuality, and political belief that result in the consolidation of white supremacist, masculinist defenses of militarized violence abroad.

One place where these various, often contradictory, elements cohere is in the chapter titled "Jesse Jackson Is Yasser Arafat." Here Beck denounces Jackson and Al Sharpton, whom he accuses of oppressing black communities through their repeated references to the damage done by slavery and the need for reparations. "They're throwing the shackles around their people, yet again," Beck claims. "They're chaining them up like slaves, yet again" (2003, loc. 1494). Black leaders and cultural atrophy, not white supremacy, are the problem. Awash in cultural racism, Beck compares Jews and blacks, claiming that Jews have ample reason to be bitter and downtrodden, and yet they think of themselves as the "Chosen People," whereas black people think of themselves as victims. Black perception, and not structural racism, is the problem. Like Arafat and the Palestinians, Beck writes, Jackson and Sharpton propagate this discourse for their own self-interest, not that of their communities. Linking Arafat and Jackson, Beck extends his antiblack cultural racism to his musings on the Middle East. On the Middle East, he asserts, "Hey, camel countries, do you know why you guys are having rock sandwiches and washing them down with glasses of sand for lunch? Because there's no security in your region. You are so busy terrorizing each other that you couldn't even build a Fiat . . . and Fiats suck" (loc. 1661). In another telling moment, Beck contends, "Arab culture looks to past glories and past humiliations and that everything is rooted in yesterday's transgressions" (loc. 1701–2). By contrast, (white) Americans, he claims, always look with optimism to the future, where the best is yet to come. The targets of Zionism and antiblack racism are decried for calling upon a historical discourse to argue that the deck is frequently stacked against them. Refusing to take responsibility for their plight, Palestinians and black Americans blame others for their situation, rather than looking to themselves.

Glenn Beck's rapid ascent in the first decade of the twenty-first century—from unknown radio DJ to celebrated commentator on Fox News—has been well documented, as has his close affiliation with the Tea Party, for whom he has been an unofficial spokesman (see, e.g., Leibovich 2010; Milbank 2010; Zaitchik 2010). What has received relatively little attention is the way in which that ascent is a telling marker of a turn to a postracial reactionary form of white identity that is dependent upon appropriating elements of civil rights history and narrating 9/11 as a world-historic form of attack on white (American) values. In addition to deploying "the real America" trope, Beck has used others from the Tea Party playbook. He was an early Obama hater, declaring him at various times to be a radical socialist, a Marxist, a "radical black nationalist," and someone out to "settle old racial scores with new social justice." Beck on many occasions has described the Obama administration as the incarnation of evil, no more so than during his months-long campaign in 2009 to get Van Jones, the president's newly appointed special adviser on green jobs—Beck called him the "Green Czar"—fired. Beck's unrelenting campaign was largely responsible for Jones resigning over controversial comments he had made years earlier. As in *The Real America*, over the last decade, Beck has most often wielded Martin Luther King Jr. as a cudgel to bash "bad" black men—Jackson, Sharpton, Obama, Jones—and any post-1968 black protest movements. Beck's gloss for post-1968 cultural reforms is the term "political correctness," which he says shuts down conservatives by mistakenly calling them racist or sexist, or homophobic or nativist. Supposedly exiled from the realm of popular rhetoric and thought are a community of "disenfranchised" white people for whom Beck speaks. Typically he does this by deploying rhetoric usually associated with blackness to represent whiteness. According to journalist Dana Milbank, in his first year on Fox News in 2009, Beck invoked slavery and slaves some two hundred times, and not to describe the historic wrongs against African-descended peoples. In one example, Obama is the engine of white enslavement, with Beck once saying: "'I think this president [Obama] is moving quickly, moving all of us quickly, into slavery. He's enslaving our children with a debt that they can never repay'"(Milbank 2010, 221). On September 12, 2009, when Beck held a rally to celebrate the ousting of Jones from the White House, one protester's sign said, "Obama's Plan = White Slavery," a not-infrequent Tea Party catchphrase. Beck has also presented prosecuting white-collar crime as akin to pre–civil rights Jim Crow laws: "'African-Americans have long understood dual justice. One set of laws for whites and one for blacks.'" Now, according to Beck, "vengeance and vigilantism was creating a dual system of justice for corporate executives" (221). In Beck world, rich is the new poor, and white is the new black.[7]

The year 2009 was also when Beck founded his 9/12 Movement, designed to bring us back to the day after 9/11, when he says unity reigned: "The day after America was attacked, we were not obsessed with Red States, Blue States or political parties" (McGrath 2010). Tellingly, the most recent version of the project's mission statement refers directly to race: "The day after America was attacked we were not obsessed with political parties, the color of your skin, or what religion you practiced. We were united as Americans, standing together to protect the greatest nation ever created" ("Our Mission" n.d.). The project is based on nine principles, including feel-good mantras such as "America is good" and more pointedly political edicts such as "I work hard for what I have and I will share it with who I want to. The government cannot force me to be charitable." The project also emphasizes twelve values, including honesty, humility, charity, and thrift, all staples of (Christian) Sunday school primers. The principles and values are at once universal and pointedly political. Though the 9/12 Movement insists it is nonpartisan, Tea Partiers swell the ranks of the various local chapters, and 9/12ers have frequently attended Tea Party rallies calling for smaller government and less taxation. In October 2009, they protested so-called liberal media bias in front of local TV stations around the country in an event dubbed "Can You

Hear Us Now?" Once again, Beck deployed the language of inclusion, community, and acceptance to attack those who question his right-wing message in celebration of small government, individual responsibility, and a return to so-called traditional American values as enshrined by the founding fathers.

The 9/12 Movement and the "Restoring Honor" rally held in its name really sought to revive a mythically simpler time, precisely the era that the civil rights movement challenged, when racial lines and gender roles left straight white men in the driver's seat and gays and lesbians firmly in the closet. As Beck claimed in his May 26, 2010, show, "This is going to be a moment that you'll never be able to paint people as haters, racists, none of it. This is a moment quite honestly that I think we reclaim the civil rights movement. It has been so distorted, and so turned upside down. It's an abomination" ("Beck Says His 8-28 Rally" n.d.). As proof of this, Beck cited Bertha Lewis's participation in a protest against Arizona's racist S.B. 1070 law. Lewis, a black woman, was the former CEO and chief organizer of the nonprofit network known as the Association of Community Organizations for Reform Now (ACORN), which had disbanded in March 2010 after right-wing media activists taped low-level ACORN workers appearing to encourage welfare fraud. The resulting controversy, fueled by Beck, who played the tapes on endless loop and repeatedly interviewed James O'Keefe, the conservative who had released the audio- and videotapes, led to federal and private defunding of ACORN and its eventual demise. Lewis and the other protesters sang "We Shall Overcome" as they were being arrested, something that supposedly outraged Beck. He railed:

> How dare you? . . . So here they are singing "We Shall Overcome." We're not even talking about the rule of law and we're not talking about equal rights, civil rights. We are talking about modern day slavery, and that is exactly what illegal immigration is, modern day slavery. Now while we're not going to talk about the issues of illegal immigration or anything that's happening in Washington because we must repair honor and integrity and honesty first, I tell you right now: We are on the right side of history. We are on the side of individual freedoms and liberties, and dammit we will reclaim the civil rights moment. We will take that movement because we were the people who did it in the first place. ("Beck Says His 8-28 Rally" n.d.)

Though Beck asked attendees to leave their political signs at home, his listeners knew the score. They knew exactly who their enemies were because Beck had been identifying them for the years and months leading up to the rally—President Obama, Van Jones, Bertha Lewis, Jesse Jackson, Al Sharpton, and so forth. Attaching Martin Luther King Jr.'s legacy to his agenda was at once a brilliant media stunt—Beck got mainstream media coverage and raised the ire of civil right leaders including Al Sharpton who held a counterdemonstration—and a nonsensical one.

Upping the ante in his linking of himself to King, in April 2010, Beck interviewed Alveda King, Dr. King's niece and a staunch pro-life, anti–gay marriage activist. The two discussed the ten-point "nonviolent pledge" King wrote in 1963, and Beck went on to analyze it over several broadcasts in the following weeks (Branch 2010). At a public event that same month, Beck read the pledge to his audience, saying it would shape the 9/12 Movement's next phase (Blow 2010). The pledge reads in part:

> I hereby pledge myself—my person and body—to the nonviolent movement. Therefore I will keep the following ten commandments:
>
> 1. Meditate daily on the teachings and life of Jesus.
> 2. Remember always that the non-violent movement seeks justice and reconciliation—not victory.
> 3. Walk and talk in the manner of love, for God is love.
> 4. Pray daily to be used by God in order that all men might be free.
> 5. Sacrifice personal wishes in order that all men might be free.
> 6. Observe with both friend and foe the ordinary rules of courtesy.
> 7. Seek to perform regular service for others and for the world.
> 8. Refrain from the violence of fist, tongue, or heart.

It is worth adding that this nonviolent pledge continues to be a centerpiece of Beck rallies. Most recently, he trotted it out for his August 2015 "Restoring Unity/Never Again Is Now/All Lives Matter" march and rally held in Birmingham, Alabama, in partnership with black pastor Jim Lowe. This time, Beck claimed to be mounting a movement of reconciliation, one designed to heal the racial wounds caused not by rampant state violence waged against black bodies but by the Black Lives Matter movement's protests against that racialized violence. The march began just a block from the Sixteenth Street Baptist Church, where four black girls were killed by a Klan bomb in September 1963, and the rally featured speakers including Alveda King and Pastor Rafael Cruz, father of presidential candidate Ted Cruz, whom Beck has since endorsed. One white marcher said he was there to heal a "racial divide" that had been caused by "people who are supposed to be the non-racist people, [but] if you pay attention, they're the ones promoting all this stuff." Not surprisingly, he went on to name "black leadership" generally and specifically Al Sharpton as examples of those widening the racial divide (Barrett 2015). One could point out that Beck's talk of making the Middle East a glowing parking lot or comparing Obama to Hitler is hardly civil or nonviolent discourse that affirms the right of all to live freely, but why bother? Use of King's pledge only makes sense if one believes that the urgent civil rights struggle of the twenty-first century is to liberate straight white men who have always been able to vote when they want, and live and work where they choose without de facto or de jure structures standing in their way. In Beck's world, ridiculous as it may seem to anyone who knows much about US history, the progressive Obama agenda is every bit as life-threatening and dehumanizing as was Jim Crow segregation.

On the actual day of the 2010 "Restoring Honor" rally, Alveda King spoke, as did former vice presidential nominee Sarah Palin. Both praised Dr. King, Lincoln, and the founding fathers, advocating a return to god that would fix much of what ails Washington. Beck also introduced members of the Black Robe Regiment (BRR), a group of religious leaders, imams, rabbis, and clergy committed to teaching the United States' constitutional principles to their congregants. In a day devoted to god and country, though, Beck still managed to plug his political agenda, suggesting that Dr. King himself would have stood against big government and lower taxes. The fact that little in King's biography supported such claims didn't matter, since it is likely that few in the audience of older white men and women knew the history any better than he did. In the best-case scenario, those at the rally had spent the civil right years blind to the plight of African Americans; at worst, they and their kin were actively defending the racial status quo. If many of Beck's on-air stances made him what Charles Blow called the "anti-King," it didn't matter to the enthusiastic crowd he addressed. Later that night on Fox News, Beck extended his efforts to restore America's honor by questioning the president's moral character and religious faith: "I don't know what that [Obama's religion] is, other than it's not Muslim, it's not Christian. It's a perversion of the gospel of Jesus Christ as most Christians know it" (Davidson 2010). This rhetoric was consistent with Beck's earlier assertions that even if Obama was not foreign-born as birthers suggested, he was "hiding something fundamental about his identity, something foreign, un-American, perhaps having to do with Kenya or Karl Marx or both" (Davidson 2010).

It is tempting to dismiss Beck's invocation of King as simply another trick in his media arsenal, but that would be to fail to see him as a symptom of a larger trend in white discourse that is both destructive and disturbing. During the 2016 presidential campaign, Ben Carson, Marco Rubio, and Ted Cruz leaned hard into xenophobic, Islamophobic, and racist rhetoric even as they insisted that their own rise was due to the achievement of equal rights made possible by the civil rights movement. They also used a defanged, inaccurate vision of the civil rights movement to bash the Black Lives Matter movement as the cause of an ongoing racial divide rather than a response to it. Meanwhile, most of the right- and left-wing media failed to interrogate ongoing examples of white racial militancy disguised as a struggle for group rights. In January 2016, an Oregon wildlife preserve was the site of an armed siege by antigovernment militia forces led by Ammon Bundy, the son of Cliven Bundy, who successfully won an armed standoff in 2014 with the Bureau of Land Management and local law enforcement over his failure to pay a decade's worth of grazing fees. Until his arrest in February 2016, Bundy was still grazing his cattle on public land free of charge, presumably pondering, as he did in one 2014 press conference, whether black people were better off as slaves. Black and brown activists on college campuses who complain about the lack of faculty of color and the racially hostile environments tolerated by university administrations are dismissed as whiners and complainers who exaggerate racial slights because they do not understand what real (read Jim Crow) racism looks or feels like. The white, conservative appropriation of civil rights rhetoric has facilitated the long march of white supremacy, while diluting the ongoing force of the civil rights movement's structural critique of US domestic and foreign policy. It threatens to make King a US icon without content, a historical remnant of a gone and forgotten racial past. If white conservatives like Glenn Beck continue to appropriate King for their racism and nativism, then they will also make King a less likely symbol for contemporary struggles against antiblack racism and poverty. Then we will know that King's image has been truly Becked-up.

Coda

In January 2017, Donald Trump became the forty-fifth president of the United States. Mobilizing a defining logic of postracial discourse, that white people are the victims of a new global order that privileges nonwhite interests over their own, Trump's "Make America Great Again" campaign slogan turned a racist dog whistle into a shout. Throughout the campaign, Trump proved himself to be an equal opportunity bigot. When Trump announced his candidacy in June 2015, he said of Mexicans: "They're bringing drugs. They're bringing crime. They're rapists." To keep them out, Trump announced he would build a wall between Mexico and the United States to be paid for by the Mexican government. In December 2015, shortly after the San Bernardino attacks by a US-born citizen of Pakistani descent and his immigrant wife, Trump called for a "total and complete shutdown" of Muslim immigration to the United States. He amended his proposed ban after the horrific shooting at an Orlando nightclub, expanding it to include any country "where there is a proven history of terrorism against the United States, Europe or allies," despite the fact that the perpetrator was a US citizen. Though such a ban was widely dismissed as unconstitutional, an NBC News/Survey Monkey poll conducted in the summer of 2016 showed that 50 percent of those polled supported it (NBC News/Survey Monkey Poll 2016). In a "nudge, nudge, wink, wink" to the radical Right, Trump and his national spokesperson Katrina Pierson, a black woman and former Tea Party candidate for Congress, denied that Trump even knew who David Duke was when the former Klan Grand Wizard endorsed him in February 2016. This, despite the fact that in 2000 Trump himself described Duke as a "bigot, a racist, a problem" (Kiely 2016). In June 2016, Trump questioned Indiana-born federal judge Gonzalo Curiel's impartiality in the civil case against Trump University. Citing his plans to build a wall to keep Mexicans out, Trump said that Judge Curiel's "Mexican heritage" posed an "inherent conflict of interest." In response, Speaker of the House Paul Ryan declared that Trump's contention was "the textbook definition of a racist comment." On the other hand, Alberto Gonzales, former attorney general under George W. Bush and himself Mexican American, defended Trump's right to question the presiding judge's impartiality, citing Judge Curiel's membership in La Raza Lawyers of San Diego and the fact that he appointed Robins Geller, a law firm that has paid nearly three-quarters of a million dollars in speaking fees to Hillary Clinton since 2009, to represent plaintiffs in the class action suit against Trump (Gonzales 2016). While both facts might indicate that Curiel had an ideological stake in the outcome of the presidential election, Gonzales's mention of Curiel's membership in La Raza Lawyers of San Diego also served to raise the image of radical Chicanx, a target of the Right and foes of so-called political correctness for decades. It also lends cover to Trump's reasoning, which was based solely on Curiel's Mexican ethnicity and not his professional affiliations. In July 2016, Trump doubled down on his Islamophobic bullying, criticizing Democratic National Convention speakers Khizr and Ghazala Khan, a Muslim immigrant family whose son was killed in Iraq, because Mrs. Khan remained silent during their appearance. Presenting himself as a champion of women's rights, Trump suggested that Mrs. Khan had not spoken because

Islam renders women silent, a framing of Islam familiar from the George W. Bush administration, which used this fig leaf as cover for the invasion of Afghanistan.

After these incidents, Democrats and Republicans alike decried Trump's actions. Prominent Republicans, including former presidents, former cabinet members, sitting governors and Congress members, as well as conservative commentators, refused to endorse him, though a substantial number of Republican leaders eventually got on board. Trump's unexpected electoral college victory confirmed what many Republicans had repeatedly tried to deny during the campaign, that is, that Trump's views, if not his precise articulations, were in keeping with the hard-right turn taken by the Republican Party in the post–Tea Party era. During the campaign, Glenn Beck himself walked this line, endorsing Ted Cruz during the primary fight as the anti-Trump. Cruz called into Beck's Blaze radio program on the day he announced his candidacy, and Beck devoted his entire radio program to singing the senator's praises. In subsequent shows, Beck explained his endorsement with varying degrees of incoherence. During one show, he said that Cruz might not be able to govern, but then the next day, he explained that what he meant was that the United States was likely to descend into martial law and that only a constitutionalist like Cruz could strike the right balance between freedom and authoritarianism: "I want Ted Cruz because I believe we are going to face tough times and we may go into martial law and I want somebody that will take that and with a velvet hand, put uprisings down if we have them and then let the hand off and restore our freedoms again" ("Washington: Glenn Beck Wants Ted Cruz's 'Velvet Hand'" 2015). When Cruz eventually endorsed Trump, Beck publicly broke with him, dismissing Cruz as just another politician: "For the very first time, I heard Ted Cruz calculate and when that happened, the whole thing fell apart for me" ("Washington: Ted Cruz Tries to Justify Trump Endorsement" 2016). Beck's public outrage and disappointment notwithstanding, Cruz's endorsement was perfectly in keeping with his own primary campaign positions. Cruz parroted the idea of building a wall between Mexico and the United States, though he refrained from suggesting that Mexico would pay for it, and after the San Bernardino attack, Cruz responded to Trump's calls for a Muslim ban by suggesting that police should begin patrolling Muslim neighborhoods.

Throughout the presidential campaign, Beck stuck to his "never Trump" stance, labeling the Republican nominee in a Charlie Rose interview "frightening" and "possibly sociopathic." Explaining his assessment, Beck asked, "Have you seen him, during the last year and a half, truly feel for someone that couldn't help him? Truly connect on a human level and say, 'This has made me stop. This has made me think. . . . I'm deeply sorry for what I have said?'" ("Glenn Beck Labels Trump a 'Sociopath'" 2016). In October 2016, after the *Washington Post* released the *Access Hollywood* video during which Trump said that when you're a star you can sexually assault women ("Grab 'em by the pussy. You can do anything."), Beck wrote a Facebook post in which he described Trump as "an immoral man who is absent decency and dignity." "If the consequence of standing against Trump," Beck continued, "and for principles is indeed the election of Hillary Clinton, so be it. At least it is a moral, ethical choice" (Beck 2016c). For a time, Beck even dangled the prospect of voting for Clinton himself before finally casting his ballot for Evan McMullin, a former CIA operations officer and fellow Mormon who ran as an Independent.

While Beck has presented his fervent opposition to Trump as the product of his own moral conviction, it was just as likely the result of his canny read of the political zeitgeist. Just as he rode previous political and cultural waves, Beck did so again. Because "Beck has remade himself again and again, from Top 40 disc jockey to morning zoo comedian to angry shock jock to sentinel of political doom," talk radio industry journalist Michael Harrison describes him as "the closest thing we have in radio to a performance artist—he's a showman and a method actor" (Fisher 2017). This time, his method actor instincts led Beck to capitalize upon Trump's unpopularity and the excessive hand-wringing and navel-gazing that followed in its wake. Many of the innumerable postmortems following the election have attributed Trump's win to white rural voters. A November 13, 2016, piece in *Politico* declared that Trump's win was the "revenge of the rural voter," a sentiment Bernie Sanders endorsed in an op-ed in the *New York Times* that same week, arguing that "working families" (read here: white working families) were "sick and tired of the economic, political and media status quo" (Evich 2016; Sanders 2016). Exit polls contradict this assessment. White voters make up 70 percent of the electorate, and 58 percent of them voted for Trump. Notably, 52 percent of white voters with a family income under $50,000 cast their ballots for Clinton, not Trump (Gould and Harrington 2016). If the current president's racism, Islamophobia, misogyny, and xenophobia, not to mention his inexperience and ineptitude, did not necessarily attract Trump voters, neither did it repel them. Scapegoating white rural voters reflects a widespread refusal to confront the deeply embedded racism and xenophobia that continues to define the United States.

Enter Beck, who halfheartedly took responsibility for our allegedly unprecedented level of divisiveness, at once positioning himself as the cause and the antidote, a conversion narrative that captured the imagination of the liberal media. Features with titles like "Glenn Beck Wants to Heal the America He Divided—One Hug at a Time," "Glenn Beck's Regrets: His Paranoid Style Paved the Road for Trumpism. Now He Fears What He Unleashed," and "Glenn Beck Tries Out Decency" appeared in outlets including the *New York Times*, the *Atlantic*, the *Washington Post*, and the *New Yorker*. In these articles, as he has for much of his career, Beck presents himself as exceedingly fallible ("I didn't notice how my language could be interpreted by half the country as racist. I lacked humility. I was the height of arrogance'" [Fisher 2017]) and prophetic ("I think, in many ways unfortunately and regretfully, I am uniquely qualified to provide this message of warning and hope" [Beck 2016a]). Beck's message was met with both appreciation and skepticism, sometimes in the same article. In the *Atlantic*, Peter Beinart lauded Beck's "unusual courage" in opposing Trump, before concluding somewhat facetiously, "Now that Donald Trump is president, Beck wants to bind the country's racial and ideological wounds. He really does" (Beinart 2017). Beck paved the way for this rehabilitation shortly before the election when he published a widely discussed *New York Times* op-ed titled "Empathy for Black Lives Matter." When the Black Lives Matter movement first emerged in 2013, Beck, like many conservatives, condemned it, embracing the "All Lives Matter" slogan, which he claimed was a truer reflection of Martin Luther King Jr.'s legacy. Announcing he had reached a "pivot point" that allowed him to empathize with sympathizers, as opposed to members, of Black Lives Matter (BLM), Beck described the former as "decent, hardworking, patriotic Americans" who feel aggrieved, just as supporters of the Tea Party or Bernie Sanders do. Empathy for BLM did not indicate his political support, Beck contended; rather, he was "acknowledging [their] pain and anger while feeling for them as human beings." He concluded, "We must follow the Rev. Dr. Martin Luther King Jr.'s message and method and move away from a pursuit of 'winning' and toward reclaiming our shared humanity" (Beck 2016b).

Previously quick to catastrophize about threats to the nation—Obama, progressivism, the liberal elite, and so forth—Beck now declared himself ready to listen and to reach across the ideological divides he had helped create and reinforce. As he wrote in an op-ed for the *New York Times* right after the election titled "Don't Move to Canada. Talk to the Other Side": "Tuesday night, as it became apparent that Mr. Trump would win, I saw myself as others may see me. Pundits were beside themselves talking about sexism, 'whitelash' and bigotry. I read three articles comparing him to Hitler. I understand what they meant. But just as President Obama was not a Manchurian candidate, Mr. Trump is not Hitler. The seeds of 1933 may have been planted, but they can grow only through our hate and divisiveness" (Beck 2016a). Conveniently, Beck omitted the fact that before the election he was one of the people comparing Trump to Hitler. This was vintage Beck: accuse others of doing what you, yourself, have done or are currently doing. Characteristically, Beck also created a false equivalence between those who oppose Trump and those who opposed Obama, ignoring the question of how racism and xenophobia fueled much of the anti-Obama sentiment, while helping to define pro-Trump forces. Birthers, Tea Partiers, and supporters of BLM and Bernie Sanders are equally impugned and excused in Beck's world. Beck expressed remorse for drawing harsh ideological lines using heightened rhetoric without actually disavowing any of his positions or altering his rhetoric across the board. Only a few months before this op-ed appeared, Beck published the book *Liars: How Progressives Exploit Our Fears for Power and Control*. There he contended that Obama's presidency was the pinnacle of progressivism's destructive, power-hungry tendencies and forecasted that the next president—clearly he imagined this would be Hilary Clinton—would also prey upon "our" fears in pursuit of political power. In this same op-ed, Beck also addressed Trump's anti-Muslim rhetoric: "If our Mr. Trump, or any future president, should decide to round up Muslims (or any group) as America did with Japanese during World War II under Franklin D. Roosevelt, I will declare, 'I am a Muslim.' My values, honor, integrity and the Bill of Rights demand I stand for those most unlike me—that is when it counts." This from the man who in 2015 capitalized on the nation's enduring Islamophobia, publishing *It Is About Islam: Exposing the Truth about ISIS, Al Qaeda, Iran and the Caliphate*, in which he argued that Islamic extremism accurately reflects the Koran's teachings, a fact that multiculturalism, political correctness, and media elites seek to obscure.

That is all to say that Beck is the same as he always was, exploiting the contemporary moment to increase his visibility. He is, as ever, addicted to hyperbole and oversimplification, strategies that enable him to insert himself time and time again into the mainstream cultural conversation. Beck relentlessly wields sentimentality, presenting himself as frequently moved by appeals to common decency, such as when he noted on his show that Michelle Obama's response to the *Access Hollywood* tape in which she said, "It doesn't matter what party you belong to—Democrat, Republican, Independent—

no woman deserves to be treated this way" was the "most effective political speech ... since Ronald Reagan" (Schmidle 2016). Whether Beck's post-Trump conversion is genuine, it has cost him both professionally and personally. His *Blaze* audience has declined precipitously, and he claims to have received death threats from members of the alt-right, whom he has roundly condemned, though his website still features ads for My Patriot Supply, which appeals to survivalists, some of whom hail from the alt-right. "'These people scare the hell out of me,'" Beck told a writer for the *New Yorker*, who adds, "Some of them are his former followers" (Schmidle 2016). On the other hand, he is part of a cultural conversation after languishing in the *Blaze* wilderness for years. In early 2017, Beck announced a national tour with Riaz Patel, a gay, secular, immigrant Muslim, a hybrid of the pro-war rallies he did in the Bush era and the civil rights marches in the Obama one. Whether Beck's latest conversion is genuine or not, he is still a consummate performer, a keen reader of the cultural tea leaves and, perhaps most essentially, a man riven with contradictions and inconsistencies. One thing, however, about which Beck has remained doggedly consistent is his insistence upon attaching Martin Luther King Jr.'s legacy to every twist and turn in his trajectory. It is the civil rights leader who now signposts Beck's turn toward empathy, just as he previously justified Beck's opposition to Black Lives Matter. Before King stood for Beck's alleged determination to work with Muslim communities to heal the nation's divisions, he stood for Beck's opposition to Islamic extremism.

If Beck has been reborn as an anti-Trumper, it is worth reflecting upon the similarities between the two men. Like Beck, Trump thrives on the element of inconsistency, has only a passing familiarity with the truth, and contradicts earlier positions without shame or compunction. The forty-fifth president has proven himself willing to stir up racist, xenophobic, and white, particularly male, fears to achieve his own political ambitions, just as Beck did before him. Trump's "Make America Great Again" slogan, his invocation of President Nixon's "silent majority," and his attacks on so-called political correctness are racist taglines that speak to a growing sense, particularly among white Republicans, that they are in danger of losing "their" country. Such attacks, particularly against "political correctness," have been part and parcel of Beck's arsenal for more than a decade. In that sense, the alt-right has it exactly right. Before Beck opposed them and their former White House insider, Steve Bannon, he created the conditions for their rise. He did so, however contradictorily, by appropriating a civil rights legacy that Trump now openly attacks. Both men, however, have long depended upon a festering white supremacy and xenophobia to increase their appeal. Rather than expanding the Republican tent to attract women and minorities, as a 2013 Republican National Committee postmortem report suggested, Trump doubled down on a white, male, working- and middle-class demographic (Republican National Committee's Growth and Opportunity Project 2013). If this has allowed mainstream journalism to place white working-class people on the table as a problem, it has also facilitated the overlooking of how right-wing corporate and political elites have wielded their power to block the voting rights of black and brown citizens via voter ID laws, mass incarceration, and gerrymandering (see, e.g., Conniff 2016; Dreher 2015; Taibbi 2015). The story of Trumpism, then, is not one of reemerging racism and xenophobia so much as it is the culmination of a nearly fifty-year-long backlash against civil rights gains. As soon as rights were nominally secured, they were under siege and have been ever since. If we can credit Trumpism with anything positive, perhaps it is this: the final nail may have been put in the postracial coffin. As I have been arguing throughout this essay, postracial rhetoric was never a way of saying the United States had moved past racial inequality; instead, it was always a way of expressing the idea that white racial inequality was a burgeoning problem that could be blamed on elites, immigrants, and civil rights activists who had allegedly gone too far. That Martin Luther King Jr. has become a right-wing symbol of a defanged antiracism that privileges white disadvantage over acknowledging black or brown is perhaps telling evidence of the progress we've made since that historic 1963 March on Washington so celebrated by Glenn Beck and his ilk.

Notes

1   I recognize that whiteness, as Nell Painter (2010) has shown, is premised on the myth of its endangered status. I am arguing, however, that 9/11 amplified this feature of whiteness.

2   For an early refutation of that view, see Dudziak 2003.

3   For an explanation of the term "therapeutic patriotism," see Aufderheide n.d.

4   Much of this essay was written prior to Donald Trump's election; nonetheless, two years later the trends I track here have been supported by polling data and academic research. See, for example, Sides, Tessler, and Vavreck 2018.

5   For Baratunde Thurston's impassioned response to President Obama releasing his long form birth certificate, see "With President Obama's Birth Certificate" 2011.

6   One notable exception to this general rule is the slogan "Keep the White in the White House," which appeared on T-shirts and signs during Mitt Romney's 2008 presidential run.

7   This phrase echoes the title of Kelefa Sanneh's "Beyond the Pale: Is White the New Black?" (2010).

6

Technological Elites, the Meritocracy, and Postracial Myths in Silicon Valley

SAFIYA UMOJA NOBLE AND SARAH T. ROBERTS

> Silicon Valley has this way of finding greatness and supporting it. . . .
> It values meritocracy more than anyplace else.
> —JOSEPH ANSANELLI, Greylock Partners

Postracialism fits within a neoliberal antiregulatory stance and technolibertarian belief system that technological solutions can remedy social ills. In this way, it operates in a circuit of paradoxical recognition and denial of racism as a problematic organizational or operational force. When these technolibertarian positions fail, the roots of the ideology are stripped bare, and its promulgators are revealed as holding good old-fashioned racist (and sexist) positions. In this case, the maintenance of power and control is done under the cover of technologically mediated neutrality. In this chapter, we seek to crystallize an understanding of how postracialism is enacted and performed in Silicon Valley, such that the attendant interventions and efforts to disrupt such commonplace thinking can be taken up by information and technology workers.

As critical race theorist and feminist legal scholar Sumi Cho defines it, postracialism is a "twenty-first-century ideology that reflects a belief that due to the significant racial progress that has been made, the state need not engage in race-based decision-making or adopt race-based remedies, and that civil society should eschew race as a central organizing principle of social action" (2009, 1594). Cho's definition of post-racialism serves as the throughpoint of our analysis of race and postracialism in the American technology industry, as represented both figuratively and concretely in the place, practices, and products of Silicon Valley. There, the ideology of postracialism serves as a key principle that both supports and perpetuates a lack of racial and gender representation and pluralism in tech—after all, if there is no longer a "race problem," what is there to fix? As Cho succinctly states: "First, post-racialism obscures the centrality of race and racism in society. Second, it more effectively achieves what the Racial Backlash movement sought to do over two decades ago—forge a national consensus around the retreat from race-based remedies on the basis that the racial eras of the past have been and should be transcended. Third, post-racialism as an ideology serves to reinstate an unchallenged white normativity" (1593).

As a legal scholar, Cho is primarily concerned with remedies and actions taken by the state. These remedies and actions have governed practices across both public and private sectors throughout the latter twentieth century, via affirmative action, equal opportunity hiring mandates, and nondiscriminatory protections. Yet, in the twenty-first century's postracialist climate, "race does not matter, and should not be taken into account or even noticed" (1595). This represents a major ideological leap beyond the related, but distinct, ideological phenomenon of color blindness. Color blindness, while fundamentally flawed, acknowledges the existence of race and racism but denies structural and other components of race and racism beyond an individual level and a visual read, and attributes the problems of racism to the discussion or acknowledgment of it.

Postracialism, on the other hand, dispenses with discussion of race altogether. This leads to an inevitable end of any action that can be taken to reverse inequities or broaden representation as concrete, tangible, or laudable goals. In this way, postracialism is the ideological basis for maintaining a racially unjust status quo, at best, and is often a mechanism for turning back the clock on a variety of gains made toward broader justice and inclusion on racial terms. Cho describes the operationalizing of postracialism as a form of racial backlash that reverses the gains of the civil rights movement in the United States since at least the 1980s:

According to post-racial logic, the move is to effectuate a "retreat from race."[1] This retreat from race takes at least three forms: material, as the retreat from state-imposed remedies; sociocultural, as the retreat from white liberal/progressive deference to Black normativity on the meaning of racial equality and justice; and political, as the retreat from collective political entities organized along racial lines and agendas as a legitimate protest or reform vehicle. (2009, 1594)

We use Cho's definitions and framings of both postracialism, as differentiated from color blindness, to deconstruct and operationalize the ways that cultural practices in Silicon Valley are explicitly working as a convenient "retreat" from race and as a cover for overt racism. We argue that these logics can also be extended to other categories like gender bias.

Activating Silicon Valley's Race/Postrace Paradox

This conceit to be both postracial and simultaneously racially aware is evident in the ways that Silicon Valley both represents itself and is represented by others in a variety of registers and dimensions. As a physical, geographically identifiable place and space, Silicon Valley is circumscribed by architectural contours serving as racial boundaries, from its physical encroachments upon historically African American neighborhoods and cities like East Palo Alto and its policies of white racial containment and control of Palo Alto, to its creeping cultural and economic impact to the north via displacement of Latino/a residents in the Mission District in San Francisco.

The criticisms of lack of hiring of underrepresented employees, again, namely, black, Latino/a, and Native American, have garnered national news media headlines, and employment discrimination against women has resulted in a federal investigation. Reporters from major technology news outlets and blogs have been documenting the problems of hiring bias against women, African Americans, and Latino/as for years, in an effort to dislodge the pervasive notion that the Valley is a meritocracy. In 2012, Andrew Keen reported for *TechCrunch* on entrepreneur Vivek Wadhwa's critique of the tech industry as a "white boys' club" that has investors who openly discriminate against minority- and women-led tech companies. Yet, despite the evidence of race and gender discrimination in Silicon Valley, technology CEOs and investors cling to notions of the industry as a meritocracy to justify their investment choices in people like themselves.

In early August 2017, an "anti-diversity manifesto" was authored by a Google software engineer, James Damore.[2] Initially posted internally for other Google employees to see, Damore's manifesto went viral within the company, throughout Silicon Valley, and, ultimately, globally, laying bare the extent to which many believe that efforts to include women and underrepresented minorities are "discriminatory" (apparently to white men). The antidiversity manifesto, as it has come to be known, argues that any remedy of hundreds of years of historical discrimination in the United States labor market is discriminatory against the presumed majority of "nonprogressives," even when complying with federal law:

> Discriminating just to increase the representation of women in tech is as misguided and biased as mandating increases for women's representation in the homeless, work-related and violent deaths, prisons, and school dropouts. There's currently very little transparency into the extend [*sic*] of our diversity programs which keeps it immune to criticism from those outside its ideological echo chamber. These programs are highly politicized which further alienates nonprogressives. I realize that some of our programs may be precautions against government accusations of discrimination, but that can easily backfire since they incentivize illegal discrimination. (Conger n.d.)

Based on his manifesto, Damore appears to be totally unaware of the long-term history of women in computing, as just one example of a historical and factual inaccuracy in the document. These contributions have been articulated by numerous scholars over past decades, to include Jennifer Light and her key paper, "When Computers Were Women" (1999), and Marie Hicks's *Programmed Inequality* (2017), a book-length history of women in Great Britain's computation teams in its Civil Service. Despite its numerous factual and logical inaccuracies, Damore's manifesto enjoyed a great deal of support among Google employees and throughout Silicon Valley. Its uptake illuminates the ideological investments of many elite technology workers in a belief that addressing the systemic and structural exclusion of women and people of color through their hiring can "incentivize illegal discrimination" (Conger n.d.). Indeed, not only have the cultures of Silicon Valley companies been places that deny meaningful participation to underrepresented people of color, but many of these companies have traded on white supremacy and postracialism by allowing and fomenting racial hatred and, in some cases, right-wing fascism and neo-Nazism through architectural mechanisms and platform characteristics that allow for anonymity and articulations of being content-neutral. Such characteristics are considered as design features in many mainstream Silicon Valley products, when they are considered at all, and ensure companies can eschew their responsibility for trafficking in hate content while continuing to neatly profit from it.

Occasionally, a momentary breakthrough in awareness of bias and exclusion occurs, mostly in service of white women rather than African Americans or Latino/as. Venture capitalist and Netscape founder Marc Andreessen, commenting on Facebook chief operating officer Sheryl Sandberg's 2013 book, *Lean In*, said:

> "Before Sheryl's book, for 20 years, the answer has been, 'Be gender blind . . . Be gender blind.' It's not important; in fact, it's not to be discussed. It certainly should not be brought into the hiring criteria and certainly should not influence how people manage. And basically have a straight meritocracy and ignore gender. Sheryl has provided a very, very provocative set of arguments that 1) That's not actually working and 2) That managers, both female and male, actually have to take gender on squarely . . . We'll have to completely retrain managers and executives of all kinds to be able to do this," he continued. "[Sandberg] argues very persuasively that it's necessary, but it's like landmine central with the way employment law works these days" (Gallagher 2013)

This sentiment of not seeing gender or color is a familiar mantra that provides cover for and a direct relationship to the more blatant sorts of misogyny (and racism) that have resulted in high-profile sexual harassment lawsuits against two major Silicon Valley venture capital firms, Kleiner Perkins Caufield & Byers, and CMEA Capital (Burleigh 2015). Despite Andreessen's enlightenment-via-Sandberg about gender bias, he is but one of many Silicon Valley gatekeepers who struggle with acknowledging the possibility that Silicon Valley may not be a meritocracy. Indeed, there are numerous public examples of racism and gender discrimination in Silicon Valley that emanate from technology company executives and board members themselves, which, in turn, are echoed in manifestos such as Damore's. After fifty years of civil rights legislation to protect women and people of color in the workplace from discrimination, Andreessen described its results in saying, "It's like landmine central with the way employment law works these days" (Gallagher 2013). The "landmines" to which Andreessen referred were not the discriminatory practices in hiring but the legislation and legal impositions brought about that were intended to counteract them. In Andreessen's eyes, the obstacles are not discrimination, but remedies to it.

"Culture Fit"

> "Like a lot of the investments that have come our way, a friend of a friend talked to us about it, and told us about it, and encouraged the founder and the CEO to come and chat with us . . . one thing led to another."
> —MIKE MORITZ, partner, Sequoia Capital, quoted in McBride (2013)

As of May 2014, only 30 percent of Google's workforce was composed of women. In July 2016, the company released updated employment numbers; in the two years since its last release, the employment of women at Google had increased by 1 percent, to 31 percent. Additionally, only 3 percent of employees were Latino/a, and only 2 percent were African American. Given the culture of meritocracy at play, how can this underrepresentation be read in the context of the purported commitment to meritocracy in hiring and retention? Based on numbers alone, the Silicon Valley meritocracy does not find value in inclusion of African Americans or Latino/as as a part of its postracial moment.

While Silicon Valley executives and venture capitalists cling to their investments in "gender blindness" and "color blindness," the evidence of their lack of bias is demonstrable, in that they only find merit in funding start-ups and companies *not* founded by African Americans and Latino/as. Meanwhile, there is disproportionate representation of East Asian and South Asian employees and leadership, which often confuses and masks the hostile disposition of Silicon Valley toward historically underrepresented minority communities in the United States that fall into federally protected classes. This is no mistake; a fundamental part of the logic of postracialism is that it refuses to deal not only with the contemporary realities of race in American society but also with the more than three hundred years of legal discrimination and disenfranchisement of African Americans, Latino/as, and Native American Indians, while pointing to the increasing numbers of South Asian, East Asian, and Asian Americans participating in the tech sector labor force as evidence of success in diversifying across racial lines. Yet the paradox of upholding Asian Americans, Asian nationals, and South Asians, Brazilians, Russians, and various foreign nationals and J-1 visa holders as model minorities serves to mask the exclusion of domestic minority groups in the United States that have been structurally marginalized without reparation and excluded from nearly every aspect of long-term social, political, educational, and economic opportunity.

Myths of a digital meritocracy premised on a technocratic postracialism emerge as key to perpetuating gender and racial exclusions. Measures of success are made on the basis of economic valuations, ability to attract investors, acquisitions, and bank account balances. Researcher Jessie Daniels articulated the functions of color-blind ideology in Silicon Valley and its embeddedness within the internet, and within the culture and practices of digital technologies, in her article "'My Brain Database Doesn't See Skin Color': Color-Blind Racism in the Technology Industry and in Theorizing the Web" (2015). In this work, she details the ways that whiteness is embedded in the architectures of the web—from "master" and "slave" drives, to deep social inequality among technology workers from the global North to the global South. She points to the investments made in middle-class and affluent immigrant labor (South Asian, Russian, Brazilian), for example, at the expense of black and Latino/a employment because these investments are consistent with the "mythology of the United States as a land of opportunity . . . thus eschewing charges of bias in hiring and promotion" (Daniels 2015, 1380).

This takes place in situations such as when investors, in their own words, fund people through their networks who are part of the well-connected, known circles within which they conduct their personal and professional lives. Often, code words like "culture fit" are ways of sorting for people most like themselves, or most like the networks they engage. Heather Hiles (the founder and former CEO of Pathbrite, a San Francisco–based educational technology firm, and one of the only openly gay black women tech leaders in Silicon Valley) put it this way: "I don't live next door to the polite white men who tout the virtues of meritocracy while pouring billions of dollars into their buddies' companies. They live in insulated little worlds, and it's hard to see color when there is none around them. Funding one's friend isn't inherently bad . . . but I challenge them to look outside their circles and also support other types of businesses—like those owned by women of color. It might be convenient to use their limited experiences to convince themselves we don't exist. But we do" (2015).

Hiles's *Recode* post about the kinds of financial redlining black women tech leaders experience went viral in March 2015. In it, she described how her degrees from Berkeley and Yale and her extensive experience had very little bearing on her ability to fairly compete in securing venture capital for her company. "Culture fit," in her case, was less about being an Ivy League graduate. Hiles said: "The anemic flow of capital to the diversity of society is a symptom of an inherently biased country and a world that shows its true nature by inefficiently investing in and giving opportunities and power to familiar, heterosexual white men. It's a hoarding of the resources that could spawn creativity and expanded opportunities for everyone. And it's a diminishing return" (2015).

Ultimately, culture fit becomes a means of instantiation of white, male heteronormativity that is explicitly, negatively felt by many of those who do not fit those identities. It is one of the many ways in which bias is operationalized in Silicon Valley, yet its poetic rendering as a simple matter of shared taste and worldview obfuscates the discrimination that is part of a larger American culture and is both reflected and reified in Silicon Valley's culture. Nevertheless, some efforts have been made to identify and remediate the crisis rendered by postracialism in the tech industry. The Kapor Center for Social Impact, founded by Mitch Kapor and Freada Kapor Klein in 2001, was created expressly to address issues of implicit bias in the tech industries. In a 2013 article entitled "Bias and Meritocracy Don't Mix," the institute reported that one of the most powerful start-up accelerators in the Valley since 2005, Y Combinator (YC), has not funded a single African American woman, bearing out Hiles's experience in stark relief.

Part of the rationale for YC's funding decisions is the notion that "fit" is part of what makes one successful in the tech industry. The Kapor Center included YC founder Paul Graham's own description, as reported in the *New York Times*, of culture fit as bias: "'I can be tricked by anyone who looks like Mark Zuckerberg. There was a guy once who we funded who was terrible. I said: 'How could he be bad? He looks like Zuckerberg!'" ("Bias and Meritocracy Don't Mix" 2013). Y Combinator has spun off many successful companies: Airbnb, Reddit, and Dropbox to name a few. But in his assessment of YC's success, Graham focused not on shared features of technology or innovation that had made those firms household names but instead on certain personal characteristics Graham believed were predictors of success in Silicon Valley tech, including being younger than thirty-two years of age and not having an accent: "'You have to go far down the list to find a CEO with a strong foreign accent,'" Graham told the Times. "'Alarmingly far down—like 100th place'" ("Bias and Meritocracy Don't Mix" 2013).

As exceptional as it often sees itself, the Silicon Valley technology sector is not the only site of elite industry access being predicated on unnamed racialized notions of meritocracy. One excellent analogous case can be found just down the California coast, in Hollywood's entertainment industry. The Hollywood Diversity Report, released annually for the past four years by UCLA sociologist Darnell Hunt and his colleagues (2017), methodically demonstrates how the lack of diversity in the professional and personal networks among Hollywood executives, cast, and crew significantly impacts workplace diversity and leads to structural exclusion of African Americans and other people of color from industry jobs. Essentially, in both Silicon Valley and Hollywood, people hire people they know or with whom they feel they can identify, just as Graham described. It is a phenomenon that manifests as a system based on meritocracy and potential, when it has much more in common with one's racial identity, gender identity, and class position.

Artifacts of the Meritocracy: Reflections
of the Technocratic Postracial Order

These principles of postracial mythology not only are inscribed in statements made by representatives at the highest corporate Silicon Valley echelons but also are found in the underlying architecture it develops (Noble 2016) and the labor practices it engenders (Jayadev 2001; S. T. Roberts 2016). These values are hardly hidden from view; in fact, they are so culturally resonant to the mainstream that they serve as the basis of humor for the American premium cable channel HBO's comedy program *Silicon Valley*. In the show, the environment of Silicon Valley's start-up and establishment culture is presented as simultaneously postracial and deeply race-aware, where postracialism is represented by the casual use of racialized, bigoted, and typically factually incorrect comments predicated on race, gender, and ethnicity. The beliefs and values espoused by white characters toward characters of color with a wink and a "we're all in on the joke" nod drive the show's plotlines. In keeping with a realistic portrayal of Silicon Valley employment demographics and culture, none of the characters in the fictional Pied Piper start-up is either black or female.

The comedy in *Silicon Valley* is frequently predicated on the casual, postracial racism of the environment—at the expense of its characters of color. This is reflected, in particular, by South Asian and East Asian characters, especially software developer "Dinesh" (Kumail Nanjiani) and "Jian Yang" (Jimmy O. Yang), the much-abused unpaid intern in the start-up incubator run by white sexist pothead Erlich Bachman (fig. 6.1).

These characters' ethnic, linguistic, and racial differences are often made the punch line for much of *Silicon Valley*'s humor. In the hipster, postracial humor of the show, race still serves as a powerful marker of difference that normalizes the whiteness and maleness of Silicon Valley's culture and success. Both the real Silicon Valley and its television parody engage the paradox of postracialism, where being South Asian or East Asian is seemingly at once acceptable and unremarkable while at the same time serves as a marker

Figure 6.1 Promotional shot for the HBO comedy *Silicon Valley* (2014–) in which the members of the start-up are depicted in the clothing and posture of the late Steve Jobs, cofounder of Apple and Silicon Valley luminary.

of otherness upon which the white male characters can capitalize as it suits their needs. In this way, the show accurately portrays the predominating postracial racist politics of Silicon Valley while also serving to reinscribe them as the natural order of things in the tech world and beyond.

Imperialism 2.0: Silicon Valley Postracialism Exported

> I do not want to miss a good chance of getting us a slice of this magnificent African cake.
> —KING LEOPOLD II of Belgium, 1876, quoted in Thomas Pakenham, "Scramble for Africa" (1992)

Postracialism does not end at hiring and representation in employment ranks. Rather, it undergirds problematic thinking on the part of a racially, educationally, and class-wise homogeneous Silicon Valley technology elite whose design and manufacturing choices have implications for populations across the globe. Against proclamations of color blindness, these same firms rely upon the legacies of colonialism, imperialism, and continued Western economic, political, and military domination for the extraction of minerals, production of goods, and provision of cheap labor in the global South, about which we have both written previously (Noble 2016; S. T. Roberts 2016b). These old and well-worn capital extractive practices are combined

Benedict Evans @BenedictEvans 1h
.@pmarca @lemonandice it's a terrible thing to offer people with no money the choice of something free.

↩   ↻ 9   ♥ 36

Vikram Chachra @lemonandice 1h
@BenedictEvans @pmarca That sounds like justification for Internet colonialism.

↩   ↻ 5   ♥ 16

Marc Andreessen ✓
@pmarca

@lemonandice @BenedictEvans Anti-colonialism has been economically catastrophic for the Indian people for decades. Why stop now?

2/9/16, 7:29 PM

Figure 6.2 Tweet by Facebook board member and Silicon Valley venture capitalist Marc Andreessen on the rejection of Free Basics product entry into India.

with versions that are newly branded as "flexible" forms that shore up transnational corporations. It does not take much for the veneer of these kinder, gentler forms of capitalism to give way to the true ideologies at their root.

Consider the February 2016 episode in which venture capitalist and Facebook board member Marc Andreessen chastised the entire nation of India for that country's Telecom Regulatory Authority rejecting the advances of Facebook's internet-lite service, Free Basics, on net neutrality grounds. "Anti-colonialism has been economically catastrophic for the Indian people for decades," Andreessen claimed with no evidence, and in the face of historical evidence to the contrary. "Why stop now?" (fig. 6.2; Mohan 2016; Wagner n.d.). With his tweet, Andreessen linked the Indian resistance to the Facebook product to anticolonialist resistance, meaning that Free Basics was in the position of a colonizing force, by Andreessen's own logic.

Technolibertarian postracialist attitudes have real-world consequences: they are invoked in order to establish, maintain, and exercise power and control. Sophisticated in his deployment of postracialist beliefs, Andreessen activated a covert racism as he tied India's supposed problem to a need for colonial control by those who know better and are in a better position to decide for that nation's people. Andreessen called on a new imperialism, much the same as the old in terms of structural belief systems: a certainty of the superiority of his group, its natural acumen and ability, as well as quasi-magical, mythic success and its ability to preternaturally determine a best path for other people. In technology and, by extension, in global policy, economics, and politics, Silicon Valley knows best. A lack of grounding in the global view of itself led to Andreessen's shock at the rejection of Facebook's freebies, which India saw as an attack on its own informational and technological, and thus economic, sovereignty. His certainty of the rightness of their products for all, and Facebook's fundamental right to the Indian marketplace and customers, showed little regard for the culture and politics of anything outside a small, privileged, and decidedly white and Western worldview.

But the new imperialism of Silicon Valley does not confine itself to targets solely in the global South. Silicon Valley values and value are frequently undergirded by practices of localized gentrification that displace, in particular, vulnerable low-income communities and/or communities of color where it comes to roost. Much has been made of the economic impossibility created for longtime residents—many of them LGBTQ, communities of color, or both—which has meant the gentrification of San Francisco and freeloading off the city's public infrastructure (Noble and Roberts 2016). Now, as Silicon Valley expands its physical footprint south to Los Angeles, in an area rebranded as "Silicon Beach," it is imposing its own system of values on that community, as well.

The Venice neighborhood in Los Angeles, California, has long been an enclave that tolerated variation between rich and poor, and a site of great racial, cultural, and ethnic mixing (Simpson 2016). Since Google and Snap arrived with a new headquarters in the heart of Venice, however, homeless persons living in the area reported being harassed by Google security, often with batons and pit bulls (Levine 2015). To maintain attractiveness for the expansion of Silicon Beach, city council members are proposing radical housing initiatives to create space for people experiencing homelessness in Venice (G. Holland 2016). This, consistent with the neoliberal economic policies that have rapidly developed in the United States and Europe since the 1980s, is more evidence of the ways that corporations eschew responsibility for building communities and contributing to public services by paying taxes, and instead increase pressure on local communities to manage the burden of displacement through public funds—funds to which they contribute very little thanks to significant tax breaks.

Now economic and gentrifying expansion has spread into Los Angeles communities of color. These neighborhoods are being targeted by unscrupulous developers who see a gold rush on their hands with the coalescing of Northern California–based firms and LA-based technology companies into a major technology hub. Rents in areas near Google and other LA outposts have increased 7 percent between 2015 and 2016 alone; this rise comes on the heels of similar increases in 2015 that saw rents in areas like Santa Monica, adjacent to or within so-called Silicon Beach, already increase 17.5 percent (Thornberg, Kleinhenz, and De Anda 2016). Despite legislative mechanisms designed to protect renters, such as the Ellis Act, residents of predominantly black neighborhoods such as Baldwin Hills and View Park are fighting gentrification by appealing to the City of Los Angeles to enter the areas in the historic registry as a way of staving off developers and real estate "flippers," people with no vested interest in living in the community who often use predatory or submarket offers to lure residents out of their homes so they can make huge profits from quick renovations and sales (Jennings 2015; Khouri 2016). In the case of Baldwin Hills, View Park, and Windsor Hills—once known as the "Black Beverly Hills," these encroachments from Silicon Beach are displacing middle-class and affluent African Americans, and elderly African Americans who are targeted with cash offers to vacate the premises in many parts of South Los Angeles (Khouri 2016).

These aspects of technology companies' tone-deaf practices in communities are not just relegated to the physical, geographic quest toward unlimited expansion, and are not simply a benign sort of libertarianism in practice. Palmer Luckey, Oculus VR founder and an outspoken Donald Trump supporter, offered a solution to those who cannot afford the lifestyle made available to the Silicon Valley elite: a VR headset to deliver the poor from their lacking material realities (Au 2016a). Oculus VR, acquired by Facebook, has been described by Luckey as having a "moral imperative," as noted by journalist W. James Au. He reported on Luckey for *Wired* magazine (Au 2016b) and expanded the abbreviated piece for his own blog:

"This is one of those crazy man topics," Luckey answered, "but it comes down to this: Everyone wants to have a happy life, but it's going to be impossible to give everyone everything they want." Instead, he went on, developers can now create virtual versions of real experiences that are only enjoyed by the planet's privileged few, which they can then bestow to the destitute of the world.

Figure 6.3 Response to Silicon Valley commentaries on Black Lives Matter. SOURCE: https://twitter.com/elogann/status/752536956286824449.

"It's easy for us to say, living in the great state of California, that VR is not as good as the real world," Luckey went on, "but a lot of people in the world don't have as good an experience in real life as we do here." (Au 2016a)

What we learn from consistently studying the discourses of Silicon Valley is that its successes come at the expense of a growing number of communities. The costs to these communities are masked by investments in an imagined postracial, postgender, postclass reality that is seemingly sympathetic to inclusion but resists it in material, quantifiable, and cultural terms.

Resistance and Reality: Pushing Back While Being Black

Postracialist silence in Silicon Valley has not been ignored by its employees of color. Black workers, in particular, have responded to the ongoing lack of remedying of inequities through their own acts of resistance. On July 7, 2016, CNN's Sara Ashley O'Brien reported that African American tech employees were "calling in 'Black'" after police murders of Philando Castile and Alton Sterling. This practice of calling in and taking a day off for mental and emotional health after the shooting deaths of unarmed African Americans allegedly began in 2015, as African Americans on social media began talking more publicly about how difficult it is to go to work and act as if they were unaffected by the social injustices and systemic racism, including the shooting of unarmed

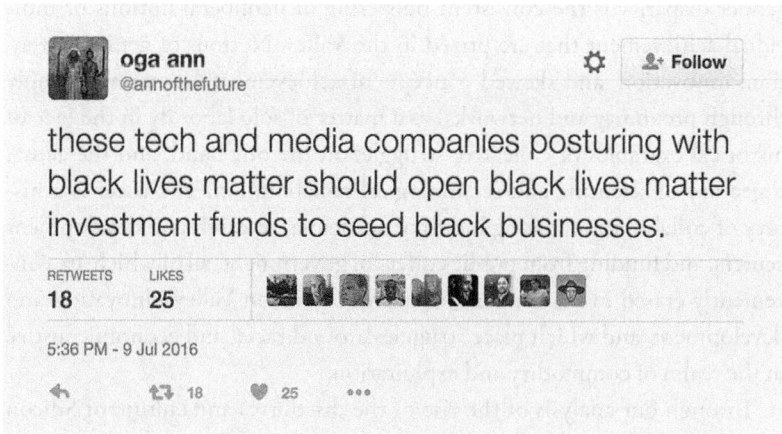

Figure 6.4 Response to Silicon Valley commentaries on Black Lives Matter. SOURCE: https://twitter.com/elogann/status/752536956286824449.

African Americans. In response, some tech firms released statements addressing the employee absences, which, despite being ostensibly supportive, were not well received in context: "But while some people expressed appreciation for the support from tech, others pointed out the deep irony of the statements coming from companies with black employees making up just 1–2% of their workforces" (Wong 2016).

Products and platforms from Silicon Valley now find themselves in the spotlight in racially motivated deaths of people like Eric Garner, Philando Castile, and Korryn Gaines through the use of their technologies like Facebook Live, Periscope, and YouTube, all of which are used to capture and circulate images and even live video. This only underscores the material consequences of the platforms, particularly as these platforms serve to benefit materially from the circulation and virality of black death and dying.

Conclusion: The Postracial as Racism, Rebooted

Postracial ideologies permeate venture capitalist funding, hiring practices, and the culture and representations of the Valley. These technolibertarian postracial projects often manifest as gentrification and in the architectures of its manufacturing and production processes. In our estimation, the postracial is racial and, in many cases, patently racist.

What is clear in the wake of the efforts by Silicon Valley companies to respond to the structural crises of racism, economic marginalization, and gender disparity is the consistent bolstering of neoliberal notions of individual achievement that are prized in the Valley. Notions of genius, invention, innovation, and skewed concepts of achievement (sometimes simply through proximity and networks) as a matter of solo labor fly in the face of historical examples of collective struggle, on the one hand, and the actual trajectory of scientific and technological collaboration. The latter is a history of collaboration among industry, academia, research and development centers, and funding from public coffers of government, all of which are conveniently erased in mainstream narratives of Silicon Valley innovation and development, and which place struggles around racial and economic justice in the realm of commodity and exploitation.

Through our analysis of the rise of the discourses and culture of Silicon Valley, a discussion of how technology elites work to mask everything from algorithmic to genetic inscriptions of race embedded in their products suggests that digital elites often elide responsibility for their postracial reinscriptions of racial visibilities (and invisibilities). Silicon Valley believes it's "post-" but then constantly appeals to the "pre-"racial models of control and exclusion when it behooves it—such as the case of calling on colonialism as an example of the "good old days" and as an ideal system for getting things done. It is also apparent in the way in which it eschews labor gains made by unions and labor organizations in the twentieth century in favor of "flexible" labor policies that benefit only the employer. Indeed, benefits from racialized systems of power are still in place and have never been dismantled, while the Valley profits from them and actually obfuscates them.

Meanwhile, Silicon Valley's corporate entities control an unprecedented amount of the world's information flow to the general public, through its solicitation of user-generated content (which it then owns); its co-opting of knowledge (through projects like Google Books' use of library books purchased and held by state research universities); its development of information-provision algorithms that prioritize information in ways that support the status quo; and its vast projects of data collection, aggregation, archiving, and storage, to the ends of advertising, surveillance, and unknown other outcomes. As the evidence shows, Silicon Valley's claim that it is "postracial" actually gives way to a reality that is not even "postracist."

American exceptionalism is not new, and it didn't start in Silicon Valley. Long-standing struggles for social, political, and economic inclusion for African Americans, women, and other legally protected classes have been predicated on the recognition of systemic exclusion, forced labor, and structural disenfranchisement. Commitments to US public policies like affirmative action have, likewise, have been fundamental to political reforms geared to economic opportunity and participation, because American corporations were not able to "self-regulate" and "innovate" an end to racial discrimination—even under federal law. Among modern digital technology elites, myths of meritocracy and intellectual superiority are used as racial and gender signifiers that disproportionately consolidate resources away from people of color, particularly African Americans, Latino/as and Native Americans. Investments in meritocratic myths suppress interrogations of racism and discrimination even as the products of digital elites are infused with racial, class, and gender markers. Thus, Silicon Valley consistently embeds its values—as white and upwardly mobile—into the architecture of its products, many of which have come under fire as racist, and extends them into its business and hiring practices. By ignoring issues of race (and, likewise, issues of class, gender, and sexual identity) by gesturing to them as being old economy problems, it actually circumvents any meaningful interventions that work toward the dismantling of barriers based on these values, and reinscribes long-standing discriminatory practices.

Notes

The authors acknowledge Ryan P. Adserias, University of Wisconsin–Madison, for advice and intellectual contributions.

Epigraph: From McBride 2013.

1 Cho invokes sociologist Dana Takagi's turn of phrase, coined by the latter in her 1993 book on affirmative action and Asian Americans, *The Retreat from Race: Asian-American Admissions and Racial Politics.*

2 Damore's manifesto was reproduced, with additional contextual notes and responses, by *Gizmodo.* See Conger n.d.

PART TWO

Performances

The second part of this collection includes chapters in which authors examine specific performances—as objects, artifacts, practices, and events—that showcase a range of difficulties and illegitimacies that attend the larger political and cultural projects of postrace. Attending to shifts in media programs and film genres, social media platforms and other DIY practices, politico-economic and policy shifts, and performances of racial identity and difference that appear increasingly "nonsensical," anachronistic, or untranslatable within the logics of postrace, these chapters show how subtle and seemingly unrelated cultural shifts cohere in dangerous new instantiations of structural racisms and vitiate the urgent politics of progressive antiracist struggle.

The chapters in this part take specific case studies—in sports, fashion, television, popular music—each as an optic to think through and within the concept of the postrace. Some of these cases consolidate the discourses and practices of postrace racism while others challenge and resist them. Each brings into relief the cultural and political contexts for complex and often contradictory performances of the postracial.

Locating their projects in the racial break between color-blind racism and postrace, these chapters explore various ways that this transition is both maintained and normalized in a range of media objects, artifacts, practices, and events. If the first half of this book theorized the assumptions that undergird the power and vulnerabilities of postrace, examining how race has taken new form in the contemporary moment, and how postracial race rearticulates powerful sets of material and discursive conditions, this second part takes up particular case studies as a way to specify and substantiate performances of the postracial across specific media and cultural industries. Common across the chapters in this part is the urgency of understanding how the concept of postrace has gained in discursive legitimacy, focusing on the ways that media representations and discourses, the performative registers and repertoires of culture, have helped to consolidate the operations of postracial power and naturalize the aesthetic and analytic gaze it engenders. These analyses illuminate the dynamics of social, cultural, and economic power that consolidate official antiracisms of neoliberalism, for example, in the global fashion industry, which is governed by neoliberal economies that mark and trade racial otherness as evidence of racial progress and even racial transcendence. Indeed, the fashion industry allows designers, editors, photographers, and stylists to articulate rainbow galas of multicultural identities even when nonwhite bodies are absent from—and have little executive control over—market celebrations of these racial performances. Popular music, likewise, capitalizes on postracial concepts of racial progress, insistently and relentlessly declaring that we should be "happy," that the postrace is a platform for feel-good emotional uplift even as it normalizes widespread social inequality. Reality television about popular music, including programs like *The Voice*, similarly position singers as repositories of a variety of "posts"—postrace, postgender, postclass—where ostensibly unmarked performances of "talent" transcend racial and gender histories and the specificities of raced and gendered power. And, in tediously analogous ways, professional sports in the United States increasingly inscribe the ambivalence of the postracial moment, vaunting sports as an "equal playing field," all the while fueling and supporting audience engagement with explicit race politics of fandom and athletic celebrity that structure the sports industries.

In other words, the chapters in the second part of the book approach the commercial media-industrial complex as particularly fecund and powerful terrain for the postracial surfacing of racial ambiguity and multiculturalism, approaching television casting, popular music, advertising, branding, social media, and fashion as the new standard-bearers of the racially flexible. Here, too, the contributors parse tensions and nuance in the performative registers of postrace. Thus, where reality television is seen as taking advantage of postracial ideals to reinscribe racial boundaries, weaving race in new forms into the stylized fabric of daily life as performed on TV, the contributors in this part also offer accounts of other media industries, including independent web-distributed media programs, which offer an opportunity to critique the ongoing hegemonic embrace of postracial representations of race as a marketing tactic. As queer perspectives on representation highlight spaces of contestation, making room for racial performances that puncture the self-assuredness of performances of postrace, these works also urge us toward intersectional specificity and cross-platform critiques that bring into view not just the adhesive and adaptive grasp of postrace but also the ambivalence and unsettledness of its performance.

7

Vocal Recognition

Racial and Sexual Difference after (Tele)Visuality

KAREN TONGSON

Tuesday, April 26, 2011, turned out to be a red-letter day for prime-time sapphism on US television. The Fox series *Glee* was still in its heyday and continuing its ham-fisted campaign against teen bullying with a subplot about the label-averse Santana scheming to bring her lesbian (or, as she joked, "Lebanese") love for co-cheerleader, Britney, to fruition. Airing opposite the "Born This Way"–anchored episode of *Glee* was the debut of the vocal reality competition series *The Voice*, NBC's bid to compete with the format's reigning champ, FOX's *American Idol*. Remarkably, two out lesbians survived the first round of the show's blind auditions: Vicci Martinez from Tacoma, Washington, and Beverly McClellan from Ft. Lauderdale, Florida, both of whom made the final four before losing to the eventual winner, Javier Colon.

Now in its fifteenth season, *The Voice* pitched itself from the very beginning as a democratic alternative to the since-decommissioned *American Idol*, which had strict age restrictions and conduct codes for contestants. *The Voice* offered itself not only as counterprogramming to *Idol*'s well-worn format but also as a kind of corrective to its failings in diversity and representation.

By redirecting its energies and systems of reward to, as its title betrays, the quality of a contestant's voice, the competition distinguished itself from the visual tyranny and disciplinary surveillance of contestants on shows like *Idol*. Whereas *Idol*'s early audition rounds derived considerable schadenfreude from oddball characters banished from the realm of "pop hot"—remember Kenneth Briggs, the much-derided "Bush Baby," or the cartoonishly Orientalized nerd William Hung, who thrust his hips provocatively to Ricky Martin's "She Bangs"?—*The Voice* eliminates looks altogether from the audition process by restricting the panel's ability to look at the singers onstage. Seated in hydraulically manipulated swivel chairs evocative of Dr. Evil's perch, the celebrity panel of coaches, not "judges," have their backs to the stage at the beginning of each performance. Only when a singer's voice sufficiently moves a coach does he or she press a button to swing around and face the talent. If none of the four coaches turns around before the song ends, the singer is eliminated and sent away with anywhere from twenty seconds to two and a half minutes of precious airtime on national television as a consolation prize. Presumably this "blind" audition process would, if not eliminate the coaches' biases altogether, at least mitigate some of the violences wrought by visual standards of beauty that are inevitably racialized, gendered, and sexualized. Judging "only the voice" manufactures the fantasy of a postracialized, postgendered subject—of a disembodied voice soaring above the murkiness of racial or sexual politics, and thus befitting the first decade of a new millennium hoping to ease seamlessly into a postracial futurity with the election of America's first biracial president, Barack Obama. On *The Voice*, the singer becomes a medium for these feelings of "postness"—postrace, postgender, postclass; a mere vessel for ostensibly pure, unmarked expressions of "talent," or in certain instances grit, strength, and determination.

As "coaches," the celebrity panel on *The Voice* is meant to cultivate and nurture raw talent rather than simply to eviscerate bad performers for the audience's amusement, as the judges on *American Idol* used to relish. As former *Voice* coach CeeLo Green opines in the premiere episode: "It's not about the judgment; it's about the journey." *Idol* has been explicitly called out on the show, from perennial coach Adam Levine's reassurance to dejected contestants that "the people we are not turning our chairs around for could win *American Idol*," to the sensational rehashing, ad nauseum, of season one contestant Frenchie Davis's disqualification from the *Idol* competition for nude photos nearly a decade earlier. Pitching itself as the anti-*Idol* or alterna-*Idol*, *The Voice*, complete with its kitschy, faux Futurist set pieces with hands forming a "V" (for voice, victory, or vendetta?), would have us believe that truly anyone from anywhere could be a vocal superstar whether they are fat, thin, brown, black, yellow, mixed-race, chinless, accented, hirsute, gorgeous, hideous, straight, gay, Mormon, or dykey. Your voice, in other words, will set you free: free from the limitations posed by your own body's significance and historical freightedness; free, in other words, from the limitations of your identity.

Taking *The Voice*'s promise of a blind American meritocracy as its starting point—a staged environment in which an individual is selected for his or her vocal talents instead of judged according to physical appearance and comportment—this essay considers the political and aesthetic ramifications posed by vocal recognition and vocal identification. Is the voice—the thing we hear but don't see—at once the first and the final frontier of what many have prematurely declared as the "postracial turn" in the second decade of this millennium? *The Voice* and the drama it manufactures around blind judgment, and implicitly also blind justice, beg the question: Can we hear what a person looks like? Do we want to? And, if so, to what ends are we listening in this manner? More specifically, can we actually hear someone's gender, race, or even *sexuality*, if we are only given access to the singing voice on a purportedly more "equal," postidentitarian playing field: the kind engineered by the reality competition format, America's puppet theater for democracy (see Meizel 2011). What difference does *audition* as a technique of perception, as well as a mode of performance, make in a US televisual politics still invested in the purportedly democratic ideals of representation and visibility across platforms into "the real"?

Beginning with accounts of how the voice becomes the figure and medium through which we sustain the fantasy of direct participation in what is structurally a representative democracy in the United States, this essay further considers how sound studies has begun to account for the vocal racialization and gendering in constitutive narratives of "the nation," as well as in critiques of rhetorics of freedom. As with most other intersectional logics, the gendering and sexualization of a voice cannot be thought apart from its racialization, and vice versa. While there is a growing body of scholarship on race, the voice, aesthetics, and politics, scholarly work on queer sexuality and vocalization is considerably more rare, though there are notable exceptions, including Wayne Koestenbaum's seminal book *The Queen's Throat* (1993), Judith Ann Peraino's *Listening to the Sirens* (2006), Allison McCracken's *Real Men Don't Sing: Crooning in American Culture* (2015), Elena Glasberg's essay on "the Butch's throat," and new scholarship (largely unpublished) on transgender vocalization by Katherine Meizel, Nina Eidsheim, Annette Schlichter, and others. This essay forges—or, perhaps more accurately, forces—a conversation between studies on racialized vocalization and queer vocalities, in order to break from the doxa, long-disputed but still prevalent, about the *universality* of the voice and the universal reach of the singing voice in particular. I do so in the effort, albeit preliminary, to explore the ways in which we sonically encounter race and sexuality in our supposedly postidentitarian landscape, as well as to move past the greater frenzy for visibility—particularly in LGBTQ efforts to win mainstream recognition. In other words, what would happen if we weren't so quick to celebrate these "aren't-we-GLAAD?" moments of prime time visibility but instead took to heart *The Voice*'s premise about prioritizing *listening*? By considering the voice and vocality, we may be able to better grasp how lesbianism and female queerness fits, or inevitably fails to fit, within popular media formats that have, to varying degrees, accommodated other marked expressions of vocality, particularly voices singing "authentically" in certain racialized idioms like rhythm and blues, soul, or jazz. Using the strange spectacle of NBC's *The Voice* as a case study, I argue that in this singing competition's overdetermined relationship to blindness, we may find enough insight to hear queerly.

The Voice of the People

Even before the venerable poet Walt Whitman heard America singing "varied carols . . . each singing what belongs to him or her and to none else," US literature and Enlightenment political philosophy conspired to bestow the nation's citizens with the sense that their individual voices mattered within the structure of our representative government. As any "American Civics 101" course reminds us, the United States is not a direct democracy with a one-to-one correspondence between the individual citizen's interests and his governance (I'm using a masculine pronoun because it refers to the citizen as it was first constituted in the United States). Instead our desires, requests, and interests are to be mediated by allegedly more learned, "reasonable," and legally adept elected representatives, hence the House of Representatives and the Senate. In the tenth of his *Federalist Papers*, James Madison articulates the founding fathers' logic for why the United States' nascent democracy should forgo direct and popular governance in favor of republicanism:

> The instability, injustice, and confusion introduced into the public councils, have, in truth, been the mortal diseases under which popular governments have everywhere perished; as they continue to be the favorite and fruitful topics from which the adversaries to liberty derive their most

specious declamations. The valuable improvements made by the American constitutions on the popular models, both ancient and modern, cannot certainly be too much admired. . . . A republic, by which I mean a government in which the scheme of representation takes place, opens a different prospect, and promises the cure for which we are seeking. (Madison n.d.)

In lieu of a direct democracy, then, as countless Americanists in history, literature, and political science have argued before me, what we have at our disposal are the tools of representation itself: the arts, literature, music, our gestures, our voices, that help manifest our "direct" relationship to the nation through metaphor, insinuation, projection, and fantasy. Having a voice and using it to advocate for one's desires, hopes, and interests, while metaphorizing that voice as a vote, is a constitutive, nationalist trope for "freedom" and citizenship in the United States, a compensatory structure for the indirectness of our democratic participation.[1] Nancy Ruttenburg describes how this manifests in various American authors' self-conscious explorations of national identity and vocality from post-Revolutionary to antebellum US literature, noting that the metaphor of the "popular voice" conjures "a spectral presence, now embodied, now disembodied; now univocal, now grotesquely polyphonic; but unfailingly, powerfully audible" (1998, 17).

Of course, the question of who actually *has* a voice in the United States' representative democracy has been unequally distributed in a blunt, material sense since the concept's incipience, even prior to the nation's constitution. Thomas Jefferson's first draft of the Declaration of Independence in 1776 famously included a paragraph decrying the British king's initiation of the slave trade, which waged (in Jefferson's words) "cruel war against human nature itself, violating its most sacred rights of life, and liberty in the persons of a distant people who never offended him, captivating and carrying them into slavery in another hemisphere" (2014, 391). Of course, this passage was excised to placate some of the southern slaveholding states in the Continental Congress. The institutionalization of slavery in the post-Revolutionary United States was further formalized in 1787 at the Constitutional Convention, when the three-fifths compromise was etched into the Constitution to guarantee the "equitable" distribution of representatives and electoral votes to slaveowning southern states, even as it was carefully calibrated to deny rights and citizenship to the slaves whose population numbers bolstered the political influence of their oppressors. Women, as we also know well through American history, were not to be granted suffrage, and thus "direct" political representation, until the Nineteenth Amendment was ratified in 1920 (King et al. 2009).

Nevertheless, the operations underscoring the modes of aesthetic representation, which help sustain political architectures like representative governments, especially failing a one-to-one correspondence between personhood and political representation, are how we arrive at the ubiquity of compensatory concepts like a vox populi, or "voice of the people," in a broader public culture. Though the notion of a vox populi has been in circulation in Anglophone contexts since the sixteenth century—and proliferating platforms for this collective voice have allegedly kept restless electorates in equilibrium as parliamentary and other republican configurations sprouted across Europe in the wake of the American and French Revolutions—it took the broadcast media age of the mid-twentieth century to revitalize the Latinate phrase. In the 1960s, the snappy abbreviation "vox pop" entered our modern lexicon, referring technically to quick-take, man-on-the-street interviews inserted into news segments on television, or on radio broadcasts as "bites." Vox pop segments became integral to indoctrinating audiences to the notion that the voice of the "common man" could be signal boosted through media technologies, and that everyone had at least random, if not equal, access to these media platforms to air one's opinion. This is how we arrive at the popular implication, capitalized upon by shows like *The Voice*, that every voice, or any voice, could be "valuable" if purely for its increased technological potential to be heard. It bears emphasis that the phrase "common man" was still taken up literally as a parameter when it came to incorporating the televisual device of vox pop to TV in the mid-twentieth century: respondents were largely white men on the street, who have historically enjoyed the freedom to move through the streets without being perceived as a threat (as people of color might be), or as women of loose morals whose propriety is measured by circumspection and privacy.

Of course, the realist, documentary style of most vox pop segments sometimes unintentionally reinforced federalist logics about why democracies should remain representative instead of direct, especially when fumbling or ill-informed commentators on the street would find themselves stunned in front of the handheld mic and camera with nothing or, worse, something utterly awful to say. The series of parodic vox pops featuring morons, eccentrics, and reactionaries in *Monty Python's Flying Circus* offer the most hilarious and incisive examples of vox pop fail, as do various segments on late night talk shows in the United States spotlighting the ignorance of the general populace about everything from geography and basic science to current events.

As many scholars in sound and voice studies have argued in response to the universalist assumption that the "voice" is a gateway to freedom (both subjective and political), the voice itself, and the singing voice in particular, is erroneously figured as a transparent medium stripped of identifying markers like race, sexuality, and in certain instances even gender. The voice, then, is sometimes construed as a conduit for "truth" precisely because it grants unmediated access to the utterer—to one's "pure" expression from the depths. Paradoxically, the voice's relationship to this purity of expression is what has also, since antiquity, raised suspicions that the voice, and the singing voice in particular, functions as the perfect medium for deception, persuasion, and fatal seduction. We need only recall the alluring song of the Sirens in Homer's *Odyssey*, "who charm all men ... the Sirens charm him with their clear-sounding song as they sit in their meadow with a huge pile of bones round them from decaying men whose skins wither round them" (Homer 1993, 184).

For musicologist Judith Ann Peraino, the song of the Sirens not only is a classical myth that establishes the voice's power to deceive and seduce but also offers one of the earliest examples of a moment in which vocalization and musicality are linked to dangerous and transgressive expressions of otherness and sexuality capable of diverting someone—even a stalwart citizen-hero like Odysseus—from the proper path. As Peraino writes, "This desire may not have a definite object, may not, in fact, be a desire *for* anything; but rather, it may be a desire to do something other than what you were just doing or simply to question what you are doing" (2006, 11). Far from maintaining the status quo or republican equilibrium, then, the voice and its mysterious sources—sometimes racialized, sometimes sexualized, sometimes gendered, or merely "other" or "otherworldly"—are sometimes difficult to pinpoint or trace, and thus threaten to destabilize and destroy political, social, and moral structures.[2]

Vocal Racialization and Critical Listening

The voice's capacity for deceit as much as truth, for destabilization as much as coherence, for identity *theft* as much as love and identification (to riff on Eric Lott's important work on "love and theft"), has also been the focus of critical studies on race, performance, musicality, and vocalization.[3] Scholars like Jennifer Stoever (2016), Daphne Brooks (2006), Tricia Rose (2004), and others have demonstrated the many instances in which the voice's purported intelligibility or lack thereof becomes a criterion for legislating a sonic color line between sense and nonsense, meaning and meaninglessness, the human and nonhuman. In her essay about Amy Winehouse's stylistic debt to black blues singers and vaudeville performers, Brooks (2008) tackles other critics' assertions, specifically Sasha Frere-Jones's, that Winehouse's "mush mouthed ... inflections and phonemes don't add up to any known style." Brooks reminds us, "These 'mush-mouthed' phrasings are anything but new. Winehouse is drawing on a known style that's a hundred years old, rooted in a tradition of female minstrelsy. . . . Her rich combination of split vocal stylings recalls Mamie Smith's sly and oscillating phrasings—moving from Northeastern vaudeville intonations in one note to early Southern blues in the next." Brooks provides the provenance for Winehouse's vocal style through phrasing, intonation, timbre, and grain, alongside her other performance-based expressions, comportment, and fashion.

In one of her earlier essays, the musicologist and voice studies scholar Nina Eidsheim anatomizes the practice of listening to and interpreting the voice, noting that "the *material* that is the singing voice, i.e., the body in its material dimension, never exists in a pre-cultural state. The vocal, material body is always already formed by the cultural and social context within which it vocalizes" (2012, 19). While it may be easy for us to imagine this relative to accented speaking voices from different regions and nations, singing voices remain susceptible to being mythologized as the media for the expression of a coherent, unified subjectivity.[4] In this sense, the notion of vocality itself in its broad, inclusive sense may be seen as the perfect medium through which to imagine and legislate—through vocal competition—a postracial, post-identitarian citizen subject. Yet instead of affirming the coherence of an un-burdened, unidentifiable subject, the voice reminds us that the articulating body is sometimes at odds within itself—among and between itself; therefore, Eidsheim implores us to "examine the voice in its concrete specificity, as an unfolding event articulated through a particular sensing and sensed body" (2012, 9). Furthermore, as listeners, we must strive to remember that our *reception* of the voice is also, at once, contextual, cultural, material, and visceral; we listen to and conjure the body or "source" when we hear the (singing) voice. As Eidsheim has pointed out through her important research bringing together dance studies and the interpretive dimensions of choreography into the analysis of vocal expression, "Each utterance (made by one's own body and by others') leaves imprints on one's ligaments, tissue, and flesh. As a result, voice is never *heard* in a state prior to the impact of cultural, social, and other outside forces" (13).

How we *hear*, in other words, is just as conditioned by our own contextualization, our own bodies, our own material conditions, and our own visceral archives; "thus we may consider how the sound of a singer's voice is in fact a co-creation to which listeners contribute" (Eidsheim 2009). This helps put into perspective how and why, for Sasha Frere-Jones, Amy Winehouse's "mush-mouthed" singing resounds as sourceless or doesn't add up to "any known style" (perhaps even conjuring a "postracial" vocality), whereas Brooks hears within it a century-long genealogy of what often remains unheard and unattributed: black women's voices lost to minstrelsy, like Mamie Smith's, Alberta Hunter's, and others,' combined with ostentatious expressions of black masculinity from Sammy Davis Jr. to "pop-ya-collar, hip-hop machismo" (Brooks 2008). The vocal source, at times seemingly and deceptively unlocatable, and at others redolent with the materiality and fleshiness of history and some of its most violent genealogies, is what brings us to the concept of vocal passing: of successfully intoning another's presumed sound, accent, and style.

As Jennifer Stoever-Ackerman argues, "Aural signifiers of race are thoroughly enmeshed with the visuality of race [because] they never really lose their ultimate reference to different types of bodies" (2010, 65). The visual echo, in other words, conspires with sonic resonance to conjure a supposedly coherent vision of the utterer or the singer. When the voice—especially the singing voice—appears to split from its source, or resonates incongruously with the performing body, structural power differentials between races, nationalities, genders, and sexualities make themselves readily apparent. Some performing bodies, more often than not white bodies, are permitted to take on multiple vocal styles and will inevitably reap praise for their agility, talent, and ingenuity: they make the style "their own" (to use the parlance of reality vocal competitions) through what is often conceived as a transformative performance.[5] These voices, in other words, might be construed as postracial, the ideation of something like *The Voice*'s mission to arrive at the "unbiased" judgment of talent. Blue-eyed soul from the 1960s and 1970s is just one among many examples of popular music genres since the early age of minstrelsy that reward white artists for "broadening the appeal" of black musical formats like soul and R&B by uncannily approximating black vocal styles.[6]

Meanwhile, other bodies—racialized, "foreign," and genderqueer bodies who adopt vocal styles and genres that fail to correspond to the expectation fostered by their embodiment—are dismissed as derivative: as flawed, accented copies out of their "natural" range.[7] While it may be tempting to extend an analogy about these regimes of vocal profiling and identity policing to institutions like the academy, where the correspondence between the subject of one's scholarly work and one's physical presentation and comportment can determine the so-called coherence of an individual's research profile, suffice it to say here that vocal passing rewards race and class mobility, and relies on the presumptive hierarchies of talent and ability, in order to be deemed successful. Vocal passing, in other words, could be seen as an apex of postracial logics, which would assimilate the coarse and complex histories of appropriation, and in some cases assimilation, into a revisionist and optimistic narrative of homage and seamless merging.[8]

As these complicated and sometimes contradictory histories of the voice's meanings and democratic resonances attest, the mere possibility that the singing voice can be apprehended without an immediate visual referent does not make it a postmillennial harbinger of a "postracial" or "postidentitarian" democracy, as *The Voice* purports to model for us. The voice has never been *pre*racial, as the scholarship on voice studies painstakingly demonstrates. Nor has it been the universal conduit to the collective soul—a voice of the people claiming to contain the common multitudes, but mostly intoning the "common sense" of elite coteries of white, male, property-owning citizen-subjects.

While shows like *The Voice* may, in many respects, reinforce scholarly accounts of how race and vocalization might work in a purportedly "democratic" voting scenario, it presents a different set of conundrums in relation to hearing sexuality. The concluding section of this essay explores how *The Voice* might extend our sense of how we assess the "lesbianism" of vocalization— perhaps as a sonic punctum to the show's halcyon imaginaries of postracial, postidentitarian justice—inspiring us further to hear queerly through the show's sonic and televisual dimensions.

Sounding Sexuality on *The Voice*

The disparate optics offered by Vicci Martinez and Beverly McClellan, the two lesbians who won over *The Voice*'s celebrity panel in season one with their raw-throated rock vocals (right in the pocket of what we might call the Etheridgean mode),[9] were dramatically crafted around the show's "blind" ethos. Martinez's audition was shot so that, just like the coaches, the TV audience couldn't see her face until she was selected a tense forty-one seconds into— or nearly a third of the way through—her blind audition. Filling screen time before CeeLo Green and Christina Aguilera pressed their buttons in quick succession to see, and thus also select Martinez for their respective teams, is a series of cutaway close-ups of the coaches' faces as they listen and confer. Martinez's performance, meanwhile, is only shot from a distance or from behind, with some screen-in-screen framing to heighten the suspense and the stakes: her friends and family are watching backstage on a monitor, anxiously waiting for one of the coaches to signal their selection by swiveling around to face her. The viewer at home is enlisted into *The Voice*'s ethos of blind judgment through these perspective shots, as well as other televisual framing devices like the biographical package leading up to her performance, in which we are made privy

Figure 7.1 Screen capture of Vicci Martinez's blind audition (opening shot).

Figure 7.2 Screen-in-screen perspective shot of Christina Aguilera listening to Martinez, preselection (TC 0:16).

to her coming-out story, offered a quick glimpse of her skinny jeans and boots (again, without seeing her face), and invited to "listen along with our coaches and see if you would pick Vicci Martinez."

As we discover after the music stops, Martinez is actually quite a little hottie: a Latina lesbian heartthrob in the making with a cute, asymmetrical shag, a winning smile, and sensibly curated fashion. Indeed, her attire could very well be labeled "standard-issue lesbian": a plain white V-neck T-shirt, dark fitted jeans tucked into motorcycle boots, multiple necklaces freighted

Figure 7.3 Front perspective and live studio audience perspective of the coaches' panel (TC 0:28).

Figure 7.4 First shot of Martinez's face and close-up of her performance after CeeLo Green is the first coach to press the button (TC 0:41).

with ample amulets, and the double-down combo of an ambiguously "eth-nic" scarf *and* a gray men's suit vest. Of course, not all lesbians elect to wear, or can pull off, this particular style. While it's obviously beyond the scope of this essay to elaborate on the many styles and expressions that would consti-tute a "lesbian look book," I've commented on her visual presentation here to initiate the type of vocal analysis Eidsheim, among others, has applied to ra-cial vocalization: one founded upon the principle that the materiality of the singing voice is also, as referenced earlier, formed and shaped by the "cultural

Figure 7.5 Martinez preparing to select Green or Aguilera as her coach (TC 1:41).

and social context within which it vocalizes." Because one *listens* and not only performs with these criteria in mind, the visual codes in Martinez's appearance resonate with the aesthetics and fashion I, as a listener and viewer, have come to understand from a lifetime immersed in lesbian culture, as well as doing the work of queer cultural studies. Upon first seeing Martinez's vest, I couldn't help but quip about her "vested interests" à la queer scholar Marjorie Garber's (1997) significant tome on "cross-dressing and cultural anxiety."

But even when we go in "blind" to Martinez's performance and attempt to isolate her vocals, as the coaches earnestly strain to demonstrate for us in their reaction shots, her vocal repertoire and style of delivery also carry within them certain "clues" to her identity, largely vectored through her sexuality. The video package revealing her coming-out story merely corroborates what has already been revealed to us through her vocal repertoire. Martinez's audition song is Adele's "Rolling in the Deep," an alto-range pop-blues hit with torchy, lyrical elements, requiring lots of impassioned vocal fry and tonal growling. As Wayne Koestenbaum, D. A. Miller, Judith Ann Peraino, and other scholars have pointed out, torch songs and other melodramatic musical modes have long been associated with queer performers and audiences (Garber 1997, 112).[10] Earlier, I described both Martinez and Beverly McClellan as singing in the "Etheridgean mode," in reference to Melissa Etheridge, the rock vocalist and nineties-era lesbian icon. Etheridge is known for her deep, gravelly alto-range vocals, which Peraino has argued amount to something of a vocal "lesbian phallus." She writes: "Etheridge's voice, like the Sirens' song, has the power to call into question the heterosexual matrix. Coming from a lesbian but emanating masculine melodrama, this voice also unites (always phallic) meaning and (always feminine) sex" (2006, 138). Stylistically, this manifests precisely in those rough-hewn intonations, the smoky, textured growls and "catching," or vocal breaking, connoting a certain damage and emotional honesty expected from her chosen musical formats, that is, rock, blues, and "women's music."

Martinez took an Adele song and delivered it in the style of "The 'Ridge" (as some lesbians affectionately call Melissa Etheridge), announcing her influences in the very first note: grainy and redolent with blues, broken hearts, and badassery. As she crescendos from the repressed urgency of the opening verse full-throatedly into the chorus, she doesn't diminish her vocal fry— something that would happen "naturally" if someone who didn't have any physical ailments or damage like nodules opened their throat to intone loudly.[11] Instead, she increases it, as one might twist hard on the gain knob of a guitar's distortion pedal for a rockin' solo. The texture of her voice, the tenacity of her delivery, and her chosen repertoire signify "queer," especially for the TV audiences at home who interpret this with the additional clues of her attire and comportment. The televisual codes at the sonic level conspire with the drama of impaired visuality staged by *The Voice* to help "identify" and taxonomize the performer and performance. Far from advancing the show's framing narratives about the postidentitarian potential of vocality, Martinez effectively flaunts that she is a queer woman of color even before we get a closer look at her.

This is not to say that all vocalists who sing in this style or through blues-influenced rock repertoires are *necessarily* lesbians or queer women, who like Janis Joplin and other such icons are also influenced by racialized rock and soul repertoires. Rather, it is to recognize that this style of vocal delivery, given its range and so-called aggressive texture, is culturally associated with artists who experiment with expressions of female masculinity and androgyny and by extension sometimes also identify as lesbian and/or queer. This style of vocalization, in other words, not only achieves a certain queer iconicity through figures like Etheridge or the Indigo Girls' contralto rocker Amy Ray but also attains the status of an oral/aural "code" hailing queers who, as Elena Glasberg (2010) has described butch lesbian efforts to vocalize, "pitched [their] voice low, threw it down that hole, tried to feel it supported from [the] solar plexus, the fundament of . . . social projection." In other words, by engaging our queer, critical listening—one freighted by our nationalist, sociocultural baggage and our fantasies about community and identification— we not only hear these women singing; we hear in them ourselves emulating

Figure 7.6 Beverly McClellan's blind audition for *The Voice*, season 1.

a particular manner of vocalization in our own efforts to *sound* queer—or at least closer to the gendered and generic aspirations of our bodies.

Beverly McClellan, Martinez's lesbian compatriot and competitor on that first season of *The Voice*, sings in a similar mode, though she sports an "edgier" look that complements her ethos of fighting, in her own words, "against the man." Unlike in Martinez's segment, TV audiences could clearly see McClellan's face and features *before* hearing her, thus fostering other elements of narrative suspense. We anxiously await "the reveal" and the reaction, should one of the coaches select McClellan for his or her team, only to swivel around to come face-to-face with a bald, tatted dyke adorned with piercings and leather wrist cuffs, chewing on Janis Joplin's "Piece of My Heart" with barroom tenacity.

Like Martinez, McClellan sports a telltale lesbian vest, although her styling skews toward the butcher end of the lesbian spectrum, not simply because of her hair (or lack thereof) but also because of the cut of her clothes, which remain tight around the calves yet hang looser around the glutes and waist. She's also wearing a crewneck T-shirt (less revealing around the décolletage), one necklace instead of two, and another iteration of the ubiquitous lesbian leather motorcycle boot.

Vocally as well as sartorially, Martinez and McClellan clearly exist within the same genus if not exactly within the same type. McClellan channels Janis Joplin's singing style, which was the inspiration for Melissa Etheridge's own vocal efforts. She also demonstrates a wider tonal range in her audition than Martinez, by mixing up her textural delivery to engage her upper registers,

strategically hitting her higher-pitched head voice for melisma to add grada-
tion and contrast, while affecting a slightly breezier swagger.

The queer blogosphere immediately picked up on both Martinez's and
McClellan's success on the show. *After Ellen* and *Unicorn Booty* posted items
immediately, encouraging queer audiences to tune in, while *After Ellen* followed up with extended interviews, first with Martinez, then with McClellan.
Both were asked about whether or not the format of *The Voice* made it "easier"
for queer contestants to succeed without being judged for their appearance.
Martinez notoriously bowed out of the Hollywood rounds of *American Idol*
because producers asked her to buy a new wardrobe (read, "femme up" even
more), so she offered a more affirmative response in line with *The Voice*'s rhetoric of leveling the playing field. McClellan, meanwhile, offered a goofy but
shrewdly diplomatic "one love"–style answer to the question, referring to a
universal vibe of human generosity in better keeping with the show's postracial, postidentitarian rhetoric. Different as their public temperaments may
be, both have been praised for amplifying lesbian visibility on network television during and after the show.

Some robust, "score TWO for the team" chest-bumping is surely in order
after the success of these Sapphic sirens and the others who followed, like
the dance- and electronica-oriented Egyptian American ladygeek, Michelle
Chamuel, runner up to season four of *The Voice*. In the wake of these successes, and by way of concluding, I'd like to reflect on how *The Voice*'s conceit
of staging a "postracial" and postidentitarian model through the implicitly
universal voice ironically brings us to a clearer sense of how the voice is actually
one of the most significant media for understanding how identity and recognition function. The voice engages our vision, even if we try to hear without
it; and more often than not, that vision of where that voice is coming from
and what it accomplishes is a projection of our own desires for identification,
which is fashioned together from the detritus of our cultural experiences.

Throughout the institutional life of queer studies, debates about lesbian
visibility have unfurled in elaborate fugue-like variations. Rather than re-
hash them here, allow me to commit the theoretical heresy of constructing
a binary to highlight some key positions. In the "real" world of mainstream
LGBTQIA organizations and cultural producers, quantifying positive representations of queer folk qualifies as measuring progress. The more gays
and lesbians we see on screens big and small, the logic goes, the better the
world gets. In the more rarefied realms of queer theory (my own habitat),
this desire for representation and belonging calls forth the very crisis inherent in politicizing visibility as an end in itself. Film and media scholar

Amy Villarejo explains this dynamic best when she remarks in her watershed book, *Lesbian Rule*, that "the common sense of visibility is that it does both [parlays representation's double meaning as 'portrait' and 'proxy']: by appearing, so it would go, we belong... [but] ... to present lesbian as image is to arrest the dynamism such a signifier can trigger" (2003, 14).

What, then, would be the sonic dynamism of lesbianism? Is it a transformative "grammar" that modifies the terms with which it becomes intimate? (Villarejo explores this possibility in her book.) Is it in the grain of a voice, as we might argue after a popular intervention like *The Voice* with its staged conceit about blindness and vocal meritocracies? Even if we hadn't been primed by the show's visualizations, did we not *hear* the lesbianism in Martinez's and McClellan's throats? In their urgent, tremulous, and toothsome strivings through the repertoires of "fierce females" like Adele and Janis Joplin? In the stubborn assertion of their identities as queer women, and in Martinez's case as a queer woman of color, can we imagine the lesbian voice as a kind of punctum to *The Voice*'s own instrumentalization of a postracial, postidentitarian logic in which prejudice no longer exists in the reality show's system of evaluation?

There is something marked, and remarkable, in the yearning and temporal drag modeled by Martinez's and McClellan's respective vocalities, voices that could only break the surface in a format that (at least initially) thwarts the edicts of visibility, of fashion, generic niches, and the envelope-pushing sensibility demanded by pop.[12] Instead of being one step ahead, Martinez and McClellan constantly pull us back to something we've heard before, often in a half-empty bar that reeks of Bud and Marlboros, both light. And in that vocal recognition of a queerness that cracks, distorts, punctures, and abjures, we may also come to acknowledge that voices in general are not inherently timeless, but mean the most for some of us when they are painfully out of time, and out of place.

Notes

An earlier, significantly shorter version of this piece originally appeared on *Sounding Out! The Sound Studies Blog* as "Hearing Queerly: NBC's *The Voice*" (May 16, 2011), https://soundstudiesblog.com/2011/05/16/hearing-queerly-nbcs-the-voice/.

1 See Jay Fliegelman's (1993) study on the very speech act of "declaring independence."
2 See Ruttenburg's (1998, 222–27) discussion of the easily manipulated and instrumentalized disembodied voice. See also Sarah Kessler's work that explores voice through ventriloquism in US political rhetoric about power and control, particularly during the George W. Bush administration (Kessler 2016), and in our coauthored essay (Kessler and Tongson 2014).

3 For more on race, musicality, appropriation, and desire, see Eric Lott's watershed study *Love and Theft: Black Face Minstrelsy and the American Working Class* (2013).

4 For a foundational philosophical account of accent, gesture, and vocalization, see Rousseau 2009.

5 For more on "making it your own" on *American Idol*, see Meizel 2011, 61–83. Elsewhere, I've also written about the imperative to "own" another's song vis-à-vis the karaoke standard on reality vocal competitions, while exploring how the invention of the karaoke machine is owed in part to touring Filipino cover bands and musicians, stoking colonial fears of debased forms of mimicry. See Tongson 2015.

6 See Taylor 1997, and Neal 2005, which accounts for the disidentifications that allow black listeners to "transcend . . . the kinds of 'affective obstacles'" that come into play when listening to white performances of black musical idioms. See also Wald 2007.

7 Eidsheim points to a sociolinguistic, educational study by Donald L. Rubin, in which groups of listeners, made up of US college undergraduates, were given the same recording of a lecture recorded by an American English native speaker but were presented with different photographs depicting this speaker. One group of listeners was given a photo of a white Anglo-American lecturer, while another group received a photo of an Asian lecturer. Unsurprisingly, the exact same recording, when paired with the photo of the Asian lecturer, was "rated less clear in speech, higher in level of accent, and poorer in coherence" (Eidsheim 2012, 10). The original study is published in Rubin 1992.

8 For more on vocal assimilation, especially among early to mid-twentieth-century white male crooners, who were under tremendous pressure to diminish the intimations of "deviance" in their minstrelized, gender-ambiguous intonations, see McCracken 2015.

9 I am riffing playfully here on the extended reading of lesbian rock icon Melissa Etheridge's vocal style, performed by Judith Ann Peraino (2006) in her chapter "Queer Ears and Icons."

10 Resonant with some of Peraino's claims about the "resistance" one may find in queer music, as well as in queer *responses* to music and lyrics, see Holman Jones: "Through parody and personal lives, irony and identity bending, consciousness and diva discourses, torch singing asks audiences to question their place in the stories of individual responsibility and victimhood. Lyrics are ideological discourses, and torch singing uses voice and music to work on those lyrics, those discourses" (2007, 113). Linda Williams (2004) also turns to the use of torch songs in Pedro Almodóvar's films to hail homosexual viewers oriented to melancholic expressions of loss. See also Koestenbaum 1993, and D. A. Miller 1998. By the second half of the twentieth century, the relationship between queers and torch songs became such a common cultural reference that creative works, most notably Harvey Fierstein's Tony Award–winning play *Torch Song Trilogy* (1983), and its film adaptation in 1988, could use the referent as a kind of shorthand for "gay."

11 Tellingly, Adele herself suffered from bleeding in her larynx and vocal nodules, requiring surgery after singing in this style throughout her career, and after an especially demanding tour schedule in the early years of the 2010s. See Adele 2012. The *New York Times* also featured a piece on vocal injuries in which a leading specialist, Dr. Natasha Mirza, comments, "Some pop singers are also more susceptible to damaging their vocal cords because they have not had classical training, and their emotive, raw-sounding vocal techniques

can place extra stress on tissues." The article also explains the range of injuries I allude to, earlier in the chapter, that account for "cracked" or granular voices: "The most common problems for singers are benign polyps, cysts, granulomas and nodules, which are growths akin to calluses that develop on the vocal cords. All these can bleed under the demands of performance. The bleeding can lead to fibrosis, or scarring. The scars leave vocal cords less pliable and soft; the voice becomes hoarse and cracks" (McKinley 2011).

12 As always, I am indebted to Elizabeth Freeman's (2010) work on "temporal drag" to describe the "visceral pull of the past on the supposedly revolutionary present."

8

More Than a Game

LeBron James and the Affective Economy of Place

VICTORIA E. JOHNSON

Sport is a site of profound ambivalence with regard to the postracial. On the one hand, sports are idealized as a uniquely public "level playing field"—a site that daily affirms the democratic possibilities of a "color-blind" meritocracy and the necessity of multiracial teamwork to any success. In the United States in particular, sports are perhaps the most visible realm in which "Black success stories lend credence to the notion that anyone, no matter how poor or how black you may be, can make it to the top if you try hard enough" (Alexander 2011, 248). Media coverage of sports regularly exemplifies the creative ways in which race is disavowed or talked around, rather than explicitly addressed (quarterbacks who are "field managers" and "gym rats"—e.g., the white Tom Brady—are regularly contrasted with those who are "instinctive," "improvisatory," "natural athletes" such as Cam Newton). And yet, sports simultaneously "remains one of the *few* places in American society where there is a consistent racial discourse" (Boyd 2000, 60) that also offers ritual, broad audience engagement with an explicit, contemporary "black aesthetic"

(Boyd 1997, 111) in its most popular and profitable US leagues—the National Basketball Association (NBA) and the National Football League (NFL).

Further, sport is one of the most powerful sites of postracial ambivalence because it is one of the few truly broadly "shared" realms of daily culture within the United States. Though sports is the most watched genre of television programming (with TV as still the most engaged form of daily media for the largest and most diversified demographic audience) even non–sports fans are inescapably aware of the top stories pertaining to the field, due to its prominence across social media, news, and other entertainment forums (V. E. Johnson 2009a, 114–37). Thus, when a sports event becomes a news event and a widely discussed controversy, it presents a key opportunity to examine the ways in which race is both avowed and disavowed in the broader discourses surrounding the event and how these rhetorical moves may both buttress and trouble understandings of the postracial.

In its "ideal" conceptualization, the postracial is allied with a "color-blind" notion of individualism that is consistent with and historically analogous to neoliberal economic and political discourses of *marketplace* equities. If the United States has "overcome" racism, then all citizens are presumed to be on equal footing in a context wherein marketplace values determine social, political, and cultural value. Failures in the market, broadly conceived, are thus due to individual shortcomings rather than systemic impediments. The postracial, in this sense, implies an idealized *placelessness* associated with finance-capital market logics. Such placelessness is, of course, only imaginable by obscuring raced labor in mappable locations (e.g., call centers or security at cloud farms; day care for telecommuters' children) and literally capitalizing upon diversity as a commodified sign of "progress" (from Mattel's new line of multiracial Ken dolls to ESPN's reliance on hip-hop to mark its youthful credibility). But outside of the concept of market relations—in the few spaces in which we might imagine that—the postracial is arguably a more unstable category. That is, while the postracial is undeniably a historic, economic, political, and juridical set of logics with ramifications in the real social world, as a lived, affective, everyday social and cultural concept, it is vulnerable. Specifically, sports represents a visible site of tension regarding the postracial because of its irrevocable connection to historic myths of *place*-identity and affective logics that feel removed from the market.

In *White by Law: The Legal Construction of Race*, Ian F. Haney López notes, "As a social construct, race depends on what people believe, rendering it an inherently unstable concept. . . . Consider the ease with which we assign racial identities knowing only that someone is from Santa Monica or South Central. Greenwich Village or Harlem.... This link between space and race functions as a matter of both external and internal identification—as a matter of what others believe of our identity, and how we think of ourselves" (1996, 120). In the sports realm, analogous logics are exceptionally powerful. To adapt the preceding, for instance, we might "consider the ease with which we assign" identities "knowing only that someone is" a Blue Demon or a Tar Heel, a 49er fan or a Raider fan. Here, I propose that the uniquely overwrought nature of the wrath and sense of "betrayal" at LeBron James's 2010 "Decision" to leave Cleveland was rooted in its exposure of local—and, apparently, shared national commitment—to *not* rewrite geographic myths of Clevelandness as shorthand for distinctly residual post–World War II–era understandings of race, industry, economy, and community. Indeed, the Decision provoked public embrace and reaffirmation of distinct, affective understandings of Cleveland as a traumatized city, iconic of an industrial and civil rights–era United States, committed to doing things "the hard way on purpose" (Giffels 2014, 4–5). James's "Return" to Cleveland in 2014 reiterated these residual logics as definitive of the region. The residual myths of Cleveland obfuscate its shrinking population, its increasing reliance on culture (of sports) as commerce, and its postindustrial economic realities. Though these myths are culturally and socially bound to the past, they still function powerfully in the present. This is not to contradict or deny the realities of the postracial as a broader cultural dominant but rather to propose that sports culture's critical conjunctures (here, LeBron James's Decision and Return) and sites (the role of and identification with teams in a community) may expose a productive ambivalence or reveal significant fissures and tensions in the construction of a "postracial" everyday in the United States.

Michelle Alexander notes that, in the postracial era, "it is no longer socially permissible to use race, explicitly, as a justification for discrimination, exclusion, and social contempt. So we don't" (2011, 2). This essay examines a specific sports media crisis to interrogate ways we don't talk about race by talking instead about *place*-identity and gendered cultural conventions. If we understand the postracial to be historically contingent, moments of public crisis may provoke a productive discursive collision between residual and emergent understandings of racialized community. Sports is a deeply affective site for fans, bound to specific places and raced histories of what is shared in a community. As such, sports crises allow us to examine how thinking through geographic frames and affectively fraught mythologies of place might trouble the postracial as a cultural dominant.

The Decision

On July 8, 2010, Akron, Ohio, native and Cleveland Cavalier professional basketball phenomenon LeBron James collaborated with the cable sports television outlet ESPN to announce "The Decision" to move to Miami, Florida, to join the NBA's Miami Heat. This prompted immediate outrage from Clevelanders and across the US sports world, with critics interpreting the move as an act of betrayal of James's previously heralded, loyal, and even self-sacrificing commitment to his home state. How does a local sports hero transform, literally overnight, from "The Chosen One" to a "breathtaking narcissist"? ("The Chosen One" 2002; Groner 2010).[1] Conversely, given such criticism, how was James's status as "redeemer" and "king" so smoothly restored with his July 2014 decision to return to Cleveland, following success with the Heat? This chapter examines LeBron James's career trajectory as a local then national and global sports media icon and returned "native son," by reading competing discursive investments in his relative rootedness or mobility as these were premised on deeply affective, residual myths of Clevelandness and accompanying understandings of community, citizenship, and the market.

As Dave Zirin has proposed, perhaps the defining ambivalence of LeBron James's career is the tension between the pull of sacrifice and that of earning.[2] During the crisis of the Decision, local and national media reduced James's choice to a question of "loyalty" and continued "sacrifice" to stay put in a small market with little hope of a championship or the "betrayal" of departure for a major market, almost guaranteed on-court success, and significantly enhanced earning power. Would LeBron be true to his native home of Cleveland and his persona as "just a kid from Akron" characterized by a sincere commitment to place, humility, and the bonds of local Rust Belt community? Or would he embrace free agency's mobile promise of material success in a largely postindustrial global city such as New York or Miami? Around the Decision, Cleveland media and sympathetic national commentators reiterated the city's defining local myths to urge LeBron to stay, implying that the Cavaliers and the region itself were rare throwbacks in their expectation of LeBron's fealty to a small market and continued service to the community that, through a "village" of mentors, coaches, and friends, raised him out of a "broken" home to success in the NBA. Pro–"Stay LeBron"/sacrifice press thus emphasized James's difficult youth as an African American child in an underresourced but supportive neighborhood of Akron in a narrative culminating in his status as the city's "native son" and "chosen one"—all stories of hardship and sacrifice based in racialized narratives of community, uplift, and exceptionalism. The "realistically, he has to go"/earn press, by contrast, began from the premise that to truly realize his potential, LeBron would have to transcend such localism, proving himself in the contemporary sports marketplace, where mobility and impermanence are the norm. Miami thus embraced its role as emblematic of "a player's league" city, and NBA franchise, where "any player who doesn't act as their own general manager is just playing themselves" (Zirin 2016). James's homecoming has restored local mythologies of hard-nosed, bootstrap, nonglamorous place-identity and has reinforced a sensibility that regional unity is, fundamentally, forged *by* sports as a uniquely shared, democratic realm of imagined, "utopian" community.

The spring before LeBron's return announcement, Destination Cleveland—the city's private, nonprofit convention and visitor's bureau—produced a promotional video that underscores this somewhat defensive but deeply held residual mythology both as definitive of the locale and as distinctively place-bound. Part of the "Positively Cleveland" campaign, the video features a balanced mix of black and white twenty- and thirty-somethings at work and play in the city, laboring to build (e.g., featuring workers at a bicycle plant) and craft (e.g., beer) while noting the rigors of place ("under the right conditions, pressure can create diamonds"). For those who stick with the pressures, Cleveland offers "world-class experiences"—explicitly, here, identified as the "passion" of Cavs basketball—"without the world-class ego." Cleveland has "never been flashy. Trendy. Perfect. And for that, you're welcome."[3] The place-bound is, here, representationally time-bound as well—evocative of a post–World War II, civil rights–era, midwestern industrial city that labored as a black and white community restored and united by a shared love for losing sports teams. In a grittily beautiful way, "Positively Cleveland" promotes shared loss as a defining Cleveland bond, emplacement (over mobility) as a sign of character, and sacrifice and stasis as tradition. It is in this context that LeBron James's stardom's persistent localness and undeniable connection to place—regardless of his real economic mobility and "world-class" achievements—are best understood.

Unlike Michael Jordan—against whom he is ceaselessly measured—LeBron James is not typically referred to through superstar clichés that he "transcends" race. The Decision outcry and Return aftermath suggest that much of the difference here is based on geographic ties.[4] While LeBron came of age in a presumptively "postracial" United States, however, his NBA career also flourishes in a league era that explicitly capitalizes on African American culture and style to market its globally popular game—particularly through the lenses of hip-hop music and fashion. James's virtuosity presents a contemporary paradox: he is not typically symbolic of the "transcendent," postracial icon, and yet, critical moments in his career have seen the perceived potential "threat" of his social and economic capital, *as* a young African American man, allayed through rhetorical displacements that—often hyperbolically—*elide* race. Specifically, when LeBron is at the center of controversies, these have been contextualized as *geographic* and *gendered* identity crises that are "not about" race but about challenges to received regional mythologies and presumptively "raceless" masculine "ideals." Thus, the public crisis and joy provided by LeBron's departure and homecoming suggest that postracial mythologies require active *work* to imagine and sustain.

Sarah Banet-Weiser notes that "to call this moment in late capitalism postracial is not to suggest that race and race relations are somehow irrelevant but rather to think seriously about recent shifts in capitalism that *contain* and *market* race and diversity in the media using new strategies" (2007, 214–15). Is it possible that—as with earlier theorizations of the postmodern as a sensibility—the logics of the postracial are unevenly dispersed and apprehended in local specificity? Might we imagine the postracial as a historic, political, cultural, and economic logic that is variably dominant? If the postracial depends upon comparatively *placeless*, historically decontextualized logics for its institutional power, might there be sites at which these logics are visibly in tension with *residual* understandings of race, rights, and social welfare grounded in mythologies of place? How might place specificity challenge the postracial as an economic, political, and cultural dominant or, at the least, reveal its tenuousness as a logic always in need of rather hyperbolic moves to shore it up?

Given that residual cultural elements are those formed in the past that are *culturally* effective in the present, analyses of the discourses of LeBron's career thus point to a continued—even unshakable—relevance of residual mythologies of place-identity. These mythologies are generally no longer explanatory of the day-to-day economic, structural, and institutional realities of place, but they remain foundational screens through which the community comprehends itself, perpetuating and defining its cultural dispositions and values both internally and to those beyond its boundaries.[5] But how is place-identity imagined, and how is this experienced and ratified through sports? According to Stuart Hall (1988, 154), a conjuncture is a historically specific moment within which a critical network of discourses forms across political, institutional, and popular sites engaged in working through a broader social dilemma. The Decision forced examination of an intersection of myths of Cleveland's political and laboring sensibilities, its industrial identity, and its overwhelming tradition of loss, as lived through and symbolized by its sports franchises. LeBron became the fulcrum around whom Cleveland worked through residual understandings of place. The Decision represented a public rupture—revealing that those key mythologies structuring affective apprehensions of community and shared identity might no longer be definitive of the region and its values. Arguably, the hyperbolic reactions to LeBron's Decision exposed the tenuousness of Cleveland's myths, while LeBron's Return arguably exposed the overcompensation required to restore them.

Sporting Community: Love, Loss, and Cleveland

A colleague of mine recently confided that his father would say, "Sports is the only thing that is true." This belief in the sports realm as one of clarity, knowability, and truth resonates particularly in relation to fallout over the Decision. Criticism and, indeed, rage over the event and James's choice were based, in large part, on two presumed "betrayals" of "shared" truths. The first of these was LeBron's apparent betrayal of an allegiance to northeast Ohio that was, previously, presumed to be *sincere*. The second was the Decision telecast's apparent betrayal of journalistic ethics: the program was resoundingly judged to violate standards expected of informational news coverage; and, arguably even more condemnable, the special was structured through gendered codes of television genre otherwise associated with "feminized" TV genres including, particularly, the soap opera and reality TV. Sports programming has historically been associated with newscasting, news event coverage, and documentary as conventionally "masculine" TV genres characterized by "objective," "fact-based" content and focus on clear outcomes and statistics as seen through "neutral" camera angles and editing practices that emphasize an "unbiased" view of the action. "Feminized" TV genres, on the other hand, are conventionally characterized by multiple and ongoing or unresolved story lines, serial engagement, and camera work and editing practices that are "intimate" (featuring the medium close-up, the close-up, and the reaction shot), "subjective," and emotionally involving. Tania Modleski, whose work is essential here, notes the broader cultural relevance of such formal and narrative conventions, noting: "In the same way that men are often concerned to show that what they are, above all, is not women, not 'feminine,' so television programs and movies will, surprisingly often, tell us that they are not a soap opera" (2008, 78; see also Modleski 1985, 67–75; Fiske 1989; M. Z. Newman and Levine 2012).

As such a belief in sports as "true" might suggest, sports represent a uniquely affective, intimate, "democratic," and potentially "utopian" forum for forging identifications and a sense of shared community in a context that is publicly valorized as representing conventionally *masculine* ideals: sporting events are public; they are rule-bound and characterized by narrative closure or clear outcomes; they are temporally limited and have tangible rewards. And yet, here again, we have a crucial sporting ambivalence. Sut Jhally has posited that "unlike other media messages, sports also involves us in other ways. There are *passions* involved, *emotional* entanglements with the events we witness that cannot simply be explained under terms such as consciousness and ideology. They are a part of how *social* identity is formed" (1989, 73). However, the emotional character of the bonds between sports team/athlete and community/fan represents a rare cultural realm in which overt display of emotion is *not* coded in feminine terms but instead through masculinized tropes of "commitment," sincerity, and *truth*.

This affective power of sports and the resultant bond between, here, professional teams and their communities thus arguably resembles Lauren Berlant's conceptualization of an "intimate public": "An intimate public operates when a market opens up to a bloc of consumers, claiming to circulate texts and things that express those people's particular core interests and desires. . . . Intimate spheres *feel* like ethical places based on the sense of capacious emotional continuity they circulate, which seems to derive from an ongoing potential for relief from the hard, cold world. Indeed, the offer of the simplicity of the rich feeling of continuity with a vaguely defined set of like others is often the central affective magnet of an intimate public" (2008, 5, 6–7). Though expressly commodified, intimate publics offer the promise of market transcendence in ineffable, affective terms. They create shared community through close identification with like-minded fans. Richard Dyer has, similarly, explained the paradoxical promise of "entertainment's" utopian thrust, as it "offers the image of 'something better' to escape into, or something we want deeply that our day-to-day lives don't provide," offering "alternatives *to* capitalism which will be provided *by* capitalism" (1993, 373).

In other words, even though modern professional sports are thoroughly commodified and deeply dependent upon market logics for their existence, our *sense* of sports tends to elide this relationship in favor of ethical ideals of shared community, intimate bonds, and utopian fantasies of major-league accomplishment and success. Teams are *loved* by their communities. Love, in this formulation, is transcendent of and unsullied by the market—it represents the realm of idealized community and actualization, a sphere of sincere *truths*. Thus, when the broader ideal of sports as something to escape into as relief from the cold, hard day-to-day is made *visible* as a profit-making endeavor, social trust *feels* breached. The love relation is newly objectified, made into hard, cold, material relation, and alienation is experienced. The relationship between the team or star and fans is rewritten as insincere and untrustworthy. When sports is "exposed," inescapably, as a market rather than a potentially utopian community—and when athletes transition from local icons to mobile commodities—the utopic fantasy is revealed to be a mystification. Perhaps the most prominent everyday venue for the valorization of masculine values is, potentially, thrown into crisis.

Historically, this paradox between sporting ideals/transcendent community and market realities/breach of communal trust has been particularly fraught in Cleveland, Ohio. Indeed, as "cities can be tagged as losers as well as winners, and attract as much publicity for futility as for success, Cleveland's image as a failed city" has been historically reiterated by its legacy of losing franchises and venues, such as "the 'mistake by the lake'" (Danielson 1997, 104). Cleveland's prominence as an industrial production center, manufactures transit hub, and technological invention site saw its brightest years from the 1920s through the mid-1960s.[6] The New Deal consensus and the economic collapses of the 1970s and 1980s hit the region particularly hard, with LeBron James's (born in 1984) hometown of Akron "at the dead center" of the newly named Rust Belt, "geographically and philosophically set squarely between the automotive and steel regions" (Giffels 2014, 4–5). Demographically, now as it was then, Cleveland is racially a predominantly black and white city that remains staunchly pro-union and largely working-class, hewing to and promoting public ideals forged during the postwar years.[7] Symbolically enough, prior to 2016, Cleveland's last professional sports championship had been in 1964. Public rehearsals of Cleveland's distinctiveness and clear "claims" to mythologies of place remain steeped in immediate post–World War II and civil rights–era understandings of local identity, race, labor, and productivity.

Before and since the economic crisis of the latest recession, Cleveland has not been shy about branding itself as a tough place to live, suited to hard-nosed, and even hardheaded, people.[8] However, while the Cleveland Clothing Company sells T-shirts with slogans such as "Factory of Sadness" and "Burning River Surf Club," it also points toward another kind of day-to-day imagined only through sports, as Cleveland's hope and democratic, unifying secular religion: "I Survived: Red Right 88, the Drive, the Fumble, the Move, Every Season since 1969, and I'm Still Here and I Still Cheer" and "Believeland."[9]

Historically, Cleveland's sports failures seemed uncannily matched to its industrial and economic downturn. While nationally, Cleveland sports fans may have seemed mired in a destructive "cruel optimism . . . maintaining an attachment to a significantly problematic object" (Berlant 2011, 24), locally, loyalty to losing organizations represents a commitment to residual ideals and values of shared community—the hard way, on purpose. According to Giffels, Cleveland fans may experience "a lifetime, one might say, of loss, but here we recognize something much different, more nuanced, more full of shadows. A lifetime of hope. And anyone who's done both—hoped and lost—knows that in many ways hoping is worse" (2014, 7). While this hoping may be focused and ritually experienced through sports, it extends to the broader region's longing for a time prior to neoliberal policies and resulting economic realities.

Thus, the emotional power of sports actively writes and reinscribes cultural mythologies of place. Though iconic of Rust Belt decline from the late 1960s through the 1980s, "since 1990, Cleveland has invested more subsidies into private playing facilities than any other community in the United States" (Rosensweig 2005, 13, 26). Progressive Field (formerly, Jacobs Field, home of Major League Baseball's "Indians"), the "Q" (home of the Cavaliers), and First Energy Stadium (home of the NFL's Browns) all occupy a new City Center with the Rock and Roll Hall of Fame, adjacent to Lake Erie, known as the Gateway District. While, according to downtowncleveland.com, the Gateway is the city's "Sports and Dining Entertainment Hub," less apparent is that prior to the construction of the sports complexes, "the activity in that section of downtown had taken place among a predominantly African American crowd," with a majority of black vendors at the old East Side market and retailers "providing merchandise targeting local black customers" (Rosensweig 2005, 130, 131). Paradoxically, however, promenades in the Gateway feature "photographic commemorative photos of African Americans who used to walk the streets there" (132). According to historian Daniel Rosensweig, the Gateway has become increasingly white in population while the Indians, Browns, and Cavaliers invoke black cultural references and appeals (e.g., Browns and Cavaliers player personnel; hip-hop sound tracks and walk-up music at Indians games,) to sell season tickets to a largely suburban, white spectator audience. Thus, Rosensweig concludes, "In places like the Gateway, 'blackness' has come to replace blacks. Yet ultimately, this replacement seems to articulate utopian longings for racial solidarity even as the renewed infrastructure . . . of the city, helps reestablish a color line" (19). Indeed, such downtown developments have been prominent "branding" iconography, particularly in cities like Cleveland, Baltimore, and Pittsburgh, each "at one time synonymous with industry and multiracial labor power" (Zirin 2015) but now increasingly reliant on tourist and service economies for civic identification and local revenues. This "sportification" of place idealizes a cultural bond with African Americanness while structurally reinforcing a "sports-driven apartheid."[10] For Cleveland, the Gateway reproduces the city's local mythologies while also presenting a bid (via televised games, championships, etc.) "producing the city as a unique cultural space with a strong communal identity that can be broadcast and sold globally" (Morgan-Parmett and Ranachan 2016).

In this context, LeBron James seemed to represent the overarching, unifying icon of communal solidarity and an unprecedented bridge between Cleveland's past and future. According to sportswriter Scott Raab, a Cleveland native, James's initial tenure with the Cleveland Cavaliers single-handedly made the team "the best thing to have happened to Cleveland—*all* of Cleveland, black and white, young and old, East Side and West—since Jim Brown walked away from the NFL 1965" (2011, 4). Indeed, LeBron was the favored native son—literally hailed as "The Chosen One"—whose presence offered to rewrite the city's legacy of losing. According to a report just prior to the Decision, "Before LeBron James . . . downtown was silent after dark. With him, every game is a sellout, and nearby bars and restaurants bustle" (Barr 2010, A10). The crisis provoked by the Decision was thus in part its exposure of the rather tenuous connection of key residual ideals (manufacture, multiracial labor, social welfare) as terms grounding Cleveland's contemporary identity, post-1970. The Decision seemed to expose the residual nature of these commitments as having been forged in the past and, though still valued in the present, no longer economically, politically, or culturally dominant. The potential loss of LeBron, in this sense, represented a broader loss of connection to grounding mythologies of place and, therefore, a genuine rupture and civic unmooring, beyond sports culture.

Pre-Decision: Geographic Lore and the Promise of a "Man-Child"

Popular press coverage of James's career before the Decision crisis portrayed his native Akron and Cleveland as residual sites of a prior America, symbolic of an industrial past that had otherwise been left behind in a finance capital–driven, global age. Effective in the present, this rhetoric suggests, remain the "time-bound" values of character, tenacity, and local bonds that mark the

Rust Belt as an imagined bedrock of community. By contrast, during the Decision process and aftermath, Miami was characterized as an emergent center of transnational capital and cultural production that was fast rising to the status of a global center and media capital (Curtin 2003, 202–28). While Cleveland was portrayed as a small market steeped in local stasis, Miami symbolized "chic" "cultural consciousness, . . . 'reflective of the changing culture of the USA'" (Horovitz 2010, 4B).

While LeBron was in high school at Akron's St. Vincent–St. Mary's, press narratives particularly focused on his story as the American Dream personi-fied: he succeeded as an honor student, "normal" teenager, and "generous" player while negotiating an impoverished and unpredictable home life (see, e.g., Wise 2012, D12). Indeed, a critical element of pre-Decision mythologies of place is a reliance on Moynihan Report era–esque conceptualizations of "the black family" as "broken," with LeBron's young, single mother, Gloria James, ritually personifying "the pathology of poor, urban, black culture" (Lubiano 1992, 335). LeBron's high school career and emerging trajectory of stardom are, here, consistently tied to prior historical narrative logics to contextual-ize his exceptionalism: in spite of his "unstable housing and financial situ-ation . . . he has managed" to overcome "a broken home" and stay "off the streets" (Dupree 2006, 1C).

Thus, while Cleveland has, historically, been the butt of jokes regarding its civic failures and may, following Pierre Bourdieu (1984), appear "lesser" in the relative distribution in nationally, socially ranked geographic space, the "LeBron Era"—from his high school stardom through his first term as a Cavalier—evidences repeated discursive alliance between LeBron and place-bound fealty, nostalgia, and tradition. Thus, the city and its "native son" are explicitly allied with sincerity, virtue, and truth. LeBron's Akronness is, in this era, iconic of the sincere as a *social* virtue. As then Cavaliers general manager Danny Ferry said in 2006, LeBron's power was a deeply *affective* one, stating, "He puts us in a situation where we can dream big" (Dupree 2006, 1C).

LeBron's explicitly raced identity at the *local* level—tied to social welfare, civic engagement, and loyal and sincere affect as an Akron native—is all in line with the region's own continued commitments in the regional imaginary to deeply *residual* ideals of place, tied to a New Deal collective, postwar, civil rights, and Great Society–era legacy of a biracial labor economy and pro-ductive culture tied to manufacture and a definable "thing-ness" to place. As neoliberal political policies and market realities effectively destroyed this lived relation to the everyday in northeast Ohio, the rhetorical, discursive commitments to the residual ideals remained powerful, particularly as focused through the lens of sports fandom and the nature of that fandom. As these examples indicate, sports point to a potentially counterintuitive, powerful *need* for residual local identifications and to the tenacity of place identification as an affective bond within late capitalism. Indeed, "sport is one of the few things that binds people to a place simply through ascription" (Danielson 1997, 8). However, coverage of the Decision and its aftermath notably effaced a key element of LeBron's local myth and narrative. From his high school years through the playoff appearances with the Cavaliers, James was always *also* understood to be transcendent of the local in ways that put him at risk of *not* belonging in Cleveland. In a feature story in the *New York Times*, for example, writer Mike Wise notes: "Watching James play basketball in high school may be akin to watching Bobby Fischer play checkers in the cafeteria at lunchtime or Dizzy Gillespie marching with the high school band at halftime. Something seems terribly out of place" (2002, D12).

While James was still in high school, biblical references routinely implied his divine, otherworldly status. And several journalists pointed out local "scandals" involving James's birthday gift of a $50,000 car from his mother and a brief suspension after being gifted with two classic jerseys by a family friend. Noted the *Times*, in a different feature, "'Maybe in New York or L.A. it wouldn't be such a huge deal,' . . . 'But when a high schooler is driving a Hummer in Akron, it's a big deal'" (Litsky 2003, D4). Later, local outcry over the Decision would also elide an ongoing, successful relationship between James and ESPN that long predated that event and clearly benefited Cleveland's own market investments in and profits from James. James's senior high school season was telecast across northeast Ohio on pay-per-view, and ESPN had telecast several of his games. The network acquired NBA telecast rights just prior to James's first season in the league with Cleveland, and the first single-sponsored episode of *Sportscenter* was underwritten by Nike upon the introduction of its Air Zoom LeBron III shoe. The Cavaliers saw game ratings increase 433 percent from the pre-LeBron to the post-LeBron era and were estimated to lose $48 million a season with James's departure (Sandoval 2003, D1).

Indeed, it became increasingly difficult for the myth of Cleveland as a throwback, small-market naïf, characterized by love over money, to hold, given its expressed dependence on James for the economic and charitable value he created for and contributed to the region. In the month leading up to the Decision, Cleveland civic leaders and regional interests invigorated campaigns whose plea was "Please Stay LeBron." Most visible and somewhat notorious among these appeals was a video produced by the city of Cleveland to the tune of "We Are the World." Featuring dozens of local

Cleveland public figures (from media celebrities to Governor Ted Strickland and Senator Sherrod Brown), the video is simultaneously earnest and self-effacing, epitomizing an overtly "square" sincerity and slight embarrassment. The lyrics contrast Cleveland's small-market, homegrown love with its crass competitors claiming, in part, "New York's overcrowded; those people are unbearable. And don't forget: the Knicks and Nets are terrible!" The chorus makes Cleveland's case to be the choice of love and community bonds over money and free agency's individual pursuits.[11] As the chorus pleads, "Please stay LeBron. We really need you. No bigger market's gonna love you half as much as we do. It's a choice you're making. You're saving our downtown, and Cleveland is a better place with you around."

The choice of "We Are the World" seems both appropriately earnest and dated to be synchronous with Cleveland mythology. However, the insistent—even defiant—parochialism of the lyrics seems jarring given the original song's "global" philanthropic intent. In the end, the video's ambivalences were in sync with a broader regional bracing for James to be "bigger" than a small market and, further, bigger than basketball itself. In a city defined by sports losses, the Decision began to seem preordained. According to one Clevelander on its eve, "'It's like being a kid on Christmas morning, except instead of presents we might be punched in the face'" (Lance Ike, quoted in Lysiak 2010, 3).

The Decision as Gendered TV Event

In spite of the proliferation of online and handheld media, traditional or "legacy" television—broadcast and cable or satellite TV delivered to the home via a TV console—remains the most heavily and meaningfully engaged daily medium across all media devices. Nielsen research indicates that US viewers spend the equivalent, on average, of 144 hours and 54 minutes a month engaged with television, as compared with the next-highest category of media engagement, which is spending 28 hours and 20 minutes a month online. African American viewers remain TV's most engaged audience (at an hour and 25 minutes, daily), followed closely by white viewers (at an hour and 16 minutes) (Nielsen Media Research 2013). Sports TV, in particular, is the site where traditional television continues to thrive. Beyond mass-spectacle sporting events such as the Super Bowl and the Olympics, daily and serially, sports generates the most "mass" and most demographically diverse audiences across the broadcast, cable, *and* "new" mediascapes. Further, sports as-seen-on-TV remains an increasingly rare, shared cultural forum for working through questions of community ideals, struggles over national mythologies, and questions of representative citizenship. Sports are a site for a "collective, cultural view of the social construction and negotiation of reality . . . a shared cultural realm through which we safely encounter and struggle with 'our most prevalent concerns, our deepest dilemmas' . . . where our most traditional views . . . as well as those that are subversive and emancipatory, are upheld, examined, maintained, and transformed" (Newcomb and Hirsch 1987, 457) in view of the broadest possible, most diversified, shared audience. Sports TV overtly references race, gender, age, sexuality, and regional "difference" in ways that appear "safely" displaced onto games and play but that, effectively, represent the shared, ritual site for significant interrogation of these culturally constructed categories.

According to Nielsen ratings, "more than 25 percent of homes with TVs" in Cleveland watched the Decision, and "of the nation's 56 biggest cities, more than 7 percent of households with TVs were watching" ("Put Off by the LeBron Spectacle?" 2010). The Decision was presented as an hour-long prime-time special telecast by ESPN but "wholly packaged by Team LeBron—from the venue to the format to the ads to the hand-picked journalists to interview him" (Jonsson 2010). Thus, even before it aired, the Decision was criticized for abdicating any semblance of news standards. Given that "Entertainment" is the first word in ESPN's name, this criticism may be somewhat curious. However, as sports journalism itself has historically fought a reputation "as the 'toy department of the news media'" (Hutchins and Rowe 2012, 125), it is clear why sportswriters, in particular, chafed at this blurring of authorial control and content. Further, the program's length, absent any information until the final two minutes, meant that its flat, studio-bound look and "interview" style was so out of sync with sports TV's textual conventions and greatest strengths—as exemplar of the most advanced audiovisual and technological aesthetics in screen culture—as to seem baffling. Indeed, the aesthetic poverty of the Decision is such that even the crawl at the bottom of the screen limps along with no information. However, if the Decision betrayed the conventions of news and sports TV, its deepest offense, it appeared, was that its "unabashedly commercial fusion of popular entertainment with a self-conscious claim to the discourse of the real" (S. Murray and Ouellette 2009, 3) *did* conform to conventions of reality TV, with all its gendered resonances and accompanying critical disdain.

Indeed, the responses to the Decision suggest it was the gender-blurring genre mash-up by which ESPN betrayed "its role as a *news* organization and [went] into the reality TV business with LeBron" that caused much critical revulsion (Wilbon 2010, D1). John Fiske has argued that "feminized address" in TV is characterized by arguably opposing conventions from those defining "masculine" TV genres, such as sports and news. Both the Decision and reality TV resist narrative closure and involve a multiplicity of characters (Cleveland? Miami? Chicago? New Jersey? New York?); their use of time parallels real time (rather than compressing, replaying, or offering more enlightening angles of view, etc.); they feature intimate conversation with an emphasis on problem solving through dialogue rather than action; and their male heroes are "sensitive men" (Fiske 1989, 179–97).

Criticism of the telecast was immediate, uniformly harsh, and premised on two key critiques: criticism of ESPN's willing allowance of prepackaged content control by the program's subject, and outrage at LeBron's "betrayal" of Cleveland for its presumed sporting and civic opposite. The latter criticism notably dovetailed with the former, as critics overwhelmingly analogized the Decision with the climactic episode of a reality TV dating series. Encapsulating much of the critical reaction to the telecast, Scott Stinson of the *National Post* called it a "much-anticipated Very Special Episode of LeBachelor. Who would get the final rose? Would it be loyal-but-dull Cleveland? The sultry Miami? That flashy temptress New York? Or that trashy, wealthy slut New Jersey?" (2010, S2).

When James "proposed" to Miami and "dumped" northeast Ohio, his iconic Clevelanderness was swiftly rewritten. In commentators' displacement of emotional distress over the Decision from the "masculine" domain of sports to the presumptively "feminine" sphere of emotion, intimacy, and open-ended narrative, LeBron's choice was recast from being a business decision, fully consistent with the logics of a "dynamic capitalist economic rationality— utilitarian, competitive, and profit-maximizing," to being "LeBronsense" (Meer 2011, 1; Lysiak 2010, 3). Further, echoing one of *The Bachelor: After the Rose* specials, within two hours of James's announcement, Cavaliers' owner Dan Gilbert posted a scathing letter to fans of the team calling James disloyal. Wrote Mike Wise of the *Washington Post*, "It's the kind of psycho ex-girlfriend letter that certifies LeBron made the right decision. When a major municipality's identity is that wrapped up in one special athlete, what does it say about Cleveland's self-worth?" (2010, D1). Striking here is commentators' effacement of characteristics of both sports culture and reality TV that might nuance their critique as well as prevailing notions of gendered capital.

As Laurie Ouellette and James Hay have carefully outlined, reality TV, in its contemporary iterations, is exemplary of neoliberalism's "normalizing of individual entrepreneurism and the branding" of the self whereby the "citizen is now conceived as an individual whose most pressing obligation to society is to empower her- or himself privately" (2008, 3), as, arguably, LeBron's free-agent move did. Further, here, James's charitable contribution to the Boys and Girls Club, resulting from the Decision telecast, underscores that now "the management and care of the self becomes an imperative in different and arguably more urgent ways," including "in the sense of replacing public services" with privatized corporate social responsibility (12). James is CEO of Brand LeBron. His move to Miami, with its added endorsements, exposure, and revenues, allowed ongoing private service endowments to sustain several organizations and populations in Akron, Ohio, that are otherwise underserved by traditional public sources of support.

In "taking his talents to South Beach" on his quest to finally win an NBA championship—in which he succeeded in 2012 and 2013—James exemplified an individualism iconic of the "modern liberal sense of political juridical right and entitlement," but inimical to residual modes of community and tradition (Meer 2011, 1). This seemed, however, a logical fit with free agency and the Miami Heat—a relatively new franchise (having entered the NBA in 1988) that already had a roster of stars and had not only made the playoffs in most of its seasons but already won one championship. Alternately praised and derided for being a team accessible to casual fans, with a national and international profile, the Heat were easily cast by Clevelanders as a high-profile, financially driven, self-serving choice for James to have made. Alternately, Miami fans hailed James's awareness of the city's and franchise's vibrancy as entities characterized by talent that would buttress his own and a legacy of hope rather than despair. Further, Miami represented a media capital worthy of James's transnational, transmedia celebrity and multiplatform endeavors.

For all the criticism, more people watched LeBron's Decision on ESPN than watched him play his first NBA final with the Cavaliers. And, more than $2.5 million was raised for the Boys and Girls Clubs of America. Notably, following the Decision, media coverage finally began to disconnect Cleveland and Akron in discussing those "jilted" by the move, noting that James never gave up his Akron home or any of his ongoing charitable organizations and work there. Notes Keith Dambrot, one of James's high school coaches and current men's basketball coach at the University of Akron, "'We're a different place. It's not like Akron is a suburb. It's separate, and I think it's different in a lot of ways. I don't think anyone from Akron says, 'I'm from outside Cleveland.' We're from Akron" (Maag 2010, 8).

If LeBron's local successes were historically contextualized as due, in part, to community support ("it takes a village" of coaches, mentors, et al.) and social welfare programs (the Boys and Girls Clubs of Akron), then his free-agent mobility and global esteem seemed, perhaps, particularly threatening: the Decision exposed the residual nature of the myth of LeBron and of the region as a producerist powerhouse. While that ethos (hardworking, masculine, union-strong, manufactures-based economy) retained value in the present, emergent neoliberal logics had, in fact, displaced it. This would, in part, help to explain what appeared to be a tremendous critical overreaction, or, the crisis provoked by the Decision. In order to alleviate the threat of rupture to regional mythology that LeBron's choice exposed, critics of the Decision had to disavow LeBron's prior iconicity of place by revising the values he seemed to now represent: if Cleveland remained defensively parochial, Miami was an explicitly global city; if Cleveland—in spite of its medical and other industries—portrayed itself as bound to Rust Belt industry, Miami thrived on an apparently fluid, "nonproductive," but tremendously profitable finance economy; if Cleveland was bound together by a legacy of loss, Miami was shiny, new, and poised for championships.

LeBron's "betrayal" was thus differently assessed at the local level and at the national level. Local critics couched LeBron's Decision to leave for Miami as a betrayal of his very core identity. If Clevelanders are defined by doing things "the hard way on purpose," then "choosing Miami was choosing to *not* do things the hard way on purpose. If there was a betrayal, that was it" (Giffels 2014, 22). LeBron further betrayed his status as "The Chosen One" and compromised his previously trusted, sincere, "native son's" commitment to community. Implicit in these local critiques was that LeBron was turning his back on his "debts" to the "village" and community services that helped raise and educate him. LeBron's local betrayal was thus, in large part, his "escape" from residual networks of social welfare and regional emplacement to embrace a self-made, entrepreneurial, individualistic ideal commensurate with the post–civil rights–era, mobile, postracial neoliberal ideal.

This is the terrain on which LeBron's Decision was excoriated in the national media: for his newly embraced status as neoliberal subject par excellence—a "self-centered" player. The national press focused criticism on LeBron's courting of the free-agency market and what it meant for the "integrity" of the game (implying that LeBron would be choosing to play with a stacked deck of superstars rather than "work" his way to the top). Instead of addressing head-on the apparent threat posed by "young black stars taking full ownership of their own legacies" (Zirin 2016), these critics displaced raced discourses onto gendered and "genre" critiques—misogyny and disdain for "reality TV" and other "women's genres" remaining, apparently, "acceptable" public discourse. LeBron's "betrayals" thus expose the active work required to *not* speak of race or to cast crisis in racialized terms.

Overall, the Decision energized conventional geographic myths about Clevelandness, and, while so doing, it mobilized gendered anxieties regarding television address. In the end, the Decision and its aftermath exposed an unresolvable tension between the residual but ongoing hope that sports is a mythic realm populated by local heroes and transcendent of commercial concerns *and* the emergent, global media context's critical discounting of the possibility of sincerity in relation to the market. Arguably, one of the reasons sportswriters and other commentators invoked the perceptively "safe"—or, safe to disdain—feminized logics of reality TV to couch their critiques was as a strategy to diffuse the otherwise exceptionally difficult theoretical problem to account for the Decision's exposure of the *raw* affective bonds of masculine public culture. By casting LeBron as "LeBachelor," critics and commentators were, possibly, able to recuperate the idea that, while reality TV is "insincere" and "beneath" emotional investment, sports is "the only thing that is true" and worthy of public displays of passion.

Cleveland Hustles: A Promise Kept, a Myth Renewed?

Herman Gray has encouraged scholars to examine where, in a plentiful yet often atomized popular culture, we might "track down the *thingness* of racism as a practice and affective materiality that takes form in bodies and feelings whose deployment, intensity, and effects we can detect, measure and map" (2013a, 257). Narratives of Cleveland's loss via the Decision used gendered conventions and geographic myth to, arguably, displace the thingness of the crisis, which was the very real social and political threat that a "25-year-old African American man with a high school diploma, commanding a global stage," posed to a "white spatial imaginary" (Rhoden 2010, 5), typically characterized by what George Lipsitz identifies as the broader culture's "phobic representations of Black people," suggesting this population is "unfit for" such "freedom" (Lipsitz 2011, 13). Arguably, critics of the Decision neutered LeBron's self-possession and real social and political capital when implying that he perpetrated a bad romance. They also posited that his native northeast Ohio, as the bedrock of Rust Belt demise, had been "betrayed" further in a "shocking act of disloyalty" when LeBron turned the page on the region's favored myth of his "bootstrap" rise and resulting "indebtedness"—geographic lore evocative of civil rights–era logics of race and one's "appropriate" place, explicitly cast(e) in black and white. Disdain for Miami in such criticisms seems like thinly veiled criticism of the "global" city's multiculturalism and arguable iconicity as such in a rhetorically postracial era. Whereas Cleveland's boosters argued that the Cavaliers put "team" and shared community first, Miami's detractors portrayed the Heat as a collection of high-priced independent contractors whose self-interest would undermine success.

Though "racial denial . . . is ubiquitously played within the sports world, pointing to the efforts to silence, minimize, and erase race from public discourse" (Leonard and Hazlewood 2014, 111), race is undeniably a significant subtext in the broader context of questions of LeBron's iconicity in a presumptively postracial era. Within the NBA—particularly given Cavaliers' owner Dan Gilbert's histrionic and near-libelous attack on James for the Decision—it is significant that all but one team owner (the presumptively "race-transcendent" Michael Jordan) is a white man over the age of forty. These are the men who write and hold the contracts for "their 20- and 30-something employees, almost 84 percent of whom are African American males" (Wise 2011, D2; Chalabi 2014). Arguably, in a contemporary US context in which "Black desires for upward mobility and intergenerational advancement" are not typically honored, James's very public, self-orchestrated Decision already risked consternation and backlash (Lipsitz 2011, 25). Yet, given the work of displacement through the Decision and LeBron's Miami Heat era, how could the "King" be restored, in his Return to Ohio, both as masculine hero, sporting community ideal *and* as sincere icon of local "truth"?

With his July 2014 announcement that he would return to the Cleveland Cavaliers, James reactivated hopes for Cleveland's reverse-of-the-curse, economic resurgence, and community unity through the utopian possibilities of sports. Announced via "letter" "as told to Lee Jenkins," in the pages of *Sports Illustrated*, the Return was greeted as "a stunning victory for maturity and perspective" (Plaschke 2014, A1), indicating "elevated . . . vision and . . . love for his community first" (L. Steinberg 2014, A13). In voluntarily returning to a place that "topped Forbes' list of the most miserable cities," James was "setting the standard for the role of the athlete today" (Love 2014). LeBron's letter itself claims that his years with the Heat were "almost like college for other kids. These past four years helped raise me into who I am. . . . I see myself as a mentor now. . . . I feel my calling here goes above basketball. . . . My presence can make a difference in Miami, but I think it can mean more where

I'm from. . . . In Northeast Ohio, nothing is given. Everything is earned. You work for what you have. I'm ready to accept the challenge. I'm coming home" (James, as told to Lee Jenkins 2014). Thus, James's successful return is assured following an exile in which he "matured," to be restored not only as favored native son but as *patriarchal* figure and redeemer. Whereas the free-agent move to Miami was portrayed as *self*-centered, market and championship bling, the Return is welcomed as about self-*actualization*, love, and social virtue.

LeBron kept his promise to bring a championship to Cleveland, with the Cavaliers' dramatic game seven victory over the Golden State Warriors in June 2016. Cleveland welcomed the team home with a victory parade including "a group equal to almost a tenth of the population of the entire state" (Jablonski 2013, C1). Notably, James never actually left northeast Ohio, maintaining his home, multiple charitable endeavors, and a growing multimedia empire from Akron.[12] James's LeBron Family Foundation and, particularly, its "Promise Project" underscore that private individuals and corporate social responsibility programs have fundamentally taken over for receding state investment in education, public resources, or social welfare. While LeBron's primary identification in his philanthropic endeavors is "Just a Kid from Akron," part of the larger Promise "Family," his autobiography as an African American child of Akron's project housing is a critical and always-already raced claim to the sincerity and commitment grounding his initiatives, which fundamentally attempt to assure that the services he grew up with in the 1990s remain viable and expand for a new generation.

Postchampionship, LeBron's media pursuits now also include local endeavors made for a national audience. Beginning in the summer of 2016, CNBC launched *Cleveland Hustles*, a series designed to "give local entrepreneurs the chance to realize their own dreams while also helping to revitalize struggling neighborhoods in their city" (CNBC News Releases 2016). Rather than the melodrama of *The Bachelor*, *Cleveland Hustles* promised to feature masculine ideals of initiative and producerism in the context of a cable outlet expressly aligned with financial news and market culture. Thus, even in its media extensions, LeBron's return home restores the residual regional myth, focusing, as Banet-Weiser notes, on "the lone, rugged, masculine entrepreneur; the individualist laborer who is nostalgically created and positioned as the only way out of what got broken" (2014, 100).

LeBron James's 2010 Decision and 2014 Return arguably represent unique critical moments that expose sports as integral to the construction and understanding of place-identity and allow for close analysis of the power and powerful ambivalence of sports in the imagination of community, its affective resonance, and gendered capital. In an ostensibly post–civil rights, postrace, global economic context, LeBron's initial decision positioned Cleveland as a space characterized by sincerity and aligned with a visibly raced, civil rights–era identity, while Miami was portrayed as iconic of flashy, postracial transnational market facility and outreach. James's Decision was thus contextualized as his movement from hardscrabble African American sports phenomenon and local hero to his reinvention as a place-"transcendent" postracial media icon. The fact that the Decision cast LeBron as a "feminine" character in a "reality TV" event allowed the patriarchal white male NBA ownership structure and media outlets to make LeBron's real capital and mobility as a young, African American global icon "safe." But the return to Cleveland as prodigal son and wise mentor-father connects LeBron with a *sincere* discourse about "knowing one's place" in all the ways that both restore him for public affection and also, arguably, circumscribe his imagined mobility, even as his entertainment and charitable venues exponentially expand.

Notably, then, when in and of Cleveland, LeBron is understood to be a tradition-honoring African American success story, role model, and community provider (e.g., giving back in all the same ways he himself benefited from through local mentoring, education, and social support services). When outside of Cleveland, James's celebrity and career have been portrayed as less focused, more rootless, and searching. After winning his second championship with the Heat in 2013, James said, "'I'm LeBron James from Akron, Ohio, . . . I'm not even supposed to be here'" (Goodman 2013, 94). While James may have meant this simply as wonder at his reaching the pinnacle of his profession (multiply) from such humble beginnings, given the success of the Return, LeBron's stated sense of self (no matter where I go, I'm from Akron) and belonging (this is not where I'm supposed to be) seems more significant. James's victorious Return does not necessarily rewrite Cleveland history or its vital sporting and community myths. LeBron returns from free agency to his "proper" place at home, both as philanthropic savior and as fulfilling a responsibility to "pay back" the social welfare he himself received as a child in Akron. James's return home is portrayed as a restoration of his human value and spirit of teamwork to the local community, after his brief experience of the world of things, materiality, and individual glory in Miami.

The Decision powerfully visualized the ambivalences LeBron embodied from his high school playing days through the championships with the Heat: between residual ties and emergent possibilities; between exposing the myths of Cleveland *as* myths and restoring and reifying them; between being the ultimate team player and individual/league-leading celebrity; between commitments to Akron and expanding global iconicity; between staying in place at home and pursuing the comparatively "placeless" open market of free agency; and between epitomizing the "postracial" and exposing its construct-edness. While LeBron's choices expose a public crisis of identity centered in the US Rust Belt, it is hoped that this example points to broader questions of geography, gender, race, community, civic identity, and the market through which to consider the complex affective power of sports; questions of citizen-ship, race, and gender; and the multivalent nature of "truth" within the logics of a postracial era.

Notes

1 "The Chosen One" (2002) was the first of twenty-four *Sports Illustrated* cover stories featuring LeBron James, to date. Throughout his high school career, James was referred to in both local and national press as, among others, "The Chosen One," the "King," and an "Apostle" of change.

2 Dave Zirin, interview with Dan Patrick, *The Dan Patrick Show*, AM 570 Los Angeles, Premiere Networks, April 6, 2016.

3 See www.thisiscle.com.

4 While Michael Jordan is a North Carolina native and UNC graduate, his career was pre-dominantly elsewhere, and his local commitments have largely been commercial rather than specific community-based endeavors.

5 On "residual" cultural elements, see R. Williams 1977, 122. I also address examples of the continued power of the residual in relation to US mythologies of politics and place in V. E. Johnson 2008.

6 The city of Cleveland's population has been shrinking remarkably rapidly. The seventh-largest US city in 1950, by 1970 it was the tenth largest, and as of the 2010 census it is the forty-fifth largest, on a par with Tulsa, Oklahoma, and Wichita, Kansas. The top five employers in Cleveland at present are government, the Ford Motor Company, the Catholic diocese, the Cleveland Clinic, and Cleveland municipal schools.

7 As of the 2010 census, Cleveland's population of 396,815 was 53.3 percent black and 37.3 percent white, with 7.3 percent Hispanic/Latino, 3.4 percent other, 2.8 percent two or more races, and 1.8 percent Asian. www.infoplease.com/ipa/A0108498.html.

8 For a close analysis of national advertising uses of Rust Belt iconography to sell "authen-ticity," see Banet-Weiser 2014, 81–106.

9 The Cleveland Clothing Company's slogan is "Wear Your Pride" (www.cleclothingco .com).

10 On "sportification of place" in racialized geographic and architectural terms, see Ra-nachan and Morgan Parmett 2016; Zirin 2015. On the marketing value of African American culture in post-1990s entertainment and advertising, see Banet-Weiser 2007; Caldwell 1995; Johnson 2009b.

11   Notably, at the juncture of the Decision, LeBron would have actually made more money had he stayed in Cleveland.

12   James's Spring Hill Entertainment is the creative source for an animated series (*The LeBrons*, 2011–present, USA Network), a live-action narrative series (*Survivor's Remorse*, 2014–present, STARZ), a DisneyXD series called *Becoming*, a multimedia platform for athletes, "Bleacher Report," a proposed prime-time game show for NBC-TV, and a partnership in a new deal with Warner Bros. (2015) for content across platforms. James also continues his commercial partnerships (Nike, McDonald's, etc.) and received rave reviews for his role in the Amy Schumer vehicle *Trainwreck* (2015). James's charities include his LeBron James Family Foundation, which underwrites educational grants and scholarships and recently partnered with the University of Akron to guarantee full college scholarships to Akron schoolchildren.

9

Clap Along If You Feel Like Happiness Is the Truth

Pharrell Williams and the False
Promises of the Postracial

KEVIN FELLEZS

> I don't live my life trying to be black.
> —PHARRELL WILLIAMS, *Oprah* interview,
> April 14, 2014

Eerily echoing Bobby McFerrin's Reagan-era breakout hit, "(Don't Worry) Be Happy," in both sentiment and sound (light, melodic pop), Pharrell Williams's hit single "Happy" similarly celebrates personal happiness as an assumed social good in which a positive attitude lifts all burdens. In interviews, Williams disregards the persistence of race as a social fact and political category. Yet race's persistence in the United States is easily recognized in the statistics that render the deleterious material effects for individuals and groups racialized as nonwhite in black and white (Alexander 2011; Lipsitz 2006, 2011; Shedd 2011; Wolfers 2015). We need look no further than, for example, the statistics outlining the maintenance of inferior educational, health, and economic conditions for aggrieved communities within the United States (Darby and Saatcioglu 2014; Haslanger 2014).[1] More tragically, the deadly interactions across the United

States between black and brown individuals and police officers, coupled with the kinds of consequences that follow in their wake—I am thinking beyond the nonindictment of police officers to highlight, for example, the situation of Ramsey Orta, the jailed videographer of Eric Garner's death—are bald instances of systemic structural racism that remain effective despite individual declarations of "can't nothing bring me down."[2]

Given these social conditions, the global success of a song titled "Happy," which encourages listeners to "clap along if you feel like happiness is the truth" given that "can't nothing bring me down" may be unsurprising. As Theodor Adorno famously argued, modernity's alienated subjects have sought emotional and psychic reprieve in the ephemeral refrains of popular song because it offers simplistic assurances in naturalized (as Adorno would underline, formulaic) musical expression. Williams tapped into a need for emotional uplift in a time of rising precarity, widespread recognition of social inequality, and a sense of the material transformation of the planet in ways that directly impact human possibilities. For example, indigenous and other marginalized populations are feeling the direct effects of global climate change the soonest, linking global climate change to the underlying racism institutionalized in the political and economic structures invested in the status quo.

Similar to the ways in which "clean coal" and natural gas are promoted as green alternatives to conventional fossil fuel resources in an effort to keep fossil fuel economies in place, Paul Taylor concludes his critique of postracialism by noting that the term "postrace" does not signal a postracist society at all but merely a "shift to the latest in a *series* of evolving—but not necessarily *progressing*—racial formations" (2014, 23; emphasis in original). This latest shift in the series, as Taylor describes it, is another adaptive formation by vested interests to keep race an invigorated part of social identity even as its (real, materially realized) presence is denied, a social parallel to global climate change denial.

In this essay, I begin by placing pop music in relation to other genres to think through the way in which Williams's song *as pop song* epitomizes a postracial political stance—a twenty-first-century blend of consumerist choice with a politics of respectability that seeks to bypass "race" as a diversion on the road to a postracial utopia. By tracking Williams's brash assertions for the power of claiming Otherness to change the world for the better through the song "Happy," as well as his commercial brand Other, Williams uses the language of the postracial to skillfully elide the very conditions of oppression to which simply "being happy" is an inadequate response. Understood this way, Williams's invocation of Otherness in the cloak of individualistic entrepreneurialism undermines his jubilant musicking, revealing it as less the radical credo he suggests and more of a tacit support for the continuation of the very racial logics he hopes to oppose. Williams's happy entrepreneurialism rests on a postracial logic that ultimately fails in determining any (new) path to a *postracist* society.

In Williams's articulation of a "politics of ambivalence," following Sarah Banet-Weiser, in which he merges identity and alterity as a brand logo for his commercial offerings, he promises his customers—his fans, his audience, his Others—a world without politics, beyond race, beyond conflict, beyond "bad news." Reinventing Otherness as individuality fully realized through entrepreneurship, Williams mobilizes alterity in the service of "wealth" acquisition, reinscribing the subordinate positioning of subaltern Others as "winners" in a capitalist game of self-promotion. I conclude the essay by contemplating two iterations of "Happy" from the 360 versions performed during the twenty-four-hour video (each version clocking in at a tad under four minutes, with a few seconds spent fading between versions) and a final few thoughts on why simply advocating "feeling happy" falls short as an antiracist agenda.

Pop Matters

From spirituals to hip-hop, black musicking has articulated alternative perspectives to US social norms (while blacks have contributed, albeit little recognized, to the formation of those very norms).[3] Certainly not all nor all of the time, and with varying successes and failures. Still, a significant amount of black soundings have been used to call into question social inequalities and to provide sonic templates not only for individual expression but also for collective action. Black musicking has imbued social dance with political resonance, public singing with social significance, and commercial music with subversive subtexts. The discourse of the postracial eviscerates the very claims black musicians have been seeking to establish for the value of their music, including those based on its social impact and widespread influence. Importantly, by offering individualized notions of "attitude adjustment" (usually involving some form of consumption that used to be called "conspicuous"), the logic of the postracial undermines black musicians' ability to continue to catalyze, inform, and motivate mass audiences to act, to organize, to dream of social transformation.[4] It is in this broad sense that the failure of Williams's "Happy," particularly in view of his efforts as a one-man brand marketing individual empowerment for economic profit, is heard most clearly.

"Happy" is not a piece of dance music per se; it is a pop song, a category of music "accessible to a general public (rather than elites or dependent on any kind of knowledge or listening skill)" and "produced commercially, for profit, as a matter of enterprise not art" (Frith 2011, 94). Williams, however, first gained widespread notice as part of the Neptunes, a production partnership with Chad Hugo, which became one of the most commercially successful production teams in hip-hop and dance music beginning with N.O.R.E.'s "Superthug" in 1998 and including Mystikal's "Shake Ya Ass" and the team's first global hit, Britney Spears's "I'm a Slave 4 U" in 2001. "Happy," written for the animated "family-friendly" comedy film *Despicable Me 2* (2013), was an unforeseen hit for Williams as a solo act and is notably distinct from older hits such as "Lapdance" and "She Wants to Move" in lyrical content and musical aesthetic. Adhering more to a pop-dance rather than a hip-hop sensibility, it is perhaps unsurprising that "Happy" crossed over in a way that "Lapdance" has not.

Pop, in any case, is not hip music. "Adult pop" such as the music of Josh Groban or Celine Dion carries with it the whiff of the musically lowbrow or middlebrow (C. Wilson 2007), and little of it ages well except for fans. Norma Coates argues that the relationship of pop to rock, a fundamental schism in popular music discourse, revolves around issues of authenticity: "Rock is metonymic with 'authenticity' while 'pop' is metonymic with 'artifice'" (1997, 52). Simon Frith is even more succinct, calling pop a "residual" category consisting of what remains once "all the other forms of popular music are stripped away" (2011, 95). We can substitute rap for rock as the two genres both occupy more artistically legitimate, even prestigious, positions vis-à-vis pop.

The song's pop status helps explain why the statistics on the discrepant education, employment, and health outcomes for blacks and whites fade into the distance throughout the twenty-four hours of the "complete" video, underlining Williams's argument that happiness is its own good. But, as Sara Ahmed (2010) reminds us, Williams's call to "be happy" rests on the unacknowledged unhappiness of others. This is the reason I call out those uncomfortable bodies in portions of the video—those figures who walk hurriedly past the cameraperson and dancer(s), who do not appear happy to be included in the video but without the need to bother with confronting or "actively resisting" their own involvement—and those bodies who *should* be uncomfortable but are not, such as a gas station attendant and a chicken-suited dancer I discuss in the concluding remarks. Even so, "because I'm happy!" is, with its rising melodic line, a great hook to sing out, alone or with others. Who doesn't want to be happy?

Ahmed tackles the question of why happiness—or the state of "I'm happy!"—is desirable. Who benefits from normative assumptions regarding the equivalence of happiness to a "well lived life" or even a "desired state of being"? Is happiness predicated on its eternal deferral? Writing "from a position of skeptical disbelief in happiness as a technique for living well," Ahmed acknowledges her debt to "feminist critiques of the figure of 'the happy housewife,' black critiques of the myth of 'the happy slave,' and queer critiques of the sentimentalization of heterosexuality as 'domestic bliss,'" which "taught me [Ahmed] most about happiness and the very terms of its appeal" (2010, 2).

Consequently, Ahmed is critical of "the recent science of happiness," particularly as described by "happiness tsar" Richard Layard with his reliance on self-reporting of levels of individual happiness, which "presumes the transparency of self-feeling (that we can say and know how we feel), as well as the unmotivated and uncomplicated nature of self-reporting" (2010, 5). Layard's larger problem, however, is his presupposing "happiness is already understood to be what you want to have," so being "asked how happy you are is not to be asked a neutral question . . . [but is an evaluation of] their life situations through categories that are value laden" (2010, 5).

In mulling over this issue, Ahmed reminds us that "within classical [Greek] models, the forms of happiness that are higher are linked to the mind, and those that are lower are linked to the body" (2010, 12). A similar high/low culture, mind/body divide lies behind the rock/pop binary in which rock is perceived as a serious musical genre, whereas pop is the commercial dreck manufactured for musical naïfs (N. Coates 1997). Additionally, it is a truism that "pop in the record industry is a euphemism for white [while] R&B means black" (Lanza 2005, 5) as it is through the imagined performing and listening bodies that music genres signify racially. In the case at hand, Williams wags his finger at the music industry: au contraire, he admonishes, being happy transcends those old colorized generic lines, blurring them in the interest of sharing happiness through singable and danceable product appealing to the mass consumer(s) but in ways that enable them to imagine themselves as individual(s) and not as a faceless member(s) of an aggregate marketing demographic.

Pointedly, Williams figures personal happiness as the zenith of political achievement, stripping aggrieved communities of their histories of struggle for liberation and social equality, which effaces, in turn, those communities of their values, efficacies, and hard-won though often partial victories.

In the wake of the success of "Happy," Williams launched i am OTHER as a "creative venture and way of life . . . a diverse group of optimistic, bright minds connected by technology and a desire to make our mark, who together can advance culture and even humanity," as declared on the iamother .com website, and marketing it through au courant retail clothing vendor Uniqlo.[5] Warning that positive psychology's mantra ("to feel better is to be better") too often and too easily aligns with neoliberalism's key incentive ("to profit is to be better"), Ahmed notes the ways in which personal happiness becomes an economic as well as ideological good. What follows, Ahmed asks, "from the idea that we have a responsibility to be happy for others, or even simply from the idea that there is a necessary and inevitable relationship of dependence between one person's happiness and the happiness of others" (2010, 9)?

In this context, how should we read Pharrell's clothing line declaring "i am OTHER" and "the same is lame"? When masses of individuals are all wearing the same T-shirt declaring "the same is lame," how has the "unique individual" been redefined?

Is "i am OTHER" a clever reversal of the power dynamics between identity and difference, at least lexically, notationally, and symbolically? Reading "identity is Difference" through the typographical inversion, in which identity becomes subsidiary to Difference (though still prioritized syntactically, which raises the question of just what this phrase is supposed to actually accomplish), the inversion of Identity and difference can be considered coterminous, dialectical, co-constitutive, binary poles, but the point of antiracist work is not to erase difference but to erase the differential opportunities, privileges, and penalties among the complex play of intersectional identity/difference formations active within a given social and historical conjuncture.

On his i am OTHER website, Williams posted a manifesto, declaring, "OTHERS are not defined by demographics or geography. OTHERS believe individuality is the new wealth. Whoever is the most individual wins."[6] Williams practices what he preaches as a one-man brand whose commercial offerings extend from music production into various high-end prestige consumer items—"redefining cool for a new generation," as claimed in the catalog description for his book, *Places and Spaces I've Seen*. More interesting and less commented on is Williams's inverting of the conventional meanings of Otherness by dismissing "demographics and geography" as nondeterminate. Is Williams seeking to reverse or simply ignore the power differentials inherent in practices of Othering?

Figure 9.1 Pharrell Williams posing in his cap and T-shirt Uniqlo offerings © Uniqlo 2014.

How, indeed, does individuality, freed of demographics and geography, translate into wealth, to use Williams's words? One T-shirt provides no answer despite offering a dictionary-styled definition, which reads: "oth•er \'e•ther\ Adjective 1. Different; Not the same 2. Being the ones or one distinguishable from that or those which is or are the uniform / Synonyms distinct, distinctive, distinguishable, diverse, dissimilar, nonidentical, opposite, different, unalike, unlike." Popular culture—with its pop song choristers leading the charge—has long traded on rebellion as individual expression for products aimed at the youth culture market, cosseting those oppositional urges into profitable consumption. Similarly, "Happy" imagines a self-aware Subject announcing her happiness through song, nonchalantly claiming Otherness as a position of power rather than subordination. In his Othering, Williams offers consumption as empowerment rather than escapism and marked as conscious rather than conspicuous by an agentive rather than passively compliant consumer. In another twist on the promotion imitating art imitating life meme, Williams can point to another of his T-shirt offerings, which states in simple block letters across the front, "The Same Is Lame."[7] Yet Williams's entrepreneurial consumerism aligned with its idiosyncratic reversal of Other-ing practically guarantees that the "same will remain."

Postrace, Postpolitics

In 2013, Williams, in collaboration with the French filmmaking duo We Are From L.A., produced the world's first twenty-four-hour-long music video for "Happy."[8] The video loops the music as a sound track to feature a number of lip-synching dancers, most of whom appear nonprofessional, though a sizable number clearly have some sort of dance training or performance experience and are meant to be representative of diversity—young, old, female, male, black, white, Latinx, Asian, multiracial, multisexual, variously attired, coiffed, and accessorized suggesting divergent class and gender positions including cameos by celebrity entertainers—giving physical expression to the song, shot in a high-gloss guerrilla style at various locations throughout Los Angeles. Williams appears in versions at the top of each hour. However, as the video approaches noon and moves into the late evening, sequences begin to trouble the sunshine-filled narrative as bemused middle-class tourist onlookers give way to the homeless and night-shift or off-shift laborers gazing quizzically at or awkwardly interacting with the dancers (or, most often, avoiding the camera crew and the dancers as much as possible). The juxtaposition of the happy dancers and these other, more perplexing participants, especially in the late, wee hours of the video, highlights the incongruencies of Williams's "feel-good" politics.

Williams's song is certainly a textbook example of an eminently pleasurable "summer single."[9] The song's insistence that "bad news, give me all you got, I'll be just fine," simply because "I'm happy, can't nothing bring me down," resonates sympathetically with his public statements on race. As I detail later, Williams claims that social norms have moved us past considerations of race and that simply "being happy" will help move us past racism. Williams's descriptions of the contemporary moment as "postracial" evince a disingenuous optimism for an *individualist* agency often expressed by the aphorism "Be the change you wish to see in the world."[10]

Williams's belief in individual rather than collective happiness as empowering is both an advertisement industry award-winning campaign (Jardine 2014) and his way of promoting positive change in the world.[11] In this sense, Williams does not shy away from using his song politically; indeed, he weaves both his consumerist politics and a call to world peace into color-blind entrepreneurial cloth. As reported in a *Rolling Stone* article in 2014: "'I'm really upset they're not letting the press out here right now, so we could show them what it looks like for 100,000 people to be happy,' said Pharrell, going on to suggest that problems in the Middle East could be alleviated if only they'd see that mass happiness was possible, or something. His later call for 'more female coders, more female doctors, more female artists' was considerably more effective, especially because there were more women onstage during his set than at any other time throughout the [Made In America 2014] festival's run" (see G. Edwards and Rosenthal 2014).

Progressive gender politics reduced to counting bodies notwithstanding, Williams's advice that the political problems of the Middle East are solvable by "mass happiness" confronts difference and, more significantly, the power differentials embedded within relationships of difference with a dancer's smile. Since the election of US president Barack Hussein Obama, the "post-racial" entered the public vocabulary as the discourses of multiculturalism and color blindness devolved into a rhetoric of diversity.[12] In considering David Hollinger's argument that current "ethnoracial vocabularies are theoretically and ethically inadequate," Paul Taylor (2014) pushes further, noting that while Hollinger's "ideological postracialism" recognizes the continuation of racism, Hollinger's concurrent assumption that racial hierarchies have disappeared leads to blaming individuals for any inadequate achievements due to their purported inability to take advantage of the opportunities now available to them (which Hollinger agrees was denied their forebears).[13]

In the wake of the deaths of unarmed young black men and women, however, the idea that race no longer matters has been given the lie. Race matters, to quote Cornel West, and identity and identification seem to matter more, not less, in a world in which death haunts the lives of black- and brown-skinned people, collective as well as individual, regardless of class position, educational achievement, or public prominence as evidenced by the 2009 arrest of Harvard University professor Henry Louis Gates Jr. in his home.

The killing of unarmed black individuals whose killers face little to no consequences, even as their communities are demonized for grieving the loss of their daughters and sons and, more significantly, for demanding justice and equality under the law, speaks back to the limits of individualized self-empowerment in the face of systemic racialized violence. What matters an individual's sense of agency when her life can end abruptly, "inconsequentially," thanks to judicial rulings that belittle the lives that expire at the hands of law enforcement officers who have been able to (re)move themselves "beyond the law" and, it appears to many, for little reason other than being black or brown?[14]

In an *Ebony* interview that took place shortly after Michael Brown's killing in Ferguson, Missouri, Williams was asked if he had seen the video footage of Brown in a convenience store shortly before he was killed. Williams admitted he had, asserting, "It looked very bully-ish; that in itself I had a problem with. Not with the kid, but with whatever happened in his life for him to arrive at a place where that behavior is OK. Why aren't we talking about that?" While acknowledging that larger social forces were also at work in Ferguson that day, Williams notes, "The boy [Michael Brown] was walking in the middle of the street when the police supposedly told him to 'get the fuck on the sidewalk.' If you don't listen to that, after just having pushed a storeowner, you're asking for trouble." Williams admits that Brown should not have been killed, but rather than protest the killing, he reasons that "displaced anger is a brushfire and the media is the wind" and advocates instead that for "every individual who gets killed, someone should build a school or teach a child."[15]

Williams's call to a politics of respectability, with its judgmental prescriptive agenda, echoes Bill Cosby, who Williams cites immediately following the preceding quotes. Linking the politics of "being happy" to his successful music career, Williams's understanding of consumerism as the answer to social and political tensions can be tethered to his reading of Cosby, a black comedian who, as Williams reminds us, "had all of us wearing Coogi sweaters [in the 1980s]. You've got to respect him." Because Williams praised Cosby prior to the elder comedian's legal troubles over allegations of serial rape, I want to remain focused on Williams's sympathies for Cosby's politics of respectability. Voicing his support for Cosby's public denouncements of the "hip hop generation" in the same interview in which he discusses the Brown killing, Williams affirms, "I agree with him [Cosby]. When Cosby [blamed black youth for their lack of achievement due to inadequate adherence to (white, "colorblind") bourgeois norms] back then, I understood; I got it." Williams continues, "Cosby can talk that talk because he created Fat Albert . . . [and] he portrayed a doctor on *The Cosby Show*," remarkably citing a comic character and a television situation comedy role as support for his endorsement. It may not be surprising, then, to note that Williams turned "Happy" into a children's book "filled with photos of children around the world 'celebrating what it means to be happy'" (Contrera 2015). In line with his admiration for Cosby's influence on fans' sweater choices and in keeping with his belief in the power of consumer choice as a means to a progressive politic, Williams's commercial offerings include Comme des Garçons fragrances, Adidas sneakers, Billionaire Boys Club high-end streetwear, and Louis Vuitton jewelry.

The multiple accusations of serial rape currently haunting Cosby tarnish his once prominent advocacy of the politics of respectability, and Williams has had his own legal entanglements concerning popular music songwriting and publishing rights, which I discuss later. While the two men are involved with distinct kinds of legal, moral, and ethical breaches that are not equivalent, they reveal, at the very least, the limits of a consumer-driven politics of upward mobility in which individual achievement, particularly in economic terms as displayed by brand-name loyalties, is the sine qua non of black liberation. As Banet-Weiser puts it, "Despite the social change rhetoric framing much commodity activism, the empowerment aimed for is ... most often personal and individual. In this context, ... the individual is a flexible commodity that can be packaged, made, and remade—a commodity that gains value through self-empowerment" (2012, 17).

In this light, Williams has clearly set a transformative agenda for his commodifying cultural moves, to use Herman Gray's apt term to describe "the shape, shifts, and effects of black struggles over identity, recognition, and representation" (2005, 3). I will grant that Williams's proclamation of moving to a space beyond race is *meant to be liberatory*. However, as Gray argued in 2005, while individual black achievements make visible black contributions to national and global culture, "they are no guarantors of progressive projects for racial justice" (186). I quote Gray at length as his prescient description glosses our present moment, conveying the complications and unintended uses of black achievement, including those "used to support political projects that deny any specific claim or warrant on the part of black folk to experiencing disproportionately the effects of social injustice, economic inequality, racism, and so on. As state and national campaigns for 'color blindness' and against affirmative action indicate, black visibility is often the basis for claims to racial equality, the elimination of social and economic injustice, and *the arrival of the time for racial invisibility*" (186; emphasis added).

Gray describes the twin-edged wedge of black achievement: "Liberals use media representation of black achievement (rather than images of, say, criminality) to persuade constituents of the importance of diversity, while conservatives use the same representations to celebrate the virtues of color blindness and individual achievement." The stakes are clear: "This state of affairs expresses the contested nature of representation, and shows why representation remains an important site of cultural politics" (2005, 186). Writing these words several years before the first election of Barack Obama to the US presidency, Gray's words continue to echo.

A current example: despite the presence of a former black US president and two consecutive black attorneys general, the list of publicly known names of blacks, including minors, who have been killed by police continues to grow as of this writing (April 2015).[16] This statistic is not attributable to gang warfare or random street violence, nor is it restricted to black male youth. Police officers, sworn to serve and protect the public, are directly involved in these deaths. Yet despite live-action video taken of the events, sometimes from multiple sources, the individual officers involved in the incidents have had little to say publicly—or been made to say—and that is saying *something*. What color as well as how much skin one might have in the game, so to speak, matters.

The point, in other words, is not to imagine an equitable social world in which we see (or hear) "*past* skin color" but to fully inhabit one "*with* skin color"—*but* without any social stigma (or prestige) or systemic disadvantage (or advantage) attached to any particular tint (or rhythm, timbre). Kathryn T. Gines writes, "*The ultimate goal is* not denying the existence of racial categories or eliminating the idea of race, but rather *the eradication of systematic institutionalized racism*. It is neither necessarily pathological to have a willful attachment to racial identities nor altogether undesirable to maintain race and ethnic based communities—even in the absence of racism and ethnocentrism" (2014, 84; emphasis added). That's quite a trick, however; indeed, the need to reconceive a social order in which hierarchies are constantly put under question is only one issue, let alone the fundamental need to address the seemingly inherent antagonisms within normative notions of identity/difference relations.[17]

In contrast, Ahmed argues that colonialism—a project justified by notions of the racial and cultural superiority of Western imperial power—set in motion the dynamics of race deeming non-European Others as requiring the civilizing effects of happy submission to colonization. Indeed, the "civilizing mission can be described as a happiness mission. For happiness to become a mission, the colonized other must first be deemed unhappy" (Ahmed 2010, 125). Williams's attempts to reverse this logic by proclaiming one's personal happiness offer little to challenge the idea that Others, in the eyes of power, are inherently *unhappy*. This logic figures people of color as pathetic, if not pathological, victims of their own inability to achieve happiness as productive citizen-consumers of the capitalist state. Is Williams convinced, in fact, that a police officer at a late-night traffic stop *won't* shoot him because he's a "billionaire playboy" convinced that "the same is lame"?

Dancing through the Intersectional

Williams actively transforms US racism's painful legacy in his response to an interviewer's question about whether "someone who is Black and in [his] income bracket still encounters racism," answering, "Yes. I think [racism] affects everyone. But I'm really concerned about how it affects my culture.

Here's the thing, though: *We're going to start seeing that it's actually less about race and more about class in the future. . . .* After all, our commander-in-chief is Black, right?" (K. Hunt 2014; emphasis added). Ignoring the lived reality of the poor, a majority for whom "race is the modality through which class is lived" (Hall 1980, 341), Williams seems unaware that much of the sharp criticisms from the Right against President Obama are explicitly racialized as when anti-Obama protesters carry signs with altered photographs suggesting he is a non–*Homo sapiens* primate.[18] By focusing on class, Williams devalues race or any number of issues subsumed beneath the still deeply divisive term "identity politics," viewing them as counterproductive diversions. Yet, pace Williams, as George Lipsitz demonstrates throughout his powerful study *How Racism Takes Place*: "In nearly every aspect of life, from the frequency and duration of layoffs to the location of branch bank closings, *race proved to be a more decisive variable than class*" (2011, 8; emphasis added).

Further, Williams displays a remarkably tin ear to the ways in which class positioning articulates social hierarchies, particularly as they intersect with other registers of identity, including race. Race, in other words, has not left the building. Williams argues, "As much as we complain about the establishment discriminating against us, we're going to start seeing that more of us are already in the establishment," erasing the assimilative nature of belonging to "the establishment." In other words, as Pierre Bourdieu (1984) argues, becoming part of the bourgeois "establishment" involves socializing into its allowable and available range of performative positionings (including certain transgressions, iconoclasm[s], and contrarians allowed to be visible and even valued at times), ideological perspectives (including certain allowable heterodoxies), and social relationships (including vocational, familial, and political) while accomplishing little to transform the differential power relations between majority and minority positionings. It encourages the reification of those power relations, in fact, by naturalizing them, layering another level of ideological sediment to the social strata.

With the inauguration of the forty-fifth president of the United States of America, the rhetoric of the nation moving beyond race has largely faded from public discourse, further obscuring the fact that the historical achievement of a black presidency has been reduced to an individual rather than a collective triumph. Indeed, raising the melanin quotient at the country club has not meant that social equality has been achieved. While Williams certainly recognizes this condition of impossibility—of black sound's inability, in other words, to begin from a superior (let alone equal) positioning—even as he celebrates entering the clubhouse through the front door, the final result is a disquieting truism: be careful what you wish for.

Conclusion

Some of Williams's Teflon-coated postracial stance may be revealing dings and scrapes. In March 2015, a jury awarded Marvin Gaye's estate $7.4 million, deciding that Robin Thicke and Pharrell Williams had plagiarized Gaye's music in creating "Blurred Lines," their 2013 hit. Perhaps tellingly, Pharrell and Thicke had initiated a suit as plaintiffs in August 2013 in an attempt to foreclose any action by Gaye's children, who hold the rights to their father's compositions ("Marvin Gaye's Family" 2015; Wood 2015). "Blurred Lines" sold more than 7.3 million copies in the United States market alone, earning Williams and Thicke more than $7 million apiece, according to court testimony (McCartney 2015).[19] News articles report the award was based on non-notational musical similarities, including attention to elements such as timbre and rhythmic style instead of note-for-note melodic or harmonic similitude as in previous court cases—a move from sheet music to recording as legal evidence.[20] In much of the reporting of the court case, Williams has purportedly earned more than $100 million. If the profits from the sales and licensing of his nonmusical business ventures are added to his already-considerable holdings, he has moved several steps closer to his dream to join "the establishment."

Before concluding, I offer a possible counter to all I have written here. Is it possible to hear "Happy" as ironic, as a signifyin(g) gesture, using a declaration of happiness not to register one's true emotional state but to shield oneself from the micro- and not-so-micro-aggressions of the day? Is it the sound track to a stance that says, "Don't let them think they're sweating you"? A twenty-first-century update of performing hep or cool (read, black) indifference, insolence, or irony?

I am almost convinced by a single iteration of "Happy" from the entire twenty-four-hour version (I watched all 360 iterations at least once initially from February 2 through 14, 2015).[21] It occurs relatively early in the video's day (beginning at midnight), at 12:20 AM, when a middle-aged black man, a gas station attendant in a previous iteration, moves from behind the cash register counter to begin his time with the song. He keeps things simple, avoiding some of the breathless quality of almost every other, usually younger, dancer's ending (including the following two dancers, who are forced to lie down on the ground to catch their breath as the song continues to churn, happily, beneath them at various points). He begins reservedly and, again in contrast to a majority of his "dance partners," ends his sequence with a slight *buildup* of energy throughout the latter part of his rendition. Bouncing in place, alternately clapping and snapping his fingers rhythmically throughout the song, he embodies "being happy" in a disarmingly open-hearted way. He lip-synchs well, offering us witty facial expressions and clever hand movements as gestural accompaniment to his "vocalizations." He is one of the few dancers in the entire twenty-four-hour period who is able to comment on as well as enact specific lyrical content by synchronizing deft and often comic hand patterns and subtle head nods, with competing eye, heel and toe, and hip and knee movements in a continuously graceful flow.

It is the loose, comfortable relationship he enjoys with his body that is remarkable. An otherwise unassuming figure, it is his joyous relationship with the song apprehended through his body that captivates. I return to his performance periodically and am always transfixed by the magic of it, which is no less enthralling with repetition. The affect is always a warm, pleasurable enactment of an individual's sense of "being happy." The scare quotes are warranted because his reality—low-wage worker, even if franchise owner, at a gas station with long, boring hours at a counter, engaged in mostly tedious interactions with others, and the issue of safety, particularly at an hour such as 12:20 AM—does not provide the conditions, one assumes, for human fulfillment, let alone happiness. And yet he never stops moving his hips, knees, or feet, his arms and hands in constant motion. His dance is more than an ironic rejoinder to the oppressive conditions of his material life; it is a celebration of the body and its joys, truths, and sheer *physicality* as a supplement to the logic of economic determination in the final instance. His head remains still, relative to his body's kinetic energy, exposing, perhaps, the reason for this ability when he temporarily abandons dance for a display of the "sweet science," shadowboxing with surprising dexterity. Can we see his brief pugilistic display as actively, physically, resisting his material condition and positioning? His happiness as agentive, purposeful, *significant*? His ending is the sharpest of any of the versions (Williams's included), miming the recording's abrupt ending with a wink while pointing directly to us, grinning slightly before folding his shoulders in and breaking his dancer's pose, no longer the happy dancer but the graveyard shift gas station attendant, break time over. Yet throughout his dance, his body is a study in contrary motion, conveying the pleasures of the flesh under conditions he did not create. Happy yet unhappy, in motion, yet still.

Perhaps, however, we should return to Sara Ahmed's cautionary aside mentioned earlier about presuming the subaltern's unhappiness. Nor do I mean to presume the gas station worker's obliviousness to the material conditions of his life, that he is a preternaturally happy soul who always glimpses the silver lining. Rather, I am suggesting that the attendant is simultaneously signaling pleasurable and critical responses to the song through facial expression and coordinated body movement that is not "about" race but is effective *through* race. The brief hint of pugilism is leavened by the slow-cooked dancing surrounding that moment, building its complexities through a continual stirring, just barely boiling physicality, bubbling in its joy. Still, anyone familiar with the sweet science knows the grace of a boxer's hands is often matched with speed and, most important, effective power. This gas station attendant's facial expression and comic timing indicate another sort of effectiveness, a kind of diffident resistance, and it is worth noting that most of his performance is a sly dance in this mode.

In contrast, at 8:48 PM a chicken-suited dancer is preening in a supermarket, as manic as the gas station attendant was fully in control. Is this the postracial body, a costumed simulacrum of physical presence? In a reverse mirror performance of the gas attendant's pugilistic skill, the dancer transforms a move to avoid dropping her "chicken head" into a gesture of abandonment and glee. The performance is leavened not only by the ridiculous chicken suit but also by the dancer's obvious pleasure in moving through the supermarket hidden beneath a ridiculous chicken suit. The suit frees the person "inside" to express herself in a number of very un-chicken-like moves: grabbing her crotch, rolling in the aisles, twerking, rearticulating gender from sexuality, feathers from skin, masks from flesh. It is a refutation of pessimism and passivity, enjoining us to a manic sort of happiness, a fevered relinquishing of decorum, a ridiculous chicken-suited clown hamming it up in front of a camera.[22]

Allow me one final word from Ahmed, expanding from Audre Lorde's position that "we should not be protected from what hurts. We have to work and struggle not so much to feel hurt but to notice what causes hurt, which means unlearning what we have learned not to notice. We have to do this work if we are to produce critical understandings of how violence, as a relation of force and harm, is directed toward some bodies and not others" (2010, 215–16). The chicken-suited dancer's energetic performance is a refutation of the killing, packaging, and marketing of the animal body for literal human consumption, items she dances past with obvious joy, abandoning inhibition, wings and legs aflutter. Her dance suggests that one cannot have happiness without its opposite. Happiness embraces many kinds of truth, including the jester's truth as she, free in her chicken skin, dances toward the butcher's cleaver.

Still, I remain unconvinced by these dancers, in the end, because Pharrell Williams wants us to hear—*insists* that we hear—"Happy" as "postracial." Seemingly deaf to the ways in which institutionalized, systemic racism results in the periodic recurrence of deaths, not to speak of all of the less-than-mortal disregard, of everyday black and brown citizens throughout the United States, Williams explicitly links political ideals to commercial consumerism. In 2014, as *Rolling Stone*'s headline described it, "Producer [Williams] encourages fans to donate to humanitarian fund while promoting global hit 'Happy'" (J. Newman 2014). Partnering with the United Nations Foundation to help celebrate the International Day of Happiness on March 20, 2014, while pursuing publicity for "Happy" as the sound track to an ideology of "happiness conquers all," Williams encouraged his fans to upload their interpretations of his song to his YouTube channel, garnering free content for a commercialized ideological pitch. The UN proclamation for the day brought attention to the "need for a more inclusive, equitable and balanced approach to economic growth that promotes sustainable development, poverty eradication, happiness, and the well-being of all peoples" (J. Newman 2014) while avoiding the language of difference (race, ethnicity, nationality) or offering substantial policy advice or direction. Lipsitz sums up the situation: "In all areas of US life, we now confront the presumption that color-bound injustices require color-blind remedies, that race-based problems should be solved by race-blind remedies. As a result, more than four decades after the civil rights activism of the 1960s, and nearly one hundred and fifty years after the abolition of slavery, *race remains the most important single variable determining opportunities and life chances in the United States*" (2011, 15; emphasis added).

To return to "Happy," a hit pop song:[23] Williams has stood as proxy for postracial discourse, which has a complicated decades-long history. So I will end with the image of a yellow chicken with bright red wings and comb, dancing in the aisles of a supermarket somewhere in Los Angeles, twirling in a beautiful circle, lip-synching "Clap along if you feel like happiness is the truth!" I clap along because I do, in fact, feel "like happiness is [a] truth." But we are all struggling in a world of often overwhelming *un*happiness (recall those dead chicken bodies being danced past in that supermarket, the factory farms from which they arrived, and the desensitization necessary to labor in their production and consumption). As we come to the end of the second half of the second decade of the twenty-first century, there is an almost palpable *absence of happiness* in large parts of the world, evincing the real tragedies just beneath the surface of many peoples' lives.[24] The fact that it has always been thus is laughable as solace and pathologically tragic if meant to belittle all the individual and collective struggles for self-realization, achievement, and personal fulfillment. And, meanwhile, the climate changes, bringing its own set of complications and requirements for coordinated human action.

Indeed, given the existential and mortal dangers with which our current social order confronts us, we do not need a postracial world so much as a post-*racist* one. As Kathryn Gines cautions, "We should not conflate *post-racialism* (the idea that eliminating racial categories or ignoring race will make racism go away) with *post-racism* (the antiracist struggle to identify and dismantle systems of racial oppression, especially institutionalized racism)" (2014, 79; emphasis added). The reason for the rise of the Black Lives Matter movement and the reactions to the movement and its raison d'être—that is, the continuing war on black and brown bodies by police and their enabling alliance with the legal establishment—continue to engulf the racial landscape of the United States despite a black president, a black attorney general, or black police officers. As David Theo Goldberg noted at the dawn of Obama's presidency, "The end of racism is confused with no more than being against race, the end of race substituting to varying degrees for the commitment to—the struggles for—ending racism. The refusal of racism reduces to racial refusal; and racial refusal is thought to exhaust antiracism" (2009, 1), aptly describing the ways in which Williams mines this discursive confusion with calls to be happy. The call to do the impossible, channeling Sun Ra, is still provocative. It is time for something more than provocations, however. It is time to realize a differently constructed social world in which power is distributed freely, coordinated collaboratively, and instrumentalized in ways that encourage trust, sincerity, and compassion among collaborators across, between, and through difference. Clap along to *that*.

Notes

1 I borrow the term "aggrieved communities" and its meaning from George Lipsitz. See also, for example, Rich 2014. There is a link to the Department of Education's Office for Civil Rights and its reports in Rich's article.

   See also Wolfers, Leonhardt, and Quealy 2015. "This article describes the fact that "[more] than one out of every six black men who today should be between 25 and 54 years old have disappeared from daily life . . . largely because of early deaths or because they are behind bars"; see also Wolfers 2015.

2 I acknowledge that Orta is no choirboy. However, his involvement in the Garner case is limited to the legal act of recording police officers acting in the public sphere on a private

citizen who, at the very least, should be treated as innocent until proven guilty. That I should have to write that said citizen should not be *dead* after the encounter is symptomatic of much current political and public discourse regarding difference. See also note 16 below.

3 Numerous texts make this point, including Floyd 1995; Small 1998; Ward 1998. For more on the ability of black musicking to play a vital role in social justice organizing, see Reed 2005; Monson 2007; Sullivan 2011.

4 Note that only forty-eight iterations of "Happy" during the entire twenty-four-hour video feature more than a solo dancer. Of those forty-eight versions, two are of women with dogs, and one woman is seen dancing with a puppet. The other couples are largely male-female or male-male duos. There are two versions of young girls dancing together and two of adult females dancing with young children. There is a single version of a woman performing in a wheelchair.

5 The site is currently reduced to a multicolored "splash" page with links to various social media sites. The manifesto, in other words, is no longer online.

6 See http://iamother.com/. I have retained the use of uppercase letters from the website.

7 The shirt also sports "Think other" in a smaller font and the logo for the company i am OTHER.

8 The twenty-four-hour video was available for viewing at www.24hoursofhappy.com/.

9 The song was initially released in November 2013 for the *Despicable Me 2* sound track. Williams reminds us of this cinematic link in the fifth iteration of "Happy" in his twenty-four-hour video version, which, instead of a live-action dancer, focuses on a vintage 1980s-era monitor on the counter of a gas station displaying scenes from the film, which acts as a self-conscious visual commentary on the lyrics. Two other iterations reference *Despicable Me 2*, both using dancing yellow "minion" characters. At 5:32 AM, a trio of minions dances uphill along a frontage road in a park. At 4:40 PM, a single minion dances through a suburban Southern California neighborhood.

10 Often attributed to Mahatma Gandhi, as Brian Morton (2010) points out in a *New York Times* editorial, it is a misquotation. As Morton notes, the actual quote—"If we could change ourselves, the tendencies in the world would also change. As a man changes his own nature, so does the attitude of the world change towards him. . . . We need not wait to see what others do"—promotes, rather, the idea that "for Gandhi, the struggle to bring about a better world involved not only stringent self-denial and rigorous adherence to the philosophy of nonviolence; it also involved a steady awareness that one person, alone, can't change anything, an awareness that unjust authority can be overturned only by great numbers of people working together with discipline and persistence."

11 There is not space here to fully engage with the debates surrounding either the political efficacy or the weighing of philosophical value between various versions of community and individualism. For more detail on this particular set of debates, see Fox-Genovese 1990; Keat 2013. There is also a substantial amount of literature devoted to these tensions in psychology and education; see, for example, Bhawuk 1992.

12 For a view from philosophy and political theory, the special issue of the *Du Bois Review: Social Science Research on Race* 1, no. 1 (March 2014) focusing on the "post-racial," with contributions from the coeditors (Robert Gooding-Williams and Charles W. Mills), as

well as Paul C. Taylor, Lawrie Balfour, Tommie Shelby, Kathryn T. Gines, and Cristina Beltrán, provides a number of productive entry points for grappling with the term.

13 Paul C. Taylor (2014, 14) also raises the significant issue of the whitewashing of history in "ideological postracialism" through its efforts to hold to the prohibition of race-talk as an antiracialist posture, thus making it difficult to raise questions regarding past injustices.

14 At the time I was finishing this essay, multiple police officers were facing felony charges for the deaths of Walter Scott and Freddie Gray (see note 16 below). This fact does not erase all the other deaths that have occurred with little to no consequence for the police officer involved and is indicative of a systemic disregard for black lives. That this is a national issue indicates its pervasive and insidious character, though it has been characterized as the actions of a few bad apples. The orchard is rotting from the roots.

15 All quotations in this and the following paragraph are from K. Hunt 2014, except where noted otherwise.

16 Regarding the attorneys general, I am thinking not only of Eric Holder but also of his successor, Loretta Lynch. She faced an unprecedented delay in her confirmation by the US Congress due, in large part, to current political positions by dominant players rather than the merits of her case.

Sadly, in April 2015, fifty-year-old Walter L. Scott joined the ranks of widely publicized black Americans shot to death by white police officers. The unarmed Scott was shot as he ran away from a traffic stop. At the time of writing, the police officer involved, Michael Slager, had been charged with first-degree murder. The footage responsible for indicting the police officer was on the internet and used by mainstream media news outlets alike. Consequently, Scott's death quickly became a national spectacle, rendering it a public matter. April 2015 also saw the death of twenty-five-year-old Freddie Gray while in police custody in Baltimore, Maryland. Six Baltimore police officers have been charged with various crimes in relation to Gray's death. We should not forget that the names of black and brown people are drawn from the list of known, i.e., reported, killings; I want to acknowledge the unreported here, as well. Indeed, there has been legalized killing of non-white people since the US colonial period. A running count of all individuals—i.e., not only blacks—killed by police in the United States can be found at *The Counted* website: www.theguardian.com/us-news/ng-interactive/2015/jun/01/the-counted-police-killings-us-database#, accessed June 6, 2015.

Even more tragically, the deaths of nine black congregants at the Emanuel African Methodist Episcopal Church in Charleston, South Carolina, at the hands of white supremacist Dylann Roof occurred just before the deadline for the submission of this essay. While Roof was not a police officer, his actions speak even more clearly to the connection of white supremacist ideology in contemporary US culture to its mortal consequences for black American lives.

17 And then, perhaps, we can begin to rationally discuss reparations, decolonization processes, and other historical dismantlings.

18 All the quotations in this paragraph are from K. Hunt 2014. For example, Obama continued to face political opposition in often undisguised racist reactions to his presidency. I am thinking here not only of Donald Trump's standing request to see Obama's "actual"

birth certificate or Tea Partiers' related emphasis on the purported foreignness of his up-bringing and heritage but also the Republican Party's obstructionist policy toward any Executive Office initiative at least partially rooted in race-based opposition to Obama's presidency. See, for example, Bouie 2012; Ramos and Fabian 2014; Slate 2014; Grunwald 2012. For a concise blog post regarding the racist imagery used against President Obama and his wife, Michelle, see Sauer 2011.

A May 21, 2015, *New York Times* story by Julie Hirschfeld Davis describes that "it took only a few minutes for Mr. Obama's account to attract racist, hate-filled posts and replies. Posts addressed him with racial slurs, called him a monkey, and one had an image of the president's neck in a noose." The left has also criticized President Obama but on issues of policy, including his inaction or unfavorable action on any number of given issues, including fracking, the closing of Guantanamo Bay prison facilities, government surveillance programs, and the use of drones.

19 However, the Associated Press reported that Williams and Thicke each earned $5 million from the sales of "Blurred Lines." In any case, it was a substantial amount of money.

20 At the Columbia University music department's fiftieth anniversary of its graduate student–run journal, *Current Musicology*, invited guest Harvard University Quincy Jones Professor of African American Music, Ingrid Monson, told the audience about her experience as an expert witness in the "Blurred Lines" case, noting that the arguments regarding *notational* distinctions, which are the historical basis of copyright law, no longer carried much rhetorical weight, and it was the argument for the correlations between audible phenomena such as the timbral affinities between the two *recordings* of music that won the day.

21 There are a number of enchanting, funny, and endearing dancers scattered throughout the twenty-four hours. However, the gas station attendant—even if simply a character—is the sole dancer to consistently rub creatively against the grain of "Happy" as I am portraying it here. The young woman at 11:24 PM may come closest in an opposite way by giving in to and embodying the song's naive charms.

22 Yet she, too, has to take a short breather at one point in her dance, simply lying coquettishly, belly down, on the floor with her feet up behind her.

23 According to Jason Newman's *Rolling Stone* article, "*Girl* [the recording featuring "Happy"] has reached Number One in more than 75 countries since its release and is Spotify's Number One album worldwide. 'Happy' has topped *Billboard*'s Hot 100 chart, *Billboard*'s Digital Songs and *Billboard*'s Radio Songs and is Number One on the iTunes chart in more than 90 countries" (J. Newman 2014). Elsewhere, "Happy" was listed by *Billboard* as the Top Single of 2014; www.billboard.com/charts/year-end/2014/hot-100 -songs, accessed April 19, 2015. Williams was awarded a 2015 Grammy award for "Best Pop Solo Performance" and "Best Music Video" for "Happy," as well as a "Best Urban Contemporary Album" Grammy for *Girl*.

24 Recent articles in the *New York Times* (A. Williams 2017) and *Japan Times* (Hoffman 2016; Editorial Board 2016) point to a small cottage industry in "we are now living in an age of anxiety" essays and articles.

10

Indie Soaps

Race and the Possibilities of TV Drama

AYMAR JEAN CHRISTIAN

The year 2015 marked a shift in broadcast television's representations of race. Earlier in the century, postracial representations dominated, with largely heteronormative characters written for actors of any race. The postracial turn followed the collapse of the black TV market around 2000 as new media competition pushed broadcast TV networks to cater to wealthier white viewers. Getting diversity on-screen required hiding it in the script. But by the 2010s, broadcast TV ratings had fallen so low that executives turned to the black market for never-before-seen representations that could attract attention amid a record number of TV shows. Representative of this shift was FOX's black drama *Empire*, created by Lee Daniels and Danny Strong. Along with *The Haves and the Have-Nots*, *Power*, and *Survivor's Remorse*, *Empire* outperformed earlier postracial narratives of *Scandal* and *How to Get Away with Murder*, which have mostly nonblack casts, less visible marks of black cultural performance, and few characters who cross lines of race, gender, sexuality, and class. *Empire* rose to the top in part by representing black gayness, steadily attracting more and more fans each week, eager to see whether "a faggot really can run this company [Empire Records]," as Lucious's ex-wife, Cookie, says in the pilot. A first in decades of prime-time serials, Jamal's coming out as gay in front of his father, Lucious, set a series high of thirteen million viewers (live plus same-day viewing), the largest audience of the night. Later episodes of *Empire* directly addressed the politics of the policing and incarceration of black men and women from an explicitly pro-black lens: season two opens with Cookie Lyon dressed as a gorilla in a cage protesting incarceration to a crowd of thousands of black fans. The trade press trumpeted *Empire*'s success as evidence of the power of diversity to revive the beleaguered broadcast prime-time drama as cable and web TV channels consistently beat them out in ratings and critical acclaim.

Watching *Empire*, one might assume that legacy television left postidentity ideologies behind and embraced complex and political representations of black people as worthy of investment. Yet a queer perspective on representation reveals how we have to critique corporate efforts to embrace explicit representations of race, gender, and sexuality as a marketing tactic, as "postidentity" narratives potentially fall out of vogue and as competition for viewer attention renders these diluted representations less likely to start conversations on social media. I argue queerness as a frame pushes our understanding of representing identity beyond authenticity (*Empire*'s explicit citation of black culture and politics through hip-hop and prisons) to intersectional specificity and sincerity, and independent web-distributed producers are best equipped to present alternatives to legacy and corporate TV production and narratives. *Empire* is an exception in the television landscape, and the depth of its break from TV's postidentity past is suspect. Even as gay representation expands in dramas like *Empire*, queer representation, which might critique the norms of gender and sexuality across specific representations of race, is all but invisible. *Empire*'s representation of black queer identity is limited by its preoccupation with heteronormativity. Even as the show strives to be post-postracial, it is still largely postfeminist and postgay. In later seasons Jamal rejects publicly discussing his interest in men, instead opting for an affair with a "down-low" hip-hop producer, and expresses disgust when a gender-nonconforming black artist requests a duet with him. Gender nonconformity is virtually invisible. Gay representation seeks acceptance within norms through visibility (Walters 2001), but queer representation treats identity as always in tension with norms and intersecting with race, class, gender, and so forth, such that they are all present and cannot be disentangled (Keeling 2014). If "gay" seeks identification with norms, "queer" is defined by constant disidentification, an understanding of the limits of capital to fully value the intersecting identifications marginalized by dominant ideologies (Ferguson 2004; Munoz 1999). Indeed, *Empire* extends from cinema an individualistic, entrepreneurial, and "ghetto fabulous" aesthetic that "works toward a consensus on black consumerism that depoliticizes African American critiques of capitalism" (Mukherjee 2006a, 613).

We see more sincerity and specificity outside of legacy, corporate development, where indie producers defy the instinct to deploy "post" identities or embrace "authentic" representations for buzz. Five years before *Empire's* climactic episode, another black queer producer, Kalup Linzy, wrote and produced a black drama series about empire set in the world of music and featuring an original sound track. Linzy uploaded his epic narrative *Melody Set Me Free* to YouTube in 2010, following a 2007 short film of the same name. He released three seasons, totaling over two and a half hours of drama: the first independently, presented on YouTube in four separate episodes, and the next two shot at MoMA PS1, produced by James Franco's Rabit Bandini production company and released as one "feature edit" on YouTube.[1] As a pilot, the short introduces a reality competition show in which Patience, Grace, and Faith vie for a record deal. Patience (played by Linzy) wins, and season one picks up with her recording her album for KK Records, owned by KK Queen, Linzy's Lucious Lyon as matriarch. *Melody Set Me Free* replaces American drama's long-standing tradition of the white male hero or antihero driven to maintain or acquire power, with an ethically complex and bedeviled black woman driven to conquer the music industry with the "nasty ass hits" that constitute the series' sound track. KK Queen invested the estate of her late husband in the company to conquer the music industry. She is powerful, and the core of the drama is her struggle to keep the company together as her artists pursue their own desires.

The heart of the drama in *Melody Set Me Free* is a struggle over capital, accumulated through the (mis)management of black queer art and relationships. KK Queen (Linzy) has started KK Records, whose *American Idol*–style competition KK premiered one month after her husband's death, and KK Queen Survey, where artists are interviewed about their practice. KK stole her late husband, Lloyd, from Hope Jones, now an alcoholic trying to wrest control of the company from KK. Working for these two women is a younger generation of artists trying to make it but with very little control over their careers: Patience O'Brien (Linzy), a sweet singer recording with her boyfriend Bill Wright (Frank Leon Roberts); Grace Jackson (Angel Tazari), a strong-willed singer who likes nasty songs; Faith Williams (Theodore Bouloukos), obsessed with nasty songs; En Strobe (Dwight O'Neal, Lawanda Hodges, Jim Hedges), a group committed to success at all costs; and Lovely (Natasha Lyonne), who will sing nasty or sweet, whatever gets the deal. Shaping their decisions are family, including KK's children, Rose and Jacob (both Linzy), and Patience's mother. Aggravating them are the duplicitous men who work for KK: Clark Gaines (Marlon Bascombe), a producer; BT (Humberto Petit), a fixer and wannabe rapper; and Isaac (Reginald Barnes), a lawyer. Changing relationships propel the story forward, as in the soap opera tradition, but this essay will show how Linzy's understanding of black women's and queer experiences reshapes prime-time drama's white and patriarchal history.

As with Lee Daniels, daytime and prime-time broadcast dramas shaped Linzy's interest in soap as an art form. Unlike Daniels, Linzy's engagement with the form is more sincere, motivated by a desire not to profit from predetermined ideas about blackness but to narrate how identity operates "between subjects" as well as within power structures (J. Jackson 2005, 15). "Sincere" narratives allow for individually specific complexity and contra-diction without foregoing power and collectivity; they are less marketable than legacy representations that are "'too tightly scripted' and corrosively mobilized to make social differences appear absolute and natural" (J. Jackson 2005, 13). Instead, Linzy's black queer narratives come from a specific, personal space. His earliest memories of television were watching *Guiding Light* with his grandmother in Florida, but he soon realized dramas were integral to the black community as a whole: "I guess it resonated in a weird way sometimes. The daytime soap operas. That they were so far-fetched but they had a realness to it.... It just got so part of your daily life and a part of your life in general ... people just *gossiped* about it."[2] Here Linzy describes the deep affective connections black viewers had with prime-time characters, despite their scant representation in them, save the short-lived *Generations*. Linzy attributes their appeal to fantasy—"so much so it became real in a dif-ferent way"—and this power drew him to watch, participate in the conversa-tion, and eventually write his own. With the help of his cousins and sister as supporting actors (none of the male-identified cousins ever participated), he released his first soap opera in 1994 for an environmental science class (see "Kalup Linzy's First Soap Opera 1994" 2011).

Linzy's interest in drama spans a period of its expansion on prime-time television. Starting in the 1970s, shows like *Dynasty*, to which both *Empire* and *Melody Set Me Free* are indebted, helped broadcast networks maintain cultural relevance and some ratings stability as new cable channels debuted. Dramas have been critical to the development of so-called new media al-ternatives to broadcast television on cable and the web. Combined with new representations of race, gender, and sexuality, and with different genres, dramas have incredible power to attract attention, as *The Sopranos* to *The Walking Dead* did for premium and ad-supported cable, along with web programs blending serial drama with other genres, such as comedy in *Orange Is The New Black* and *Transparent*, and action in *Video Game High School* on YouTube and *Luke Cage* on Netflix. Since the 1990s, serial dramas have shaped the brands of new cable and web TV channels, allowing them to market themselves as either "edgy" or "cutting edge," selling the newness of new technological platforms with "new" cultural narratives. This branding strategy, a process Sarah Banet-Weiser attests is as much cultural as economic, uses the casting of black, Latinx, and LGBTQ characters in narratives with greater violence and sex than broadcast television to appear on the cutting edge of cultural production and maintain fans' loyalty to the sponsors and distributors (networks) that finance and develop original series (Banet-Weiser 2012; Fuller 2010).[3]

As often as black, Latinx, and GLBTQ characters are cast in shows intent on representing their diverse experiences specifically, as *Empire* claims to do, they have been cast "postrace" to add "color" to the narrative and obscure historical inequalities in TV production and development. Postracial casting evacuates race from histories of inequality, legacies of survival, and intersections of identity in service of race as a skin-deep brand of authenticity for attention and capital. As Kristen Warner argues of color-blind casting: "Skin color, then, becomes the primary lens through which we understand racism. . . . [R]acism and white supremacy are treated as rare and aberrational rather than as systemic and ingrained" (2015, 8). Catherine Squires argues "post racial discourses . . . blame continuing racial inequalities on individuals who make poor choices for themselves and their families" (2014, 6). Thus postracial programming decisions center race as skin color for its ability to grab attention but without a historical or collective understanding of race, so differences between and within races (gender expression and sexuality especially, but also geographic location and class) become less salient, both in production and in narratives. Warner states: "The non-recognition of difference ensures many systemic inequalities go unchallenged and enables the maintenance of white supremacy as the status quo" (2015, 8).

Postidentity ideologies maintain historic inequalities in series development by minimizing the depth, complexity, and specificity of identities within and outside television narratives. Denying specificity and complexity by subsuming collective realities for individual ones maintains white heteropatriarchy as a norm. Thus, postidentity narratives persist because they do not challenge the historically disproportionate investment in white hetero-normative representation in television drama, even as viewers have grown more diverse and difficult to retain. Since dramas brand television networks and attract attention from fans, critics, and more casual viewers, networks have to devote considerable resources to produce lengthy narratives and avoid intersections of race, gender, and sexuality for fear of deviating from past success. The most expensive television episodes are invariably dramas, with production budgets averaging more than double those of comedies (Biller 2014; Magder 2009). Networks and studios invest in complex narratives that will sustain attention. Serial narrative breaks stories into installments, interrupting our listening, viewing, or reading; these interruptions encourage viewers to return and continue the narrative (R. C. Allen 1995). As drama shifted from daytime to prime time in the latter twentieth century, it changed fans' mode of engagement and increased their value for networks, as has been the case historically (Meyers 2015). As Jason Mittell writes: "For prime time programs, the weekly gaps, and even longer breaks between seasons, make each episode seem more eventful and encourage fans to bridge those gaps with paratextual engagement and speculation" (2015, 239). This is serial narrative's historical role: building regular audiences for institutions looking to "exploit new technologies of narrative production and distribution" (R. C. Allen 1995, 1).

Legacy TV's disproportionate investment has material effects on the value viewers place on narratives. Who is both worthy of complex narratives and national attention, and also capable of securing the resources to achieve it? Until very recently with a handful of shows like *Empire*, the answer has always been white, cisgender, heterosexual people. The large investment in money and network programming to tell such robust stories has made dramas about nonwhite and queer communities too risky for network executives. Deregulation, which allowed corporations to vertically integrate, made executives more averse to risk and less diverse in their professional networks, leading to stagnant or declining diversity on and behind the screen (Hunt 2014; Hunt and Ramón 2015). Even as dramas encourage fan participation, television executives have spent decades advancing a very limited view of the form in terms of race, gender, and sexuality. By advancing starkly different performances of intersectional identities on a legacy broadcast network with comparable "production value," *Empire* earned intense fan participation in a market with many more networks releasing original programs.

Yet viewers are spreading their attention across media and among networks within each media form (Webster 2014). As such, while dramas developed by corporate broadcast, cable, and web networks continue to garner all the funding, critical attention, and credit for ushering in a golden age of television, fans marginalized by the industry have always sought alternative narratives from independent producers. Viewers still spend the most of their time watching broadcast and cable dramas, daytime and prime time, but indie dramas have proved resilient in the web TV market and capture significant fan attention. Indeed, as interest in dramas rose on corporate on-air networks from 2000 to 2010, a small but disciplined cohort of showrunners created a slate of web-based programs rivaling corporate counterparts in their diversity of representations and in production and distribution strategies. A number of these programs innovated new stories and new ways of telling them, presaging developments in the better-funded corporate market (Christian 2018). *Melody Set Me Free* and Linzy's other dramas preceded *Empire* by many years.

Examining the production and distribution of independent web television series appealing to black queer people, I argue that indie serial drama resists and reconfigures historical and contemporary trends toward network branding that relies on postracial narratives to amass large audiences, a holdover of the broadcast legacy. Integrating scholarship on black web series and interviews with Linzy and the creators of similar black and queer series, I argue that indie TV dramas are spaces of innovation in television because they can expand notions of production value and narrative complexity by working through and with blackness and queerness. While low budgets preclude many indie dramas from competing with corporate television in technical production value, freedom from corporate development supports producers' pursuit of artistic and cultural production value: creating stories representing sincerely intersectional identities in their local, political, social, and individual complexity. Indie dramas may lack the big-budget grandeur of *Empire*, but in their focus on entertaining smaller, specific fans, producers must be sincere about the experiences of those living through racial, gender, and sexual difference.

Drama remains an underexplored aspect of the web series market, yet since the early 2000s, streaming media dramas and soaps have played an important role in the independent television economy, and particularly for groups marginalized in corporate production such as black, Latinx, queer, Asian, and Pacific Islander Americans. I will focus on dramas at the intersection of blackness and queerness. Black queer narratives are particularly fruitful objects for analysis because of the ways in which black sexuality exists in a "glass closet" of hypervisibiliy and invisibility within the mainstream media sphere (Snorton 2014). Snorton's notion of the glass closet provides a useful framework for understanding the problem of postracial and postgender representations for the ways they render difference visible while rendering invisible specificities of diverse experiences. Specificity must come from producers who have sincere connections to their communities and who are empowered to produce their stories without intervention from development executives who see race as marketing. Black queer—or "quare" (E. P. Johnson 2005)—indie series develop through "quare shared recognition":

> Quaring and shared recognition undergird the reading practices that viewers bring to performances of black queer and femme identities in indie TV, framing the discourse through which they negotiate the paradoxical invisibility and hypervisibility of blackness and queerness—the glass closet frames the reality of black queer productions and publics. In their use of quare-shared recognition, black queer Web producers quare legacy television production by demonstrating the value of black queer identity. This is accomplished through producing series and pilots that expand the diversity of black queer performances, as well as bringing viewers into the production process by encouraging recognition and interaction with the media text. (Day and Christian 2017)

Thus, narratives produced by and about black queer peoples across genders and sexualities are a potent site for understanding the value of independent digital media and serial drama in general, because of the ways producers like Linzy work through the intersections of race, gender, and sexuality through both production and narrative.

Drama and the Development of New Media

When "new media" came to audiences and distributors in the form of cable in the early 1980s, drama resurged as an important part of the prime-time television economy and American culture (Ang 2013). Broadcast networks' fear of competition allowed soap operas to migrate from daytime to prime time starting in the late 1970s. By 2012, when Netflix purchased *House of Cards*, budgets, production value, and narrative complexity for prime-time dramas increased across broadcast, cable, and premium networks, with many paying upwards of $3 million per episode—and in some cases $5 million to $6 million—for lush narratives about power. Thirst for power fuels drama. Characters are often on a mission—typically wealth, power, or security—but fans are equally attracted to the aspirations of networks and studios: their ability (and often inability) to manage multiple plots, reconfigure casts, attract stars, and produce glamour or violence.

Sexuality, race, and gender undergird all narratives producers create, but legacy TV narratives are more likely to evade gender and sexual differences within races, marking white straight men as neutral and ideal, racism and patriarchy as order (Ferguson 2004). A strong narrative tradition in the post-1970s prime-time serial is the white protagonist's pursuit or maintenance of empire, typically in industry, as seen in shows such as *Dynasty*, *Twin Peaks*, *The Sopranos*, and *Breaking Bad*, or in politics, from *West Wing* to *Game of Thrones*. Violence, death, and state power are near-ubiquitous themes in episodic drama (medical, legal, criminal procedurals). The irony of much of American drama is its capacity to construct complex narratives about politics and culture but its infrequent engagement with how race, intersecting with sexuality and gender, might shift these narratives and expand their complexity. After short-lived attempts to produce black dramas amid the success of black comedies in the 1980s—particularly *Frank's Place* and *Generations*—broadcast networks left racial melodrama to new cable networks in the 1990s and early 2000s, many of which eventually canceled shows about black and Latino people (*Soul Train*, *Oz*, *Resurrection Boulevard*) for "broader" period and franchise series.

More recent dramas opt for narratives in which characters of color are on similar quests for power, and their race is visible but rarely affects the plot. With the premieres of *Sleepy Hollow*, *Scandal*, *Power*, *Survivor's Remorse*, *How To Get Away with Murder*, and of course *Empire* chief among them, broadcast networks have again used epic dramas to undercut cable network dominance over later-hour prime-time viewing (10:00 PM) and to reconnect web audiences ("black Twitter") with live television viewing, where most profits are made. When dramas are diverse, characters are cast to engage viewers across media and cultures, as in global sales and in cross-platform marketing for network-owned intellectual property—as in the case of *The Event*, *Heroes*, and *Lost*, or in the musical dramas *Glee*, *Smash*, *Nashville*, and *Empire*. This evades racial specificity in service of global branding, even as digital networks shift how fans engage with narratives by promoting what they feel compelled to share. As Kara Keeling explores in *The Witch's Flight* (2007), film and television companies benefit from viewers' affective connections with reconstructed cinematic reality, and cinematic reality is always already encoded with norms of race, gender, and sexuality. If studios allow underserved audiences to see themselves, they can monetize pent-up demand for representation, but historic inequalities in representation ensure viewers have fewer alternatives to normative reality and so will accept representations that are "skin deep" as opposed to specific: black characters who seek white supremacy. But Warner reminds us that "details make characters real and their realness is what makes them relatable, not their 'similarity to me.' Specificity adds those details and enables characters to become more than types" (2015, 7).

The need to attract audiences, to "pull" as opposed to "push" programming to mass audiences with limited options, has pressured major networks to take some marginal risk in attending to complex relationships between race, gender, and sexuality. Yet even corporate dramas that purport to explicitly engage race still rely on the power of white supremacy to give the drama its heft and narrative tension. *Scandal* marked the revival of the black-led drama on broadcast television since the cancellation of *Julia* and *Frank's Place*. The cliffhanger of its pilot reveals Olivia Pope (Kerry Washington), a black woman lawyer working as crisis manager, having an affair with a white, Republican president of the United States. While Olivia is the show's protagonist, her importance in the narrative rests on her relationship with the most powerful man in the world, to the extent that in the fifth season she auctions herself on the international black market as the one person whose life, through sex, shapes the president's decisions on policy and war. *Sleepy Hollow* started with Nicole Beharie as the black female detective partnered with an American Revolutionary to ward off supernatural forces. The pilot for *How to Get Away with Murder* reveals Annalise Keating (Viola Davis) cheating on her white, tenured husband, accused of raping a student before he dies mysteriously. Jenji Kohan, the creator of *Orange Is the New Black*, one of the most diverse dramas ever produced, confessed that she shaped the narrative around a white woman in order to sell it to executives ("'Orange' Creator Jenji Kohan" 2013). Meanwhile, cable dramas mostly focus on white men achieving supremacy; when black men appear, they are often in criminal settings—*Oz*, *The Wire*, *Power*, and *Survivor's Remorse*.

As dramas proliferate, they are failing to become more representative of the country. Indie producers making series for the web struggle to correct systemic imbalances by crafting intimate, epic narratives about women and queer people of color. After Vimeo and YouTube's debut around 2005, series like *Anacostia*, *If I Was Your Girl*, *No Shade*, *East Los High*, and *Mythomania*, to name just a few, provide vivid portraits of a range of individuals across gender expression, class, and ethnicity in and far outside New York and Los Angeles. In the context of a conglomerate-controlled industry, this is an innovation in the development and distribution of new series and vital to scholarly debates over net neutrality, media ownership, and cultural representation in the postnetwork era. Indie TV creators innovate by expanding "production value" and redefining narrative complexity to position cultural specificity based on regional, cultural, racial, gender, or sexual differences as central to series' production and narratives.

Cultural Production Value: Identity, Place, and Black Queer Performance in Indie Drama

When I first came across *Anacostia* shortly after its premiere in 2009, I found it difficult to make it past the first episode. The sound was inconsistent. Awkwardly composed shots dragged on without any cuts. The acting was committed but difficult to connect with after noticing technical inconsistencies. After interviewing creator Anthony Anderson, I forgot about *Anacostia*. When I checked back in at the end of the season, the episodes were averaging more than ten thousand plays on Vimeo. Clearly, I had missed something: the writing, a plot constructed to keep story lines open-ended propelled by dialogue uttered by actors committed to their characters and representing a specific community—Anacostia, once a black middle-class neighborhood now known in the mainstream press mostly for crime. The pilot for *Anacostia* begins with a shooting, and viewers needed to stay tuned to get the story, which revolves around a black gay relationship. In this way, *Anacostia* situates violence within black *life*—not death, as mainstream news does. As Anderson says: "The show is escapism. . . . It shows Anacostia in a completely different way that I don't think people get a chance to see. People usually see 'local teen gets shot,' but, they don't see everyday that there are people out there working, striving and have great lives" (Ali-Coleman 2009). But violence is only one theme in *Anacostia*; the plot also explores adultery, addiction, financial struggles, and homophobia, the latter theme unfolding through a story line with Anderson in a starring role. *Anacostia* narrates black urban life outside DC with a focus on how sexuality and violence shape families and communities, featuring a rare black gay story line within a drama, six years before *Empire* (one of YouTube's first dramas, *Chump ChangeS* [2006], also does this). As Darnell Hunt argues in his analysis of *Anacostia* as "the end of television as we know it":

> *Anacostia* captures the flavor of a community not typically represented in network productions shot on carefully constructed studio sets or at iconic locations. At the expense of acting that may be a little uneven at

times, it provides its audiences with regular peeks inside the homes and offices of regular Anacostia folk. It features in its establishing shots area landmarks, such as the "Big Chair," that only locals would know. And most importantly, Anderson took plotlines one might see on network television and converted them into altogether different stories by placing black characters, a black community and contemporary black issues at the very center of the web series' narratives. (2014, 169)

Hunt identifies a mode of drama production scaled to the entertainment demands of local and marginalized communities, for whom place, race, gender, and sexuality shape their everyday lives in subtle and explicit ways.

I narrate this story to distinguish between different kinds of "production value," a term industry workers use to describe the investments necessary to deliver the highest-quality product to consumers. Most invocations of production value by workers refer to technical crafts performed by below-the-line workers, especially camera work and cinematography but including sound, editing, and design, including makeup, costume, set, and location (Caldwell 2008). The standard for "high production value" is set by studio films, which spend the most time and money per page of the script. Television production values are lower: shots are simpler; scenes are often shot in studios, not on location, special effects budgets are lower, and so forth. Web television production values are often deemed too low for critics and network executives to give them attention. But, as my story suggests, a focus on technical production value prevents critics from seeing what is seen by fans of certain genres and with certain identities *undervalued* by the industry. This is particularly true for drama, which unlike comedy requires more screen time to narrate complex and interlocking stories from larger ensembles to give fans time to get to know characters. More time requires more investment, since shoots are longer and technical crews need to be paid. As such, indie dramas are often weakest in technical production value, though they often improve as the series progresses.

Yet the most innovative indie dramas compensate for lower funds for technical production by situating narratives within specific community concerns or fantasies and often within their personal experiences. Race shapes how narratives unfold, and many of the most popular black queer dramas show how race intersects with gender, sexuality, place, state and economic institutions, and social norms. In this way, indie drama creators are reshaping television's role in the culture: redefining its "choric" or "bardic" functions to speak not to the nation—as Horace Newcomb, Robert Alley, John Hartley, and John

Fiske theorize from mass-mediated TV—but to marginalized communities, while simultaneously deepening its "lyric" function, less social and more personal, to connect to individual realities and fantasies in those groups (Newcomb and Alley 1983; Hartley and Fiske 2003). The goal is to represent identities more fully than is possible in corporate television. Or, as LAWeb Fest founder Michael Ajakwe told Christine Acham: "Webisode producers are covering every aspect of Black life online. African Americans are no longer begging the networks to produce their shows and their ideas" (Acham 2012, 66).

The range of production contexts and politics in the indie TV market reflects how producers respond differently to the resources they have as artists and the needs they see in their communities. Black queer communities have greater need for representation, but producers have fewer resources, so they have to be creative to tell complex dramatic narratives. Casting, for instance, is particularly complicated when narratives require an ensemble of characters to interact, love, conspire, betray, and so forth, constructing identities and furthering the plot. Linzy has spent much of his career negotiating the politics of casting on low budgets. While Linzy's first cast members were family, Linzy initially cast himself in his narratives. In our interview he recalled voicing dialogue into tape recorders with music playing in the background; it was easier than trying to entice family and friends to act.

Voicing all his dialogue became an art practice for Linzy, a way to ground his representations in his black, queer, and southern identities. While his student work features actors using their own voices, *Melody Set Me Free* has Linzy doing the voices for all twenty-one characters in dialogue and song. This technique offers efficiencies and creates value. It relieves actors of some of the burden of interpretation; production involves actors performing in "drag" to Linzy's voice. Linzy's vocal performance shapes their behavior as they make sense of changes in pitch, space, and volume. The characters' voices feature a range of intonations and styles, but in many Linzy displays his very specific black southern accent. This gives the narrative a sense of specificity around place, despite the range of actors hired and (most of) it shooting on sets at PS1. According to Linzy: "My dialect is based on the region I'm from. But you can't put everybody from the South in that category. You can't even put everybody in my family in that category cause it's different styles of speaking, but if you went there and listened to different people talk, you would kind of hear similarities, but since mine's so performative, I'm often . . . taking stuff from pop mainstream television culture as well, and not just . . . my hometown."

Linzy sets his narratives in a small, stateless, black town in the South, with voices mostly, but not exclusively, inspired by his hometown. Linzy said he finds it difficult to imagine his characters in places he has not been. *Melody Set Me Free* contains no exterior establishing shots, partly to allow Linzy to shoot anywhere he has the resources. It also empowers or inspires viewers to construct a place while keeping them rooted in the "emotional" and "physical" space of the characters' performances. Linzy compensates for his lack of budget for location-based shooting by focusing the performance on mannerisms and body language. He explained: "I sometimes think it helps push me more when some of my resources are limited. Not that I want my resources to always be limited. But, that's when I have to get, like, *really creative.*" Linzy's practice of producing identities and their place through his voice is an innovation borne of having lower resources for technical production. Yet Linzy embraces national culture. It influences this idea of the show, its production, and the performances in it, even if national television would not develop his work. According to Tavia Nyong'o: "Linzy's adoption of the soap opera form approaches it with the historical affect of its rural, Southern black female audience, which he refuses to relinquish for an affirmative vision of television in which minorities are adequately represented" (2010, 76). Linzy's own identity anchors the enterprise, putting black, queer, southern, and American performance in constant, productive tension.

Because it takes considerable skill to produce multiple identities across lengthy narratives, Linzy uses a core practice of drag—the lip-synch—as the foundation for production. He records all the dialogue and music before filming. All the voices are his; actors are lip-synching to him. Structuring his dramas with histories of queer performance (through the lip-synching body) and new queer production practices (through the actor as drag queen), Linzy expands and queers the art of serial drama. In production it allows Linzy to cast and recast a range of actors who are diverse in identity and craft— outside himself, as he plays a plurality of the roles. For instance, the role of Hope, the series' scheming antagonist whose husband left his fortune to KK Queen, has been played by three different performance artists due to scheduling: in the short film, Justin Vivian Bond, a singer and white transwoman; in season one by Isabelle Lumpkin, a conceptual artist and biracial cis-woman who performs as Narcissister; and the feature edit by Jibz Cameron, a white and cis-woman who performs as Dynasty Handbag. The late Sahara Davenport starred in the short but had to be recast because she landed a role on *RuPaul's Drag Race*. The series' cast features industry veterans of television drama Natasha Lyonne (*Orange Is the New Black*) and January LaVoy

(*One Life to Live*) alongside black queer academics (Frank Leon Roberts), visual artists (Wardell Milan), web series producers (Dwight Allen O'Neal of *Christopher Street TV*), and rappers (Malik So Chic). Beyond casting, the lip-synch method saves the cost of paying a crew member to capture sound, freeing Linzy as a director to focus on the actors' performance with their own bodies. In performance, the act of drag and Linzy's asynchronous voice mark it as queer, adding another layer of drama to the narrative. The rupture of body with voice, of interior feeling with exterior performance, of sincerity with authenticity forces viewers to critically engage at every moment with identity and narrative as constructed. Linzy's project opens up control over the narrative beyond the creator-artist to a community of artists, producers, and the viewers of the show.

It is also a feat to behold, but a different kind of feat than legacy TV's fantasies of white patriarchal empire. Without access to a green screen, Linzy has performed multiple characters in the same scene on the same day. Recalling a day in which he performed KK Queen and her children Rose, Jacob, and Patience, Linzy details the struggles of managing photography—a consistent shot—and trying to bring out in performance the subtle differences between characters who are kin: "I was literally crazy by the end of the day, trying to switch in and out. People think they're all alike, but it's like, trying to slide in and get the differences, so they read somewhat different, even though you know they're all me." At each level of production—script, vocal performance, visual performance, and editing—Linzy manages character and narrative development with a focus on specificity and sincerity. His taking on multiple roles facilitates production and highlights the creative loss of Hollywood's exclusion of queer people of color from those roles, all while providing an entertaining narrative about the struggles of black women in society and the music industry.

Narrative Complexity as Intersectional Drama

Viewers demand character development from dramatic narratives as material for social interaction. Historically, corporate television networks in America have met this need with large and constantly changing ensembles in daytime and with slightly smaller ensembles but higher technical production values and mythic narratives in prime time—the so-called complex narratives of the second golden age of television. With less funding for large casts and lavish sets and costumes, indie producers must rescale drama fans' demand for robust narratives in innovative ways. The work of digital production studio

Pemberley Digital provides a case. Started by Hank Green, a writer known on YouTube, with his brother John, as Vlogbrothers, the studio debuted with a hit, *The Lizzie Bennet Diaries*. Writer Bernie Su adapted Jane Austen's *Pride and Prejudice* for YouTube by making Elizabeth Bennet a communications grad student who vlogs. The entire series is shot with characters speaking to the audience in direct address. Pemberley Digital advanced the innovations of earlier vlog series *lonelygirl15* and *The Guild*, both of which eventually moved past the vlog format. By telling the story through a narrative device where characters are in the same location and are composed in a single shot, all narrative time is spent on character development and interaction. It also costs less, so Pemberley was able to make one hundred episodes of *Lizzie Bennet*, along with four other series, in just two years. The focus on character also made the narrative easily transferrable to other platforms, such that each series has concurrent narratives on social media sites Twitter, Pinterest, Instagram, Facebook, and/or Tumblr. All these innovative series focus on young, white women, creating community around (almost always white) "culture of feels" (Stein 2015).

Gender, sexuality, and race structure the narratives and technologies of serial drama, from daytime serials (soap operas) to contemporary prime-time serials and indie web dramas working at smaller scale. The daytime formats derive from the early twentieth century when white, middle-class women were expected to be at home and have leisure time. Daytime serials offered narratives with expansive casts, slow forward plot movement, and constant recapitulation of events and character reactions to them to meet the daily production demand, allowing fans to keep up and networks to fill less marketable daytime hours. Many innovative web dramas like those of Pemberly Digital extend the daytime tradition, altering how narratives are structured and released without necessarily changing their racialized address.

Because the entire family is assumed to be home by night, prime-time hours are more valuable, so legacy networks are spending more money on production, make fewer episodes, and historically focus narratives on white, straight, and gender-conforming characters as a hedge against the risks of high-cost production. Casts are smaller, plots move faster, and episodes are increasingly expensive and designed to stand alone. Competition has also made dramas' gendered appeal more complex. The differences in production and distribution affect narrative structures: for one, daytime serials spend more time showing connections between relationships, "feminizing" their critical reception (Mittell 2015). Building on the work of Robyn Warhol on the Victorian novel, Linda Williams's work on melodrama, and John Fiske's theorization of television narrative in the 1980s, Jason Mittell deconstructs the "feminization" of daytime "soaps" and the presumed "masculinization" of prime-time serial dramas: "It becomes clear that most complex television offers a blend of gendered appeals. These gender mixtures are a comparatively recent phenomenon within mainstream fictional television.... Fiske contrasts the feminine facets of open narrative deferment, emotional expressiveness, domestic settings, and character complexity against masculine norms of exclusively male professional spheres, rational actions, and narrative closure. What is striking is how difficult it is to find a contemporary prime-time drama that fits neatly into his feminine or masculine paradigms" (251). Mittell's reading of serial melodrama in contemporary complex television identifies how contemporary series about men deconstruct masculinity (e.g., *Breaking Bad*), and series about women can hew to Fiske's masculine norms (e.g., *The Good Wife*).[4] This gender mixing reflects changes in the function of dramatic narratives in the television industry. As Mittell has written, genre differences reflect industrial, cultural, and social factors in how programs are produced, distributed, and received by the public.

A competitive market in search of new sources of value has expanded norms of gender, race, and sexuality in serial drama, but legacy TV networks have been slow to develop truly intersectional drama. Emboldened by small-scale production and networked distribution, *Melody Set Me Free* and Linzy's larger body of work intervene in the genre's narrative traditions by integrating race and sexuality into their representation of gender, which networks and studios do not. Linzy's story reflects a thorough critique of media empire and its near-complete denial of the gender and sexual diversity within racialized communities in its pursuit of the affective attachments of mass (white) audiences. The narrative of *Melody Set Me Free* revolves around KK Queen's pursuit of empire: in music, pursuing "nasty ass hits," and in art, pursuing information. In her quest, KK Queen tries to rise to the top on her own, to leave her black family and community behind or put them in conflict, but her efforts consistently backfire. Using narrative conventions of daytime serials (open-ended episodes, recapitulation of events and relationships, studio-set domestic settings) and contemporary prime-time serials (genre-mixing, the focus on an antihero, event-based episodes), Linzy crafts a narrative about a black woman's quest for power made complex by her attachments to black family, community, and artists.

Over the course of three seasons, we see how KK's plans fail, partly due to her blindness to what her artists want and her desire to consolidate power with little regard for its impact on black and queer art and community. The first episode, "Return to the Battlefield," depicts KK at her strongest, giving the audience a glimpse into her business and relationships, narrated through queer dialogue, song, and performance. It starts with Patience and Bill singing with Clark, "Pain in My Butt," describing love through anal lubrication, and Faith, singing her own tune, "my pussy won't run dry." These are KK's star artists, on whom she has pinned hopes of owning "one of the top nasty ass record companies." Both songs describe frictionless intercourse from characters played by cisgender men, suggesting KK's sexual supremacy. The other song in the episode is a pop piece of braggadocio, pitched by Grace to KK, who likes it even though "it's not as nasty as it could have been." Linzy gives the audience hope for KK's queer music empire, built on reality stardom and sexual explicitness, but her art empire is crumbling. Survey counts are down. KK's art business frames the series, being mentioned only in the first and last episode of the third season. Indeed, the first scene with dialogue is in an art gallery, where Bill expresses his passion for art over music, much to Patience's dismay. He's trying to sell work, and Hope, KK's rival, barges in wanting to buy: "I need a new painting to discuss at my next cocktail party," which is funny because she too never mentions either of those things again; still, we later learn she did buy Bill's work to woo him away from Patience and bring him closer to her side of the family. Ignoring art and family while dressed in an ornate Proenza Schouler coat, KK spends the episode seducing two men to shore up her music empire: Clark, to motivate him to produce a hit, and BT, to thwart Hope.

The narrative of the series unpacks the richness and depth of black sexuality by slowly revealing, by season three, the sexual interconnectedness of the characters: this is one big family. Linzy's portrayal of KK's sexual assertion in the first episode—we see her take the men she wants—is not characteristic of the series. There are no visual representations of sex in *Melody Set Me Free*. Sex appears in songs and in the stories characters tell about their lives and each other. Often sex is secret, and its products—children—kept in the dark about their origins. Patience is KK's daughter, given to Mama because she'd given away a child (Grace) years earlier, and KK's dad was going to press charges against Patience's father. We learn Hope is KK's cousin after it's revealed that Hope's niece, Summer (January LaVoy), is pregnant with Bill's child (Summer runs the art residency he left for). The narrative peels away decades of family secrets, buried for fear of public and state condemnation. Linzy delves deep into tropes of black representations of sexuality, revealing "how black sexualities are characterized by hypervisibility and confinement and subject to regulation and surveillance" (Snorton 2014, 14). Rather than craft a narrative about the "down low," Linzy's body and voice make black male sexuality visible in a myriad of ways: dressed as women with makeup and wigs; represented literally by black cis-male actors playing sexually violent or dishonest characters; and manifested sonically by Linzy's voice digitally manipulated to reach the lowest and highest octaves. Freed from literal representation, black sexuality can operate organically, shaping relationships based on character interdependencies and the threat and actions of institutions like corporations, hospitals, the police, and the media.

Linzy queers the black family and its representation through a narrative focused both on struggles over capital and on reconciliation across gender, sexuality, age, and class. As KK's family changes, so does ownership and management of the company. Once she discovers she is KK's daughter, Patience serves as acting CEO while KK is in a coma—she was shot by Faith for cutting her song. KK's children Jacob and Rose return, only to find out Isaac—who sexually preyed on Rose when she was younger—finagled part ownership for Hope, who gets her own label after shooting Isaac ("Courts felt sorry for her. She never had any good lawyers," says Rose, in a nod to broader inequalities). KK awakes from a coma to find Patience peddling "mushy wushy songs" instead of "nasty ass hits." While that strategy worked from En Strobe, renamed Chastity's Churen by KK, KK wants to stay nasty by doing a compilation record and by putting Hope and her artists on a reality show to embarrass them. Yet she is the one embarrassed in the penultimate episode by her estranged sister Mimi Queen, who goes on to public access to sermonize against KK, her business, and her family: "I will / lead y'all / to a better place / yes I will / See my name / is Mimi Queen / Yes it is / Unlike my sister KK queen / y'all don't hear me / See she got all the churen / running right here / singing that nasty so and so / But I'm here to tell y'all / my sister might be doomed / y'all don't hear me / Cuz all she do / is keep a bunch of ole mess."

Mimi's gospel-style speech about KK, her "churen" and "mess," is designed to shame KK into believing it was self-sabotage that caused her to get shot and end up in a coma. KK believes Mimi is starting a "fight in the name of inspiration" and "using me to get ratings." In the show's moral universe, where most people are focused on advancing their own careers, she is probably right, but with Hope working for her, KK should probably learn to keep her family close. Instead, the third season ends with KK telling off her daughter Rose, who has a crush on the family doctor, Dr. Goodfeel, who KK has asked out. The sexual feud excavates deep roots. KK had crushed on Isaac years ago, when Isaac was having sex with a young Rose: "This will not be the sequel to Fuck Mama's Man. I promise you if you *try it again!*"

The drama's narrative shifts in the end by asking the viewer to question the relationship between art, capital, and identity. The final episode of the third season cuts to a voice that sounds like Faith's. KK has called to check in on the art survey company, and the voice responds: "Nice to meet the Queen." While the voice administers the survey, the viewer sees books and magazines like *Artforum* on a shelf, and a special-edition book from Sundance. The survey is interesting in how it foregrounds issues of labor, identity, and community in the art world:

Q: *What should be the minimum age an artist should be allowed to emerge?*
A: 16, B: 18, C: 21, D: 25, E: 30, F: 50
Q: *What should be the maximum age an artist should be allowed to emerge?*
A: 30, B: 40, C: 50, D: 65, E: 80, F: 125
Q: *In your art community how would you describe the powers that be?*
A: Amazing, B: Alright, C: Above Average, D: Balanced, E: Touch, or F: Psycho

Melody Set Me Free thus ends by querying KK, but also the audience, on their position on/in capitalism. The first two questions raise the specter of aging, when artists are known and valued. It cannot be the same for every artist, and after sitting through almost three hours of narrative about black artists, one thinks of the limits placed on black bodies for success. Who imposes those limits? "The powers that be." Linzy forces KK to confront her own power while asking us to reflect broadly on the structures behind the valuing of art, ending the season with the word "psycho." Is KK psycho? She has power in this narrative, but we've seen how it is circumscribed, particularly by sex and family. Moreover, there are other powers in art: How do we feel about them?

It may seem strange to end three seasons so focused on a black woman's pursuit of power with a questioning of power from a voice whose body we have not seen. We know it is Linzy's voice, because they all are, but it has no character, so it has been evacuated of agency, perhaps in some ways of gender and race. At this point in the narrative, it may as well represent the postidentity "powers that be." *Melody Set Me Free* ends with "uncompromising withdrawal," which as Tavia Nyong'o (2010), in his analysis of *SweetBerry Sonnet*, Linzy's 2008 video song cycle, has suggested, is an evacuation that is political. Theorizing the artist as a "punk"—both the anarchic artist and the "passive" black queer—Nyong'o suggests that Linzy's performance is neither full critique nor an embrace of national culture and its erasure of black queer genius. It could not be. While it is a monumental achievement, *Melody Set Me Free* cannot correct decades of exclusion. As a corrective, it is set up to fail. Instead, it opens up space in history—here, television, art, and media history—for the engagement of black sexual difference in ways that disrupt discourses of authenticity. It is a small space, so small it is almost invisible. The promise of full representation of black life on television has not been fulfilled, despite the importance of blackness to the technological and industrial transformation of television after the introduction of new media—see, notably, broadcasters' rapid adoption of the black sitcoms in the 1990s in response to white flight to cable and other media (H. Gray 1995). As viewers we must assess the value of the drama we have experienced and its place in our appreciation of media and art: "What the ethics of sublimation effect is not a transcendence of sex, but the puncturing of history at its core. . . . The anticipation of eternal return—itself an antagonistic refusal of the breathless expectations of a post-racial world, or one where sexual difference will no longer matter—opens out both history and futurity" (Nyong'o 2010, 85).

José Muñoz picks up Nyong'o's analysis by theorizing how Linzy's work represents queer virtuosity and failure, in the tradition of midcentury art filmmaker Jack Smith. There are several feats in *Melody Set Me Free*. That the credits read "written, edited, all voices and songs by Kalup Linzy" reflects this clearly. Linzy's shouldering the historical burdens of representing black sexual life amid ambivalent desires for inclusion in white fantasies (the daytime and prime-time serial) can only lead to exhaustion and be sustained through a certain evacuation of the self into the drama. While the queer nature of *Melody Set Me Free* may distance most viewers—the videos average three to five thousand plays on YouTube—Linzy rewards those who take the journey, who lose themselves in his drama, with an invitation to a different time and space. Through its production, narrative, and distribution *Melody Set Me Free* gives audiences a vision of the black queer soap opera they never had and of the art community they could have in the future if they embrace and question the history and future of television drama.

Notes

1 In 2014 Linzy released the first episode of the fourth season, "We Kiki," costarring Macaulay Culkin and the Pizza Underground.

2 Personal interview, July 13, 2013, Brooklyn, NY.

3 This is part of a long-standing American tradition in which racialized or racist melodramas, in particular around blackness, function to validate new audiovisual media. We can think of *Birth of a Nation* as cinema's first blockbuster (Diawara 1993; Guerrero 1993;

hooks 1992); *Amos 'n' Andy* as being "the most popular and influential early radio fiction program" (Mittell 2015); the civil rights movement as national melodrama validating television's power of representation while blaxploitation revitalizes cinema in a period of stagnation (Keeling 2007); spectacular performances of black excellence in popular arts and sports as defining early cable channels, like Michael Jackson's *Thriller* for MTV or *Thrilla in Manila* for HBO (Tannenbaum and Marks 2011); and black viewers sustaining broadcast television amid this competition, particularly NBC, Fox, and UPN (H. Gray 2005; Havens 2013; Zook 1999).

4 Amanda D. Lotz (2014) offers this analysis of deconstructing masculinity.

11

Debt by Design

Race and Home Valorization on Reality TV

EVA C. HAGEMAN

In May 2009, Home and Garden Television (HGTV) premiered *$250,000 Challenge*, a reality show focused on a bloc of homeowners competing to achieve the best renovation, judged by a panel of expert HGTV designers and hosts. The show had particularly high stakes for those who faced possible foreclosure and looked to the cash prize to rescue their mortgage. If they failed to impress at the design challenge, they could lose more than just the game. This show literalizes the union of debt and design in real estate reality television. Here the possibility of success is reserved for those contestants who work within the aesthetic parameters of the network and invest in a normalizing project of what I later describe as "home valorization." As the second-place Marquezes say in the finale: "The truth is while we didn't win the $250,000, we did add a lot of value to our house" (Kreisberg and 495 Productions 2009).

The HGTV network was launched in 1994 as part of the Scripps Networks, and it grew during the very same years as the buildup to the financial and housing crisis of 2008. Its programs reflect many of the features of this crisis, including its often unacknowledged racialized aspects, and primarily revolve around the creation of real estate value, design aesthetics, and narratives about the conceptual framework of "home." This essay focuses on HGTV's reality programming about real estate, and the relationship between property, taste, and race. In particular, I am interested in how race and class stratification come to be represented through ideas of *lifestyle* in which certain rituals of everyday life are aestheticized and, in turn, measured on an affective scale from pleasure to disgust and used to determine the value of everything from job worthiness to real estate appraisal.

Scholars have argued that multiculturalism under neoliberalism erases the lived effects of structural inequality by equating the increased or improved representation of minorities (racial and sexual as well as women) in the media with greater forms of equality in society at large (Bonilla-Silva 2014; H. Gray 2005; Melamed 2011; Mukherjee 2006b). Key to this imaginary is an understanding that inequality is best remedied through individual responsibility and participation. In other (perhaps more televisual) words, structures like racism are presumed to no longer have an audience and are therefore "over." But in many cultural contexts, including reality television, these so-called postracial ideals are used to reinscribe racial boundaries. This essay looks at real estate–themed reality television to analyze how race is woven into the highly stylized fabric of daily life and represented on TV. How does race operate in a genre of television and an economic process in which its significance is obscured? I focus in particular on the racialization of the abstract concept of value in the housing market.

The rise of reality television is a particularly useful phenomenon for examining the specific disciplinary and pedagogical technologies and affective registers of neoliberalism (see Hearn 2008; McCarthy 2007; Ouellette 2008). A number of commentators have focused on the function of neoliberalism in reality television through an analysis of the effects of deregulation, union busting, and other aspects of the economic restructuring of the television industry, as well as through studies that emphasize the entrepreneurial and citizen-making pedagogies of the genre (see, e.g., Hearn 2008; Ouellette and Hay 2008). Fewer studies highlight how race specifically operates as a part of these neoliberal transformations in reality television.[1] But as this essay shows, the process by which the structural forces of race and racism are produced within the aesthetic forms of neoliberal multicultural economics, what I call the "lifestyling of race," is an essential feature of the genre. As a result, an analysis of postracial ideologies provides a uniquely helpful framework for understanding the popularity of reality television under neoliberalism.

Building on existing scholarship about race, branding, and lifestyle television, I further illustrate "the quiet operations of race" in the network HGTV.[2] Reality television quite literally capitalizes on the politics of multicultural representation to cast race and racial difference as merely a matter of individual choice and taste that can be mobilized for individual profit. Thus, when the racial politics of neoliberalism are included in our analytic lens, we get an expanded understanding not only of the place of race in reality television's representations, as is the focus of this essay, but also in its development and production, the participation of its actors, and the pleasures of its fans.[3]

The Postrace Lifestyle

Although this essay focuses on real estate television, the dynamic by which racialization is stylized as the main accessory of daily life is a feature of reality television in general, be it the *Real Housewives* fascination with the embodiment of classy, or how the *Bad Girls Club* showcases it. Laurie Ouellette (2016) shows how lifestyle has emerged as a key component of the fragmentation of the mass market and the rise of niche programming in television. Or, as I explore here, HGTV's instruction on how to choose the right tenant for your income property by looking at prospective tenants' cars and then making the rent *just high enough*. According to this strategy, good tenants are the ones who can afford premium market rates and cars (that are clean inside, of course). Here racial distinction emerges through a highly aestheticized code that is often referred to as lifestyle. Lifestyle blurs racial and class divides by maintaining an imagined color-blind and postracial ideology where the economic playing field has been leveled through privately funded transformations—in other words, where classy women are self-possessed, drive a clean car, and pay premium rent. That is, on reality real estate programming, the seemingly mundane and unremarkable characteristics of daily life are produced as stylized commodities that, in turn, create the context that situates certain life circumstances and choices within a hierarchy of value.

In HGTV real estate shows, lifestyle is a branded and sanitized form of racialization that is produced as both authentic and uniform. Sarah Banet-Weiser demonstrates how ideas of authenticity are used within branding strategies as a "creative production . . . within and between residual and emergent codes of capital and aesthetics" (2012, 96). Using the example of street art, she argues that authentic markers are used by both street artists and corporate brand managers to capitalize on the racialized aesthetics originally associated with graffiti by making them nonthreatening to white consumers. One example of how this mode of branding translates into the lifestyling of race is the motto of the Oprah Winfrey Network (OWN), "It's your life, OWN it," which suggests that "life" is an individualized commodity that can only be authenticated through branded ownership (Oprah Winfrey Network 2011). Race is indirectly referenced through the connection to Oprah, who is one of the world's most famous black women but for whom race is not cast as an impediment to her own branded success. On HGTV, this kind of sanitized authenticity is then used to develop and extract value from real estate as a cultural commodity.

David Harvey's theory of rent is useful for exploring how value functions here. Harvey outlines the nature of the relationship between culture and capital through the concept of monopoly rent. In brief, rent is extracted by withholding a commodity from the marketplace while speculating on the future values of the object. Harvey also shows how the symbolic capital involved in the process of monopoly rent relies on a contradiction that at once demands uniqueness and homogeneity. This concept shows how taste becomes important to the production of value within a cultural commodity (Harvey 2002). For the lifestyles featured on HGTV, this means a constant tension to remain irreplaceable while also blending in with the crowd. Building on Ouellette's concept of the "lifestyling of television," which asserts the mass fragmentation of the television market into a myriad of instructional programming, I argue that within the postracial representations of reality television, lifestyle and its concomitant characterizations act as stand-ins for race where it is purportedly absent. This lifestyling of race helps not only to produce differential values in real estate but also to develop equity in land values as well as real estate television franchises. The lifestyling of race is thus a process of aestheticizing certain cultural and racial referents to maximize capital returns.

The shows examined in this essay use the lifestyling of race as a narrative device to produce pleasurable stories of postracial upward mobility and success in real estate investment. The stories on these shows feature a multicultural cast of mostly "inoffensive" people with seemingly banal characteristics looking for and achieving an average-sized (or sometimes larger) piece of the American Dream. The ease and predictability of these shows' narratives make them pleasing and easy to watch for viewers. The story is brief, with normatively attractive aesthetics (including both cast and design features), and nearly always offers a satisfying transformation and/or conclusion. Like most television programming, these narratives are of course offered in service to advertising and are thus attached to an array of multinational brands that are featured throughout the episodes. This partnership works to maintain the relationship between branding and authenticity asserted by Banet-Weiser, where the creative transformation is shown to reveal the potential capital gains on both the property and its imagined associated lifestyle. However, the aesthetic pleasures of these shows also obscure the real racialized exclusions that are manifest in and help to maintain the real estate market.

For example, HGTV shows actively promote certain aesthetic parameters as the true determinants of value in the real estate market. These programs formulate specific guidelines that direct all aspects of the design inside and outside the home so as to add more equity to the real estate investment. Although race is rarely directly referenced within the design guidelines, flourishes that are often associated with different racial and ethnic groups, such as bright colors that are characterized as "loud" and "overpowering," are actively discouraged as devaluing while so-called neutral elements that are figured as "calm" and "inviting" are said to bring more value.[4] The HGTV shows that seek to provide instruction on building home equity often encourage home renovators to stick with "neutral" color palates that include colors such as white, beige, and gray, so as not to deter potential home buyers. The hosts and real estate professionals featured on these shows assert that these color schemes allow potential buyers to imagine themselves in the home, whereas bright and bold colors are seen as specific choices that will only speak to a narrow range of buyers. While these claims in themselves do not make any overt references to race, the homes and episodes in which these bold colors are featured carry deeply racialized connotations. For instance, the B-roll shots of houses in international locations such as Latin America or the Caribbean, as well as urban areas within and outside of the United States, frequently feature people of color in the background. At the same time, episodes featuring homes in suburban enclaves, such as in the midwestern United States, rarely show people of color in the background (even though we know that people of color live and work in a variety of locations in the Midwest as well).

In this way, postracial ideas work to reinscribe racial boundaries, and lifestyle becomes a sort of de facto (popular) cultural policy in which taste is part of a normalization process. These shows produce standards of taste within the marketing of houses that position the house as cultural object. The lifestyle of the owner is outlined by race and class and lends value to the house as a *home*, making it so the house is valorized as a *home*. This is promoted through assessments that calculate the aesthetic elements of a house. As another example, on a number of shows an important feature is stainless steel appliances or white cabinets, and homes without these are understood as "fixer-uppers" in need of repair. Lifestyle programming promotes certain aesthetic choices and cultural ideals as a way to manage property values within a stratified racialized landscape. Racialized characterizations of people of color, especially black and brown people, as loud and aggressive are repackaged as aesthetic choices. At the same time, these descriptions create whiteness as a neutral category of "everyman" by normalizing descriptions of white people who are then figured as calm and reasonable. This essay shows that terms like "neutral" color are anything but, and that they mask the racialized biases in the world of real estate and design that deeply affect the prospects for certain racialized groups to gain real estate equity.

Booms and Bursts

Much has been written about the final burst of the so-called housing bubble in 2008. It is generally agreed that this most recent boom to bust ran from the late 1990s to about 2006, with the ensuing economic collapse approximately two years later when mortgage-backed securities lost value due to increasing foreclosures and several banks, including the nation's largest mortgage backers, Fannie Mae and Freddie Mac, went bankrupt. These bankruptcies had a domino effect in the economy, causing job loss, which in turn caused more foreclosures. In an article for the *Nation*, Dean Baker argues that after the stock market crash of 2000, housing investment was viewed as safe. In turn, this increased investment caused housing prices to rise at incomparable rates between 1999 and 2006. Ultimately, the bust was caused by a cycle of speculative financing practices using adjustable-rate or subprime loans with interest rates (and thus the corresponding mortgage payments) that "ballooned" or increased dramatically after an initial period. Millions of moderate-income families suffered under these ballooning payment structures and faced foreclosure.[5]

It is interesting, then, that the birth and initial heyday of HGTV roughly corresponded to these years, and the development of its programming provides a useful way to map out some of the major dynamics that unfolded. In 1994, HGTV was launched as the anchor for the Scripps Networks. Owned by the Cincinnati-based EW Scripps Company, Scripps has since become the parent company to five other networks, all of which it markets under the category of "lifestyle" television, including *The Food Network*, DIY, *Fine Living*, and *Great American Country*. Its CEO, Ken Lowe, pitched the idea of HGTV to the networks "by drawing them a house and then explaining how each room could be the subject of its own show. The board bit, and in 1994, HGTV was born." Lowe was a "weekend architect" and "home buff," who became frustrated with his projects and thought there should be a network dedicated to these home improvement visions. Scripps invested $75 million, and the network launched in December 1994 with 90 percent original programming, much of it reality-based. The shows focused on the five prime categories of Remodeling, Gardening, Crafts, Decorating, and At Home. These original categories were later expanded between 1995 and 1996 to include niche programming in food, real estate, and collectibles (Albiniak 2007).

The year 1999 gave a start not only to the housing bubble but also to the show *House Hunters* on HGTV. *House Hunters* follows home buyers as they move through a foreshortened version of buying a house. In a formulaic half hour, the buyer or buyers look at three houses, weigh the pros and cons of each, decide on one to purchase, make an offer, and buy (and sometimes renovate) the house. The show concludes with a follow-up to showcase how the homeowners have settled in. During the years before the collapse, programming about real estate on HGTV continued to increase as the housing market bubble expanded. These shows informed viewers how to buy and sell and, *most important*, how to "flip" houses for profit. These stories featured a cast of supposedly diverse, "postracial" elites even as racial segregation and class stratification remained stable, or even grew. This obscures the long history of exclusionary housing practices that helped to produce the national ideology of homeownership and incorporates calls for redress (through diversity of access) into neoliberal practices that fold "diversity" into home valorization.

House Hunters was soon joined by several other home-buying shows on HGTV, each with a slightly different formula offering insight into a range of standard real estate issues, from first-time home buying to how to strengthen your investment and improve your possible return. Shows that were on air just around 2008 included *Property Virgins*, *My First Place*, and *Hidden Potential*; the first two offered slightly different takes on the first-time home buyer experience, the third show illustrated ideas for how to transform a so-called fixer-upper into the house of your dreams. More recent programs offer information on investment potential, such as *Property Brothers*, a show hosted by twins, one a contractor and the other a real estate broker, who help people buy and renovate older properties into "dream homes." Yet another is *Fixer Upper*, in which a husband and wife design-and-contracting team do the same.[6]

Complementing these shows have been house-selling programs, which offer advice on how to make one's house most attractive to buyers. These shows too reflected the changing real estate market. Just after the 2008 burst, they ranged from shows that instruct basic house selling and capitalization like *Income Property*, *Buy and Sell*, and *Curb Appeal* to more anxious topics like *My House Is Worth What?*, *Get It Sold!*, *The Unsellables*, and *Buy Me*. In these programs homeowners are shown how to increase the value of their home in ways such as building a rental suite in a portion of the property or through renovations and staging to increase the appeal to larger portions of the buying market. The more anxious shows instruct homeowners and viewers in the harsh aesthetic realities of property value as well as the difficulties of value decline within the market.

It is important to note that the housing crisis was motored not only by the use of subprime loans in general but by those targeted to people of color in particular. Subprime loans are a direct descendant of earlier loan practices that systematically excluded people of color, such as redlining. Lenders instead targeted these groups, and then, as Catherine Squires shows, the media used postracial and neoliberal logics of race to cast the people of color who consumed these loans as greedy individuals who took on too much debt (Squires 2012). These representations figure the high rate of foreclosure in black and brown communities as a result of poor choices rather than a system of deregulation that targeted communities of color. This dynamic is part of uneven development, in which global capital needs both depressed and speculative markets so as to produce a gap for profit, on both a local and a global scale (N. Smith 1996). Instead of being framed as areas that were depressed for and through speculation, the foreclosures were framed as so-called poor choices that were inherent in the lifestyles of black and brown people. Black and brown communities were represented as unable to maintain and uphold certain ways of living that are structured through debt and rely on specific indebted investment strategies. This was the case even though, at the same time, these speculative practices placed these communities as always already foreclosed.

Indeed, foreclosure emerged as an essential transmedia narrative for HGTV. From 2006 to 2015, HGTV.com also ran an online real estate listing site, FrontDoor.com. FrontDoor and HGTV were partnered with several of the top real estate brokerages and listing sites in the country, including Prudential Real Estate and Zillow ("FrontDoor.com Continues to Grow" 2008). The site offered ample advice on all aspects of home buying, owning, and selling in conjunction with the content available on HGTV.com (which includes archived programming). In continuing the narrative of speculative and failed investment in the real estate market, FrontDoor began to list foreclosures post-2008 along with guides on how to deal with foreclosure from all perspectives (i.e., both how to purchase foreclosed property and how to avoid or manage foreclosure).

The dynamics of uneven development continue to be dramatized on more recent HGTV shows, such as *Fixer Upper* and *Home Town*, which demonstrate how value is extracted from purposefully depressed communities through certain design choices that are crafted as lifestyle preferences. Later in this essay, I examine these shows and their representative relationship to the towns to which they are attached to illustrate how this form of speculation affects communities of color. With this brief history in mind, the remainder of this essay explores HGTV's programming in relation to the housing market and postracial racializations. I highlight programs that demonstrate the racialization of lifestyle and the lifestyling of race through characterization, design, and so-called revitalization.

The Characters of Lifestyle

In 2012, HGTV introduced its audience to the characters of lifestyle through some briefly aired promotional spots for *House Hunters* and *House Hunters International*. In all, there were four advertisements, each of which featured a different type of house. The house types are directly related to the HGTV FrontDoor.com website, which offers links to view houses by the type of lifestyle you think you live. The ads feature a suburban home, a 1970s ranch, a rural cabin, and a Paris pied-à-terre, each style of which the ads attach to a human personality. For example, the suburban home is represented by a middle-aged white woman looking frazzled in a kitchen, as kids run screaming in the background. The woman says, "I'm a suburban family home in a five-star school district. Sure my walls are covered in crayon and I'm drowning in an endless amount of toys and clutter, but [takes off glasses shakes out hair] underneath it all I'm still the same immaculate premier listing I've always been [wink]."

The implications within this advertisement are not subtle. The woman's body is used to represent the home as attached to a lifestyle that is encoded with certain race and class markers that are, in turn, tied to a narrative of value that is relayed by the woman. The woman tells us that her house, and therefore her lifestyle, will maintain its value even with some age. By contrast, the 1970s ranch house is represented by a young black woman with an Afro and a brightly colored 1970s-style outfit lounging in a chair in a living room with a fire burning in an orange Malm fireplace. She says, "I'm a seventies ranch style home. I've got wall-to-wall shag rugs, beaded curtains instead of doors, and a fire pit in my living room. Oh, you can act like you're not digging this groovy, dated scene, but this [waves hands to accentuate her body] is classic baby! Aaaaaoooowww!"

The difference between these two representations is stark. The description of the decor of the house is tied to the woman's physicality through her gestural reference to her body. Thus, this house is linked to a certain type of black female sexuality, which, we then learn, is given certain aesthetic value characteristics such as "dated yet classic." In this way, the ad characterizes black lifestyles within an aesthetic and temporal frame that is used to construe value. In other words, the black lifestyle of the house is situated in the past, behind the times, and in need of repair in order to regain any value.

There is a long history that marks blackness and black sexuality as primitive (see Gilman 1985; Somerville 2000). In the context of the narrative of capital accumulation, this fixes blackness as unable to advance and thus unable to increase in value. On HGTV, blackness and black bodies are often marked as wholly outside of Western advancements through advertisements for charities that work to alleviate poverty in underdeveloped nations and feature malnourished children looking sad and playing in dirt, as well as B-roll shots of people of color laboring under the supervision of white bodies. Neighborhoods associated with blackness are cast as places of poverty, through the use of B-rolls of not only black bodies but also aesthetic symbols, such as graffiti, that link urban neglect and blackness. These shows rely on a familiarity with these representations of blackness in order to create their narrative about real estate speculation. The result is to show blackness and black people as unable to cope with modern-day life under capitalism, even as it shows some black people as house hunters. By including some black people who are able to participate in the real estate market, the shows situate unequal access to the market as a matter of individual choice. Thus, the representations of poverty associated with blackness are cast within the specious terms of the "culture of poverty," which makes poverty appear to be the result of underdeveloped thinking skills, primitive technological capabilities, or supposedly backward *lifestyles*, rather than the result of economic policy that maintains unequal access to resources and services.

These neighborhoods are also described as ripe for investment by show hosts, realtors, and narrators through the use of words and phrases such as "up and coming," "transitional," "emerging," "on the rise," "revitalizing," and other euphemisms that ignore and/or downgrade the neighborhoods' existing populations as insignificant and undeveloped. Potential buyers are then framed within a colonialist logic as "pioneers" and the neighborhood as a "new frontier" primed for settlement and investment ventures.[7] (This coincides with a parallel narrative about bringing neighborhoods back to their "former glory" that trades on histories of white flight. I return to this later.) In this story of speculation and good investment, the only way for increased equity is for the so-called primitive frontier of the "up-and-coming" neighborhood to be developed *by replacing existing communities with newer and wealthier ones.* There is no possibility for return on speculation if the neighborhood does not "transition." What is left unsaid is that this transition requires a shift away from the neighborhood's racialized embodiments. Blackness is thus positioned as an aesthetic marker that is at once desirable and out of date and must be displaced in order for the story to progress and the land value to increase.

In the context of the advertisement for the 1970s ranch house, the possibility of uplift affixed to this house/body requires that the groovy black woman must be made over into a more respectable house/body in order to increase her value. Both ads rely on racially coded notions of sexuality and femininity, but the difference between these two representations is in how they affix value to the homes they feature. For instance, the description of the 1970s decor is tied to the woman through her gestural reference to her body, while the white woman shakes out her hair as if to reveal her inner beauty. Thus the houses manifest women's race and sexuality as an inherent part of value: in other words, blackness comes to be situated as never quite as modern and therefore deeply discounted (see Miller-Young 2014). The 1970s ranch does not maintain its value in the same way as the suburban. Instead, it is understood as "used goods" that will require cleaning and renovation to bring it up to date. Thus, the property value does not appreciate at the same rate as for the suburban home.

The gendered dimensions of lifestyle also become evident when race is affixed to the object through its relation to whiteness. In this case, a black woman's physical embodiment is set up against the white woman as an oppositional outline that is used to define a white heteronormative structure of value. In this frame the two women are situated within an implied "Madonna/whore" dichotomy in which the white woman is figured as a mother and homemaker by placing her in the kitchen and referencing her care for children, while the black woman is lounging in an easy chair using dialogue and gestures filled with sexual innuendo.

These examples show how lifestyle is measured through ideals of status and taste and then connected to race. Lifestyle is thus a normalizing process where taste is the key measure of differentiation in a society within a postracial or multicultural framework. Taste is situated as informing the hierarchical positioning of the cultural object and its related subject (Bourdieu 1984). Standards of taste at HGTV are used to market real estate and thus position the house as cultural object. In this dynamic, the lifestyle of the owner, which is understood through race and class markers of taste, affixes value to the house as a *home*. As such, not just the *house*, but the *home*, becomes valorized.

Kitchen Stories: Combing Out Race and Value

Just as characterizations of lifestyle are attached to certain homes to determine house value in these programs, the material objects of the house also give or take away value as shows leave the identities of residents largely unspoken. Like the classic home renovation show *This Old House*, the HGTV/DIY network show *Rehab Addict* (2010–present) with the host Nicole Curtis also features a "classic" old home that is refurbished over several episodes (Departure Films 2015). In particular, *Rehab Addict* focuses on the revitalization and preservation of homes that have been auctioned off for reasons that may include abandonment and foreclosure.[8] One of the show's advertisers is Quicken Loans, a mortgage loan company based in Detroit that is deeply invested in the "revitalization" of Detroit and even sponsored the rehabilitation of the season seven house known as the Detroit House.

The sixth season of *Rehab Addict* is also located in Detroit and focuses on a 1912 Tudor house in the Islandview Village neighborhood. In an episode focused on the kitchen renovation, during the demolition phase, Nicole and her crew find "a comb" behind the stove. Nicole declares she doesn't know what a comb is doing back there, but she knows that even though she didn't brush her hair that day, she is still going to "pass on that!" The camera gets a close-up of the comb, and it is then that (at least a portion of) the viewing audience understands exactly what kind of comb it is and what it was doing back there. The comb is a hot comb, a popular grooming device used primarily by black women to straighten kinky, curly hair. The comb itself is made of metal, and to harness its straightening powers it is placed in an open flame burner until it is hot and then combed through oiled hair. The result is shiny, straight hair. Many black women's ears know the fear of the hot comb.

The hot comb exists mainly in the black cultural world. As a white woman, Nicole Curtis may really not have known or interacted enough with black people to know what a hot comb is or how it works. However, because Detroit has a long history as a black city and Curtis identifies as a Detroiter, the comb incident illustrates at the very least how black culture is situated within the terms of home valorization. The comb acts as a device to help the audience imagine, and make value judgments about, who would use grooming devices in the kitchen and, even more, under what circumstances such a device would have fallen and been abandoned behind a stove. While hot combing hair may not be familiar to the entire audience, and does not get a lot of representation in popular culture, Detroit's status as a black city with decimated housing is more familiar. If we combine these popular cultural references with the premise of Curtis's show, we begin to see how race and class are embedded in the narrative of revitalization. The comb shows us how postracial ideals operate quietly in the production and development of real estate television and land value.

As I mentioned earlier, the show's producers may not know what the comb is or how it might be seen, and yet they can still understand the comb as an important narrative device to use for a story about "revitalizing" an abandoned and abject property. However, what the producers do not understand or see does not necessarily carry over into audience ignorance, so for the audiences who watch the show, the comb may hold a number of significant meanings that are distinctly racialized. In this case, the comb is used to signal abandonment and disrepair without acknowledging the previous black tenants of the house. Many viewers of color will be familiar with displacement or the threat of it. The comb here stands in for those people who are all too familiar with this history while leaving them unnamed. The comb stands in for the person of color who may have been right at home near the stove but is now pushed behind the stove and when seen is viewed as out of place, confusing, and abject. In this way, black bodies in these neighborhoods function as a signal of misuse and neglect because the very idea of a comb by the stove or a black body in a historic neighborhood is utterly unfamiliar. This is the case even as black bodies haunt the narratives of historic homes throughout the history of the United States in a variety of quite familiar ways.[9]

It is also interesting to note that *Rehab Addict* is set mainly in neighborhoods of a majority people of color that have been marked as "blighted" and slated for revitalization, but Curtis's show nonetheless features very few people of color. In the beginning of each season/project, Curtis invites the public to come view the "before" of the house. In the shots of the crowd that the audience is to understand are "the public" invited to view the "before" house, the bodies the camera shows mostly read as white. Further, Curtis does use local craftspeople and workers for her jobs, but the ones the camera shows appear to be overwhelmingly white. Curtis has stated that one of her missions is to get people to move back to Detroit from the suburbs and to show them how to not be scared of Detroit (Departure Films 2015). A 2010 census coded for race reveals that coming back to Detroit from the suburbs is a code for the return of a white professional class (Cable 2013). So, when *Rehab Addict* shows a hot comb in the first act, it probably means a black person will be displaced in the end. Not all "kitchens" are valued the same.[10]

A Unique Homogeneity: Valuing Identity

This connection between real estate–focused television programming and speculative markets is not new. *This Old House* aired during another period of rampant housing speculation and also featured homes that were facing foreclosure; however, a key difference with this generation of shows is its temporal nature. Although *Rehab Addict* follows a similar pace in which one house is renovated throughout the season, on other house-flipping shows the pace is much quicker. The renovations happen in a half hour versus a thirteen-episode season. Through the process of foreshortening, the narrative of increased equity through creative design strategies is made more dramatic. Making the show shorter then creates a space for the next novel design/project/property. In other words, the shorter time span of the show allows for the use of leftover airtime to produce more shows.

The construction of authenticity is important here because of the deconstructed aspect of these shows. The way in which the show creates a sense of reality within condensed time is ruptured through an exposure of those methods within the production. For instance, on some programs the viewer will see outtakes, or a host or other participant will make explicit the difference in time span. These rhetorical strategies accelerate time to capitalize on the affective reaction participants have to their purchase/renovation/redesign. Furthermore, this time speedup heightens the ideal of fast profits through the risk-based debt schemes known as house flipping.

Managing the debt-based investment in flipping requires design strategies that normalize and flatten racial, gender, or sexual difference and obscure the racial and gendered features of financial debt. This normalization process then capitalizes on the flattening of difference, which becomes packaged into easily portable *lifestyles*. Like Ikea furniture and Sears Modern Homes before it, both of which are packaged in flat boxes for ease of transport, these lifestyles can be moved around interchangeably into suitable neighborhoods and homes that become retrofit or custom-fit and "revitalized" through the process. Thus the design strategies of house flippers make apparent the function of the lifestyle aesthetic as a form of capital. This Ikea-like flattening of difference places the viewer as participant observer. In this, the viewer/character's creativity is a deconstructed and quantifiable lifestyle that is simply defined and as such is easily reproducible. This easy reproduction becomes a commodity to be exchanged with a value that is determined through markers of taste and used to assert ideas of authenticity. Here, "readable" styles can be received as authentically representing specific packaged identities.[11]

Some specific content of the website for HGTV (content that was once based in the now closed FrontDoor.com partner site) provides a prime example of how this unique homogeneity of packaged identities of difference is cultivated. The site lists and describes twelve types of neighborhoods: "Urban Core (Downtown), Urban Pioneer (Up-and-Coming), New Urban, Cul-de-Sacs & Kids (Bedroom), Pedestrian, Historic, Status/Destination, Ethnic, Active/Resort, Golf, Retirement, and Rural" (HGTV n.d.). One can then read more information to find out which type of neighborhood is right for one's imagined and presupposed desires and needs. Coordinated programming is offered that allows viewers to design their home or neighborhood around their lifestyle. Buyers search for the property that fits within their chosen parameters, and sellers attempt to style their home to attract and fit within the lifestyle boundaries of their given location. Here, the broker's creed, "location, location, location," is laid bare.

This is precisely in line with Richard Florida's thinking in his best-selling book *The Rise of the Creative Class: And How It's Transforming Work, Leisure, Community and Everyday Life* (2002). Florida argues that cities should make efforts to attract the so-called creative class to ensure future economic survival and growth. He bases this assertion on his creativity index, which shows the most economically viable urban centers to be those with a large creative pool. These areas are identified by what Florida refers to as the 3T's: talent, technology, and tolerance. In other words, these are people who work in the creative or technology sector and have a high level of "tolerance" for difference, most importantly, for gay people. This is important because his index denotes a correlation between a large gay population and a successful creative economy. Here again is "location, location, location!" For Florida, if your location doesn't have these markers, it is important to find a way to incorporate them.[12] The HGTV network and its corresponding website act as both a guide and testimony to this line of thinking. The shows on HGTV illustrate this principle through their insistence on matching the house hunter to a neighborhood with the proper "fit." This is evident again on the website through the manufacture of the types of neighborhoods and the corresponding list of what types of people are appropriate matches for those neighborhoods.

For instance, the website provides five categories (with examples listed for each) to help buyers understand neighborhood types. The subheading for this page reads: "Whether you like big yards or hip nightclubs, there's a community type that fits your lifestyle." The lifestyle categories are "Where to Find It," "What You Can Call Home," "Your Neighbors," "Why You'll Like It," and "Why You May Not," as well as a list of examples for each neighborhood type. In these categories, buyers can find information to help them assess how a neighborhood might suit their tastes.

A number of telling clues illustrate how certain design ideas are shaped by assumptions about identity as well as location as a way to figure out property value (as it is attached to lifestyle). For instance, only three neighborhood types list any sort of "diversity" under the "Your Neighbors" section. Those neighborhoods are Urban Core (Downtown), Urban Pioneer (Up-and-Coming), or Ethnic (no parenthetical needed, apparently). The remaining nine neighborhoods have no diversity as an "attraction," according to HGTV. This in fact fits into Richard Florida's paradigm, especially in the context of the first two categories, which are mainly urban. The HGTV website and network try to match the shopper to the neighborhood in the "Why You'll Like It" and "Why You May Not" categories. These categories group difference on a design scale, by situating ethnicity as an aesthetic part of a neighborhood.

For instance, the neighbors of an Urban Pioneer might be an "ethnically diverse mix of young singles and couples, recently divorced and single parents, aging retirees who have lived in the neighborhood for years, immigrants," but they may not like the "construction noise and eyesores, neighbors who can't renovate their homes." In the "Ethnic" neighborhood we can see how ethnic diversity in your neighbors is set as an attractive quality in one form but may also be unappealing. In this case, your neighbors may be "immigrants from a particular ethnicity, young couples, budget-conscious singles," which will offer, on the one hand, "affordable housing, interesting cuisine and products," but, on the other hand, "If you're not the same ethnicity, you may feel like an outsider." In another example, the site offers that if you want to live in the "Urban Core," your neighbors will be an "ethnically diverse mix of young single professionals, low to middle income families and seniors," which may positively offer "affordable housing, eclectic mix of high-end and modest, close to nightlife and city attractions," but may also have the drawbacks such as "little to no public parking, typically has higher rate of crime, transients" (HGTV n.d.).

In all these examples, "ethnicity" and thus people of color more generally are used to describe both attraction and aversion in mostly aesthetic terms.

In these neighborhood lifestyles, the idealized buyer has an unspoken whiteness, and difference is used to measure lifestyle comforts along varying levels of abstraction from inferring high crime rates to addressing one's comfort as an "outsider" in the "ethnic" neighborhood model. Thus, in this formula of matching neighborhood to lifestyle, people of color are equated to design props for "curb appeal" and are (both positively and negatively) figured in the overall value of the home.

As Anna Everett (2004) notes, on HGTV, "successful non-white couples" are represented without marking, making them out to be nonthreatening everyday people. Also not bracketed out as special are gay/lesbian or interracial couples and families. As Everett argues, these different families "underscore the new 'reality' of American life that most other 'reality' shows fail to engage, or problematically sensationalize" (175). By doing this, the network normalizes the lives of these people within the context of their desired neighborhoods. However, normalization in this context is not necessarily ideal. Everett explains, "The most central ideology of these shows is that of an idealized consumer culture. These transformations only happen through an acceptance of these shows' consumerist logics, at both the high-end and more budget conscious levels" (176). In this way, the shows work not just to normalize the lives of these people in and of themselves. Instead, the process of normalization goes hand in hand with the use of race and culture to increase rent through home valorization.

This dynamic demonstrates HGTV's use of the creative index and the 3T's. The network clearly has incorporated talent, technology, and tolerance within its narrative structure. It does this by weaving together design and web and video interfaces to showcase the process of house hunting and including people of color and "alternative" lifestyles as main actors in the frame. In this way, HGTV illustrates, even exemplifies, how to attract the capital associated with the so-called creative class. To further Everett's point that diversity and difference in this context lay in the service of profit we can turn again to Florida. Florida's indices that show a positive correlation between diversity and the rise of the creative class indicate a "diversity of elites." And yet, he highlights that there is "a gaping hole" that is made by the negative correlation, or lack of representation within the creative class, of African Americans and "other non-whites" (Florida 2002, 80). Interestingly, Florida cannot quite make sense of this "negative correlation," leaving the obvious racialized exclusions unexplored in the interest of rent increases.[13] Thus his creative cities can be read as a revitalization and rebranding of the same redlining practices that have excluded certain communities from histories (and futures) of inherited wealth. What is made apparent in the example of HGTV is that people of color and LGBTQ couples and families are important not in and of themselves as good neighbors and people to know. Instead, they are situated as a type of global capital called "diversity" and utilized to add value to the debt-based investment strategy that obscures real estate speculation by calling it "homeownership." These are the specifics of home valorization that commodify every aspect of life into a highly stylized form of capital that can be called a lifestyle.

Uneven Representation: Lifestyle Speculation

Richard Florida's ideas have been shown to be limited, but the history of urban and suburban development demonstrates that economic and socio-cultural forces have long worked together to produce differential home value (Florida 2012). In particular, government subsidies backed the white middle class purchase of houses and land in suburban communities where normalization became increasingly attached to segregated enclaves and individual consumer practices (see Fraad Baxandall and Ewen 2000; K. T. Jackson 1985). In essence, then, this history points to a state-sanctioned investment in consumer culture and to a history of making race into lifestyle through homeownership (Gans 1982; Tongson 2011).

Fixer Upper (2013–18) is a show on HGTV that is focused on buying and renovating homes for families in the Waco, Texas, area. It features hosts Chip and Joanna Gaines, who are locally well-known house flippers turned real estate moguls and owners of a number of real estate–focused businesses that all share the name Magnolia. Each episode of the show is one hour and follows the same format. First Chip and Joanna show the buyer three houses to choose from. Usually the buyers are a white heterosexual couple, but occasionally there are couples of different races and ethnicities; the episodes also sometimes feature single women. Chip and Joanna are themselves an interracial couple (Chip is white, and Joanna is Korean American), and this fact is sometimes referenced within the show. At each house Chip explains its price with the possible renovation budget, and Joanna explains design and renovation options. After seeing all the choices, the buyers then tell Chip and Joanna which house they want to purchase. After the decision scene, the buyer meets with Joanna, who outlines her design plans and gives the buyer an option to choose one of three bonus features.

The second half of the show features the renovation scenes and the "reveal." The renovation sequence always begins with demolition, which is portrayed as being exciting and cathartic. After demolition, the renovation is begun in earnest. These scenes often include the basic renovation show shots such as long shots of laborers (who on this show are often Spanish-speaking Latino men) and close-ups on tools, laborers' hands, and hosts/carpenters in action nailing and sawing (and sometimes even slow-motion shots of sawdust and power tools). (This format is fairly standard for home renovation shows. But *Fixer Upper* adds a twist in this section when it follows a short, personal narrative about the development of the hosts' real estate empire, such as the renovation of their own farmhouse in the first season or of silos located in downtown Waco the Magnolia compound that will be home to their many real estate and design businesses by the third season.) In the next scene, Joanna visits a local furniture designer/carpenter named Clint, who helps her to build a special piece of furniture just for this family. The scene that follows generally focuses on a problem or snag in the house construction process that poses a challenge to the design. This challenge is overcome through compromise or by adding more money to the budget or a combination of the two. Joanna then stages the property. The final scenes are the reveal of the transformed house.

The renovation show *Home Town* (2017–present) follows a similar format as *Fixer Upper*. The show is set in the small town of Laurel, Mississippi, and features the host couple, Erin and Ben Napier. *Home Town* thus far has had two seasons, but it is useful to analyze the show alongside *Fixer Upper*. Both shows illustrate how renovation television narrativizes postracial real estate markets through the use of racialized bodies that are and are not represented on screen. In the pilot episode of *Home Town*, we meet the host couple, both of whom are white, and the buyers, who are also white. In the opening credits, we see a montage of people in a small town, whose aesthetic is conveyed through images of American flags and people driving around and stopping to talk to one another. Throughout the seasons we see very few people of color. Though the opening montage of the pilot shows a black policeman stopping to talk and laugh with a white man on the street, the B-roll features mainly white people. The representation here marks the small-town aesthetic within a logic of cultural sameness, even as it includes black bodies in the lens. While the first episode following the pilot does indeed feature a black family, the majority of the episodes feature white heterosexual couples. Through these montages and B-roll the show trades on the idea that everyone in a small town looks the same and has similar desires.

In this way the representational strategy of the show inserts an idea of homogeneity that doesn't really exist by making postracial, racialized inclusions and exclusions. For instance, the black family featured in the first episode is cast as simply wanting to enjoy the small-town life, and the decision to feature a black police officer during an era of heightened attention to police violence against black people is telling. Another example of this type of exclusion is through a renaming strategy that is part of the show's format. During the house-hunting phase of each episode, Erin and Ben give names and short histories to each house according to who lived there previously, and then during the reveal, Erin produces another drawing of the house in which it has been renamed for the featured family/buyers. For instance, in the third episode of season one, the "Chancellor" house becomes the "Warren" house. This renaming strategy works to marginally include racialized histories, but as means of systematic erasure. Although no racialized information is given, viewers are left to imagine (through the B-roll of a few black bodies) that some of these houses have histories in the black community. Further, while Erin and Ben and their producers may or may not know these histories of difference within the community, this seemingly small erasure helps to manifest the town of Laurel within a homogeneous aesthetic, even though it is not.

To repeat, HGTV is a network with diverse representations that include people with various racial, ethnic, and sexual identities. In *Home Town*, however, mostly white people are made visible with the exception of the police officer. During its pilot episode, a lot of work is done to set up the history of the town as home to a once thriving lumber industry that needs to be brought back to its "former glory." The term "former glory" can allude to something more than just lost industry, especially (but not only) when speaking of the Deep South. The episode suggests that it gestures back to a time of prosperity and wholesomeness, but it also begs the question, for whom? In each episode, the house that the house-hunting couple decides to purchase is given a small nostalgic narrative that imagines an idealized past of the previous owners and their relationship to the neighborhood. Again, while the race of the previous owners is never directly referenced, the language of idealized goodness suggests an implicitly racialized narrative of respectability. This is reinforced in the final scene of the pilot, when the new buyers of the home are given a certificate of appreciation from the mayor, a black man, for investing in the town.

The representational strategies of *Home Town* and *Fixer Upper* are curious given the racial demographics of the actual towns in which they are staged. The census data on Laurel, where *Home Town* is set, reveals the town has just over 18,000 residents and, since at least 2000, an increasing African American population and a steadily decreasing white population (US Census Bureau n.d.). The census points to a similar demographic change in Waco, the setting of *Fixer Upper*, a town of about 124,000. However, in Waco the rising population is Latino, with both white and African American populations showing slight declines. And although people of color laborers are shown in the background and Joanna (from *Fixer Upper*) is of mixed race, the overall representation of both towns is majority white.

This homogenized representation is particularly interesting given the fact that Waco and Laurel are well-known historic sites of racially motivated, brutally violent lynching murders of black people.[14] Magnolia Market at the Silos is just one half mile from Waco City Hall.[15] This is the site of the 1916 lynching murder known as the "Waco Horror" that is notable not only because it was heavily photographed but also because the photographs revealed the banal excitement in the gathering of thousands of so-called ordinary (white) people (Allen 2000; J. B. Smith 2015). The town of Laurel and neighboring town of Shubuta have lynching murders linked to a bridge known as the Hanging Bridge (Frankman and Raphael 2016). In 1942 a man named Howard Wash was taken from the town jail by a mob of fifty people and hung from the bridge (J. M. Ward, 2016). The histories of racialized violence I outline here are never referenced within the shows' narratives; nevertheless, they constitute an important part of the overall story about the serene and bucolic small-town life that is being constructed. Although not all producers or viewers may know of them, these violent histories are not unfamiliar. Even more so, it is the fact of this history of violence and exclusion that is used to maintain the superficial appeals of the homogeneous and genteel small town to land speculators. Thus, these histories make and facilitate the operations of monopoly rent and the present-day profits of the land market. "Former glory," indeed.

Considering these shows alongside the vision of Detroit in *Rehab Addict* emphasizes how efforts to represent "revitalization" markedly proscribe representations of black and brown populations. Black and brown people are mainly figured to outline and make more evident these renovation transformations. Even when black and brown people are included in the narrative, these racialized tropes of revitalization are situated in a way that masks long histories of violent displacement and profit. Further, the obfuscation of these exclusionary practices is what the lifestyling of race relies on: a culture of poverty and other racialized assumptions masked as a simple question of design aesthetics.

Conclusion

The HGTV network works with corporate, artist, and audience interests in its manufacture of lifestyles and is thus a part of today's much vaunted creative economy. The creative industry of HGTV develops ideals of taste, status, and value that contribute to creating "home valorization." In this context, all aspects of one's lifestyle, both in and outside of the home, are seen to contribute to the overall market value of real estate. In line with the neoliberal ideals associated with the period in which reality television gained popularity, the logics of the free market incorporate all facets of life as they move into more and more social and cultural domains.

In *The Expediency of Culture*, George Yúdice (2003) lays out how culture is positioned as an expedient that rationalizes and naturalizes the uneven investment and distribution of social resources. In this way, culture acts as a performative resource "for attaining an end," that is, profit. Even the seemingly most mundane aspects of everyday living are increasingly turned into creative and aesthetic products. Within the context of HGTV, the expediency of culture to serve as a resource facilitates the network's capitalization on all aspects of a person's life. These are congealed together into a "lifestyle." Accordingly, home means not only the physical property of the house but also all aspects of one's lifestyle that structure the house as a cultural object. These aspects are not limited to the activities that take place inside the physical space of the house but also encompass all expressions of the daily life of its inhabitants; these include work, leisure, social interactions, and even travel. Thus, HGTV is actively engaged in the production of home value (home valorization) as a way to promote the further growth of a (corporate) creative economy within neoliberalism.

As I have shown, lifestyle is not just an abstract cultural concept but is specifically raced, albeit in a postracial idiom. Home valorization is promoted through assessments of value that calculate the physical elements of the house alongside specific design features of the home. The aesthetic parameters laid out in these shows reconstruct hierarchies of race (and other forms of identity) within a supposedly multicultural and postracial framework. What I term "home valorization" shows how the idea of home is given value through distinct racial and identity markers. In this way, lifestyle programming promotes certain cultural ideals as a way to market and manage property values through the use of elements of design and construction that are seemingly non-racially coded. This is the lifestyling of race: structural racial inequalities in the real estate market that are represented and capitalized upon as style and aesthetic choices. "Homeownership" is masked as a product of individual lifestyle choice that obscures the real effects of displacement and racialization within the housing market. This racialized value is then turned into profit, or equity, that is unequally distributed through debt.

Videography of Shows Referenced in the Text

Bad Girls Club (2006–present), Bunim-Murray Productions/Oxygen Networks
Buy Me (2006–9), Whalley Abbey Media/HGTV/HGTV Canada
Curb Appeal (1999–present), Edelman Productions/HGTV
Fixer Upper (2013–present), High Noon Entertainment/HGTV
Get It Sold! (2007–9), HGTV
HGTV $250,000 Challenge (2009), 495 Productions/HGTV (producer)
Hidden Potential (2006–9), Leopard Films/HGTV
Home Town (2016–present), RTR Media/HGTV
House Hunters (1999–present), Pie Town Productions/HGTV
House Hunters International (2006–present), Pie Town Productions/HGTV
Income Property (2008–present), RTR Media/HGTV/HGTV Canada
My First Place (2007–present), High Noon Entertainment/HGTV
My House Is Worth What? (2006–2011), Pie Town Productions/HGTV
Property Brothers (2011–present), Cineflix/W Network/HGTV
Property Virgins (2007–present), Cineflix Productions/HGTV
Real Housewives of . . . (franchise, 2006–present), Bravo
Rehab Addict (2010–present), Departure Films/Magnetic Productions/Scripps Networks
The Unsellables (2008–10), HGTV
This Old House (1979–present), This Old House Productions/This Old House Ventures/
    WGBH/PBS/PBS International

Notes

1 For pieces that do thematize race, see Everett 2012; R. Gates 2012; Ouellette 2004.
2 The phrase the "quiet operations of race" is borrowed from the editors of this collection.
3 This essay is culled from a larger project that examines reality television and the role it plays in shaping articulations of race in the twenty-first century. I examine development, consumption, and participation through an ethnography and close readings of particular shows, networks, industry professionals, and industry marketing materials. In that project I try to account for the large number of viewers of color, who are dismissed as inferior consumers of cast off entertainments.
4 For further discussion of the links between design colors and race, see Londoño 2012; Taussig 2010.
5 See Baker 2007, 5. In describing the characteristics of the bubble, Baker writes, "Soaring home prices pushed construction and home sales to record levels. Even more important,

the run-up in home prices created more than $8 trillion in housing bubble wealth. This wealth fueled a consumption boom, as homeowners withdrew equity from their homes almost as it was created. . . . This pattern of growth could not be sustained. Record house prices were supported by a tidal wave of speculation. . . . As prices soared, financing arrangements became ever more questionable. . . . The worst of the speculative financing was in the subprime market, where moderate-income home buyers were persuaded to take out adjustable-rate mortgages, which generally feature very low 'teaser rates,' typically reset after three years, often to levels that are five or six percentage points higher. Millions of families who could afford the teaser rates cannot possibly afford the higher rates."

6 It should be stated that these shows cast buyers who are already in escrow. This means that on *House Hunters* two of the three homes were never really being considered by prospective tenants. In fact, some of the show's participants have reported on internet blogs that they are sometimes filmed visiting a friend's house. We should expect this type of production cost cutting from reality television. The reason for casting people already in escrow seems to be to make sure the narrative is already set, limit production time to just five days of filming for both the shopping scenes and the after, and make it easier to secure location filming permits.

7 For a discussion of the frontier myth in gentrification narratives, see N. Smith 1996.

8 *This Old House* began airing on PBS in 1979. Each season of *This Old House* features a thirteen-part series that follows the renovation of one historic house. The show continues to air, with more recent seasons focusing on more upscale renovation and design and featuring two or three houses over a season.

9 A foundational essay is DeHave Newsom 1971.

10 "Kitchen" is also a black cultural term for the tight curls at the nape of the neck that cannot be reached by the hot comb.

11 This is also a feature in other culture industries; see Negus 2013.

12 For more extensive critiques of Florida's argument, see Hanhardt 2013; Tongson 2011.

13 Also interesting here is Florida's lack of any intersectional analysis that would allow him to consider the possibility that African Americans and LGBT people may be overlapping populations. Further, this limited viewpoint certainly contributes to his skewed index.

14 This section owes to Shelleen Greene for her helpful comments and discussion with me about the Waco Horror after I presented this paper at the annual meeting of the Society for Cinema and Media Studies in 2015.

15 For more information on the sites of lynching murders in the United States, see the Monroe Work Today interactive map 2016.

12

"Haute [Ghetto] Mess"

Postracial Aesthetics and the Seduction
of Blackness in High Fashion

BRANDI THOMPSON SUMMERS

In the fashion industry, aesthetics not only define blackness in particular ways but also allow designers, editors, photographers, and stylists to play with the fluidity of blackness even (especially) when black bodies are not present. As Herman Gray writes, considering "the level of saturation of the media with representations of blackness, the mediascape can no longer be characterized using such terms as *invisibility*. Rather, we might well describe ours as a moment of 'hyperblackness'" (1995, 230). Aesthetics, in general, have tremendous influence on how we make sense of and affectively respond to the world—what we "see" contextualizes what we make of individuals, environments, and events. We need visual accounts to assign value to subjects, so in this way vision acts as a technology of power. Recognizing the power of fashion imagery in contemporary culture, I analyze how fashion images express knowledge about race. As an aesthetic realm, fashion is the place where vision, visual discourse, and stylized bodies meet. In terms of race, I am curious how the aesthetic value of blackness today reflects the current conjuncture.

In this essay, I analyze the "Haute Mess" editorial spread in the March 2012 issue of *Vogue Italia* to demonstrate that "hyperblackness" does not only require the presentation of blackness in bodily form but also can reference symbolic renderings of blackness—without being named as such. "Haute Mess" is a colorful, cartoonish, fantastical spread featuring several popular high-fashion models like Coco Rocha, Joan Smalls, and Jessica Stam. The cover and corresponding editorial story, styled by Lori Goldstein, were received with both praise and backlash. First, the magazine was touted for featuring a black cover model, Afro-Latina Joan Smalls, for the first time in four years. But, because the (mostly white) models in the story wore extralong and excessively decorated fingernails and toenails, elaborate hairpieces, and gold teeth, the issue received criticism for its blatant use of stereotypical imagery of poor, black women.

Criticism of the "Haute Mess" story was particularly resonant because *Vogue Italia* had received significant attention for its focus on blackness and black models just four years earlier. In July 2008, it released "A Black Issue" exclusively featuring black models as well as commentary on topics that would seemingly interest a black American audience (e.g., profiles of Michelle Obama, Spike Lee's *Miracle at St. Anna*, and pieces about *Ebony* and *Essence* magazines). "A Black Issue" quickly became the highest-grossing issue of *Vogue Italia*. The first run of the July 2008 issue sold out in the United States and Britain, which led *Vogue Italia* to reprint several thousand copies for American and British audiences—it did not sell particularly well in Italy—the first time a Condé Nast magazine was reprinted to satisfy high demand. Interviewed by several media outlets, *Vogue Italia* editor Franca Sozzani credited the success of Oprah Winfrey and future president Obama for her growing interest in promoting and supporting black models and designers. That Sozzani's inspiration to produce an issue of *Vogue Italia* exclusively featuring black models stemmed from two exemplary and iconic black American public figures allows us to think about how the longing for a postracial America provokes more attention to blackness, as opposed to less.[1] Again, while postrace attempts to minimize the significance of race in daily life, it also gives us permission to play with it.

The production of the "Haute Mess" spread four years later shocked, disrupted, and contradicted the seamless celebration of blackness in the July 2008 "Black Issue"—but operated as a product of the same logic. While "A Black Issue" is offered up as evidence that we are beyond the bounds of racism inasmuch as the individual black models who appear in the issue have achieved success in the high fashion industry (despite the presentation of some as eroticized, sexualized, and primitivized visual subjects), I became particularly interested in how "Haute Mess" amplified and perverted the excess of a constructed and stereotyped black cultural aesthetic. Both issues expose a space for postracial and postracist discourse to flourish. Where the notion of postracial suggests that we are beyond conversations about race in the determination of the economic, political, and social lives of individuals, postracism belies a similar logic. Postracism moves us away from conversations about the structural embeddedness and implications of racial discrimination and instead suggests that racism can be eradicated through postracial inclusion and assimilation. The presentations of bodies featured in both issues are produced at the intersection of heightened visual technology, commodity consumption, globalization, increased urbanization, and spectacularization. The "Black Issue" of *Vogue Italia* demonstrated the necessity of visible black bodies, while "Haute Mess" shows why black bodies are not necessary to display blackness and fulfill the postracial neoliberal diversity project.

Hailed as both brilliant and racist, the spread is a visual smorgasbord complete with model "characters" wearing high-priced, high fashion clothing, adorned with junk food, candy wrappers, and other symbols of American overconsumption, while the obscured faces of infants and male companions appear in the distance. Even the cover text, "#overthetop," connotes excess, a particularly black excess that can be most notably linked to imagery of Saartjie Baartman, colloquially known as the Hottentot Venus, whose spectacularization points to the representation of the black female body as perverted and excessive in the public imagination. The spectral presence of Baartman can be linked to contemporary black female public figures like Nicki Minaj, Lil' Kim, and Serena Williams, whose bodies are always already exposed, accessible, erotic, grotesque, and as Nicole Fleetwood (2011) observes, troubling to the field of vision.

Contained within the cover image is a complete "string of signifiers, associations, mythologies, and obsessions about blacks and blackness [that] are also being sold" (Russell 1998, 114), with the implicit association of black femininity and excessiveness being just one pair. The spread features a global circulation of symbols and is a creative production of an Italian-based high fashion magazine shot on location in Los Angeles.

As image activist and former model Bethann Hardison has said, modeling is probably the only industry in which you have the freedom to refer to people by their color and accordingly reject them in their work. It certainly is one of the few industries where segregation is still acceptable—claims for

"Caucasian only" or "no blacks" are neither uncommon nor deemed socially, politically, or professionally reprehensible. I argue that race is both made and unmade in fashion through, on the one hand, the production/performance of "difference" and, on the other hand, the flattening of difference where difference generates cultural and economic value through consumption and celebration. I consider high fashion magazines as visual and discursive fields that according to Fleetwood (2011) mark the (black) subject within systems of visual discourse that exist prior to the subject.

I first discuss fashion's engagement with the visual discourse of diversity, where notions of postrace and multiculturalism encourage fashion to play with race and difference as an aesthetic—therefore, racial performances and spectacles are not deemed racist. "Haute Mess" shows why black bodies are not necessary to display blackness and fulfill a postracial diversity project. I consider the discursive power of "race neutrality" in the visual presentation of difference and how the economic market and technology are used to privilege white bodies. Then, I discuss how the high fashion industry creates a space for blackness through the performance of race as an aestheticized category. Recognizing whiteness as "the universal empty point" (Puwar 2002) highlights the ability of white bodies to occupy blackness because their bodies are racially unmarked. Racial performances in high fashion, like black-face, draw attention to this privilege especially. Finally, I read the production and consumption of blackness through racial performance by analyzing images from the "Haute Mess" editorial.

Through my examination of "Haute Mess," I identify the ways in which blackness is deployed as an aesthetic, rather than an identity, that can be inhabited then removed without significant political consequence. In other words, I consider blackness as constituted outside the category of race and identity, and instead constructed through aesthetics—while aesthetics are concurrently structured in and by race. Power produces blackness as color and culture in the fashion industry, where the historical absence of black bodies in this exclusive space is overshadowed—black matters as an aesthetic or to provide "edge" or "cool." In his influential piece "Ethnicity and Internationality: New British Art and Diaspora-Based Blackness," Kobena Mercer (1999) argues that the hypervisibility of blackness was a consequence of corporate internationalism, which resulted in blackness being designated as cool and an accepted part of mainstream culture. The marketability of difference became a vital component of "new" British arts, and Mercer highlights the practice of black artists conforming to the aesthetic norms in order to become visible. Similar to Mercer's analysis of British art, I propose that blackness needs to be "seen," regardless of the fashion industry's preoccupation with multiculturalism.

The Aesthetic Value of Diversity

In August 2013, the *New York Times* featured a story on the cover of its "Fashion and Style" section that explored the racial dynamics of the fashion industry. In the article, Eric Wilson details various accounts of discrimination by fashion designers, stylists, and photographers based on their "persistent lack of diversity." Although the article focuses on the dearth of black models on the runway despite fashion's claims of change and social progressiveness, one of the more interesting aspects of the article was a comment by Francisco Costa, the women's creative director for Calvin Klein. Costa has been repeatedly criticized for selecting an overwhelmingly white cast of models since becoming the principal designer of Calvin Klein in 2003. In response, Costa claimed that there are not enough "top-level professionally trained" black models from which to select, and that "we try to present a unique and interesting cast with as many exclusives as possible to create and emphasize that season's aesthetic" (Wilson 2013, E1). In other words, blackness is assigned a particular meaning in the aesthetic system of fashion—a space that retains a particular value to the fashion system itself. In a conversation I had with fashion writer Robin Givhan, she supported Costa's assertion that he preferred a more diverse runway, but because he had only recently been charged to lead design efforts at Calvin Klein, and the brand was one of the creators of the "waif look," he did not believe he could completely change course because the waif aesthetic and minimalism defined the brand. For Costa, it was not a matter of introducing diversity; instead, he considered aesthetics and what the Calvin Klein brand represented in the fashion world—sameness as a desirable goal. Hence, diversity (as an aesthetic) was not part of the desired vision for Calvin Klein. Givhan added that once Costa feels comfortable and feels that his personal vision has become part of the Calvin Klein aesthetic, he can add more models of color (telephone conversation, December 20, 2011). By establishing whiteness as an aesthetic norm for the Calvin Klein brand through the exclusion of black bodies, Costa's position furthers the dominating aesthetic system of postracialism in which visible representations of cultural diversity operate as style—a style that cannot be considered part of the Calvin Klein brand aesthetic.

The exclusive fashion house Dior, like Calvin Klein, has also been publicly criticized for not presenting diverse casts of models. Nevertheless, in July 2013, Dior revealed its collection and included six black models. Ironically, Dior and Calvin Klein share the same casting director, Maida Gregori Boina, who suggested that the Dior casting "was the result of the multicultural concept of the collection, not the criticism." For the designer and casting director, the selection of mostly white models is purely an aesthetic matter—what Patricia Williams (1989) calls an "aesthetic of uniformity," where whiteness on the runway represents precision, balance, and inconspicuousness. Here we see that black bodies are used to provide and represent a particular "multicultural" aesthetic rather than representing racial and ethnic difference both as an issue of a relations of power and as a source of protest or political empowerment. The deployment of black bodies used to realize a multicultural aesthetic and the presence of black bodies as legible resistance to racism are illustrations of separate spheres that are no longer linked. This decoupling makes these spheres become unintelligible, and different from previous eras, since blackness no longer signifies particular conditions of inequality but is instead aestheticized to function as an element of a multicultural aesthetic and an optional identity, ushering in a new regime Kobena Mercer (1999) calls "multicultural normalization."

Hegemonic narratives of difference and diversity are part of a postracial framework that relies primarily on "celebration" and/or fun and play, which allows for the representation of specific types of difference in the popular imagination. This emphasis on diversity only seeks to obfuscate various forms of inequality that depend on the maintenance of systemic racism, sexism, classism, and so forth in order to prevail. Only specific forms of diversity are allowed to roam freely. Accordingly, a fundamental prerequisite of the increased visibility of difference is that these representations exist to thwart conversations about the presence of continued inequality.

Diversity is specifically profitable within a commercial versus editorial fashion space. The color divide is evident where black women and other women of color are represented in high numbers within commercial modeling versus editorial modeling: "Diversity is strategically sought—not to be obvious or too closely aligned with an affirmative action agenda—but just enough to increase the commercial enterprises' market share by representing the demographic base" (Mears 2010, 34). Therefore, in the fashion space, difference is depoliticized and diversity becomes an economically valued commodity where it is relegated to the field of culture to be consumed, celebrated, and enjoyed.

Overexposure: The Problem of Race as/in Technology

Richard Dyer (1997) writes about the impact of race on the technological function of photography. He theorizes that while all technologies are technical in terms of their material features and function, they are also social—having economic, cultural, and ideological properties—and are therefore not race-neutral. In fact, the development of camera, film stocks, and lighting to normalize the white face provided an apparatus that "came to be seen as fixed and inevitable, existing independently of the fact that it was humanly constructed" (Dyer 1997, 90). Photographic lighting relies on "controlled visibility," or, as Dyer claims, its guiding principle is controlled visibility, which ensures "that what is important in a shot is clearly visible to the audience" (86). The method of lighting (dim, spotlight, etc.) depends on the desired expression. Furthermore, photography and moving image lighting both privilege and constitute whiteness. According to Dyer, this apparatus "was developed with white people in mind and habitual use and instruction continued in the same vein, so much so that photographing non-white people is typically constructed as a problem" (89). Elaborating on Dyer's theorization of the aesthetic technology of photography, I argue that within high fashion iconography this inherent problem of blackness upholds an aesthetic preference for whiteness.

Here, I am suggesting that the umbrella of "aesthetics" also includes the aesthetic technology of photography, which favors, assumes, and constructs an image of white bodies within a discursive field that is organized according to a logic. It is this constructedness of the photographic medium that upholds preference for white. I agree with Dyer, who argues that it might be true that the photographic apparatus has "seemed to work better with light-skinned peoples, but that is because [it was] made that way, not because [it] could be no other way" (1997, 90).

Again, photographic technology has historically been calibrated to privilege whiteness and has also impacted how blackness is seen in the visual field. Photography is where the conventions of seeing meet the racial politics of meaning. The technology of images was originally designed to disregard the multiple and subtle shadings of darker skin. The racial politics of image production "extended into the aesthetics of the medium itself, which from its very beginnings was predicated on the denigration and erasure of the black body" (Hornaday 2013). Even today, photographers must manage the inherent bias of their tools to capture an "accurate" depiction of darker skin. In my own experience, I was surprised to learn that the complexions of several popular new black models, particularly Chanel Iman and Joan Smalls, are significantly lighter in person than how they appear in magazine images and on television. Clearly, the impact of lighting on set continues to privilege white skin while rendering black skin darker than in reality, since cameras and lighting were developed to take the white face as the benchmark. In this way, technology is effective in assigning value to race and difference. Nevertheless, as Dyer argues, linking human subjects and the photographic apparatus is not just about achieving accuracy, because "getting the right image meant getting the one which conformed to prevalent ideas of humanity. This included ideas of whiteness, of what color—what range of hue—white people wanted white people to be" (1997, 90) and, I would add, what color white people wanted black people to be. Therefore, both the aesthetic and the technological construction of beauty shape racial representation in fashion.

The high fashion industry relies on a commonsense notion of how race is represented and seen in image. I am suggesting that cultural, market, and technological structures impact decision making, as well as how blackness is "seen" in high fashion. The norms that define and exclude black bodies in fashion are embedded in the system, and technological apparatus, so that they become unrecognizable as having such power over the decision making and ways of seeing.

Blackness as Cultural Commodity: Defining a Market for Blackness in High Fashion

In her *New York Magazine* article titled "Why Fashion Keeps Tripping Over Race," Robin Givhan notes that fashion's global reach means that "everyone isn't hauling around the same societal baggage" (2001). She goes on to offer examples in France and Holland, where the former embraces "exoticism" as well as the historical migration of expatriate African American artists, and the latter is known for its association of blackface with "Black Peters," who are recognized as Santa's little helpers. Nevertheless, the celebration of exoticism and the practice of Dutch revelers wearing blackface during the Christmas holiday season both have deep historical roots in the relationship between two colonial powers and their complex and patriarchal relationship with various African nations. In the same article, Givhan rhetorically asks if she should not have been "horrified" by Viktor and Rolf's spring/summer 2001 decision to paint the faces and bodies of their models black for a collection called "The Black Hole" that "focuses on silhouettes."[2] Givhan suggests that these images and performances are a sign of the contemporary moment (in fashion) where people feel more comfortable playing with images that refer to race. But she acknowledges the difficulty of disaggregating these images from the historical legacy of blackface. She suggests when "it comes from an industry that is hurtful and dismissive it comes across as suspect" (Givhan 2011).

Although black bodies may not be desirable to the average fashion consumer, the popularity of blackface, "urban" shoots, and African-themed spreads shows that there is a particular interest in blackness despite the fact that most of these spreads do not include black professional models (in some cases black bodies are included in the background to add authenticity to the image). The preponderance of these images highlights the fashion industry's strong fascination with black bodies and black culture. It is through the discourse of postracialism that high fashion purveyors enjoy blackness as exotic and fun, since blackness is deployed as a method of celebrating difference as novelty. In other words, postracialism structures race so that it deploys blackness as a commodified style, a fashion accessory that can be used or discarded according to demands of the market—therefore, blackness serves a particular aesthetic function in fashion.

The cover image of a 2006 issue of *The Independent* features supermodel Kate Moss covered in black paint with the caption: "NOT a fashion statement—The Africa Issue." Here, Africa is signified not through landscape or fabric colors but through the blackening of Kate Moss's skin, as if her darker hue evokes kinship with, devotion to, or empathy for the fight against AIDS in Africa. This cover, in the most obvious way, attempts to simulate bodily features associated with blackness/Africanness by projecting a "direct quotation" of blackness through the appropriation of black skin (Black 2009). That same year, in February, photographer Steven Klein shot an editorial for *Vogue Italia* where white models were featured with obviously blackened skin.

One of the most provocative editorials of 2007 was in the August issue of *iD* magazine where black Jamaican model Sasha Gaye-Hunt donned blackface and a colorful head wrap for a short feature on the controversial clothing store American Apparel. The caption for the image read, "Sweeter than candy. Better than cake," proclaiming Gaye-Hunt's body as edible. In her study of the relationship between food, flesh, and racial identity formation, Kyla Wazana Tompkins identifies racist images from the nineteenth and early twentieth centuries that feature "the edible and delicious black subject" whose presence "reveals something larger about the relationship between eating and racial identity" (2012, 1). In contrast to blackface, where blackness is "put on," with images of the delicious, edible black body, Gaye-Hunt's hyper-blackness is "put in" (11).

Following the immensely popular July 2008 *Vogue Italia* "Black Issue," Naomi Campbell was featured in the September 2009 issue of the American *Harper's Bazaar* in an editorial called "Wild Things," where she was styled in various animal skins in an unnamed desert location. The shoot references images of Donyale Luna in the April 1965 issue of *Harper's Bazaar*, photographed by Richard Avedon, with Luna in African garb. Like Luna, Campbell is styled in leopard print; however, whereas Luna's hands gestured "in a claw-like action in one image" and she was pictured "on all fours in another" (Cheddie 2002, 66), Campbell is photographed in action. Her superimposed image is running alongside a leopard as if they are in a race. In this African-themed shoot, the landscape, colors, and Campbell's body are used to signify "Africa" and "blackness" while still pointing to her primitive exoticism.

Despite claims of achieving a postracial America, since the election of President Barack Obama and the July 2008 release of *Vogue Italia*'s "Black Issue," the high fashion industry saw a significant increase in the production of visual representations of racial drag and/or models in blackface for editorial spreads. In any other conjuncture, following the historic election of the first black president, one might be shocked to see so many instances of blatant racism; however, now blackness can be classified as an aesthetic rather than an identity, and the decision to play with these symbols reflects creativity and art. The following list describes some of the most controversial editorial images that were featured in global high fashion magazines between 2009 and 2012:

- October 2009—The body of Dutch model Lara Stone was covered from head to toe in a dark brown lacquer for the supermodel issue of French *Vogue*. The fourteen-page editorial spread, photographed by Steven Klein, featured Stone in various poses, scenes, and garb, including embellished headpieces and outerwear.
- November 2009—Sasha Pivovarova's nude body was covered in black makeup as she modeled opposite Heidi Mount (sans black makeup) for the "Beauty" editorial in *V* magazine. Pivavorova and Mount, both with mouths agape, pose in an embrace above a caption beneath that reads: "Black is the new Black."
- June 2010—Claudia Schiffer performs various instances of racial drag for the sixtieth issue of the quarterly German magazine *Stern Foto-*

grafie. In one of the images, Schiffer dons blackened skin and an Afro wig and assumes a fierce stance as she glares at the camera.

- October 2010—In an editorial entitled "The Kid," Constance Jablonski poses with a black toddler in numerous shots as she is styled with darkened skin and both blond and dark-brown Afro wigs. The spread, for *Numéro* magazine, was reportedly a comment on the growing trend of white celebrities adopting African children.
- May 2010—For *Interview* magazine's "Let's Get Lost" editorial, Daria Werbowy was the only white model photographed among a collection of black male and female models. The black bodies of the accompanying models act as the background to highlight both the clothing and Werbowy's white body.
- February 2011—African American singer and actress Beyoncé Knowles "voluntarily" darkened her skin for *L'Officiel Paris* magazine's editorial honoring Nigerian singer and activist Fela Kuti. She appears in both blackface and tribal makeup and wears garments that were designed by her mother, Tina Knowles.
- Spring/summer 2012—Brazilian model Adriana Lima was photographed for Donna Karan's campaign following the devastating earthquake in Haiti. The campaign features several images of Lima in the foreground with young, black, presumably Haitian bodies lurking in the shadows of the background.

Blackface images in fashion are especially jarring in a contemporary context, not only because of the history of blackface minstrelsy but because the discourse of postracial neoliberalism breaks the equivalency of race and identity to link race and aesthetics so that black is understood as color (skin, fabric—as we saw with the repetition of black in text, fabric, skin, and paint in the beauty spread of "A Black Issue" featuring Chanel Iman), or black signifies wild and exotic. According to fashion historian Colin McDowell, "Models with non-white skin are increasingly visible—although rarely in the world of couture—as a way to give clothes a hint of exoticism and the glamour that comes along with it" (2013, 19). Various scholars have used content analysis of fashion media to explore the ways in which women of color are represented (Arnold 2001; Baumann 2008; hooks 1992). In general, they have found that if darker-hued women are included at all, they tend to be posed and styled "in exotic juxtaposition to the normatively white female body" (Mears 2010, 24). Nevertheless, I disagree with communications scholar Anjali Vats, who suggests that the fashion industry's display of white models in blackface "highlights the underrepresentation of Black models in the fashion industry" (2014, 123), since I argue that blackface in fashion (as in the late nineteenth and early twentieth centuries) has more to do with constructing boundaries of whiteness than representing blackness. In other words, white women in blackface are not taking modeling jobs away from black women, despite what some white models may believe.[3]

The importance of whiteness as "the universal empty point" (Puwar 2002) matters here, since white models can dress in and remove blackness at will, therefore playing with blackness without assuming the burden of race (Pham 2011). Referencing blackface and other racial performances, blackness must be both present and absent to be valuable in the fashion system. The absence of an actual black body allows the darkened white body to operate as a "black" figure, which is "shaped to the demands of desire; [black figures] were screens on which audience fantasy could rest" (Lott 1992, 28). Hence, what is desired is a proximity to blackness. Blackness is a productive association that becomes a category to assign value vis-à-vis whiteness. Therefore, different bodies can now occupy the location of "blackness," which had very specific meaning prior to this "post-" moment, before blackness was deployed as an aesthetic.

Vogue Italia and the Messiness of Race

The title "Haute Mess" is a play on the phrase "hot ghetto mess," popularized by the website hotghettomess.com, which satirizes various constructions of black poor and working-class culture through the use of spectacular images. According to its creator, attorney Jam Donaldson, the website was established "to usher in a new era of self-examination" by displaying a gallery of "the worst of hip-hop culture" (Donaldson n.d.). Donaldson uses the website as a technology of neoliberalism to police the boundaries of blackness by placing the bodies of poor black people under surveillance—in contrast to the cultural norms that position "respectable" black people as worthy of respect and citizenship. Donaldson employs respectability politics to manage the self-improvement and self-regulation of black bodies. As a result, she succeeds in reinscribing racist stereotypes of black people while supporting the postracial narrative that racism is no longer as prevalent or destructive as in the past. Instead, what holds people back is inappropriate individual conduct, which includes personal style. By putting these individuals on display, Donaldson provided an opportunity for a range of interests, including the news media, marketers, new media entrepreneurs, and the high fashion industry, to co-opt these images and turn them into valuable and marketable racialized commodities.

The "Haute Mess" spread and commentary produced in reaction to it are indicative of the current palette of arguments about race and this conjunctural moment. The available commentary by left cultural critics starts with the assumption that producers are extracting or parlaying race. I questioned whether the scene simply depicted the "ghetto-fabulous" or "bling" cultural aesthetic, which Roopali Mukherjee argues is racial spectacle. Mukherjee points to "excess" as a response to late-stage capitalism, which positions blackness as a "social asset" and the ghetto as a "reservoir" of creative and aesthetic inspiration (2006a, 600). Upon its introduction in the late twentieth century, the ghetto-fabulous aesthetic was once a political comment to capitalism and a signifier of youth rebellion. Ghetto-fabulousness displays conspicuous black consumption and connotes a rags-to-riches, class trajectory. The aesthetic signifiers include designer clothes, expensive gold and diamond jewelry, and so forth. Like many cultural productions and performances, the ghetto-fabulous aesthetic was reintroduced as a market commodity. By amplifying the excessiveness and hypervisualizing this aesthetic, the "Haute Mess" spread succeeds in memorializing a static and outdated racial performance. The "playful" use of this aesthetic freezes blackness in the form of a particular black "look."

The "Haute Mess" editorial story also refers directly to the infamous Bronner Brothers trade show that takes place in Atlanta, Georgia, every year. The showcase, which annually features more than fifty thousand hairstylists, exhibitors, distributors, and students, ends with a festive hair show (highlighted in Chris Rock's controversial docu-comedy *Good Hair*) in which stylists from all over the country display their most outlandish creations for a large audience. To imagine the aesthetic style and design of the Bronner Brothers' show (a black American production, with a black American audience and circulation) in an Italian, high fashion, minimally distributed magazine spread would be impossible at any other historical conjuncture but this one, where markers of race are hypervisible commodities *and* actively disavowed. Nevertheless, glancing at web pages such as "Gallery of Ghetto-Fabulous, Edible Hair-Dos" (2011), you see where primary photographer Steven Meisel, Lori Goldstein, and their style team derived their inspiration. The bodies of these women are produced through both consumerism and creativity, becoming the consumable commodities (candy-wrapper hair and nails) and allegedly canvases for their artistic expression.

The images presented in the story, according to Meisel and editor Sozzani, are supposed to represent extravagant, "messy" drag queen culture. Sozzani responded to the uproar and cries of racism (again), from various blogs, by proclaiming innocence to any racist agenda. She defended the spread against charges of racism by suggesting that unlike previous spreads in the magazine, it was not at all controversial (Moss 2012). She explained that the shoot was an attempt to push people to be more creative and extravagant, since the fashion world is too bland and uniform. Sozzani's use of "messy" drag queen culture to combat the "blandness" of the fashion world can be invoked by bell hooks's astute argument that the commodification of otherness "has been so successful because it is offered as a new delight, more intense and more satisfying than normal ways of doing and feeling.... Ethnicity becomes a spice, seasoning that can liven up the dull dish that is mainstream white culture" (1992, 21).

Sozzani claims that those who criticized the spread as classist are "sick" and unable to read the images like a "normal" person. That Sozzani denies any connection to stereotypical representations of black culture and instead claims that the spread was generated as harmless fun and a nod to drag queens only highlights the fact that deployments of race today are delinked from traditional understandings of race—where historical links to racism apparently no longer apply. Sozzani is able to deflect cries of racism and instead attaches signifiers to drag queens, whose performances are rooted in black women's culture. Rather than recognizing drag queen culture as linked to blackness, she supports her project using the language of aesthetic creativity—where race becomes a depoliticized social construct. Here, Sozzani seemingly stages "messy" drag queen culture as an image of commoditized hybridity that conflates race, class, gender, and sexuality within the particular totalizing logic of neoliberalism. She effectively silences the voices and visions of black cultural producers by employing what Stuart Hall calls "regressive modernization" in her "creative" assembling of editorial fashion and popular culture. By "regressive modernization," Hall speaks to an attempt to discipline and "educate" society "into a particularly regressive version of modernity by, paradoxically, dragging it backwards through an equally regressive version of the past" (1988, 2). The producers of "Haute Mess" deny race as an organizing and driving factor in their "messy" drag queen performance. It is this performance that is conditioned by proximation to blackness and the "language of creative license." Such performances dislodge common cultural practices of racism from their repugnant history and reframe them as aesthetic choice.

As I mentioned earlier, the image of cover girl Joan Smalls acts as a tour guide to the fantastic and "#overthetop" world of a "Haute Mess." At first glance, the image refers to stereotypical overrepresentations of black women as excessive, creative, gluttonous, lascivious, fertile, perverse, complexly un/feminine, irresponsible, and wasteful. Black women have historically been produced through visual signs as in excess of idealized white femininity; from mammy to the passing woman to the jezebel. The explicit white woman's body, on the other hand, follows the norm of idealized femininity. Puerto Rican beauty Smalls's lithe figure and light-brown skin do little to disrupt the visual field. However, Smalls is placed in the scene to provide visual evidence that black and white bodies are interchangeable in this space. In this multicultural era when racial performance and racial markers lack the political significance they held in the past, both black bodies and white bodies can play with race.

Picturing a "Hot Ghetto Mess"

I use the remaining space of the chapter to delve into a closer analysis of "Haute Mess." I argue for the necessity of examining these images in order to frame the aesthetic of blackness that is explicitly and implicitly embedded within each image—including those images in which a human body is not displayed.

The first image of the spread, presented beside a cover page illustrating the "Haute Mess" title in colorful graffiti print, features a seemingly pregnant model who is dressed in a tight tube dress, seated at a diner booth. On her table are items from McDonald's, Burger King, and Popeye's fast-food outlets. The model is also styled in an ostentatious way, with her pink hair reaching epic heights, interwoven with pink silk flowers and other garish accessories. Her eyes are decorated with colorful eye shadow featuring the Louis Vuitton logo. An adult bystander and a baby in a stroller, presumably her partner and child, stand in the distance with their faces blurred. Although only one black body is visually present, the setting enables the audience to fantasize about how additional black bodies could occupy the space.

Again, at first glance, the shoot appears to reference a stereotypical presentation of a particular black aesthetic, a modernized form of blackface. Explicit racial markers (e.g., cans of Colt 45 malt liquor) deploy blackness despite the fact that all but one of the models are nonblack. The use of these materials in the spread evokes what Henry Louis Gates (1984) describes as a "naturalist fallacy," which suggests that there is an expectation that visual signifiers of race consistently and authentically represent black people rather than social relations. Through the presentation of blackness as style worn by nonblack bodies, we are led to believe that "the boundaries of racial identity can be crossed, or at least blurred slightly" (Black 2009, 247). It is through these discursive markers that blackness comes to life in image.

With its display of hair weave tracks, colorful wigs, gold teeth, decorative finger- and toenails, and so forth, the "Haute Mess" spread reproduces what Nirmal Puwar calls the "amnesia of celebration"—the practice of forgetting the violence (in the form of harassment, discrimination, and fetishization) against women of color for wearing garments and accessories that are now celebrated on white bodies or deemed as fun play through aesthetic transformation. The white bodies that are adorned with these accessories remain white and look white, while maintaining the pleasure of whiteness, since white female bodies occupy the powerful, universal, unmarked empty space (Dyer 1997), which enables them to "play with the assigned particularity of ethnicized female bodies" (Puwar 2002, 76).

In this age of postracialism, black bodies are not necessary for blackness to be observed. As Harry Elam argues, blackness can now "travel on its own, separate and distinct from black people." Blackness, according to Elam, is of particular material value: "Blackness functions as something that you can apply, put on, wear, that you use to assuage social anxiety and perceived threat: the desire to be included without the necessity of including black folk." The problem, as Elam identifies it, is that "it remains exceedingly attractive and possible in this post-black, postsoul age of black cultural traffic to love black cool and not love black people" (2005, 386). Racial markers act as consumable elements of a black aesthetic. In this postracial period, race no longer occupies the same space of identity in the ways it did during and immediately following the civil rights movement; therefore, race is reduced to explicit and crude markers/accessories like the weave extensions, acrylic nails, wigs, and excessive cosmetics, as well as fast food, baby strollers, and "fierce" bodily poses. Here, we see the disciplining of the white body to adopt racial dispositions in a two-dimensional space.

Imani Perry (2011) discusses the popularity and profitability of racial performances, which are "repeatedly bought and sold." She continues by arguing that the performance of race roles generates profits; however, "they also operate to implicitly thwart the recognition of people of color who don't occupy such roles. Moreover, the consumer package of the role or performance becomes overdetermined and collapses within it cultural attributes that become further devalued by virtue of their association with stereotype"

(Perry 2011, 173). Blackness as a performance requires a particular attitude, body position, glance, and look that transcend the medium of print, enabling the performer to profess knowledge about the experience of being black and therefore accessorizing identity with cultural add-ons.

The practice and performance of blackface during the nineteenth century, as Eric Lott suggests, were a way to make blackness "into a marketable thing of white interest . . . commodification is, in a sense, its *attraction*; it is what seems 'blackest' about [the racial economy]" (1992, 44). This form of "fun" is distinguished from blackface, where the constructedness of "Haute Mess" is considered laughable rather than being a representation of natural or real characteristics of black women. The images reflect a racial structure "whose ideological and psychological instability required its boundaries to be continually staged, and which regularly exceeded the dominant culture's capacity to fix such boundaries," as Lott has written of nineteenth-century blackface performances (27). I would argue that "Haute Mess" visually projects more than overt racial stereotypes—it literally exceeds the mere language of the stereotype. Unlike recent fashion spreads and advertisements where white models are literally painted black, the "Haute Mess" spread disengages from more overt historical references to racist performances and instead fosters a shrewder variety. Nevertheless, I lean on Stuart Hall's (1978) claim that forms of racism that occupied previous historical eras can be in accord with new and emerging discourses of race and racial meaning.

Given the current moment in race relations, as Bonilla-Silva (2014) identifies, race and racism operate in a subtler manner than in the past. Race, in this conjuncture, operates more like the "cheesy" films and television programs highlighted by Newitz (2000), since it does not take for granted that black women (and Americans) are "naturally" excessive. Instead, the spread laughs at the history of black women being constructed in that way. This form of parody fixes the instability and ambivalence of race. Race is therefore commodified, rendered equivalent, and sold as a sensation. In fashion, history becomes fetish. Fashion images displace, justify, and recognize history and its importance by producing aesthetic references to it, while at the same time disavowing it with the removal of certain aesthetics from their contexts and placement in a seemingly unrelated mode.

The images hail a particularly American version of cultural politics, one that appeals to Americanness, not just black Americanness. The images provide more than exaggerations of black women in the service of subordination. Instead, "Haute Mess" evokes notions of branding, consumption, commodity, and nation. Furthermore, the spread designates different cultures as equivalent, where their equivalences operate as humorous, fashionable, and marketable as entertainment. "Haute Mess" invites laughter "at something that seems utterly horrifying in its complexity: the totality of social connections and disconnections we call multinationalism" (Newitz 2000, 61).

Hence, the reversal of white bodies as wasteful, hypersexual, excessive, immoral, unhealthy, and irresponsible for those of black bodies brings with them a shield against critiques of black excess and abuse of the state—since they are white. The spread, in particular, allows us (and the featured models) to enjoy the story and avoid the "upsetting implications of objects" that speak to the reality of poverty (Newitz 2000, 75). The logic of using skin color to identify blackness allows for symbolic forms of blackness, as objects and accessories, to roam freely, unregulated by the same technologies, on the bodies of nonblack persons. In this way, blackness is no longer tied to skin and instead can be exchangeable, distributed as style. According to Homi K. Bhabha, the threat of mimicry "comes from the prodigious and strategic production of conflictual, fantastic, discriminatory 'identity effects' in the play of power that is elusive because it hides no essence, no 'itself'" ([1994] 2005, 90). The interaction of mimicry with neoliberalism seems to reattach the fractured pieces of race in that it makes blackness exportable and stylized. It is in fact the excessiveness of the performance that makes the image/style black. Nevertheless, the whiteness of the white bodies in a black space brings with it insurance against charges of abuse of the symbolic system. This reversal of bodies assures protection against the critique of black excess and racism more generally.

In a conversation about the contemporary music period and the appropriation of black music by white artists, Imani Perry notes: "I think what it reflects is that there is a sonic preference for blackness—the sounds of blackness—but there is a visual preference for whiteness in our culture, and a human preference for whiteness."[4] So, too, is the case in the fashion industry with the performance of blackness (using racial markers) by white models. What remains important is that the models in the images (with the exception of Joan Smalls—whose blackness is exemplified by her skin, hair, heritage, and so forth) are obviously white—their visible whiteness is at the center of the artistic intent. The characters in the "Haute Mess" story must appear to be submerged in the culture of blackness. If mostly black or Latina models were to be used for the editorial, the implied pleasure and fun of the performance would be compromised and possibly deemed racist.

"Haute Mess" has only one black body, but blackness is everywhere—so, excess operates within the symbolic codes. This conjuncture allows both to happen simultaneously because in the postracial and neoliberal renderings of the moment, this particularly American version of cultural politics presents excess as blackness, because it cannot portray excess as white. Similarly, "feminine racialization as a lucrative flexible personal asset creates a neoliberal racial visibility that requires profound blindness to current and historical injustices" (Hasinoff 2008, 326). In other words, neoliberalism is inscribed on bodies/spaces in the name of representation and diversity through the aestheticization of blackness.

Notes

1 I define "postrace" as the theoretical extraction of race from any meaningful dialogue about our economic, social, and political conditions—or, put simply, we are "beyond" race, since race is no longer a factor when considering the life chances of individuals. Postracial discourse rests on the strategic disregard of racism by ignoring the implications of race

2 Ironically, Viktor and Rolf followed their 2001 effort with a corresponding "White" collection spring/summer 2002. In this runway show, none of the models were covered with white makeup to represent the "white" aesthetic.

3 Crystal Renn was interviewed by *Jezebel*'s Jenna Sauers about her controversial shoot for *Vogue Japan* in which she donned eye tape to presumably make her look "more Asian." In the midst of the interview, Sauers asked Renn about her thoughts on blackface in fashion. She replied: "I am not 100% morally okay with [blackface shoots]—I would feel that I'm taking a job from one of them. I would feel that I'm taking a job from a black girl who deserved it" (Sauers 2011).

4 For the conversation between Perry and Marc Lamont Hill, see "Justin Timberlake: 'The 20/20 Experience'" 2013.

13

Veiled Visibility

Racial Performances and Hegemonic Leaks in Pakistani Fashion Week

INNA ARZUMANOVA

In 2009, colorful abayas, embroidered headscarves, and jeweled face veils made their way down fashion catwalks in Karachi, Pakistan. Saturated, busy color palettes and volumes of billowing silks were weighed down by delicate but plentiful embroidery and beadwork. Chains from jhoomar head orna-ments held models' hair in place. These were the scenes of Pakistan's first official fashion week. The pieces on display at that 2009 event were created by designers who nearly uniformly attribute their textile designs, fabric in-spirations, patterns, and preferred cuts to their shared Pakistani heritage. There were also aesthetics heavily informed by Islamic fashion—saris were accompanied by chaddors; shawls hung casually but reliably on models' heads; scarves covered shoulders and, often, faces; variations of hijab were as plentiful on the catwalk as they were in the audience. Through social media and press coverage, images and representations of these collections gained transnational circulation, simultaneously introducing Pakistan as the new-est citizen of global high fashion's creative geography and catapulting the aesthetic sensibilities of Pakistani designers into global visibility.

Since 2009, Pakistan's fashion industry has grown significantly and become more institutionalized. The country now hosts four fashion weeks, two in Karachi and two in Lahore, all overseen by the country's two primary fashion councils. In 2014, the Pakistani fashion market was estimated at roughly $7.3 billion (Rehman 2015).[1] Reviewing the 2015 Telenor Fashion Pakistan Week, Faiza Virani observes that "the industry has evolved, the onslaught of fashion weeks has made not only designers more competitive, it has also made for a more discerning audience" (2015).

Global Fashion, Fracturing Maps

That Pakistan's foray into the international fashion calendar represents a perceptible shift in the maps that govern the global fashion industry's typical distribution of value and visibility is undeniable. In fact, in the past several years, owing in part to the establishment of off-center industrial manufacturing and production sites, as well as the deregulation of the global garment industry, the locations from which fashion's aesthetic creativity has traditionally emanated have shifted, enabling creative visibility for previously uncovered cities.[2] Global fashion weeks have popped up in places like Mumbai, Mexico City, Moscow, Johannesburg, and São Paulo, testifying to those cities' growing fashion industries, as well as their designers' visibility as creative citizens. "The scales," according to one journalist, "are tipping fast between 'the West' and 'the Rest' and boy does the fashion industry know it" (R. Young 2015). Writing of Pakistan's 2011 fashion season, Huma Qureshi triumphantly declared: "Forget the catwalks of London, Paris, New York and Milan. This year, there's only one fashion week making history: the world's very first Islamabad fashion week" (2011). *Vice* magazine's documentary series "Fashion Week Internationale" operates according to one governing principle: "anywhere but New York, London, or Paris" (the home page image is a close-up shot of five Nigerian models from Lagos Fashion Week).

This multiplication and fracturing of global fashion's traditional geography (a geography that counts Paris, Milan, New York, and London as its capitals) is a new landscape that demands an equally new response from the stalwarts of the fashion industry. Formal silence about racial difference and quiet but routine appropriation of racial "otherness" will no longer do. Organizers of the four major fashion weeks as well as leading figures in these Eurocentric fashion industries must account for this fractured geography, for the emergence of what Okwui Enwezor (2009) would call the creative off-center, as both creative hub and potential market.[3] For the global fashion industry, managing this new reality has meant espousing a kind of adapted postracial philosophy. This form of postracialism is born out of neoliberalism's wider commitment to multiculturalism. As Jodi Melamed argues, neoliberal industries fetishize multiculturalism as a way of both exploiting its market possibilities and, importantly, concealing the ways in which neoliberal markets rely on the "hyperextraction of surplus value from racialized bodies... naturalizing a system of capital accumulation that grossly favors the global North over the global South" (2006, 1). The global fashion industry, governed by neoliberal economies, in turn, builds on these logics in order to produce its own variation: an adapted postracial philosophy. That is, this industry does not simply deny the urgency of racial critique or representation, as postracial logics often urge; doing so would mean ignoring the economic shifts within the industry and among its consumers. Instead, figures within the industry (designers, stylists, journalists, etc.) mark racial "otherness," only to then bring it into the fold, neutralizing its power and then using its visibility as evidence of racial progress, at best, and racial transcendence, at worst. Within this economic context, this type of doubled move can be seen as a form of crisis management.

One example is the fact that the reigning fashion capitals, as they are typically called, are now engaged in "a competitive recruitment drive... to lure in designers from around the globe" (R. Young 2015). This recruitment results in initiatives like the International Fashion Showcase, sponsored by the British Fashion Council and held during London Fashion Week, intended to pluck young designers of color from around the globe, grant them visibility within the purview of London Fashion Week, and win their lifelong loyalty to the British fashion industry. What ostensibly looks like commitment to racial and cultural heterogeneity is, in fact, an increasing economic necessity. Furthermore, this frenzied international scouting is also driven in part by major transformations in the luxury goods consumer market, where "consumers from emerging markets dominate the equation by holding the purse strings" (R. Young 2015).

Parallel to these considerable efforts to incorporate and neutralize the economic threat posed by the off-center, however, is the global fashion industry's determined adherence to postracial logics. Reviewing Dolce & Gabbana's spring 2013 collection, Robin Givhan (2012), a well-known US fashion journalist who has often spoken about fashion's glaring racial gaps, discussed the Italian designers' use of the golliwog image as part of their collection. She writes: "There was nothing ponderous or political about this collection—no matter how gut-clenchingly odd it might be to see a kind of Golliwogg face on a designer shirt worn by a white model. . . . The Golliwogg is not fully freed of its burden. But it is thought-provoking to see it in the context of another culture's sweet memories—a reminder that our world is both vast and tiny, as well as exceedingly complex" (Givhan 2012).

It is worth noting that Givhan isn't so much denying that there is racial connotation embedded in the golliwog image; rather, she is implying that its global circulation and deployment by Italian designers strip that connotation and achieve a reinscription, one that is nearer to joy than it is to pain (her piece is called "Ode to Joy"). Givhan's is probably the more complicated of these postracial declarations. When asked about their unwillingness to grapple with race, many fashion figures will claim that they simply focus on beauty, which they suggest as a neutral, deracialized category that should easily solve fashion's problems with racial othering, silence, and absence. Barbara Nicoli, fashion model casting director for several leading fashion houses, told James Lim that she doesn't "like to talk in terms of white, Asian, black, etc., because a model is a model and that's it. To me, if we want to talk about diversity, it's about the model and not the color of their skin. It's more about the body, the face, and the attitude" (Nicoli quoted in Lim 2013).

In a podcast interview, Anna Wintour, editor of US *Vogue*, tells André Leon Talley that she is particularly proud of her September 2015 Beyoncé cover because it is a testament "of how far we've come, how much the world has changed," adding that the singer is "every woman." In the same interview, however, in the midst of congratulating the magazine on contributing to what she positions as racial "progress," Wintour also says "race was very much on our mind but we didn't consciously set out to represent black culture or black politics or race; it just all came together" ("ALT Interviews Anna Wintour" 2015). *Why bother with race, they all seem to ask in their own way, we've come so far that simple merit and beauty are enough.*

The off-center then—creative cultures like Pakistan's fashion industry—gains visibility within a global fashion climate that has embraced an adapted postracial ethos. This is a climate that necessarily marks them as racial or cultural others; a climate that retains its allegiances to Eurocentric value attribution and stubbornly praises a merit-based system where aesthetics and beauty are somehow divorced from their racial histories; a climate that, at the same time, finds itself needing to invest, both literally and figuratively, in racial "difference."

It is under these conditions that Pakistan's fashion industry becomes visible within the circuits of global fashion. For Pakistan's fashion industry, which was considered an "off-center" entrant into the international fashion week cohort, becoming visible as a creative industry means entering into an arrangement wherein designers and their aesthetics are compelled both to compete for visual significance in fashion's Eurocentric, geographically rigid symbolic imaginary and to accommodate that imaginary's grammars of race, nationhood, and citizenship by adopting, in part, the industry's mythological mantle of postracial citizenship. To become visible within the global fashion arena, where consumer power may be shifting but visibility is nevertheless dictated and governed by the stalwart fashion capitals and their institutions, Pakistan's fashion industry must perform its own presence on the global fashion stage. It must enter into a strategic dialogue with its own conditions of visibility. In fact, the case of Pakistan's fashion industry and its newly visible fashion weeks reminds us that it is not enough to celebrate this industry's visibility within the circuits of global fashion. The existing celebration is one in which racial indexing crosses with the demands of neoliberal capital. Instead, it is necessary to consider the economic and legislative conditions that both make that visibility possible and contain its racially marked articulations and operations.

If the concurrent and imbricated processes of neoliberal market expansion (and trade policies) and the fashion industry's mutated postracial philosophy enable the existence and global visibility of Pakistan's fashion industry and fashion weeks, then how do these global markets dictate the visual consumption and legibility of Pakistani fashion? And how do Pakistani designers perform to accommodate those regimes of visual and commercial consumption? Finally, what do these performances tell us about the racially inflected requirements of a global creative citizenship that is underwritten by neoliberal economies of visibility? The last question is a critical one as it provides some insight into the conditions under which off-center cultural and arts industries gain symbolic citizenship as creative global citizens.

The Pakistani Fashion Industry: Deregulation and Institutionalization

The histories of Pakistan's fashion industry are linked to the global garment trade, local Pakistani textile manufacturing, and neoliberal trade policy. The industry itself is some thirty years in the making. Frieha Altaf, former model, CEO of Pakistan's Catwalk Productions, and one of the pioneers of the Pakistani fashion industry, traces the institutionalization of the industry to the early 1980s (Rashed 2005). The industry underwent a period of maturation in the late 1980s and 1990s, especially under the rule of Prime Minister

Benazir Bhutto, who sponsored fashion shows in the early 1990s. Throughout the 1990s and into the first decade of the 2000s, design institutes and fashion councils were established with the help of the Trade Development Authority and the Ministry of Commerce; the annual Lux Style Awards were introduced; luxury department stores were opened; and fashion magazines were launched. By 2007, Ayesha Tammy Haq, CEO of Fashion Pakistan, described it as the "nascent fashion industry taking its first baby steps" ("About Xpozé" 2009).

The increasing institutionalization of fashion creativity was also propelled by the needs of the Pakistani textile industry, which accounts for nearly 60 percent of Pakistan's total exports and is the eighth-largest exporter of textile products in Asia (Mukhtar 2008). Yasin Ahmed of Horizon Securities reported in 2009 that the "textile and clothing industry has been the main driver of the economy for the last 50 years," with a significant "investment boom" in most of its textile industry segments from 2003 to 2007 (2009, 2, 3). This investment boom can be traced back to the massive deregulation that began in 1995 and was brought to full fruition in 2005 in the global textile and garment trade industries.[4] The deregulation, or the Agreement on Textiles and Clothing (ATC), began in 1995 and was meant to gradually lift quotas on textile exports over a ten-year period, culminating in what was intended to be complete deregulation and liberalization of the textile trade and garment industry by 2005.[5]

It was precisely this global postquota climate of liberalization and deregulation that produced the investment boom in the Pakistani textile industry through 2007. The development of Pakistan's fashion industry has been, at least in part, a function of the nation's economic reinvestment in the domestic textile industry. The Pakistan Institute of Fashion and Design (PIFD) includes the demands posed by the cotton and textile industries as primary drivers of its own origin story. At its inception, the institute's objective was to furnish the textile industry with the professionals it required in order to compete in the global fashion industry. Meanwhile, the Pakistan Fashion Design Council (PFDC) vows to "work closely with textile mills in Pakistan to develop fabric and manufacture value added garments . . . [which] will help in promoting value added exports in the textile sector," ultimately leading to national economic growth.[6]

These pronouncements of commitment to the nation's textile industry suggest that the development of the Pakistani fashion industry is intimately linked to the nation's investment in its textile industry as a route to competing within the global apparel trade and its economic structures of globalization. In other words, the visibility and subsidized growth of Pakistan's fashion industry are conditioned by the development of the nation's neo-liberal trade practices and its ability to position itself as a market available for foreign investment—deregulated and amenable to privatization (India Pakistan Trade Unit 2011). The industry's institutionalization (its objectives and its existence) cannot be divorced from the neoliberal, economic ambitions of the state.

Propelled to the forefront of global fashion's visual imaginary by these economic practices, Pakistani designers and their aesthetics nevertheless enter the circuits of global fashion visibility as othered representatives of the off-center, forced to manage their own threatening presences on the global stage. And it is precisely these tactics of performative self-management that demonstrate the compromised and uneasy nature of global visibility best of all. As the following examination of Pakistani designers and their treatment of aesthetics demonstrates, for representatives of the off-center, global creative visibility is structured by a compulsory performance of racially indexed and legible racial subjectivity. The management and accommodation of identity and aesthetics that Pakistani designers engage in are most readily evident in two particular areas: (1) the industry's treatment of garment manufacturing and its gendered labor, and (2) the aesthetics of the collections on display.

Strategic Performances: Gendered Labor

Pakistan is one of the world's leading cotton producers and the chief manufacturer and exporter of embroidery on the subcontinent, making local textile manufacturing fundamental to Pakistan's GDP and even more significant to its growing clothing sector and fashion industry. Importantly, the clothing sector's primary geographic clustering is dictated by the availability of "sufficient ladies labor" (Y. Ahmed 2009, 2). Indeed, women make up the majority of the Pakistani garment industry's labor force, subject to the injustices of an industry that operates seasonally, by contract, and by piece rates. Karin Astrid Siegmann and Nazima Shaheen call these laborers the "weakest link in the global textile chain" (2008, 628). The conditions that female Pakistani garment workers face are neither new nor exclusive to this nation. Scholars like Ellen Israel Rosen (2002) and Grace Kyungwon Hong (2006) have written at length about the gendered labor that shores up the continual expansion of the global apparel trade.[7]

That female garment workers are the most vulnerable link in this chain, as Siegmann and Shaheen describe, is only exacerbated by the Pakistani industry's rapid deregulation. Because the industry's growth and global participation have been accelerated by global neoliberal trade policies and economies, the industry has been modeled in neoliberalism's vision. Local labor deregulation has been pursued relentlessly. For example, the 2003 Punjab Industrial Policy abolished labor regulations in several industries, including textiles, to make those industries more attractive to business investment.

These economic and neoliberal realities are, unsurprisingly, not conducive to the performance of global creative citizenship; they are serious wrinkles in the fashion industry's celebratory pronouncements about racial transcendence and shifting scales of power. As the realities of Pakistani garment workers and cotton pickers' labor conditions enter into dialogue with the global fashion industry, they are instead envisioned as crafts, artisanal manufacturing, and hand embroidery. Descriptions invoke images of local artists carefully and diligently embroidering unique pieces, rather than garment workers laboring in deregulated neoliberal industries that exploit their labor in order to compete in the global garment trade. The UK-based company Fashion Compassion, which often works with Pakistani designers, is a good example of the ways in which the labor of garment workers in Pakistan, as well as other participating regions, transforms into a myth of artist craftswomen and traditional, regional skill. Ayesha Mustafa, the company's founder, has said that the "consumer is told that each order placed is handled with love and care by artisans possessing immense ability. From the artisans['] angle they are trained to give the product their heart and soul and when it comes out for delivery it is unique and exquisite and a brand" ("Ayesha Mustafa" 2012). More to the point, the Pakistani brand Inaaya is described as a "socially conscious fashion brand" that "currently works with female artisans in rural impoverished areas of Pakistan where the infrastructure and poverty issues are compounded by women's rights issues" ("New to Fashion Compassion" 2013).

Furthermore, the international press is primarily interested in exactly how "war-torn" the region of craftsmanship might be, often focusing on frameworks of terrorism, extremism, and war. Reporting for *Business of Fashion*, Maliha Rehman framed her review of the 2015 Telenor Fashion Pakistan Week around what she saw as the disjuncture between religious reality and the fashion fantasy bubble. "On a more sordid note," she writes, "with parts of the country spiraling towards violent extremism, the fashion fraternity has to worry that the threats they receive may actually be carried out" (Rehman 2015). Reporting for the *London Extra*, Tim Bale describes the 2015 Lahore fashion week he attended as no less than a "battle for Pakistan's survival" (Paracha 2015).

But the parameters for this discourse were established long before the 2015 fashion season. In the aftermath of Pakistan's first fashion week in 2009, for example, the Western press typically focused on the threats posed by the Taliban and the event's constant security issues. In light of this discourse, and attesting to the types of performances that globalization demands of the off-center, designer Sonya Battla aligned her own collection with the empowerment of women. "I'm a very brave woman," Battla told the *UK Telegraph*. "I'm not going to be scared and no one's going to judge me" (Allbritton 2009). Here, Battla is unproblematically positioning her own design sensibilities in opposition to the Taliban and, therefore, in close alliance with the Eurocentric and Western-oriented fashion world. And Battla was not alone. Female designers, speaking to the foreign (and particularly the US and European) press, frequently cited vague liberal feminist principles as the force driving their decisions to participate in the fashion week. Ayesha Tammy Haq, CEO of Pakistan Fashion Week (PFW), was quoted by the *UK Telegraph* as saying that the entire event should be viewed as a "gesture of defiance to the Taliban" ("Taliban Defied by Pakistani Models" 2009). Tooba Sheikh, one of the organizers of the event, told a journalist that she views fashion shows as "challenging the extremist mind-set proliferating in the Pakistani society" (Paracha 2015). Providing a concise summary for this discourse, designer Fahad Hussayn chose "Democrats Midsummer" as the name for his 2015 collection for the PFDC Sunsilk Fashion Show.

The designers and organizers, in dialogue with the Eurocentric global fashion world gaze, produce themselves as what Chandra Mohanty (2003) calls "the Third World woman." Mohanty argues that this trope, favored by Western feminism, consolidates the experiences and identities of all women from the global East and global South into a singular mode of common oppression and dependency. Inside this discourse, women of color are defined in terms of "object status," universally described as victims of violence (male and capitalist), as powerless and exploited, and in need of political saving from the West (Mohanty 2003, 23). It is precisely this discourse that Battla and other designers deploy when they publicly pledge their visibility to Western feminism, producing and positioning themselves as successful "Third World Women" subjects. This production of subjecthood brings to mind Malek Alloula's (1986) collection of colonial postcards, which featured Algerian women, typically veiled, and performed several key tasks: they provided French audiences with a racialized fantasy that would authorize colonial practice, and they represented French possession of Arab women as a proxy for France's possession of Algeria and its future. In the introduction to this collection, Barbara Harlow observes that the women on the post-cards served as "phantasmic representations of Western designs on the Orient" (Alloula 1986, xiv). In stitching themselves together as "Third World Women" subjects, Pakistani designers like Battla are joining this visual legacy but from a radically different site of production. Rather than being the objects of the colonial gaze, these designers are producing their own subject-hood and doing so strategically, in order to negotiate their presence within fashion's economies of visibility. Alloula's collection of postcards, however, remains a useful reference point because the cards allow us to see the ways in which these contemporary strategic performances, as I will discuss later in this chapter, yield drastically different and potentially subversive results.

Consolidating their political positionalities into this identity performance allows these Pakistani female designers to become legible as creative bodies in the discursive structures of fashion's geographic and racial hierarchies—hierarchies that refuse to see them (indeed, make them visible) as anything but "Third World Women." That their initiation into legibility as creative citizens requires their adoption of Western liberal feminist sensibilities, wherein their own bodies are made to work toward capital's racially asymmetric structures and toward fashion's postracial myth, is a telling characteristic of the requirements for global creative citizenship.[8]

Consequently, when it comes to the Pakistani industry's global visibility, the discourses that designers and their aesthetics undertake produce a system of tripled labor for the industry's female labor force (garment workers and designers). These workers' bodies become responsible both for material production, physically supporting the nation-state's global neoliberal ambitions, and for symbolic production, performatively invoked in the narratives of artisan craftswomen. Finally, in producing their own bodies as contestations to what is rendered as fundamentalism, these designers and garment workers' bodies also labor to validate Western capitalist democracy, drawing on the West's long-standing discursive tradition of using tropes of oppressed women to validate invasion and foreign policy (Alloula 1986; Mohanty 2003). To gain entry into global fashion's circuits of visibility, which prefer an adapted postracial ethos, the newly minted postracial subjects (in this case, the Pakistani designers) must simultaneously invoke their own racial selves and then announce their own transcendence of that self. Here, that invocation is routed through religion, relying on the ways in which the Orientalist and Eurocentric imagination tethers religious difference (specifically, Islam) to racial difference. In other words, in making references to religious difference within this context, these subjects are always also gesturing to their own racialization, guaranteeing that racialization and sowing the conditions necessary for the industry's postracial claims. While these are the discursive stakes of global creative citizenship within the fashion industry, strategic deployments of aesthetics provide a second area where the off-center enters into a strategic dialogue with global fashion's circuits of visibility.

Strategic Performances: The Aesthetics of Heterogeneity

Describing the expansion objectives embraced by the design house Monica Couture, the brand's designer explains that her plan for growth hinges on aesthetic heterogeneity, combining "traditional patterns and motifs inspired from Ottoman and Mughal periods" with the "latest trends and cuts" ("Fashion Designer Monica Paracha" 2012). Aesthetic heterogeneity, in fact, is the centerpiece of the Pakistani fashion industry's growth strategy. This heterogeneity is a particular one; it refers specifically to the mix of what is understood—and commonly named—as "Western" and "Eastern" aesthetics. Designs on display on Pakistan's catwalks from 2009 and into the present represent a combination of traditional Pakistani fabrics and styles, as well as entire collections that make no references to Pakistan's sartorial heritage at all.

This preference for aesthetic diversity has only grown since the fashion week events began in 2009. The 2012 collection ("Colonial Transgression") by rising young designer Misha Lakhani combined high-waisted skinny pants, narrow belts, and simply draped monochromatic silk tops with heavy, entirely embroidered dupattas as jackets. The designer used a wide range of fabrics, including both screen prints and digital prints. She told Pakistan's *Daily Times* that the collection is about "refining the extravagance of old India by fusing it with the lexicon of international chic" (Agha 2012, B8). Showing again at the 2013 PFW, she opted for limited ornamentation, minimalist cuts, and tailoring that, in some cases, cited traditions prevalent in European menswear. Similar to other designers, like Zaheer Abbas, Lakhani stuck to a subdued color palette; in two pieces, she showed dresses in stark black and white, a color combination that rarely appears in traditional Pakistani clothing. Other designers have combined Pakistani textiles with small pleats, Peter Pan collars, and geometric tailoring.

In line with their commitment to aesthetic heterogeneity, Pakistani designers have also consistently offered variations on garments intended as Islamic fashion (silk headscarves, chaddors, etc.). At the 2009 PFW, designer Ather Hafeez sent traditional yellow and orange gowns, complete with headscarves, down the runway, and at one point, a model encased in layers of a heavy, bright pink and green hijab made her way down the ramp. During the same event, Zarmina Khan's costumes included jewel-embellished, loosely worn headscarves. A model for Rizwanullah's show wore a completely white ensemble, covering everything but her face (she even kept her hands tucked firmly in her pockets as she walked down the runway). For the spring 2015 shows, the designer Yousuf Bashir Qureshi (known as YBQ) showcased his "Laal, Shah, Mast" collection, inspired by three Sufi saints. The models, who walked to Sufi music, wore heavy black and red turbans, draped tunics and gowns, and churidars; some of them held flags bearing prayer texts.

As the earlier quote from Misha Lakhani demonstrates, designers often point to this trend of aesthetic heterogeneity to explain their artistic inspirations. Ali Xeeshan told Pakistan's *Sunday Plus Magazine*, for example, that his collection "The Paradox" was inspired by "a combination of two extremes . . . creating a harmony between traditional and the avant-garde style" (Kunwar 2011, 10). The collection he showed at the 2011 PFW was a combination of chaddors with face veils, in some cases, and brightly colored short shorts, in others. Designer Saim Ali understands her aesthetic as a mix of the same categories, remarking: "I work on Western cuts while the embellishments are pretty Eastern so I have a lot of fusion in my designs" ("Showbiz Pakistan—Interview Saim Ali" 2011). And Nosheen Rana of NSR defines her own sense of style as "an amalgamation of the East and West, and of traditions and modernity" (Deen 2012). Over and over, designers not only present a wide range of aesthetic sensibilities, borrowing from diverse design traditions and cultural dress norms, but also consistently envision these aesthetics as fusions of "East" and "West."

And there is evidence to suggest that an invocation of the "East" and its presumed "traditionalism" is both functional and strategically performative here. Designer Madiha Ibrar says that in order for young Pakistani designers to be recognized internationally, they must use their Pakistani culture as a "tool" and "focus on more traditional outfits" ("Fashion Designer Madiha Ibrar" 2012). As the Pakistani industry grows and expands internationally, joining the ranks of other newly visible fashion production sites, Ibrar worries that "there are certain areas where one feels that the fashion industry is fast leaving its traditional roots that had made it exotic and appealing in the first place. There is a need to hold onto those ideas" ("Fashion Designer Madiha Ibrar" 2012). Others in the industry follow suit. Tariq Amin, a Pakistani stylist and TV personality working at the 2011 fashion week in Islamabad, told US-based *Vice* magazine that the models' "waist-length tribal braided black extensions [were] inspired 'by a fusion of Rasta and northern

Pakistani tribal dress'" (Duboc 2011, 41). Exoticism, for both Ibrar and Amin, is strategic. While a complicated modernity is the staple of fashion aesthetics, this designer and stylist urge the industry to err on the side of the "exotic" and "traditional" to manage international growth and global visibility. In other words, not only is this "exoticism" intended to appeal to the Eurocentric global fashion industry and its gaze, but the implication is also that this strategy, considering the discussed broadening of global fashion's maps, will help Pakistani designers maintain their distinct aesthetic identity in a rapidly multiplying landscape.

What is noteworthy in these discussions of aesthetics is that Pakistani designers frequently employ the Orientalist strategy of reifying the East and the West as mutually exclusive, autonomous categories that can be juxtaposed but are in no way constitutive of one another. It is a strategy not unlike the one deployed by Western journalists and, consequently, a reminder of the accommodation and dialogue that Pakistani aesthetics need to embrace in order to be legible as creative global citizens in fashion. The version of postraciality adopted by the global fashion industry doesn't just shine the spotlight of visibility on the off-center. It marks Pakistani designers and aesthetics as citizens of the off-center and compels them to perform to gain visibility, all the while touting itself as racially transcendent and congratulating itself on its host of "new" fashion locales.

Of course, no dialogue and no accommodation of power are so tightly controlled or guaranteed. The differences in perspectives—between the Pakistani designers and an Orientalist treatment that emanates from more overt positions of geopolitical power—are contained in the value the designers ascribe to that heterogeneity. The Pakistani designers view the "East" as an insurgent in the existing narrative of "Western" design, while the more Eurocentric fashion industry views the "East" as the mainstream fashion world's necessary exotic and opportunity for crisis management (Shohat and Stam 1994).

This cohort of Pakistani designers unilaterally imagines their aesthetics as the reinvention of modernity.[9] Rarely does an interview with a designer proceed without mention of an aesthetic that reroutes modernity through traditionalism. Ali Xeeshan's collections are said to be "mystic yet restrained, ornate yet elegant" (Kunwar 2011, 10). The designer Rizwan Beyg has described his 2009 collection as an aesthetic that travels "from the rural to the runway," making direct gestures to this intersection of modernity and tradition (Beyg quoted in Syed 2009). The Pakistani fashion website Fashion Central PK describes designer Rabia's 2010 collection of veils as "mystical modernity" ("Rabia at Fashion Pakistan" 2010). Explaining the inspiration for her 2014

"Arabesque" collection, Nida Azwer said that her "latest collection paid homage to the traditional Islamic art of Arabesque . . . an endeavour to revive the age old handicraft and art form again in a more modern reimagining but without fundamentally altering the craft itself" ("Nida Azwer Collection" 2014). The modern, as it is imagined by these designers, is an aesthetic mode that is simultaneously oppositional and constitutive of tradition and that accompanies the cultivation of cultural industry.

This emphasis on aesthetic modernity demonstrates a complicated tension with the concept's usual deployment, since it is typically colonized by European narratives of progress and liberal humanism, including Western democracy and the growth of capitalist industry. As many scholars have explained, the concept of the modern is inseparable from histories of colonialism and the racial difference that it has produced. The modern is a cornerstone of those Eurocentric discourses of history that would render the postcolonial subject and the non-European subject (indeed, the Pakistani subject) ahistorical and antimodern, foreclosing the possibility of that subject's speech. While Pakistani designers do frequently invoke "modernity" as an explanation for their design parameters, their use of the term is more complicated, suggesting that designers imagine their own participation in modernity as inseparable from traditionalism and history. The designers, in a nod to the Eurocentric global fashion market's circuits of visibility, maintain the East and the West as mutually exclusive spatiotemporal concepts. Nevertheless, their vision of modernity is neither exclusively Eurocentric nor historically linear. "History" and "tradition" are, for these designers, not the foils of a disconnected place and time; they are present and currently active in what is seen as modernity. These self-representations are the off-center's reinterpretation of modernity through the traditionalism that is constitutive of the present moment. It is a vision of the modern that is in conversation with its historical legacies—one that sees those temporalities as constitutive loops rather than linear trajectories.

The Performative Excesses of Aesthetics

While designers' strategic identity performances suggest that the off-center's conditions of visibility are rigidly reproductive of Orientalist discourses and far from a domain where global visibility or multicultural self-representation can warrant celebration, designers' use of what is positioned as Islamic or otherwise rendered as "traditional" or "Eastern" dress creates moments that implode these performances from within and are worth exploring. For

Pakistani designers, complying with the requirements of fashion's global creative visibility has meant, in part, accentuating the "traditional," the "Eastern," and the Islamic influences of their designs to ensure global visibility, both in terms of the physical travel of collections and in terms of visual circulation through photography in the mainstream, Western press. While these performances certainly fit squarely within the practices of racial domination that structure both fashion's Orientalist discourses and its postracial fantasy, these practices also yield an excess visual domain surrounding aesthetics read as Islamic, particularly the Islamic veil. In fashion's racially policed circuits of visibility, the veil not only gains visibility but also is rescripted as an object of art. However contaminated and conflicted its route to this compromised visibility might be, the veil nevertheless becomes visible in a context of Western artistic practice, destabilizing the very idea of Western artistic practice from within some of fashion's most hallowed circuits of both symbolism and commerce. If the strategic performative dialogues described in this chapter accommodate the fashion world's racial and geographic hegemony, then the presence and visibility of aesthetics that gesture to Islam and to Muslim bodies, and especially the veil, are that hegemony's unintended leak. These aesthetics work to symbolically recast the terms of global Islamic citizenship, by offering a decentered visual imaginary that deposits itself into discourses of cultural futurity. In short, these aesthetics' compromised visibility is a hegemonic leak that betrays the static Orientalism (and the postracial myth that this Orientalism paradoxically labors to uphold), which its designers are compelled to mobilize, offering its would-be consumers a different way to visually travel through time and space.

When it comes to Pakistan's fashion weeks, aspects of Islamic fashion have appeared consistently in numerous designers' collections from 2009 to the present. Nomi Ansari's 2009 collection, for example, included black gauzy veils, reminiscent of bridal veils but, significantly, black. At the 2011 fashion week, Ali Xeeshan showed a variety of richly colored chaddors as well as heavily embroidered face veils in jewel tones. Showing at the 2010 fashion week, the designer Rabia was the first Muslim designer to take the stage, and she presented an array of veils. Designer Fahad Hussayn's 2009 line included a veiled black bridal gown. Hussayn's collection also included a costume with a golden brown, jewel-embellished, gauzy veil, fixed at the top by a hat, covering the model's entire face. The photo of this look reveals that the model's face was visible through the fabric, but only ambiguously so. At the end of the 2011 Saai show, the brand's two designers took their celebratory walk on the runway in matching abbayas, fully covered in loose pants, long-sleeved tunics, and a cowl around their heads, reminding viewers that the Islamic garb on display at these particular shows is not intended as fashion's theater but, rather, as consumable, practical clothing.

Furthermore, interpretations of the hijab and niqab are plentiful on these catwalks. At the 2009 fashion week, some of these examples were loose cowls, framing models' faces; others were tied tightly so as to encase the model's face completely. Perhaps most important, at Pakistani fashion weeks, these variations of dress are neither novelty nor theater. The practical functionality of these veils is critical here. That is, veils have of course been used by Western designers in numerous collections as theatrical accoutrements, meant to cultivate a particular, temporary climate for the show. What differentiates Western designers' uses of the veil from those shown by Pakistani designers is that the former use these objects as styling elements, intending them as theater, not commodities that are manufactured and offered to consumers. The hijab, niqab, and veil offered by Pakistani designers, however, are consumable objects, meant to enter the marketplace.

What makes these aesthetic elements' presence within global fashion's visual landscape so significant is that these veils and headscarves are stylistic elements that are difficult to divorce from the notions of Islam and regional politics in this sociohistorical moment. As discussed earlier in this chapter, this was certainly the case with the colonial postcards collected by Malek Alloula. Additionally, Leila Ahmed (1992) has argued that the veil served as a key signifier of "Muslim backwardness" during colonization, and Saba Mahmood has added that it has "more than any other Islamic practice . . . become the . . . evidence of the violence Islam has inflicted upon women" (2005, 195). For Dana Cloud (2004), the image of the veiled woman, as consumed in the West, is an ideograph that activates the rhetoric of "the clash of civilizations," naturalizing that image as an authentic narrative but also asking the (Western) consumer of the image to disidentify with what is framed as abjection.

In the West, the veil functions as an easy and normalized point of disidentification with what is rendered as senseless (and, thus, antithetical to modernity) terror and oppression. In fact, one need only look to the enduring legacy of banning veils in Western nations to see that the Islamic veil is synonymous with fundamentalism, terrorism, and antimodernity in contemporary Western discourse. In 2010, after France passed a resolution making face-covering veils illegal in public, André Gerin, who served as the head of the information panel in these proceedings, opined that "veils transform women into 'phantoms,' 'walking coffins' and represent the 'barbarism' of Muslim extremists" (Ganley 2010). Since then, a Muslim woman has been fined nearly 500 euros for wearing a burqa in Italy, Belgium has passed its own ban on the burqa and niqab, and Britain has continued debating the ban, since 2006 occasionally polling its public ("Survey Finds Support" 2006).

Hegemonic Leaks and Global Creative Citizenship

Within this geopolitical context, aesthetics citing Islam are sent down the runway at Pakistani fashion weeks and made visually consumable through global fashion's neoliberal circuits of visibility. The work these aesthetics perform registers mostly in the symbolic realm. Here, these aesthetics in general and the veil in particular work to articulate the terms of their own presence, performing their own temporalities and shifting the terms of what it means to be a global Muslim citizen. As I noted in the previous section, in the Western imagination the veil, as the perceived symbol of Islamic aesthetics in general, is inextricably linked to what is often dismissed as backwardness, antithetical to a teleological, progressive, linear view of historical movement. Furthermore, for consumers living in the diaspora, it is an object that ritualizes and animates symbolic connections to a homeland, serving as a "depository of memory" (Balasescu 2007, 314). In both instances, the affect that both Islamic aesthetics and the veil's presence initiate becomes a sort of shadowy weight on the accelerated, progressive temporalities that inform the global fashion industry.

The global fashion industry's accelerated temporalities are deeply imbricated with a symbolic futurity, with designers' primary task consisting of aesthetic speculation: constantly reinventing and reenvisioning fashion's relationship to a future as well as to an imagined modernity. It is not an exaggeration to suggest that a notion of a futurity accessible through aesthetics is constitutive of the work fashion designers lay claim to. Partly due to its historical commitments to the avant-garde, and partly because the capitalist production of fashion fads mandates a near obsession with novelty, fashion aesthetics are always in conversation with futurity (Lipovetsky 1994; McRobbie 2002). Fashion's very currency in the traditional global fashion market is its ability to foretell the aesthetic future (even if that often means reinterpreting the past).

In light of this fundamental process of the global fashion industry, then, the presentation of aesthetics that invoke Islam as fashion inserts those aesthetics and the Muslim citizen they inadvertently drag along into the grammars of aesthetic futurity. Despite designers' conservative strategic performances, securing ideological safety and continued visibility for their own designs, laboring to offer themselves as evidence of global fashion's postracial "successes," their use of legibly Islamic aesthetics constitutes a leak in this constructed hegemony. On the one hand, the veil, hijab, and niqab all labor to communicate the Orientalist tropes of "mysticism" and "antimodernity" that designers and their aesthetics must perform in order to participate in global fashion's spotlight. Their very presence and visibility preserve the illusion that global fashion is beyond racial hierarchies while the Orientalist tropes that index that visibility keep the power differentials just as they were, before fashion weeks multiplied and before new fashion markets began to force the Eurocentric fashion industry's proverbial hand. On the other hand, the veil's presence as an aesthetic object at a creative event estranges the Western gaze that informs global fashion's circuits of value.[10]

In the Western imagination, which informs global fashion practices and rhetorics, the "ideographs" of the veil and the future are irreconcilable. If the veil is shorthand for backwardness, operating in its own stagnant economy of desire and consumption, then it is not in easy compliance with the Western fashion world's temporalities. Consequently, the veil's presence on a global fashion stage unleashes its connotations onto the congealed understandings of what a future global citizen embodies, prying that signification open and dwelling in the dissonances that result. The veil, by depositing itself into aesthetic futurity, into a landscape that refuses to account for its presence outside of the norms of Orientalism, insists on an expanded present that critiques the conditions of its own existence, undermining the fashion industry's carefully adapted version of postracial philosophy.

Okwui Enwezor (2009) has said of artistic practice in the age of economic globalization that its cultural productions are not only aware of history but, in a marked departure from the postmodern, engage in a deliberate play with its narratives. Here, Islamic aesthetics articulate that play, becoming, as Balasescu argues, "a prompter for times past, and spaces lost" (2007, 314). The play with attire marked as traditional is committed to "adapting the clothes to a mobile body that needs to move continuously, a modern body circulating in an urban environment" (313). Balasescu's quote is especially urgent here as it references movement and a reinscription of the modern, a process that Pakistani designers mobilize despite the nearly obligatory invocations of an oppositional "East" and "West." As the Pakistani model, whose face is covered by one of Fahad Hussayn's light, brown, and bejeweled veils, glides down the runway, she recasts the terms assigned to global Islamic citizenship and rejects the postracial ethos that makes her visible in the first place. She represents a leak in the neoliberal, postracial logics that would use the aesthetics of Islamic dress as a resource for the global fashion economy and then neutralize their signification to claim a postracial reality. For a moment, the veil intervenes in global fashion's visual regimes, insisting that Islam cannot simply be relegated and affixed to history's "backwardness." Instead, the veil as fashionable object reminds the viewer that Muslim global citizenship is not only salient in the present but also mobile, reasserting Muslim citizenship in the present by routing it through a figuration of an aesthetic future, muddying progressive, linear temporalities in the process.

Notes

1. According to Maliha Rehman (2015), this estimate comes from Euromonitor data.
2. For more on this shift within the fashion world, see Emling 2006; Gilbert 2006.
3. Enwezor argues that artistic practice in the contemporary global moment is characterized by "jagged maps." Within these maps, the off-center rises to global visibility, fracturing previously centralized circuits of perceived artistic value.
4. From 1974 to 1995, the global trade in textiles was regulated through the Multi-Fibre Arrangement (MFA), which imposed quotas on textile exports for World Trade Organization member nations. Scholars have argued that the MFA was "originally created to protect European and U.S. domestic industries from low-cost production sites in developing countries" (Tu 2010, 10). The 1995 phaseout of the MFA is known as the Agreement on Textiles and Clothing (ATC).
5. As Thuy Linh Nguyen Tu and others point out, full liberalization did not, in fact, happen as nations signed bilateral and regional agreements in order to regulate exports.
6. The quote comes from the PFDC website "About" page, http://pfdc.org/about/, accessed in 2009. The text on that page has since been changed.
7. Ellen Israel Rosen, for example, argues that as the sophistication of technology deskilled the production process, jobs in the global garment trade have been increasingly "designed specifically to employ women, often women who are young and unmarried" (2002, 240). Grace Kyungwon Hong adds that "racialized women—often very young—are the preferred workforce for transnational capital in the contemporary era" (2006, 108).
8. Elizabeth Wissinger's (2011) examination of the ways in which models of color must engage in "aesthetic labor," specifically with regard to their bodies' racial characteristics, in order to accommodate the imbrication of the "white gaze" and the "corporate gaze" provides some important points for this discussion, from the standpoint of modeling.
9. Ammara Maqsood's (2014) study of the conditions of middle-class consumption in Lahore, Pakistan, and the reliance on a discourse of modernity are a useful extension of the present conversation.
10. Subversive uses of these aesthetics have a historical legacy within a variety of political contexts. For example, Gillo Pontecorvo's film *The Battle of Algiers* (1967) depicts the National Liberation Front's uses of hijab and its meanings within the Orientalist imagination for purposes of political subversion.

Epilogue

Incantation

> Hard times are coming, when we'll be wanting the voices of writers
> who can see alternatives to how we live now, can see through our fear-
> stricken society and its obsessive technologies to other ways of being,
> and even imagine real grounds for hope.
> —URSULA K. LE GUIN, "Freedom," 2014

I repeat the words, aloud:

We stand, in resolve, between hope and despair.

My friend and colleague approached me after I finished the lecture in which
I spoke this incantation. He asked me, quite sincerely and urgently, to help
him understand *how* we could stand between hope and despair, how we
could find such a stance when things in the world were so terribly wrong. I
told him I would work on that.

Like any good alchemist, I returned to my study, to my trove of books, to
revisit the origins of these words. I examined my notes on their etymological

essence to better understand what I was trying to bring out of the ether and into view.

Despair: n. the complete loss or absence of hope; v. to lose or be without hope

The 2016 US presidential election shook many people to their foundation; the outcome and aftermath demonstrated the razor-thin line between hope and despair, and how vast the chasm seems between the latter and the former once one's hopes are dashed. The Latin roots of the word "despair" are clear: *de* (reversal, fall down from); *sperare* (hope). One is pushed into a spiraling fall, turning away from hope, descending into despair.

Hope: n. a feeling of expectation or desire for a thing to happen; archaic—a feeling of trust

Hope, of course, according to the myth of Pandora, is all that is left once the enchanted box is opened and all the evils are released into the world: sickness, prejudice, war, ignorance.

Resolve: n. firm determination to do something; in chemistry or photography, to turn into a different form when seen more clearly

The Latin origins of "resolve" help explain my attraction to this phrase, and my thinking that it is fit for inclusion in our investigations of the postracial: *re* (expressing intensive force); *solver* (to loosen).

Standing in resolve, in this hybrid, paradoxical space of expressing intensive force and loosening simultaneously, is what I believe we need in these troubling postracial times to relocate ourselves, to reimagine our world, and to be patient as we are presented with contradictions that are not yet to the point of being *resolved* in the other sense of our alchemical term's meaning, to solve a problem. But we can, as the authors of this collection do, find different lenses for understanding postracial dilemmas—that is, turning them *into a different form* once scholarship helps us *see more clearly*.

Clear vision is a necessity when one is making a new map of the world in times when each new headline or tweet makes one want to rub her eyes to test if it's just a trick of the light, or fatigue conjuring the latest racist, sexist, and xenophobic disaster-in-progress. *Was it just my imagination that they were marching with tiki torches and making Nazi salutes? Am I going crazy to hear they want teachers to bring guns to schools?*

No. It's not just you.

To paraphrase poet Claudia Rankine, it is the out-of-control imaginations of white supremacists trying to rewrite history and dominate the future, spinning fantasies of feminazis and black brutes and immigrants run amok. These grotesqueries continue to influence public perceptions, algorithms, and more.

(I don't know if it was scarier when racism was insisting it didn't exist anymore or when the racists held the tiki torches high to spotlight their faces and they proclaimed their faith in the full glare of CNN cameras. Was it a relief to have it all in the open (again), to not be feeling gaslighted and alone in one's suspicions? The color-blind era's complaint of "racial fatigue" disappeared into the night as the torchlight parade and Twitter trolls gnashed their teeth and screamed for blood.)

We need quite a bit of resolve these days. And a generous dose of liberatory imagination alongside our determination to wrestle with our troubling history and present. We need fierce imagination guided by an ethic of care. Despair thrives when we feel alone, abandoned, without fellow travelers on our fog-clouded path. Despair swallows hope whole in the waning present, leaving a vortex of nothingness in its place. Despair displaces us from the rhythm of time, making us feel nothing we have done in the past has been productive, and we have no future.

Our preference for nostalgia and for a history that never happened is not without consequence.

—HASAN KWAME JEFFRIES (2018)

Perhaps the "post" in "postracial" is so slippery, seductive, and ultimately disillusioning because our society has so little awareness of that which preceded the alleged post. We rarely have time or make space to grapple with, and then loosen our grip on, difficult knowledge from the past. We are rarely called upon to stretch our imaginations to envision a future without white supremacist patriarchy. This is why, as I write, the release of *Black Panther* is causing such a stir, a stirring that reverberates with some imaginations of pasts, presents, and futures that could have been, or could be. The movie depicts an African nation that was untouched by European colonialism, that was able to develop its natural resources and cultural expressions with total autonomy. The landscape is not undone by colonial incursions and extractive industry. Black people, self-determined.

In the year that marked the fiftieth anniversary of the assassination of Dr. Martin Luther King Jr. and the one hundredth anniversary of the end of World War I, a war in which European powers fought (in part) to preserve their preferred parceling of the African continent among themselves, the success of *Black Panther* is interesting, to say the least. What so many people, from the theaters to the Twittersphere, commented on (beyond the delightful Afrofuturist mise-en-scène) was the overwhelming sense of solidarity and care among the characters. Whatever you may think about its narrative or ideological flaws, for many people, *Black Panther* provided a vision of a history that *could have been* if it were not for white supremacist imperialism.

The historical traumas of imperialism, indigenous genocide, and slavery aren't difficult knowledge only because it is hard to witness the testimony of those who were oppressed, or to hear the contempt of those who inflicted the wounds. It is literally difficult for many people to envision a map of the world that includes traces of that violence rather than require its erasure. The imperial maps have used white ignorance to draw convincing facsimiles of our globe, of lands that did not and do not look the way they do in the Western history books and atlases. Most people have a hard time imagining that indigenous peoples of the Americas and Africans were not predestined for genocide and enslavement, that these diverse peoples were dynamic agents negotiating and struggling with the incursions of Europeans. The maps charted by white supremacy and patriarchy have made it difficult for us to see where we actually are. It is unsettling to discover you are lost without a reliable map. One might lose hope.

Resolve is our bridge back to hope. Resolve helps us imagine the impossible, like Sylvia Wynter's call for us to forget five hundred years of history in order to make truly humane ways of being in the world. She does not mean we undertake a project of postracial amnesia; rather, we must experience loss, we must loosen our grip on those habits of mind we inherited from the brutal past. We must let go in order to have the capacity to imagine and embrace the challenge of making the world that could have been if colonialism, slavery, indigenous genocide, patriarchy, and all the other demons had not been let out of the box. In other words, to explore and inscribe a map of a better world, we must heal our current one. And in so doing we must become acquainted with the losses that come with facing difficult, traumatic histories. We must loosen our grip on the past in order to intensify our vision of it, to allow ourselves to get lost and dream possible futures.

ST. PAUL, Minnesota, or Wakanda or Earthsea

References

"About Xpozé." 2009. *Xpozé Monthly Magazine*. http://xpozemonthly.com/about.html.

Abrajano, Marisa, and Zoltan L. Hajnal. 2015. *White Backlash: Immigration, Race and American Politics*. Princeton, NJ: Princeton University Press.

Acham, Christine. 2012. "Blacks in the Future: Braving the Frontier of the Web Series." In *Watching While Black: Centering the Television of Black Audiences*, edited by Beretta E. Smith-Shomade, 63–76. New Brunswick, NJ: Rutgers University Press.

Adele. 2012. Interview for *60 Minutes*. February 12. www.cbsnews.com/news/adele-opens-up-about-vocal-cord-surgery/.

Agha, S. 2012. "Misha Lakhani Adds Wave of Freshness to the Fashion Industry." *Daily Times*, September 17, B8.

Ahmed, Leila. 1992. *Women and Gender in Islam: Historical Roots of a Modern Debate*. New Haven, CT: Yale University Press.

Ahmed, Sara. 2010. *The Promise of Happiness*. Durham, NC: Duke University Press.

Ahmed, Sara. 2012. *On Being Included: Racism and Diversity in Institutional Life*. Durham, NC: Duke University Press.

Ahmed, Y. 2009. *Report on Textile Industry of Pakistan*. Lahore: Horizon Securities Ltd.

Albiniak, Paige. 2007. "Ken Lowe: Designed to Succeed." *Broadcasting and Cable*, February 23.

Alexander, Michelle. 2011. *The New Jim Crow: Mass Incarceration in the Age of Colorblindness*. New York: New Press.

Ali-Coleman, Khadijah. 2009. "New Web Series Highlights DC's Anacostia Community." *Examiner*, August 28. www.examiner.com/article/new-web-series-highlights-dc-s-anacostia-community.

Allbritton, Chris. 2009. "Pakistan Fashion Week Defies Taliban with Non-Islamic Dress." *UK Telegraph*, November 5. www.telegraph.co.uk/news/worldnews/asia/pakistan/6504709/Pakistan-fashion-week-defies-Taliban-with-non-Islamic-dress.html.

Allen, James. 2000. *Without Sanctuary: Lynching Photography in America*. Santa Fe: Twin Palms.

Allen, Robert C., ed. 1995. *To Be Continued—: Soap Operas around the World*. New York: Routledge.

"Allen West CPAC Speech Closes Conservative Conference (Video)." 2011. *Huffington Post*, February 12; updated December 6, 2017. www.huffingtonpost.com/2011/02/12/allen-west-cpac-speech-_n_822423.html.

"Allen West The Revolution." 2009. YouTube, posted by Channel1Images, October 21 www.youtube.com/watch?v=VP2p9idvm6M.

Alloula, Malek. 1986. *The Colonial Harem.* Translated by Myrna Godzich and Wlad Godzich. Introduction by Barbara Harlow. Minneapolis: University of Minnesota Press.

"ALT [André Leon Talley] Interviews Anna Wintour." 2015. *Vogue Podcast*, episode 1, September 14. www.vogue.com/article/vogue-podcast.

Alter, Jonathan. 2006. "Is America Ready: Hillary's Hair and Hemline Won't Be Issues." *Newsweek*, December 25, 28.

Amurao, Carla. 2013. "Fact Sheet: How Bad Is the School-to-Prison Pipeline?" *Tavis Smiley Reports.* www.pbs.org/wnet/tavissmiley/tsr/education-under-arrest/school -to-prison-pipeline-fact-sheet/.

Andersen, Margaret L., and Patricia Hill Collins, eds. 2012. *Race, Class and Gender: An Anthology.* Belmont, CA: Wadsworth.

Ang, Ien. 2013. *Watching Dallas: Soap Opera and the Melodramatic Imagination.* New York: Routledge.

Arnold, Rebecca. 2001. *Fashion, Desire, and Anxiety: Image and Morality in the 20th Century.* New Brunswick, NJ: Rutgers University Press.

Ashikari, Mikiko. 2005. "Cultivating Japanese Whiteness: The Whitening Cosmetics Boom and the Japanese Identity." *Journal of Material Culture* 10 (1): 73–91.

Au, Wagner James. 2016a. "Palmer Luckey's Support for Pro-Trump Group Reminds Me of His Support for Pacifying the Poor with VR—UPDATE, 7:10pm: Luckey Posts Confusing Apology on Facebook." *New World Notes*, September 23. http://nwn .blogs.com/nwn/2016/09/palmer-luckey-trump-supporter-poor-vr.html.

Au, Wagner James. 2016b. "VR Will Make Life Better—or Just Be an Opiate for the Masses." *Wired*, February 25. www.wired.com/2016/02/vr-moral-imperative-or -opiate-of-masses/.

Aufderheide, Pat. n.d. "Therapeutic Patriotism and Beyond." *Television Archive: A Library of World Perspectives on 9/11.* Last modified 2001. www.televisionarchive.org /html/article_pa1.html.

Austin, Regina. 2004. "Kwanzaa and the Commodification of Black Culture." *Black Renaissance/Renaissance Noire* 6 (1): 8–18.

"Ayesha Mustafa of Fashion Compassion UK Talks to Fashion Central." 2012. *Fashion Central PK*, December 5. www.fashioncentral.pk/people-parties/celebrity -interviews/story-1343-ayesha-mustafa-of-fashion-compassion-uk-talks-to-central/.

Bai, Matt. 2008. "Post-race: Is Obama the End of Black Politics?" *New York Times Magazine*, August 10, 34–41.

Baker, Dean. 2007. "The Housing Bubble Pops." *The Nation* 285 (9): 5.

Bakhtin, M. M. 1981. *The Dialogical Imagination: Four Essays.* Edited by Michael Holquist. Translated by Caryl Emerson and Michael Holquist. Austin: University of Texas Press.

Balasescu, Alexandru. 2007. "*Haute Couture* in Tehran: Two Faces of an Emerging Fashion Scene." *Fashion Theory* 11 (2/3): 299–318.

Baldwin, James. 1985. "The Fire Next Time: Letter to My Nephew." In *The Price of the Ticket*, edited by James Baldwin, 333–81. New York: St. Martin's/Marek.

Banet-Weiser, Sarah. 2007. "'What's Your Flava?': Race and Postfeminism in Media Culture." In *Interrogating Postfeminism: Gender and the Politics of Popular Culture*, edited by Diane Negra and Yvonne Tasker, 201–26. Durham, NC: Duke University Press.

Banet-Weiser, Sarah. 2012. *Authentic^{TM}: The Politics of Ambivalence in a Brand Culture.* New York: NYU Press.

Banet-Weiser, Sarah. 2014. "'We Are All Workers': Economic Crisis, Masculinity, and the American Working Class." In *Gendering the Recession: Media and Culture in an Age of Austerity*, edited by Diane Negra and Yvonne Tasker, 81–106. Durham, NC: Duke University Press.

Barr, Meghan. 2010. "More Than a Basketball Star at Stake." *Washington Post*, July 5.

Barrett, Brian. 2015. "A Day inside Glenn Beck's America." *New Yorker*, September 1. www.newyorker.com/news/news-desk/a-day-inside-glenn-becks-america.

Baumann, Shyon. 2008. "The Moral Underpinnings of Beauty: A Meaning-Based Explanation for Light and Dark Complexions in Advertising." *Poetics* 36 (1): 2–23.

Beck, Glenn. 2003. *The Real America: Messages from the Heart and Heartland.* New York: Pocket Books, Kindle edition.

Beck, Glenn. 2016a. "Don't Move to Canada. Talk to the Other Side." *New York Times*, November 11. www.nytimes.com/2016/11/11/opinion/glenn-beck-dont-move-to -canada-talk-to-the-other-side.html.

Beck, Glenn. 2016b. "Empathy for Black Lives Matter." *New York Times*, September 7. www.nytimes.com/2016/09/07/opinion/glenn-beck-empathy-for-black-lives-matter .html?_r=0.

Beck, Glenn. 2016c. Facebook. October 8. www.facebook.com/GlennBeck/posts /10154622008673188.

"Beck Says His 8-28 Rally Will 'Reclaim the Civil Rights Movement. . . . We Were the People That Did It in the First Place.'" n.d. *Media Matters for America.* Audio last modified May 26, 2010. http://mediamatters.org/video/2010/05/26/beck-says-his -8–28-rally-will-reclaim-the-civil/165327.

Beinart, Peter. 2017. "Glenn Beck's Regrets: His Paranoid Style Paved the Road for Trumpism. Now He Fears What's Been Unleashed." *Atlantic*, January/February. www.theatlantic.com/magazine/archive/2017/01/glenn-becks-regrets/508763/.

Beltrán, Mary C. 2005. "The New Hollywood Racelessness: Only the Fast, Furious, (and Multiracial) Will Survive." *Cinema Journal* 44 (2): 50–67.

Beltrán, Mary, and Camilla Fojas, eds. 2008. *Mixed Race Hollywood.* New York: NYU Press.

Berlant, Lauren. 2008. *The Female Complaint: The Unfinished Business of Sentimentality in American Culture.* Durham, NC: Duke University Press, 2008.

Berlant, Lauren. 2011. *Cruel Optimism.* Durham, NC: Duke University Press.

Berlet, Chip, and Matthew Lyons. 2000. *Right-Wing Populism in America: Too Close for Comfort.* New York: Guilford Press.

Bhabha, Homi K. (1994) 2005. *The Location of Culture.* London: Routledge.

Bhawuk, D. P. S. 1992. "The Measurement of Intercultural Sensitivity Using the Concepts of Individualism and Collectivism." *International Journal of Intercultural Relations* 16: 413–36.

"Bias and Meritocracy Don't Mix." 2013. Kapor Center. Accessed August 19, 2017. www .kaporcenter.org/bias-and-meritocracy-dont-mix/.

Biller, Diana. 2014. "The 10 Most Expensive Flops in Television History." Gizmodo, October 23. http://io9.com/the-10-most-expensive-flops-in-television-history -1649881502.

Black, Daniel. 2009. "Wearing Out Racial Discourse: Tokyo Street Fashion and Race as Style." *Journal of Popular Culture* 42 (2): 239–56.

Black Demographics. 2012. *Poverty.* http://blackdemographics.com/households /poverty/.

Blow, Charles. 2010. "I Had a Nightmare." *New York Times*, August 27. www.nytimes .com/2010/08/28/opinion/28blow.html.

Bobo, Lawrence D. 2014. "The Stickiness of Race: Re-articulating Racial Inequality." *Du Bois Review* 11 (2): 189–93.

Bonilla-Silva, Eduardo. 2014. *Racism without Racists: Color-Blind Racism and the Persistence of Racial Inequality in America.* 4th ed. Lanham, MD: Rowman and Littlefield.

Bottemiller Evich, Helena. 2016. "Revenge of the Rural Voter: Rural Voters Turned Out in a Big Way This Presidential Cycle—and They Voted Overwhelmingly for Donald Trump." *Politico*, November 13. www.politico.com/story/2016/11/hillary-clinton -rural-voters-trump-231266.

Bouie, Jamelle. 2012. "Yes, Race Influences Opposition to Obama." *The Nation*, September 14. www.thenation.com/blog/169961/yes-race-influences-opposition-obama#.

Bourdieu, Pierre. 1984. *Distinction: A Social Critique of the Judgement of Taste.* Translated by Richard Nice. Cambridge, MA: Harvard University Press.

Bourdieu, Pierre. 1993. *The Field of Cultural Production.* New York: Columbia University Press.

Boyd, Todd. 1997. *Am I Black Enough for You? Popular Culture from the 'Hood and Beyond.* Bloomington: Indiana University Press.

Boyd, Todd. 2000. "Mo' Money, Mo' Problems: Keepin' It Real in the Post-Jordan Era." In *Basketball Jones: America Above the Rim*, edited by Todd Boyd and Kenneth Shropshire, 59–67. New York: NYU Press.

Branch, Taylor. 2010. "Dr. King's Newest Marcher." *New York Times*, September 4. www .nytimes.com/2010/09/05/opinion/05branch.html?_r=0.

Brooks, Daphne. 2006. *Bodies in Dissent: Spectacular Performances of Race and Freedom, 1850–1910.* Durham, NC: Duke University Press.

Brooks, Daphne. 2008. "Amy Winehouse and the (Black) Art of Appropriation." *The Nation*, September 10. www.thenation.com/article/amy-winehouse-and-black-art -appropriation/.

Burghardt, David, and Leonard Zeskin. 2010. *Tea Party Nationalism.* Kansas City, MO: Institute for Research and Education on Human Rights.

Burghardt, David, and Leonard Zeskind. 2012. *Beyond FAIR: The Decline of the Established Anti-immigrant Organizations and the Rise of Tea Party Nativism.* Kansas City, MO: Institute for Research and Education on Human Rights.

Burke, Meghan. 2015. *Race, Class, Gender and the Tea Party: What the Movement Reflects about Mainstream Ideologies.* Lanham, MD: Lexington Books.

Burleigh, Nina. 2015. "What Silicon Valley Thinks of Women." *Newsweek*, January 28. www.newsweek.com/2015/02/06/what-silicon-valley-thinks-women-302821.html.

Bush, George W. 2006. Speech, NAACP annual convention, Washington, DC, July 20.

Cable, Dustin. 2013. "The Racial Dot Map: One Dot Per Person for the Entire United States." July. Racial Dot Map of Detroit. September 2010. https://demographics .coopercenter.org/racial-dot-map.

Caldwell, John Thornton. 1995. *Televisuality: Style, Crisis, and Authority in American Television*. New Brunswick, NJ: Rutgers University Press.

Caldwell, John Thornton. 2008. *Production Culture: Industrial Reflexivity and Critical Practice in Film and Television*. Durham, NC: Duke University Press.

Chalabi, Mona. 2014. "Three Leagues, 92 Teams and One Black Principal Owner." *ESPN FiveThirtyEight/DataLab*, April 28. http://fivethirtyeight.edu/datalab/diversity-in -the-nba-the-nfl-and-mlb/.

Chambers, Jason. 2011. *Madison Avenue and the Color Line: African Americans in the Advertising Industry*. Philadelphia: University of Pennsylvania Press.

Chan, Brenda. 2005. "Imagining the Homeland: The Internet and Diasporic Discourse of Homeland." *Journal of Communication Inquiry* 29 (4): 336–68.

Cheddie, Janice. 2002. "Politics of the First: The Emergence of the Black Model in the Civil Rights Era." *Fashion Theory* 6 (1): 61–82.

Cho, Sumi K. 2009. "Post-racialism." *Iowa Law Review* 94: 1589–645.

"The Chosen One: High School Junior LeBron James Would Be an NBA Lottery Pick Right Now." 2002. *Sports Illustrated*, February 18.

Christian, Aymar Jean. 2018. *Open TV: Innovation beyond Hollywood and the Rise of Web Television*. New York: NYU Press.

Christian, Aymar Jean. Forthcoming. "Scarcity to Capacity: Scaling Production Value in Networked Television." *Critical Studies in Television*.

Cloud, Dana L. 2004. "To Veil the Threat of Terror: Afghan Women and the Clash of Civilizations in the Imagery of the U.S. War on Terrorism." *Quarterly Journal of Speech* 90 (3): 285–306.

CNBC News Releases. 2016. "CNBC Greenlights 'Cleveland Hustles' with NBA Superstar LeBron James and 'The Partner' with Marcus Lemonis." CNBC, January 14. www .cnbc.com/2016/01/14/cnbc-greenlights-cleveland-hustles-with-nba-superstar -lebron-james-and-the-partner-with-marcus-lemonis.html.

Coates, Norma. 1997. "(R)evolution Now? Rock and the Political Potential of Gender." In *Sexing the Groove: Popular Music and Gender*, edited by Sheila Whiteley, 50–64. New York: Routledge.

Coates, Ta-Nehisi. 2015. "Post-racial Society Is Still a Distant Dream . . ." *Atlantic*, July/ August, 85–86.

Cobb, Jasmine Nicole. 2011. "No We Can't! Postracialism and the Popular Appearance of a Rhetorical Fiction." *Communication Studies* 62 (4): 406–21.

"Coca-Cola Acts to Aid Minority Enterprises: Airing Special TV Show July 24." 1970. *New York Amsterdam News*, July 4, 58.

"Coca Cola Opening Up to Minority Investors." 1984. *Brooklyn News*, November 10, n.p.

"Coke Faces Mass Race Bias Lawsuit." 1999. *Sunday Mail*, April 25.

Colapinto, John. 2008. "Outside Man: Spike Lee's Celluloid Struggles." *New Yorker*, September 22, 52.

Conger, Kate. n.d. "Exclusive: Here's the Full 10-Page Anti-diversity Screed Circulating Internally at Google [Updated]." *Gizmodo*. Accessed August 19, 2017. http:// gizmodo.com/exclusive-heres-the-full-10-page-anti-diversity-screed-1797564320.

Conniff, Ruth. 2016. "RNC 2016: White Rage in Cleveland." *Progressive*, July 22. www .progressive.org/news/2016/07/188874/rnc-2016-white-rage-cleveland.

Contrera, Jesse. 2015. "Pharrell Williams Is Writing a Children's Book. You'll Never Guess What It's Based On: And You Thought You Were Going to Go a Little While without Having 'Happy' Stuck in Your Head." *Washington Post—Blogs*, February 17. http:// search.proquest.com/docview/1657631630?pq-origsite=summon&accountid=10226.

Cooper, David, Mary Gable, and Algernon Austin. 2012. "The Public-Sector Jobs Crisis: Women and African Americans Hit Hardest by Job Losses in State and Local Governments." Economic Policy Institute, May 2. www.epi.org/publication/bp339 -public-sector-jobs-crisis/.

Craig, Maureen A., and Jennifer A. Richeson. 2014. "More Diverse Yet Less Tolerant? How the Increasingly Diverse Racial Landscape Affects White Americans' Racial Attitudes." *Personality and Social Psychology Bulletin* 40 (6): 750–61.

Crenshaw, Kimberlé Williams. 1995. "Race, Reform, and Retrenchment: Transformation and Legitimation in Anti-discrimination Law." In *Critical Race Theory: The Key Writings That Formed the Movement*, edited by Kimberlé Williams Crenshaw, Neil Gotanda, Gary Peller, and Kendall Thomas, 103–22. New York: New Press.

Crenshaw, Kimberlé Williams. 1997. "Color-Blind Dreams and Racial Nightmares: Reconfiguring Racism in the Post–Civil Rights Era." In *Birth of a Nation'hood: Gaze, Script, and Spectacle in the O.J. Simpson Trial*, edited by Toni Morrison and Claudia Brodsky LaCour, 97–168. New York: Pantheon.

Crenshaw, Kimberlé Williams. 2011. "Twenty Years of Critical Race Theory: Looking Back to Move Forward." *Connecticut Law Review* 43 (5): 1253–352.

Curtin, Michael. 2003. "Media Capital: Towards the Study of Spatial Flows." *International Journal of Cultural Studies* 6 (2): 202–28.

Da Costa, Alexandre Emboaba. 2016. "Thinking 'Post-racial' Ideology Transnationally: The Contemporary Politics of Race and Indigeneity in the Americas." *Critical Sociology* 42 (4/5): 475–90.

Daniels, Jessie. 2015. "'My Brain Database Doesn't See Skin Color': Color-Blind Racism in the Technology Industry and in Theorizing the Web." *American Behavioral Scientist* 59 (11): 1377–93. doi:10.1177/0002764215578728.

Danielson, Michael N. 1997. *Home Team: Professional Sports and the American Metropolis*. Princeton, NJ: Princeton University Press.

Darby, Derrick, and Argun Saatcioglu. 2014. "Race, Justice, and Desegregation." *Du Bois Review* 11 (1): 87–108.

Dasgupta, Debarshi. 2009. "Our True Colors." *Outlook*, June 29. Accessed September 17, 2012. www.outlookindia.com/article.aspx?250314.

David, Mario. 2007. "Afrofuturism and Post-soul Possibility in Black Popular Music." *African American Review* 41 (4): 695–707.

Davidson, Amy. 2010. "Beck on the Mall." *New Yorker*, August 30. www.newyorker.com /news/amy-davidson/beck-on-the-mall.

Davis, Angela. 1972. "Reflections on the Black Woman's Role in the Community of
Slaves." *Massachusetts Review* 13 (1/2): 81–100.

Davis, Julie Hirschfeld. 2015. "Obama's Twitter Debut, @POTUS, Attracts Hate-Filled
Posts." *New York Times*, May 21. www.nytimes.com/2015/05/22/us/politics/obamas
-twitter-debut-potus-attracts-hate-filled-posts.html.

Day, Faithe, and Aymar Jean Christian. 2017. "Locating Black Queer TV: Fans, Producers, and Networked Publics on YouTube." *Transformative Works and Cultures* 24.
http://dx.doi.org/10.3983/twc.2017.867.

Deen, Marium. 2012. NSR Exclusive Interview with Fashion Central. *Fashion Central PK*,
October 18. www.fashioncentral.pk/people-parties/celebrity-interviews/story-1304
-nsr-exclusive-interview-with-fashion-central/.

de Goede, Marieke. 2005. "Carnival of Money: Politics of Dissent in an Era of Globalizing Finance." In *The Global Resistance Reader*, edited by Louise Amoore, 379–91.
New York: Routledge.

DeHaven Newsom, Michael. 1971. "Blacks and Historic Preservation." *Law and Contemporary Problems* 36 (3): 423–31.

Deleuze, Gilles, and Félix Guattari. 1987. *A Thousand Plateaus: Capitalism and Schizo-
phrenia*. Minneapolis: University of Minnesota Press.

Delmont, Matthew F. 2016. *Why Busing Failed: Race, Media, and the National Resistance
to School Desegregation*. Oakland: University of California Press.

DeNavas-Walt, Carmen, Bernadette D. Proctor, and Jessica C. Smith. 2013. *Income, Pov-
erty, and Health Insurance Coverage in the United States: 2012*. U.S. Census Bureau,
Current Population Reports, P60-245. Washington, DC: U.S. Government Printing
Office.

Departure Films, prod. 2015. *Rehab Addict*. "Kitchen Overhaul." Aired February 12, on
DIY/HGTV.

DeSilver, Denise. 2013. "Black Unemployment Rate Is Consistently Twice That of
Whites." *Pew Research Center*, August. www.pewresearch.org/fact-tank/2013/08/21
/through-good-times-and-bad-black-unemployment-is-consistently-double-that-of
-whites/.

Diawara, Manthia. 1993. "Black American Cinema: The New Realism." In *Black American Cinema*, edited by Manthia Diawara, 3–25. New York: Routledge.

Donaldson, Jam. n.d. "Hot Ghetto Mess—From the Editor." Accessed December 7, 2011.
hotghettomess.com.

Draz, Marie. 2017. "Born This Way? Time and the Coloniality of Gender." *Journal of
Speculative Philosophy* 31 (3): 372–84.

Dreher, Rod. 2015. "Why Trump Matters." *The American Conservative*, November 6.
www.theamericanconservative.com/dreher/why-trump-matters-middle-aged-white
-men-dying/.

Duboc, Charlet. 2011. "Islamabad Fashion Week." *Vice* 18 (3): 40–41.

Dudziak, Mary, ed. 2003. *September 11 in History: A Watershed Moment*. Durham, NC:
Duke University Press.

Duggan, Lisa. 2004. *The Twilight of Equality: Neoliberalism, Cultural Politics, and the
Attack on Democracy*. Boston: Beacon.

Dupree, David. 2006. "King James' Next Conquest." *USA Today*, April 21.

Duster, Troy. 2012. "The Combustible Intersection: Genomics, Forensics and Race." In *Race after the Internet*, edited by Lisa Nakamura and Peter Chow-White, 310–28. New York: Routledge.

Dyer, Richard. 1993. "Entertainment and Utopia." In *The Cultural Studies Reader*, edited by Simon During, 371–81. London: Routledge.

Dyer, Richard. 1997. *White: Essays on Race and Culture*. New York: Routledge.

Early, Gerald L. 2008. "The End of Race as We Know It." *Chronicle of Higher Education* 55 (7): B11–B13.

Editorial Board. 2016. "Happiness in Short Supply." *Japan Times*, March 26.

Edwards, Breanna. 2014. "Pharrell Williams: Why Aren't We Talking about Michael Brown's 'Bullyish' Behavior?" *The Root*, November 25. www.theroot.com/pharrell -williams-why-aren-t-we-talking-about-michael-1790877844.

Edwards, Erica R. 2011. "The Black President Hokum." *American Quarterly* 63 (1): 33–59.

Edwards, Gavin, and Jeff Rosenthal. 2014. "20 Best Things We Saw at Made in America 2014." *Rolling Stone*, September 1. www.rollingstone.com/music/music-lists/20-best -things-we-saw-at-made-in-america-2014-165843/best-philadelphia-performance -kanye-west-171029/.

Eidsheim, Nina. 2009. "Synthesizing Race: Towards an Analysis of the Performativity of Vocal Timbre." *Trans: Transcultural Music Review* 13. Accessed July 30, 2015. www .sibetrans.com/trans/articulo/57/synthesizing-race-towards-an-analysis-of-the -performativity-of-vocal-timbre.

Eidsheim, Nina. 2012. "Voice as Action: Toward a Model for Analyzing the Dynamic Construction of Racialized Voice." *Current Musicology* 93 (Spring): 9–32.

Elam, Harry J., Jr. 2005. "Change Clothes and Go: A Postscript to Postblackness." In *Black Cultural Traffic: Crossroads in Global Performance and Popular Culture*, edited by Harry J. Elam Jr. and Kennell Jackson, 379–88. Ann Arbor: University of Michigan Press.

Elam, Michele. 2011. *The Souls of Mixed Folk: Race, Politics, and Aesthetics in the New Millenium*. Palo Alto, CA: Stanford University Press.

Elan, Priya. 2014. "Why Pharrell Williams Believes in 'The New Black.'" *Guardian*, April 22. www.theguardian.com/music/shortcuts/2014/apr/22/trouble-with -pharrell-williams-new-black-theory.

Ellis, Trey. 1989. "The New Black Aesthetic." *Callaloo* 38: 233–43.

El Marzouki, Mohamed. 2015. "Satire as Counter-discourse: Dissent, Cultural Citizenship, and Youth Culture in Morocco." *International Communication Gazette* 77 (3): 282–96.

Emling, S. 2006 "Big 4 Fashion Weeks Get New Company." *New York Times*, October 3. www.nytimes.com/2006/10/03/style/03iht-Rweeks.3015966.html.

Enck-Wanzer, Darrel, ed. 2010. *The Young Lords: A Reader*. New York: NYU Press.

Enck-Wanzer, Darrel. 2011. "Barack Obama, the Tea Party, and the Threat of Race: On Racial Neoliberalism and Born Again Racism." *Communication, Culture and Critique* 4: 23–30.

Enwezor, Okwui. 2009. "Modernity and Postcolonial Ambivalence." In *Tate Triennial*, edited by Nicolas Bourriaud, n.p. London: Tate Britain.

Epstein, Reid J. 2011. "U.S. Consulate in India Apologizes for Diplomat's Gaffe." *Politico*, August 15. www.politico.com/news/stories/0811/61377.html.

Everett, Anna. 2004. "Trading Private and Public Spaces @ HGTV and TLC: On New Genre Formations in Transformation TV." *Journal of Visual Culture* 3 (2): 157–81.

"Fair and Lovely." 2007. YouTube, posted by pachaaaspaisa, February 1. www.youtube.com/watch?v=0Is-9F4kPJk.

"Fair and Lovely." 2012. YouTube, posted by Infinitoid, April 8. www.youtube.com/watch?v=ouCr1NkhhRg.

"Fair and Lovely Commercial Spoof." 2010. YouTube, posted by Fawzia Mirza, September 15. www.youtube.com/watch?v=20ubDRNFpa4.

"Fair and Lovely Spoof—Extended Ad." 2010. YouTube, posted by RZ8990, May 23. www.youtube.com/watch?v=MIqPhX6VHuo.

"Fair and Lowly | Short Film | By Nicholas Kharkongor." 2012. YouTube, posted by humaramovie, June 25. www.youtube.com/watch?v=PP_Dgb-Ehfk.

"Fashion Designer Madiha Ibrar Talks to Fashion Central." 2012. *Fashion Central PK*, October 15. www.fashioncentral.pk/people-parties/celebrity-interviews/story-1300-fashion-designer-madiha-ibrar-talks-to-central/.

"Fashion Designer Monica Paracha Talks to Fashion Central." 2012. *Fashion Central PK*, November 22. www.fashioncentral.pk/people-parties/celebrity-interviews/story-1330-fashion-designer-monica-paracha-talks-to-central/.

Feldmann, Linda. 2008. "Obama's Victory Signals New Push for Unity." *Christian Science Monitor*, November 6, 25.

Ferguson, Roderick. 2004. *Aberrations in Black: Toward a Queer of Color Critique*. Minneapolis: University of Minnesota Press.

Ferguson, Roderick. 2012. *The Reorder of Things: The University and Its Pedagogies of Minority Difference*. Minneapolis: University of Minnesota Press.

Fields, Barbara Jeanne. 1990. "Slavery, Race and Ideology in the United States of America." *New Left Review* I/181 (May–June): 95–118.

Fields, Karen E., and Barbara J. Fields. 2014. *Racecraft: The Soul of Inequality in American Life*. London: Verso.

Fisher, Marc. 2017. "Glenn Beck Wants to Heal the America He Divided—One Hug at a Time." *Washington Post*, March 14. www.washingtonpost.com/lifestyle/style/glenn-beck-wants-to-heal-the-america-he-divided—one-hug-at-a-time/2017/03/14/70067648-f970-11e6-be05-1a3817ac21a5_story.html?utm_term=.27ae8348cc11.

Fiske, John. 1989. *Television Culture*. New York: Routledge.

Fleetwood, Nicole. 2011. *Troubling Vision: Performance, Visuality, and Blackness*. Chicago: University of Chicago Press.

Fliegelman, Jay. 1993. *Declaring Independence: Jefferson, Natural Language, and the Culture of Performance*. Palo Alto, CA: Stanford University Press.

Flores, Lisa A., Dreama G. Moon, and Thomas K. Nakayama. 2006. "Dynamic Rhetorics of Race: California's Racial Privacy Initiative and the Shifting Grounds of Racial Politics." *Communication and Critical/Cultural Studies* 3 (3): 181–201.

Florida, Richard L. 2002. *The Rise of the Creative Class: And How It's Transforming Work, Leisure, Community, and Everyday Life*. New York: Basic Books.

Florida, Richard. 2012. "What Critics Get Wrong about Creative Cities." May 30. www
.citylab.com/work/2012/05/what-critics-get-wrong-about-creative-cities/2119/.

Floyd, Samuel, Jr. 1995. *The Power of Black Music: Interpreting Its History from Africa to
the United States*. Oxford: Oxford University Press.

Fluet, Lisa. 2010. "Hit-Man Modernism." In *Bad Modernisms*, edited by Douglas Mao
and Rebecca L. Walkowitz, 269–97. Durham, NC: Duke University Press.

Foucault, Michel. 1977. *Discipline and Punish: The Birth of the Prison*. 2nd ed. New York:
Vintage Books.

Foucault, Michel. 1990. *The History of Sexuality: An Introduction, Volume 1*. New York:
Vintage Books.

Foucault, Michel. 2004. *The Birth of Biopolitics: Lectures at the College of France
1978–1979*. New York: Picador.

Foucault, Michel. 2007. *Security, Territory, Population: Lectures at the College of France
1977–1978*. New York: Vintage Books.

Fox-Genovese, Elizabeth. 1990. "Between Individualism and Fragmentation: American
Culture and the New Literary Studies of Race and Gender." *American Quarterly* 42
(1): 7–34.

Fraad Baxandall, Rosalyn, and Elizabeth Ewen. 2000. *Picture Windows: How the Suburbs
Happened*. New York: Basic Books.

Frankman, Ellen, and T. J. Raphael. 2016. "Searching for the Truth of the 'Hanging
Bridge.'" WNYC, May 2. www.wnyc.org/story/searching-truth-hanging-bridge/.

Freeman, Elizabeth. 2010. *Time Binds: Queer Temporalities, Queer Histories*. Durham,
NC: Duke University Press.

Freeman, Richard B., and Eunice Han. 2012. "The War against Public Sector Collective
Bargaining in the US." *Journal of Industrial Relations* 54 (3): 386–408.

Frith, Simon. 2011. "Pop Music." In *The Cambridge Companion to Rock and Pop*, edited
by Simon Frith, Will Straw, and John Street, 93–108. Cambridge: Cambridge University Press.

"FrontDoor.com Continues to Grow—Web Site Powered by HGTV Now Offers More
Than 3 Million Home Listings." 2008. *Business Wire*, July 18. www.businesswire.
com/news/home/20080718005506/en/FrontDoor.com-Continues-Grow—-Web-
Site-Powered.

Fuller, Jennifer. 2010. "Branding Blackness on US Cable Television." *Media, Culture and
Society* 32 (2): 285–305.

Gallagher, Billy. 2013. "Marc Andreessen: The World Would Be Much Better If We Had
50 More Silicon Valleys." *TechCrunch*, April 20. http://social.techcrunch.com/2013
/04/20/marc-andreessen-the-world-would-be-much-better-if-we-had-50-more
-silicon-valleys/.

"Gallery of Ghetto-Fabulous, Edible Hair-Dos." 2011. YumYucky, March 8. www
.yumyucky.com/2011/03/gallery-of-ghetto-fabulous-edible-hair-dos.html.

Ganley, E. 2010. "Veil Ban In France: Parliament Lays Groundwork, Sarkozy Wants Full
Ban." *Huffington Post*, May 11. www.huffingtonpost.com/2010/05/11/veil-ban-in
-france-parlia_n_571328.html.

Gans, Herbert. 1982. *The Levittowners*. New York: Columbia University Press.

Garber, Marjorie. 1997. *Vested Interests: Cross-Dressing and Cultural Anxiety*. New York: Routledge.

Gaspar, Michelle. 1977. "McDonald's Does It All to Help Minorities." *Chicago Daily Tribune*, December 27, E8.

Gates, Henry Louis, Jr. 1984. *Black Literature and Literary Theory*. New York: Methuen.

Gates, Racquel. 2012. "Keeping It Real(ity) Television." In *Watching While Black*, edited by Beretta Smith-Shomade, 141–57. New Brunswick, NJ: Rutgers University Press.

Giffels, David. 2014. *The Hard Way on Purpose*. New York: Scribner, Kindle edition.

Gilbert, David. 2006. "From Paris to Shanghai: The Changing Geographies of Fashion's World Cities." In *Fashion's World Cities*, edited by Christopher Breward and David Gilbert, 3–32. New York: Berg.

Gilman, Sander L. 1985. *Difference and Pathology: Stereotypes of Sexuality, Race, and Madness*. Ithaca, NY: Cornell University Press.

Gilroy, Paul. 2002. *Against Race: Imagining Political Culture beyond the Color Line*. Cambridge, MA: Harvard University Press.

Gines, Kathryn T. 2014. "A Critique of Postracialism: Conserving Race and Complicating Blackness beyond the Black-White Binary." *Du Bois Review* 11 (1): 75–86.

Giroux, Henry A. 2008. "Beyond the Biopolitics of Disposability: Rethinking Neoliberalism in the New Gilded Age." *Social Identities* 14 (5): 587–620.

Givhan, Robin. 2011. "Why Fashion Keeps Tripping over Race." *New York Magazine*, February 13. http://nymag.com/fashion/11/spring/71654/.

Givhan, Robin. 2012. "Ode to Joy: Dolce, Versace and Bottega in Milan for Spring 2013." *The Daily Beast*, September 23. www.thedailybeast.com/articles/2012/09/23/ode-to -joy-dolce-versace-and-bottega-in-milan-for-spring-2013.html.

Glasberg, Elena. 2010. "Our Amy Ray Earworms: The Butch's Throat: 'She's Got To Be' and 'Stand and Deliver.'"*Junebug versus Hurricane*, March 11. junebugvshurricane .wordpress.com/2010/03/11/our-amy-ray-earworms/.

"Glenn Beck Labels Trump a 'Sociopath.'" 2016. *AOL News*, October 25. www.aol.com /article/news/2016/10/25/glenn-beck-labels-trump-a-sociopath/21591444/.

Glissant, Edouard. 1992. *Caribbean Discourse: Selected Essays*. Translated by J. Michael Dash. Charlottesville: University of Virginia Press.

Goldberg, David T. 2002. *The Racial State*. Malden, MA: Blackwell.

Goldberg, David T. 2007. "Neoliberalizing Race." *Macalester Civic Forum* 1 (1): article 14. digitalcommons.macalester.edu/maccivicf/vol1/iss1/14.

Goldberg, David T. 2008. "Racial Palestinianization." In *Thinking Palestine*, edited by Ronit Levin, 25–46. London: Zed Books.

Goldberg, David T. 2009. *The Threat of Race: Reflections on Racial Neoliberalism*. Malden, MA: Wiley-Blackwell.

Gonzales, Alberto. 2016. "Trump Has a Right to Question Whether Judge Gonzalo Curiel Is Fair." *Washington Post*, June 4. www.washingtonpost.com/posteverything /wp/2016/06/04/alberto-r-gonzales-trump-has-a-right-to-question-whether-hes -getting-a-fair-trial/?utm_term=.c498ea6cd935.

Goodings-William, Robert, and Charles W. Mills. 2014. "Race in a 'Postracial' Epoch." *Du Bois Review* 11 (1): 1–8.

Goodman, Joseph. 2013. "King James Crowned Again." *Advertiser*, June 22.

Gordon, Linda, and Nancy Fraser. 1994. "A Genealogy of Dependency: Tracing a Keyword of the U.S. Welfare State." *Signs* 19 (2): 309–36.

"Gore Gote: India's Number 1 Testicular Fairness Cream." 2014. YouTube, posted by SnG Comedy, March 14. www.youtube.com/watch?v=S745IK1G23k.

Gotanda, Neil. 2000. "A Critique of 'Our Constitution Is Colorblind.'" In *Critical Race Theory: The Cutting Edge*, edited by Richard Delgado and Jean Stefancic, 35–38. 2nd ed. Philadelphia: Temple University Press.

Gould, Skye, and Rebecca Harrington. 2016. "7 Charts Show Who Propelled Trump to Victory." *Business Insider*, November 10. www.businessinsider.com/exit-polls-who-voted-for-trump-clinton-2016–11/#by-income-clinton-led-only-among-voters-with-a-2015-family-income-under-50000-a-group-that-included-36-of-the-voters-in-the-exit-polls-4.

Grabham, Emily. 2009. "Flagging the Skin: Corporeal Nationalism and the Properties of Belonging." *Body and Society* 15: 63–82.

Gramsci, Antonio. 1971. *Selections from the Prison Notebooks*. London: Lawrence and Wishart.

Gray, Herman. 1995. *Watching Race: Television and the Struggle for Blackness*. Minneapolis: University of Minnesota Press.

Gray, Herman. 2005. *Cultural Moves: African Americans and the Politics of Representation*. Berkeley: University of California Press.

Gray, Herman. 2013a. "Race, Media, and the Cultivation of Concern." *Communication and Critical/Cultural Studies* 10 (2–3): 253–58.

Gray, Herman. 2013b. "Subject(ed) to Recognition." *American Quarterly* 65 (4): 771–98.

Gray, Kevin Alexander, Jeffrey St. Clair, and JoAnn Wypijewski, eds. 2014. *Killing Trayvons: An Anthology of American Violence*. Petrolia, CA: CounterPunch.

Greenhouse, Steven. 2011. "Strained States Turning to Laws to Curb Labor Unions." *New York Times*, January 3.

Groner, Danny. 2010. "The Decision: 2010's Worst Sports Moment?" *Huffington Post*, December 27. www.huffingtonpost.com/danny-groner/the-decision-2010s-worst_b_801657.html.

Grunwald, Michael. 2012. *The New New Deal: The Hidden Story of Change in the Obama Era*. New York: Simon and Schuster.

Guerrero, Ed. 1993. *Framing Blackness*. Philadelphia: Temple University Press.

Gutiérrez, Elena R. 2008. *Fertile Matters: The Politics of Mexican-Origin Women's Reproduction*. Austin: University of Texas Press.

Hades. 2008. "Fair and Lovely Disappointed with Obama Win." *The Times of Bullshit*, November 16. http://thetimesofbullshit.blogspot.com/2008/11/fair-and-lovely-dissapointed-with-obama.html.

Hades. 2012. "Bollywood Blackface." *The Times of Bullshit*, August 19. http://thetimesofbullshit.blogspot.com/2012/08/bollywood-blackface.html.

Hall, Stuart. 1978. *Racism and Reaction: Five Views of Multiracial Britain*. London: Commission on Racial Equality.

Hall, Stuart. 1980. "Race, Articulation and Societies Structured in Dominance." In *Socio-logical Theories: Race and Colonialism*, 305–45. Paris: UNESCO.

Hall, Stuart. 1988. *The Hard Road to Renewal: Thatcherism and the Crisis of the Left*. London: Verso Books.

Hall, Stuart, Doreen Massey, and Michael Rustin. 2013. "After Neoliberalism? The Kilburn Manifesto: Framing Statement." *Soundings: A Journal of Politics and Culture*, no. 53: 3–19.

Hall, Stuart, and Alan O'Shea. 2013. "Common-Sense Neoliberalism." *Soundings: A Journal of Politics and Culture*, no. 55: 8–24.

Hancock, Ange-Marie. 2004. *The Politics of Disgust: The Public Identity of the Welfare Queen*. New York: NYU Press.

Haney López, Ian F. 1996. *White by Law: The Legal Construction of Race*. New York: NYU Press.

Haney López, Ian F. 2010. "Post-racial Racism: Racial Stratification and Mass Incarceration in the Age of Obama." *California Law Review* 98: 1023–73.

Haney López, Ian F. 2011. "Is the 'Post' in Post-racial the 'Blind' in Colorblind?" *Cardozo Law Review* 32 (3): 807–31.

Haney López, Ian F. 2014. *Dog Whistle Politics: How Coded Racial Appeals Have Reinvented Racism and Wrecked the Middle Class*. Oxford: Oxford University Press.

Hanhardt, Christina B. 2013. *Safe Space: Gay Neighborhood History and the Politics of Violence*. Durham, NC: Duke University Press.

Hannah-Jones, Nikole. 2017. "The Resegregation of Jefferson County." *New York Times Magazine*, September 6. www.nytimes.com/2017/09/06/magazine/the-resegregation-of-jefferson-county.html?emc=edit_ne_20170908&nl=evening-briefing&nlid=52544459&te=1&_r=0.

Hariman, Robert. 2008. "Political Parody and Public Culture." *Quarterly Journal of Speech* 94 (3): 247–72.

Harold, Christine. 2004. "Pranking Rhetoric: 'Cultural Jamming' as Media Activism." *Critical Studies in Media Communication* 21 (3): 189–211.

Harris, Anita. 2004. "Jamming Girl Culture: Young Women and Consumer Citizenship." In *All about the Girl: Culture, Power, and Identity*, edited by Anita Harris, 163–72. New York: Routledge.

Harris, Cheryl I. 1993. "Whiteness as Property." *Harvard Law Review* 106 (8): 1709–95.

Hartley, John. 2010. "Silly Citizenship." *Critical Discourse Studies* 7 (4): 233–48.

Hartley, John, and John Fiske. 2003. *Reading Television*, 2nd edition. New York: Routledge.

Hartman, Saidiya. 2007. *Lose Your Mother*. New York: Farrar, Straus and Giroux.

Harvey, David. 2002. "The Art of Rent: Globalisation, Monopoly and the Commodification of Culture." *Socialist Register* 38: 93–110.

Hasinoff, Amy Adele. 2008. "Fashioning Race for the Free Market on America's Next Top Model." *Critical Studies in Media Communication* 25 (3): 324–43.

Haslanger, Sally. 2014. "Studying While Black: Trust, Opportunity, and Disrespect." *Du Bois Review* 11 (1): 109–36.

Havens, Tim. 2013. *Black Television Travels: African American Media around the Globe*. New York: NYU Press.

Hearn, Alison. 2008. "Insecure: Narratives and Economies of the Branded Self in Transformation Television." *Continuum: Journal of Media and Cultural Studies* 22 (4): 495–504.

Hearn, Alison. 2010. "Reality Television, *The Hills* and the Limits of the Immaterial Labour Thesis." *TripleC: Communication, Capitalism and Critique. Open Access Journal for a Global Sustainable Information Society* 8 (1): 60–76.

Heckman, James J. 2011. "The American Family in Black and White: A Post-racial Strategy for Improving Skills to Promote Equality." *Daedalus* 140 (2): 70–89.

Hegde, Radha S. 2011. "Introduction." In *Circuits of Visibility: Gender and Transnational Media Cultures*, edited by R. S. Hegde, 1–17. New York: NYU Press.

Herbert, Bob. 2008. "The Obama Phenomenon." *New York Times*, January 5, A15.

Herrnstein, Richard, and Charles Murray. 1994. *The Bell Curve*. New York: Free Press.

HGTV. n.d. "12 Kinds of Neighborhoods." Accessed October 5, 2016. www.hgtv.com /design/real-estate/12-kinds-of-neighborhoods.

Hicks, Marie. 2017. *Programmed Inequality: How Britain Discarded Women Technologists and Lost Its Edge in Computing*. Cambridge, MA: MIT Press.

Hiles, Heather. 2015. "Silicon Valley Venture Capital Has a Diversity Problem." *Recode*, March 18. www.recode.net/2015/3/18/11560426/silicon-valley-venture-capital-has-a -diversity-problem.

Hill, Dave. 1986. *Designer Boys and Material Girls: Manufacturing the 80's Pop Dream*. London: Blandford Press.

Hoffman, Michael. 2016. "Japan Is as Happy as It Feels—Miserable." *Japan Times*, April 9.

Holland, Gale. 2016. "L.A. Considers Providing Homeless in Venice with Housing, Bathrooms and Storage." *Los Angeles Times*, April 17. www.latimes.com/local/lanow /la-me-homeless-bathrooms-venice-20160415-story.html.

Holland, Sharon. 2012. *The Erotic Life of Racism*. Durham, NC: Duke University Press.

Holman Jones, Stacy. 2007. *Torch Singing: Performing Resistance and Desire from Billie Holiday to Edith Piaf*. Walnut Creek, CA: AltaMira Press.

Homer. 1993. *The Odyssey: Translation and Analysis*. Translated by R. D. Dawe. Sussex: Book Guild.

Hong, Grace Kyungwon. 2006. *The Ruptures of American Capital: Women of Color Feminism and the Culture of Immigrant Labor*. Minneapolis: University of Minnesota Press.

hooks, bell. 1992. *Black Looks: Race and Representation*. Boston: South End Press.

Hornaday, Ann. 2013. "'12 Years a Slave,' 'Mother of George,' and the Aesthetic Politics of Filming Black Skin." *Washington Post*, October 17. www.washingtonpost.com /entertainment/movies/12-years-a-slave-mother-of-george-and-the-aesthetic-politics-of -filming-black-skin/2013/10/17/282af868–35cd-11e3–80c6–7e6dd8d22d8f_story.html.

Horovitz, Bruce. 2010. "Miami's Star Power Rises with LeBron." *USA Today*, July 12.

HoSang, Daniel M. 2010. *Racial Propositions: Ballot Initiatives and the Making of Postwar California*. Oakland: University of California Press.

Hsu, Hua. 2009. "The End of White America." *Atlantic*, January/February, 46–55.

Hunt, Darnell. 2014. "Hollywood Story: Diversity, Writing and the End of Television as We Know It." In *Sage Handbook of Television Studies*, edited by Manuel Alvarado, Milly Buonanno, Herman Gray, and Toby Miller, 163–73. London: Sage.

Hunt, Darnell. 2016. "Renaissance in Reverse?" *The 2016 Hollywood Writers Report*, March. www.wga.org/uploadedFiles/who_we_are/HWR16.pdf.

Hunt, Darnell, Ana-Cristina Ramón, Michael Tran, Amberia Sargent, and Vanessa Díaz. 2017. "2017 Hollywood Diversity Report: Setting the Record Straight." UCLA, February 21. www.bunchecenter.ucla.edu/wp-content/uploads/2017/04/2017 -Hollywood-Diversity-Report-2-21-17.pdf.

Hunt, Kenya. 2014. "Pharrell Williams Talks Race, Black Women and Social Justice." *Ebony*, November. www.ebony.com/entertainment-culture/pharrell-williams-talks -race-black-women-and-social-justice-cover-story#axzz3Uo886bHJ.

Hunter, M. L. 2002. "If You're Light, You're Alright: Light Skin Color as Social Capital for Women of Color." *Gender and Society* 16 (2): 175–93.

Hutcheon, L. 1985. *A Theory of Parody: The Teachings of Twentieth-Century Art Forms*. New York: Methuen.

Hutchins, Brett, and David Rowe. 2012. *Sport beyond Television: The Internet, Digital Media and the Rise of Networked Media Sport*. New York: Routledge.

India Pakistan Trade Unit. 2011. "Pakistan: Competitive Advantages." Accessed May 12, 2010. www.iptu.co.uk/content/pakistan_compet_advant.asp.

Jablonski, David. 2013. "All In for a Party." *Dayton Daily News*, June 23, C1.

Jackson, John L., Jr. 2005. *Real Black: Adventures in Racial Sincerity*. Chicago: University of Chicago Press.

Jackson, John L., Jr. 2006. "Gentrification, Globalization, and Georaciality." In *Globalization and Race: Transformations in the Cultural Production of Blackness*, edited by K. M. Clarke and D. Thomas, 188–205. Durham, NC: Duke University Press.

Jackson, Kenneth T. 1985. *Crabgrass Frontier: The Suburbanization of the United States*. New York: Oxford University Press.

James, LeBron, as told to Lee Jenkins. 2014. "I'm Coming Home." *Sports Illustrated*, July 11. www.si.com/nba/2014/07/11/lebron-james-cleveland-cavaliers.

Jardine, Alexandra. 2014. "Creativity 50; Pharrell Williams Musician, Entrepreneur." *Advertising Age*, December 29, 15.

Jayadev, Raj. 2001. "South Asian Workers in Silicon Valley: An Account of Work in the IT Industry." In *Sarai Reader 01: The Public Domain*, edited by Raqs Media Collective and Geert Lovink, 1:167–70. New Delhi, India: Sarai Programme, Center for the Study of Developing Societies.

Jefferson, Thomas. 2014. "Draft of the Declaration of Independence." In *The Bedford Anthology of American Literature*, edited by Susan Belasco and Linck Johnson, 387–93. New York: Bedford/St. Martin's.

Jeffries, Hasan K. 2018. Preface to *Teaching Hard History: American Slavery*. Southern Poverty Law Center. www.splcenter.org/20180131/teaching-hard-history.

Jennings, Angel. 2015. "'Black Beverly Hills' Debates Historic Status vs. White Gentrification." *Los Angeles Times*, July 18. www.latimes.com/local/la-me-adv-view-park -20150719-story.html.

Jha, S., and M. Adelman. 2009. "Looking for Love in All the White Places: A Study of Skin Color Preferences on Indian Matrimonial and Mate-Seeking Websites." *Studies in South Asian Film and Media* 1 (1): 65–83.

Jhally, Sut. 1989. "Cultural Studies and the Sports/Media Complex." In *Media, Sports, and Society*, edited by Lawrence A. Wenner, 70–93. Newbury Park, CA: Sage.

Johnson, E. Patrick. 2005. "'Quare' Studies, or (Almost) Everything I Know about Queer Studies I Learned from My Grandmother." In *Black Queer Studies: A Critical Anthology*, edited by E. Patrick Johnson and Mae G. Henderson, 124–60. Durham, NC: Duke University Press.

Johnson, Victoria E. 2008. *Heartland TV: Prime Time Television and the Struggle for U.S. Identity*. New York: NYU Press.

Johnson, Victoria E. 2009a. "Everything New Is Old Again: Sport Television, Innovation and Tradition for a Multi-platform Era." In *Beyond Prime Time: Television Programming in the Post-network Era*, edited by Amanda D. Lotz, 114–37. New York: Routledge.

Johnson, Victoria E. 2009b. "Historicizing TV Networking: Broadcasting, Cable, and the Case of ESPN." In *Media Industries: History, Theory, and Method*, edited by Jennifer Holt and Alisa Perren, 57–68. Malden, MA: Wiley-Blackwell.

Jones, Jacqueline. 2013. *A Dreadful Deceit: The Myth of Race from the Colonial Era to Obama's America*. New York: Basic Books.

Jones, Nicholas A., and Jungmiwha Bullock. 2012. "The Two or More Races Population: 2010." *Census Briefs 2010*, September. No. C2010BR-13. U.S. Department of Commerce, Economics and Statistics Administration, U.S. Census Bureau. www.census .gov/prod/cen2010/briefs/c2010br-13.pdf.

Jonsson, Patrik. 2010. "LeBron James Show: A One-Hour Ticket to His Fabulous Universe." *Christian Science Monitor*, July 8. www.csmonitor.com/USA/2010/0708 /LeBron-James-show-a-one-hour-ticket-to-his-fabulous-universe.

Joseph, Ralina L. 2011. "Imagining Obama: Reading Overtly and Inferentially Racist Images of Our 44th President, 2007–2008." *Communication Studies* 62 (4): 389–405.

Joseph, Ralina L. 2012. *Transcending Blackness: From the New Millennium Mulatta to the Exceptional Multi-racial*. Durham, NC: Duke University Press.

Joseph, Ralina L. 2017. "What's the Difference with 'Difference'? Equity, Communiation, and the Politics of Difference." *International Journal of Communication* 11:3306–26.

"Justin Timberlake: 'The 20/20 Experience': Is There a Visual Preference for Whiteness?" 2013. *Huffington Post*, March 27. www.huffingtonpost.com/2013/03/27/justin -timberlake-the-2020-experience-is-there-a-visual-preference-for-whiteness_n _2965509.html.

"Kalup Linzy's First Soap Opera 1994." 2011. YouTube, posted by Kalup Linzy, July 9. www.youtube.com/watch?v=I-zEy5ga1VM.

Katznelson, Ira. 2005. *When Affirmative Action Was White: An Untold History of Racial Inequality in Twentieth-Century America*. New York: W. W. Norton.

Keat, Russell. 2013. "Individualism and Community in Socialist Thought." In *Issues in Marxist Philosophy*, edited by J. Mepham and D-H. Ruben, 127–52. Brighton: Harvester Press.

Keeling, Kara. 2007. *The Witch's Flight: The Cinematic, the Black Femme, and the Image of Common Sense*. Durham, NC: Duke University Press.

Keeling, Kara. 2014. "Queer OS." *Cinema Journal* 53 (2): 152–57.

Keeling, Kara. 2019. *Queer Times, Black Futures*. New York: NYU Press.

Keen, Andrew. 2012. "Keen on . . . Vivek Wadhwa: Why There Are So Few Black or Female Entrepreneurs in Silicon Valley [TCTV]." *TechCrunch*, April 3. http://social .techcrunch.com/2012/04/03/keen-on-vivek-wadhwa-why-there-are-so-few-black -or-female-entrepreneurs-in-silicon-valley-tctv/.

Keightley, Keir. 2011. "The Historical Consciousness of Sunshine Pop." *Journal of Popular Music Studies* 23 (3): 343–61.

Kelley, Robin D. G. 2000. "Foreword." In *Black Marxism: The Making of the Black Radical Tradition*, by Cedric Robinson, xi–xxxiii. Chapel Hill: University of North Carolina Press.

Kelley, Robin D. G. 2011. "'He's Got the Whole World in His Hands': US History and Its Discontents in the Obama Era." *Journal of American Studies* 45 (1): 185–200.

Kenway, J., and E. Bullen. 2011. "Skin Pedagogies and Abject Bodies." *Sport, Education, and Society* 16 (3): 279–94.

Kessler, Sarah. 2016. "Anachronism Effects: Ventriloquism and Popular Media." PhD diss., University of California, Irvine.

Kessler, Sarah, and Karen Tongson. 2014. "Karaoke and Ventriloquism: Echoes and Divergences." *Sounding Out! The Sound Studies Blog*, May 12. http://soundstudiesblog .com/2014/05/12/karaoke-and-ventriloquism-echoes-and-divergences/.

Khouri, Andrew. 2016. "Tenant Buyouts Lead to Protests and a Crackdown Plan by L.A. City Council." *Los Angeles Times*, September 23. www.latimes.com/business/la-fi -tenant-buyouts-20160919-snap-story.html.

Kiely, Eugene. 2016. "Trump's David Duke Amnesia." *Factcheck.org*, March 1. www .factcheck.org/2016/03/trumps-david-duke-amnesia/.

King, Desmond, Robert C. Lieberman, Gretchen Ritter, and Laurence Whitehead, eds. 2009. *Democratization in America: A Comparative-Historical Analysis*. Baltimore: Johns Hopkins University Press.

Knowles, Eric D., Brian S. Lowery, Elizabeth P. Shulman, and Rebecca L. Schaumberg. 2013. "Race, Ideology and the Tea Party: A Longitudinal Study." *PLoS One* 8 (6): e67110. https://doi.org/10.1371/journal.pone.0067110.

Koestenbaum, Wayne. 2001. *The Queen's Throat*. Cambridge, MA: DaCapo.

Kreisberg, B., dir., and 495 Productions, prod. 2009. *HGTV $250,000 Challenge*. Episode 4, "You Gotta Be a Garden Warrior." Aired May 31, on HGTV.

Kuku, D. 2009. "India Is Racist and Happy about It." *Outlook*, June 29. www .outlookindia.com/article.aspx?250317.

Kumar, S. 2015. "Contagious Memes, Viral Videos and Subversive Parody: The Grammar of Contention on the Indian Web." *International Communication Gazette* 77 (3): 232–47.

Kunwar, B. 2011. "Ali Xeeshan: The Neo-Traditionalist." *Sunday Plus Magazine*, April 24.

La Ferla, Ruth. 2003. "Generation EA: Ethnically Ambiguous." *New York Times*, December 28. www.nytimes.com/2008/12/28/fashion/28ETHN.html?pagewanted=2.

Lanza, Joseph. 2005. *Vanilla Pop: Sweet Sounds from Frankie Avalon to ABBA*. Chicago: Chicago Review Press.

Le Guin, Ursula K. 2016. "Freedom: A Speech in acceptance of the National Book Foundation Medal for Distinguished Contribution to American Letters, November 2014." In *Words Are My Matter: Writings about Life and Books, 2000–2016*. Easthampton, MA: Small Beer Press.

Leibovich, Mark. 2010. "Being Glenn Beck." *New York Times Magazine*, September 29.

Leonard, David J., and Bruce Lee Hazlewood. 2014. "The Race Denial Card: The NBA Lockout, LeBron James, and the Politics of New Racism." In *The Colorblind Screen: Television in Post-racial America*, edited by Sarah Nilsen and Sarah E. Turner, 108–39. New York: NYU Press.

Leong, Solomon. 2006. "Who's the Fairest of Them All? Television Ad for Skin-Lightening Cosmetics in Hong Kong." *Asian Ethnicity* 7 (2): 167–81.

Levine, Yasha. 2015. "'We Got Geeks': Inside Google's Ugly War against the Homeless in LA." *Pando*, June 22. https://pando.com/2015/06/22/we-got-geeks/.

Light, Jennifer S. 1999. "When Computers Were Women." *Technology and Culture* 40 (3): 455–83.

Lim, J. 2013. "5 Top Casting Directors Explain Why Runways Are So White." *Buzzfeed*, March 19. www.buzzfeed.com/jameslim/5-top-casting-directors-explain-why-runways-are-so-white.

Limbaugh, Rush. 2010. "Union Thugs: 'Raise My Taxes!'" *The Rush Limbaugh Show*, April 22. www.rushlimbaugh.com/daily/2010/04/22/union_thugs_raise_my_taxes_2.

Limbaugh, Rush. 2011. "We've Reached the Tipping Point." *The Rush Limbaugh Show*, February 18. www.rushlimbaugh.com/daily/2011/02/18/we_ve_reached_the_tipping_point.

Lio, Shoon, Scott Melzer, and Ellen Reese. 2008. "Constructing Threat and Appropriating 'Civil Rights': Rhetorical Strategies of Gun Rights and English Only Leaders." *Symbolic Interaction* 31 (3): 5–31. doi:10.1525/si.2008.31.1.5.

Lipovetsky, Gilles. 1994. *The Empire of Fashion: Dressing Modern Democracy*. Translated by Catherine Porter. Princeton, NJ: Princeton University Press.

Lipsitz, George. 1998. *The Possessive Investment in Whiteness: How White People Profit from Identity Politics*. Philadelphia: Temple University Press.

Lipsitz, George. 2006. *The Possessive Investment in Whiteness: How White People Profit from Identity Politics*. Revised and expanded edition. Philadelphia: Temple University Press.

Lipsitz, George. 2007. *Footsteps in the Dark: The Hidden Histories of Popular Music*. Minneapolis: University of Minnesota Press.

Lipsitz, George. 2011. *How Racism Takes Place*. Philadelphia: Temple University Press.

Litsky, Frank. 2003. "LeBron James' SUV Prompts an Investigation." *New York Times*, January 14.

Londoño, Johana. 2012. "Aesthetic Belonging: The Latinization and Renewal of Union City, New Jersey." In *Latino Urbanism: The Politics of Planning, Policy, and Redevelopment*, edited by David R. Diaz and Rodolfo D. Torres, 47–64. New York: NYU Press.

Lott, Eric. 1989. "Response to Trey Ellis's 'The New Black Aesthetic.'" *Callaloo* 38:244–46.

Lott, Eric. 1992. "Love and Theft: The Racial Unconscious of Blackface Minstrelsy." *Representations* 39:23–50.

Lott, Eric. 2013. *Love and Theft: Black Face Minstrelsy and the American Working Class.* Twentieth anniversary edition. Oxford: Oxford University Press.

Lotz, Amanda D. 2014. *Cable Guys: Television and Masculinities in the 21st Century.* New York: NYU Press.

Love, David A. 2014. "Return to Cleveland Spotlights Urban Problems." *Philadelphia Inquirer*, July 18.

Lowe, Lisa. 1996. *Immigrant Acts: On Asian American Cultural Politics.* Durham, NC: Duke University Press.

Lowndes, Joseph. 2008. *From the New Deal to the New Right: Race and the Southern Origins of Modern Conservatism.* New Haven, CT: Yale University Press.

Lubiano, Wahneema. 1992. "Black Ladies, Welfare Queens, and State Minstrels: Ideological War by Narrative Means." In *Race-ing Justice, En-gendering Power: Essays on Anita Hill, Clarence Thomas, and the Construction of Social Reality*, edited by Toni Morrison, 323–63. New York: Pantheon Books.

Lysiak, Matthew. 2010. "A Final Day of Lebronsense!" *New York Daily News*, July 8.

Maag, Christopher. 2010. "Back in His Hometown, James Remains Royalty." *New York Times*, August 8.

Madison, James. n.d. *The Federalist Papers*. No. 10, "The Same Subject Continued: The Union as a Safeguard against Domestic Faction and Insurrection." From the New York Packet (Friday, November 23, 1787), Yale Law School Avalon Project. Accessed August 5, 2015. http://avalon.law.yale.edu/18th_century/fed10.asp.

Maese, Rick. 2011. "LeBron's Home Team." *Washington Post*, June 7.

Magder, Ted. 2009. "Television 2.0: The Business of American Television in Transition." In *Reality TV: Remaking Television Culture*, edited by Susan Murray and Laurie Ouellette, 141–64. New York: NYU Press.

Mahmood, Saba. 2005. *Politics of Piety: The Islamic Revival and the Feminist Subject.* Princeton, NJ: Princeton University Press.

"Make Me White." 2010. YouTube, posted by SamosaTv, March 26. www.youtube.com /watch?v=3MPVjdA90Gk.

Maqsood, A. 2014. "'Buying Modern': Muslim Subjectivity, the West and Patterns of Islamic Consumption in Lahore, Pakistan." *Cultural Studies* 28 (1): 84–107.

Marable, Manning. 2009. "Racializing Obama: The Enigma of Post-black Politics and Leadership." *Souls* 11 (1): 1–15.

"Marvin Gaye's Family Says Pharrell's Happy Is Another Copy." 2015. *Guardian*, March 13. www.theguardian.com/music/2015/mar/13/marvin-gayes-family-says -pharrells-happy-is-another-copy?CMP=ema_565.

Marx, Karl. 1978. "On the Jewish Question." In *The Marx-Engels Reader*, edited by Robert Tucker, 26–52. New York: W. W. Norton.

Marx, Karl, and Friedrich Engels. 1956. *The Holy Family or Critique of Cultural Critique.* Moscow: Foreign Languages Publishing House.

Marx, Karl, and Friedrich Engels. 1964. *The Communist Manifesto.* New York: Simon and Schuster.

Maxwell, Angie, and T. Wayne Parent. 2012. "The Obama Trigger: Presidential Approval and Tea Party Membership." *Social Science Quarterly* 93 (5): 1384–401.

Mayes, Keith. 2009. *Kwanzaa: Black Power and the Making of the African-American Holiday Tradition.* London: Routledge.

McBride, Sarah. 2013. "Insight: In Silicon Valley Start-Up World, Pedigree Counts." *Reuters,* September 12. www.reuters.com/article/us-usa-startup-connections-insight -idUSBRE98B15U20130912.

McCarthy, Anna. 2007. "Reality Television: A Neoliberal Theater of Suffering." *Social Text* 25 (4): 17–42.

McCartin, Joseph. 2011. "Convenient Scapegoat: Public Workers under Assault." *Dissent* (spring): 45–50.

McCartney, Anthony. 2015. "Jury Says Pharrell Williams, Robin Thicke Copied Marvin Gaye Song for 'Blurred Lines.'" *Christian Science Monitor,* March 11. www.csmonitor .com/The-Culture/Music/2015/0311/Jury-says-Pharrell-Williams-Robin-Thicke -copied-Marvin-Gaye-song-for-Blurred-Lines.

McCracken, Allison. 2015. *Real Men Don't Sing: Crooning in American Culture.* Durham, NC: Duke University Press.

McDowell, Colin. 2013. *The Anatomy of Fashion: Why We Dress the Way We Do.* London: Phaidon Press.

McGrath, Ben. 2010. "The Movement: The Rise of Tea Party Activism." *New Yorker,* February 1. www.newyorker.com/magazine/2010/02/01/the-movement.

McKinley, James C., Jr. 2011. "Advances in Medicine Lead Stars to Surgery." *New York Times,* November 8. www.nytimes.com/2011/11/19/arts/music/why-voices-of -singers-like-adele-and-john-mayer-are-stilled.html?_r=0.

McKissick, Floyd. 1968. "Black Capitalism." *New York Amsterdam News,* December 21, 7.

McMillan Cottom, Tressie. 2017. "The Coded Language of For-Profit Colleges." *Atlantic,* February 22. www.theatlantic.com/education/archive/2017/02/the-coded-language -of-for-profit-colleges/516810/.

McRobbie, A. 2002. "Clubs to Companies: Notes on the Decline of Political Culture in Speeded Up Creative Worlds." *Cultural Studies* 16 (4): 516–31.

Mears, Ashley. 2010. "Size Zero High-End Ethnic: Cultural Production and the Repro- duction of Culture in Fashion Modeling." *Poetics* 38 (1): 21–46.

Medved, Michael. 2003. "Hollywood Finally Moves beyond Racial Obsession." *USA Today,* June 10, 13A.

Meer, Zubin. 2011. *Individualism: The Cultural Logic of Modernity.* New York: Lexington Books.

Meizel, Katherine. 2011. *Idolized: Music, Media, and Identity in* American Idol. Bloom- ington: Indiana University Press.

Melamed, Jodi. 2006. "The Spirit of Neoliberalism: From Racial Liberalism to Neolib- eral Multiculturalism." *Social Text* 89 24 (4): 1–24.

Melamed, Jodi. 2011. *Represent and Destroy: Rationalizing Violence in the New Racial Capitalism.* Minneapolis: University of Minnesota Press.

Mercer, Kobena. 1994. "1968: Periodizing Politics and Identity." In *Welcome to the Jungle,* 287–309. London: Routledge.

Mercer, Kobena. 1999. "Ethnicity and Internationality: New British Art and Diaspora-Based Blackness." *Third Text* 13 (49): 51–62.

Meyers, Erin. 2015. "Don't Cry Because It's Over, Smile Because It Was: American Soap Operas and Convergence Culture." *Critical Studies in Media Communication* 32 (5): 333–46.

Milbank, Dana. 2010. *Tears of a Clown: Glenn Beck and the Tea Bagging of America.* New York: Doubleday.

Miller, D. A. 1998. *Place for Us: Essay on the Broadway Musical.* Cambridge, MA: Harvard University Press.

Miller, Toby. 2007. *Cultural Citizenship: Cosmopolitanism, Consumerism, and Television in a Neoliberal Age.* Philadelphia: Temple University Press.

Miller-Young, Mireille. 2014. *A Taste for Brown Sugar: Black Women in Pornography.* Durham, NC: Duke University Press.

Mire, Amina. 2005. "Pigmentation and Empire." *Counterpunch*, July 28. www .counterpunch.org/2005/07/28/the-emerging-skin-whitening-industry/.

Mittell, Jason. 2015. *Complex TV: The Poetics of Contemporary Television Storytelling.* New York: NYU Press.

Modleski, Tania. 1985. "The Rhythms of Reception: Daytime Television and Women's Work." In *Regarding Television*, edited by E. Ann Kaplan, 67–75. Frederick, MD: Greenwood.

Modleski, Tania. 2008. *Loving with a Vengeance: Mass-Produced Fantasies for Women.* 2nd ed. New York: Routledge.

Mohan, Pavithra. 2016. "Marc Andreessen Riles Up Twitter after Defending Colonialism in India." *Fast Company*, February 16. www.fastcompany.com/3056581/marc -andreessen-riles-up-twitter-after-defending-colonialism-in-india.

Mohanty, C. 2003. *Feminism without Borders: Decolonizing Theory, Practicing Solidarity.* Durham, NC: Duke University Press.

Molina, Natalia. 2014. *How Race Is Made in America.* Berkeley: University of California Press.

Monroe Work Today interactive map. 2016. Accessed October 5, 2016. www .monroeworktoday.org/explore/.

Monson, Ingrid. 2007. *Freedom Sounds: Civil Rights Call Out to Jazz and Africa.* New York: Oxford University Press.

Moreno, Carolina. 2015. "9 Outrageous Things Donald Trump Has Said about Latinos." *Huffington Post*, August 31 (updated November 9, 2016). www.huffingtonpost .com/entry/9-outrageous-things-donald-trump-has-said-about-latinos_us _55e483a1e4b0c818f618904b.

Morgan-Parmett, Helen, and Kate Ranachan. 2016. "There Goes the Neighborhood: Centurylink Field and the Transformation of Seattle's Sodo Neighborhood." *Mediapolis: A Journal of Cities and Culture*, December 28. http://www .mediapolisjournal.com/2016/12/there-goes-the-neighborhood/.

Morris, Dick. 2007. "Obama's Selma Bounce." *RealClearPolitics.com*, March 8. RealClear-Politics.com/articles/2007/03/obama_selma_bounce.html.

Morrison, Toni. 1998. "Comment." *New Yorker*, October 5. www.newyorker.com /magazine/1998/10/05/comment-6543.

Morton, Brian. 2011. "Falser Words Were Never Spoken." *New York Times*, August 29. www.nytimes.com/2011/08/30/opinion/falser-words-were-never-spoken.html.

Moss, Hilary. 2012. "Franca Sozzani on 'Haute Mess': A Racist Image, I Really Do Not Understand." *New York Magazine*, March 19. http://nymag.com/daily/fashion/2012/03/franca-sozzani-talks-about-her-haute-mess.html.

Moynihan, Daniel Patrick. 1965. *The Negro Family: The Case for National Action*. Office of Policy Planning and Research. United States Department of Labor. March.

Mukherjee, Roopali. 2006a. "The Ghetto Fabulous Aesthetic in Contemporary Black Culture: Class and Consumption in the *Barbershop* Films." *Cultural Studies* 20 (6): 599–629.

Mukherjee, Roopali. 2006b. *The Racial Order of Things: Cultural Imaginaries of the Post-soul Era*. Minneapolis: University of Minnesota Press.

Mukherjee, Roopali. 2016. "Antiracism Limited: A Pre-history of Post-race." *Cultural Studies* 30 (1): 47–77.

Mukhtar, Abida. 2008. "Insight into the Problems Facing Pakistan's Textile Industry." *CHUP!—Changing Up Pakistan*, April 17. http://changinguppakistan.wordpress.com/2008/04/17/contribution-insight-into-the-problems-facing-pakistans-textile-industry-by-abida-mukhtar/.

Muñoz, José E. 1999. *Disidentifications: Queers of Color and the Performance of Politics*. Minneapolis: University of Minnesota Press.

Muñoz, José E. 2009. *Cruising Utopia: The Then and There of Queer Futurity*. New York: NYU Press.

Munshi, Shoma. 1998. "Wife/Mother/Daughter-in-Law: Multiple Avatars of Home-maker in 1990s Indian Advertising." *Media, Culture and Society* 20 (4): 573–91.

Murray, Charles. 2012. *Coming Apart: The State of White America 1960–2010*. New York: Crown Forum.

Murray, Susan, and Laurie Ouellette, eds. 2009. *Reality TV: Remaking Television Culture*. New York: NYU Press.

Nakamura, Lisa, and Peter A. Chow-White, eds. 2012. *Race after the Internet*. New York: Routledge.

Narisetti, Kim Barrington. 2014. "Racism Alive in India: Story of Kim Barrington Narisetti, an African-American Professional." *Economic Times*, January 25. https://economictimes.indiatimes.com/racism-alive-in-india-story-of-kim-barrington-narisetti-an-african-american-professional/articleshow/29319888.cms.

NBC News/Survey Monkey Poll. 2016. June 16. www.scribd.com/doc/315926515/NBC-News-SurveyMonkey-Post-Orlando-Toplines-Methodology-616-final?secret_password=pJVSdx2XqAtU7xJtMWPB.

Neal, Mark Anthony. 2005. "White Chocolate Soul: Teena Marie and Lewis Taylor." *Popular Music* 24 (3): 369–80.

Negus, Keith. 2013. *Music Genres and Corporate Cultures*. New York: Routledge.

Nelson, Alondra. 2016. *The Social Life of DNA: Race, Reparations, and Reconciliation after the Genome*. Boston: Beacon.

Newcomb, Horace, and Robert S. Alley. 1983. *The Producer's Medium: Conversations with Creators of American TV*. Oxford: Oxford University Press.

Newcomb, Horace, and Paul M. Hirsch. 1987. "Television as Cultural Forum." In *Television: The Critical View*, 4th ed., edited by Horace Newcomb, 455–70. New York: Oxford University Press.

Newitz, Annalee. 2000. "What Makes Things Cheesy? Satire, Multinationalism, and B-Movies." *Social Text* 18 (2): 59–82.

Newman, Jason. 2014. "Pharrell Partners with UN for 'International Day of Happiness.'" *Rolling Stone*, March 7. www.rollingstone.com/music/news/pharrell-partners-with -un-for-international-day-of-happiness-20140307.

Newman, Michael Z., and Elana Levine. 2012. *Legitimating Television: Media Convergence and Cultural Status*. New York: Routledge.

Newport, Frank. n.d. "Tea Party Support Holds at 24%." Gallup. Last modified October 1, 2014. www.gallup.com/poll/177788/tea-party-support-holds.aspx.

"New to Fashion Compassion—Inaaya Jewellery." 2013. *FCEdit*, January 17. www .fashioncompassion.co.uk/new-to-fashion-compassion-inaaya-jewellery/.

Newton, Huey. 1995. "Huey Newton Talks to the Movement about the Black Panther Party, Cultural Nationalism, SNCC, Liberals and White Revolutionaries." In *The Black Panthers Speak*, edited by Philip S. Foner, 50–66. New York: Da Capo Press.

Nicholls, David. 2014. "Pharrell Williams Interview: The Smell of Success." *Telegraph*, August 29. www.telegraph.co.uk/men/fashion-and-style/11059026/Pharrell -Williams-interview-the-smell-of-success.html.

"Nida Azwer Collection at Fashion Pakistan Week 2014 Day 1." 2014. *Fashion Central PK*. Accessed July 28, 2015. www.fashioncentral.pk/pakistani/ramp/review-1287 -nida-azwer-collection-at-fashion-pakistan-week-2014-day-1/.

Nielsen Media Research. 2013. *State of the Media: U.S. Consumer Usage Report, 2012*. www.nielsen.com/us/en/reports/2013/state-of-the-media—u-s—consumer-usage -report.html.

Noble, Safiya Umoja. 2016. "A Future for Intersectional Black Feminist Technology Studies." *Scholar and Feminist Online*, nos. 13.3–14.1. http://sfonline.barnard.edu /traversing-technologies/safiya-umoja-noble-a-future-for-intersectional-black -feminist-technology-studies/.

Noble, Safiya Umoja, and Sarah T. Roberts. 2016. "Through Google-Colored Glass(es): Design, Emotion, Class, and Wearables as Commodity and Control." In *Emotions, Technology and Design*, edited by Sharon Tettegah and Safiya Umoja Noble, 188–212. San Diego: Elsevier Academic Press.

Norton, Michael, and Samuel R. Sommers. 2011. "Whites See Racism as a Zero-Sum Game That They Are Now Losing." *Perspectives on Psychological Science* 6 (3): 215–18.

Norwood, Kimberly Jade, ed. 2014. *Color Matters: Skin Tone Bias and the Myth of a Postracial America*. New York: Routledge.

Norwood, Kimberly Jade, and Violeta Solonova Foreman. 2014. "The Ubiquitousness of Colorism: Then and Now." In *Color Matters: Skin Tone Bias and the Myth of a Postracial America*, edited by Kimberly Jade Norwood, 9–28. New York: Routledge.

Nyong'o, Tavia. 2010. "Brown Punk: Kalup Linzy's Musical Anticipations." *TDR: The Drama Review* 54 (3): 71–86.

O'Brien, Sarah Ashley. 2016. "Some Silicon Valley Tech Workers Are Calling in 'Black' to Work." *CNN Tech*, July 7. http://money.cnn.com/2016/07/07/technology/philando -castile-tech-workers-calling-in-black/.

Oliver, Melvin, and Thomas Shapiro. 2006. *Black Wealth/White Wealth: A New Perspective on Racial Inequality*. New York: Routledge.

Omi, Michael, and Howard Winant. 1994. *Racial Formation in the United States*. New York: Routledge.

"'Orange' Creator Jenji Kohan: 'Piper Was My Trojan Horse.'" 2013. *Fresh Air*, August 13. www.npr.org/2013/08/13/211639989/orange-creator-jenji-kohan-piper-was-my -trojan-horse.

Orbe, Mark P., and Ewa L. Urban. 2011. "'Race Matters' in the Obama Era." *Communication Studies* 62 (4): 349–52.

Osnos, Evan. 2015. "The Fearful and the Frustrated: Donald Trump's Nationalist Coalition Takes Shape for Now." *New Yorker*, August 31. www.newyorker.com/magazine /2015/08/31/the-fearful-and-the-frustrated.

Ouellette, Laurie. 2008. "'Take Responsibility for Yourself': Judge Judy and the Neoliberal Citizen." In *Feminist Television Criticism: A Reader*, 2nd ed., edited by Charlotte Brunsdon and Lynn Spigel, 139–53. Maidenhead, UK: Open University Press.

Ouellette, Laurie. 2016. *Lifestyle TV*. New York: Taylor and Francis.

Ouellette, Laurie, and James Hay. 2008. *Better Living through Reality TV: Television and Post-welfare Citizenship*. Malden, MA: Blackwell.

"Our Mission." n.d. The 9/12 Project. www.the912-project.com/about/about-the-912 -project/.

Painter, Nell Irvin. 2010. *The History of White People*. New York: Houghton Mifflin.

Pakenham, Thomas. 1992. *Scramble for Africa*. London: Abacus.

Paracha, Nadeem F. 2015. "The Bookstalls and Catwalks of Defiance in Pakistan." *Dawn News*, February 19. www.dawn.com/news/1164428.

Parameswaran, Radhika. 2011. "E-raceing Color: Gender and Transnational Visual Economies of Beauty." In *Tracking Visibilities: Gender and Transnational Media Cultures*, edited by Radha Hegde, 68–86. New York: NYU Press.

Parameswaran, Radhika. 2013. "Exfoliating Colorism: Contestations, Comedy, and Critique in a Transnational Field." Paper presented at the annual conference of the International Communication Association, London, June 17–21.

Parameswaran, Radhika, and Kavitha Cardoza. 2009. "Melanin on the Margins: Advertising and the Cultural Politics of Fair/Light/White Beauty in India." *Journalism and Communication Monographs* 11 (3): 213–74.

Parker, Christopher S., and Matt Barreto. 2014. *Change They Can't Believe In: The Tea Party and Reactionary Politics in America*. Princeton, NJ: Princeton University Press.

Patten, Eileen. 2016. "Racial, Gender Wage Gaps Persist in U.S. Despite Some Progress." *Pew Research Center Fact Tank*, July. www.pewresearch.org/fact-tank/2016/07/01 /racial-gender-wage-gaps-persist-in-u-s-despite-some-progress/.

Pawlenty, Tim. 2010. "Government Unions vs. Taxpayers." *Wall Street Journal*, December 13. www.wsj.com/articles/SB10001424052748703766704576009350303578410.

Payne, S. 2014. "Gore Gote: Spoof Testicular Cream Advert Mocks India's Skin-Lightening Craze." *International BusinessTimes*, March 21. www.ibtimes.co.uk/gore-gote-spoof-testicular-cream-advert-mocks-indias-skin-lightening-craze-1441309.

Peraino, Judith Ann. 2006. *Listening to the Sirens: Musical Technologies of Queer Identity from Homer to Hedwig.* Berkeley: University of California Press.

Perlman, Allison. 2016. *Public Interests: Media Advocacy and Struggles over Television.* New Brunswick, NJ: Rutgers University Press.

Perry, Imani. 2011. *More Beautiful and More Terrible: The Embrace and Transcendence of Racial Equality in the United States.* New York: NYU Press.

Pham, Minh-Ha. 2011. "Unintentionally Eating the Other." *Threadbared*, September 12. http://iheartthreadbared.wordpress.com/2011/09/12/unintentional-eating/.

"Pharrell Williams Interview." 2014. *Oprah Prime*, April 14. Oprah Winfrey Network. Television broadcast.

Piacenza, Joanna. 2014. "Americans' Racial Disconnect on Fairness and Discrimination." PRRI American Values Survey, October 6. www.prri.org/spotlight/graphic-of-the-week-americans-racial-disconnect-on-fairness-and-discrimination/.

Plaschke, Bill. 2014. "James Proves He Can Go Home Again." *Los Angeles Times*, July 12.

Pontecorvo, Gillo, dir. 1967. *The Battle of Algiers*. Algiers, Rome: Casbah Film, Igor Films.

Potok, Mark. 2012. "The Patriot Movement Explodes." *Southern Poverty Law Center Intelligence Report*, March 1. www.splcenter.org/fighting-hate/intelligence-report/2012/patriot-movement-explodes.

Putnam, Robert. 2015. *Our Kids: The American Dream in Crisis*. New York: Simon and Schuster.

"Put Off by the LeBron Spectacle? Here's a Redeeming Virtue." 2010. *Christian Science Monitor*, July 9.

Puwar, Nirmal. 2002. "Multicultural Fashion . . . Stirrings of Another Sense of Aesthetics and Memory." *Feminist Review* 71 (1): 63–87.

Quadagno, Jill. 1994. *The Color of Welfare: How Racism Undermined the War on Poverty*. Oxford: Oxford University Press.

"Quaker, McDonald's Expand Minority Hiring." 1975. *Chicago Tribune*, November 28, 16.

Qureshi, Huma. 2011. "Islamabad's First Fashion Week." *Guardian*, January 24. www.theguardian.com/world/2011/jan/24/islamabad-fashion-week-pakistan.

Raab, Scott. 2011. *The Whore of Akron: One Man's Search for the Soul of LeBron James*. New York: HarperCollins.

"Rabia at Fashion Pakistan Week 2010." 2010. *Fashion Central PK*. Accessed January 30, 2010. www.fashioncentral.pk/pakistani/ramp/review-202-rabia-at-fashion-pakistan-week-2010/.

Rachleff, Peter. 2012. "The Right to Work Offensive: Tracking the Spread of the Anti-union Virus." *New Labor Forum* 21 (1): 22–29.

Rajagopal, Arvind. 1998. "Advertising, Politics, and the Sentimental Education of the Indian Consumer." *Visual Anthropology Review* 14 (2): 14–31.

Ramos, Jorge, and Jordan Fabian. 2014. "Crist: Race Motivates GOP Opposition to Obama." *Fusion*, May 6. http://fusion.net/story/5527/crist-race-motivates-gop-opposition-to-obama/.

Ranachan, Kate, and Helen Morgan Parmett. 2016. "Fortune Favors the Braves? Race and the Suburban Rebranding of Baseball in Atlanta." Paper presented at the Annual Conference Society for Cinema and Media Studies, Atlanta, GA, March 30–April 3.

Rashed, F. 2005. "Frieha Altaf–Unveiled!" *Influence Lifestyles, Spring/Summer 2005*. Accessed July 27, 2005. http://fariharashed.blogspot.com/2005/07/frieha-altaf-unvelied.html.

Reardon, Sean F., Elena Grewal, Demetra Kalogrides, and Erica Greenberg. 2012. "Brown Fades: The End of Court-Ordered School Desegregation and the Resegregation of American Public Schools." *Journal of Policy Analysis and Management* 31 (4): 876–904.

Reed, Adolph, Jr., and Merlin Chowkwanyun. 2012. "Race, Class, Crisis: The Discourse of Racial Disparity and Its Analytical Discontents." *Socialist Register* 48:149–75.

Reed, T. V. 2005. *Art of Protest: Culture and Activism from the Civil Rights Movement to the Streets of Seattle*. Minneapolis: University of Minnesota Press.

Rehman, Maliha. 2015. "The Moral Fabric of Pakistan's Fashion Week." *Business of Fashion*, April 29. www.businessoffashion.com/articles/global-currents/the-moral-fabric-of-pakistans-fashion-week.

Republican National Committee's Growth and Opportunity Project. 2013. Accessed July 23, 2017. http://s3.documentcloud.org/documents/623664/republican-national-committees-growth-and.pdf.

Rhoden, William C. 2010. "It Was Only Business, but Then It Got Personal." *New York Times*, July 10.

Rich, Motoko. 2014. "School Data Finds Pattern of Inequality along Racial Lines." *New York Times*, March 21. www.nytimes.com/2014/03/21/us/school-data-finds-pattern-of-inequality-along-racial-lines.html?_r=0.

Roberts, Dorothy. 2011. *Fatal Invention: How Science, Politics, and Big Business Re-create Race in the Twenty-First Century*. New York: New Press.

Roberts, Sarah T. 2016a. "Commercial Content Moderation: Digital Laborers' Dirty Work." In *The Intersectional Internet: Race, Sex, Class and Culture Online*, edited by Safiya Umoja Noble and Brendesha Tynes. New York: Peter Lang.

Roberts, Sarah T. 2016b. "Digital Refuse: Canadian Garbage, Commercial Content Moderation and the Global Circulation of Social Media's Waste." *Wi: Journal of Mobile Media* 10 (1): 1–18.

Robinson, Cedric J. 2000. *Black Marxism: The Making of the Black Radical Tradition*. Chapel Hill: University of North Carolina Press.

Robinson, Cedric J. 2007. *Forgeries of Memory and Meaning: Blacks and the Regimes of Race in American Theater and Film before World War II*. Chapel Hill: University of North Carolina Press.

Roediger, David R. 2006. "The Retreat from Race and Class." *Monthly Review* 58 (3). monthlyreview.org/author/davidroediger.

Roediger, David R. 2008. "Race Will Survive the Obama Phenomenon." *Chronicle of Higher Education* 55 (7): B6. chronicle.com/article/Race-Will-Survive-the-Obama/21983.

Rondilla, Joanne L. 2009. "Filipinos and the Color Complex: Ideal Asian Beauty." In *Shades of Difference: Why Skin Color Matters*, edited by Evelyn Nakano Glenn, 63–80. Stanford, CA: Stanford University Press.

Rose, Nikolas. 1996. "Governing Advanced Liberal Democracies." In *Foucault and Political Reason: Liberalism, Neo-liberalism, and Rationalities of Government*, edited by Andrew Barry, Thomas Osborne, and Nikolas Rose, 37–64. Chicago: University of Chicago Press.

Rose, Tricia. 1994. *Black Noise: Rap Music and Black Culture in Contemporary America*. Middletown, CT: Wesleyan University Press.

Rosen, Ellen Israel. 2002. *Making Sweatshops: The Globalization of the US Apparel Industry*. Berkeley: University of California Press.

Rosensweig, Daniel. 2005. *Retro Ball Parks: Instant History, Baseball, and the New American City*. Knoxville: University of Tennessee Press.

Rossing, Jonathan P. 2012. "Deconstructing Postracialism: Humor as a Critical, Cultural Project." *Journal of Communication Inquiry* 36 (1): 44–61.

Rousseau, Jean-Jacques. 2009. "Essay on the Origin of Languages." In *Essay on the Origin of Languages and Writings Related to Music*, edited and translated by John T. Scott, 289–332. Hanover, NH: University Press of New England.

Rubin, Donald L. 1992. "Nonlanguage Factors Affecting Undergraduates' Judgments of Nonnative English-Speaking Teaching Assistants." *Research in Higher Education* 33 (3): 511–31.

Russell, John G. 1998. "Consuming Passions: Spectacle, Self-Transformation, and the Commodification of Blackness in Japan." *Positions* 6 (1): 113–77.

Ruttenberg, Nancy. 1998. *Democratic Personality: Popular Voice and the Trial of American Authorship*. Princeton, NJ: Princeton University Press.

Ryzik, Melena. 2013. "Round-the-Clock Giddiness in a 24-Hour Music Video." *New York Times*, December 25.

Sakala, Leah. 2014. "Breaking Down Mass Incarceration in the 2010 Census: State-by-State Incarceration Rates by Race/Ethnicity." *Prison Policy.org*, May. www .prisonpolicy.org/reports/rates.html.

Sanders, Bernie. 2016. "Where the Democrats Go from Here." *New York Times*, November 11. www.nytimes.com/2016/11/12/opinion/bernie-sanders-where-the-democrats -go-from-here.html.

Sandlin, Jennifer A. 2007. "Popular Culture, Cultural Resistance, and Anti-consumption Activism: An Exploration of Culture Jamming as Critical Adult Education." *New Directions for Adult and Continuing Education* 115:73–82.

Sandoval, Greg. 2003. "James Makes All the Right Moves." *Washington Post*, October 31.

Sanneh, Kalefa. 2010. "Beyond the Pale: Is White the New Black?" *New Yorker*, April 12, 2.

Saraswati, L. Ayu. 2010. "*Cosmopolitan* Whiteness: The Effects and Affects of Skin-Whitening Advertisements in a Transnational Women's Magazine in Indonesia." *Meridians: Feminism, Race, Transnationalism* 10 (2): 15–41.

Sauer, Abe. 2011. "Primate in Chief: A Guide to Racist Obama Monkey Photoshops." *The Awl*, April 19. www.theawl.com/2011/04/primate-in-chief-a-guide-to-racist-obama -monkey-photoshops.

Sauers, Jenna. 2011. "Crystal Renn Wasn't Trying to 'Look Asian' in That Eye Tape Shoot." *Jezebel*, September 7. http://jezebel.com/5838088/crystal-renn-wasnt-trying -to-look-asian-in-that-eye-tape-shoot.

Schmidle, Nicolas. 2016. "Glenn Beck Tries Out Decency." *New Yorker*, November 14. www.newyorker.com/magazine/2016/11/14/glenn-beck-tries-out-decency.

Schwen, Christine. n.d. "One Year after Calling Obama a Racist, Glenn Beck Is Still Busy Race-Baiting." *Media Matters for America*. Last modified July 28, 2010. http:// mediamatters.org/research/2010/07/28/one-year-after-calling-obama-a-racist-beck -is-s/168358.

Scott, James C. 1990. *Domination and the Arts of Resistance: Hidden Transcripts.* New Haven, CT: Yale University Press.

Semati, Mehdi. 2012. "The Geopolitics of Parazit, the Iranian Television Sphere, and the Global Infrastructure of Political Humor." *Popular Communication* 10 (1–2): 119–30.

Shedd, Carla. 2011. "Countering the Carceral Continuum: The Legacy of Mass Incarceration." *Criminology and Public Policy* 10 (3): 865–71.

Shohat, Ella, and Robert Stam. 1994. *Unthinking Eurocentrism: Multiculturalism and the Media.* New York: Routledge.

Shome, Raka. 2010. "Internationalizing Critical Race Communication Studies." In *The Handbook of Critical Intercultural Communication*, edited by Thomas K. Nakayama and Rona Tamiko Halualani, 149–70. Malden, MA: Blackwell.

"Showbiz Pakistan—Interview Saim Ali." 2011. *Showbiz Pakistan*. http://showbizpak .com/Saim-Ali.php [no longer available].

Shuker, Roy. (1998) 2005. *Popular Music: The Key Concepts.* New York: Routledge.

Sides, John, Michael Tessler, and Lynn Vavreck. 2018. *Identity Crisis: The 2016 Presidential Campaign and the Battle for the Meaning of America.* Princeton, NJ: Princeton University Press.

Siegmann, Karin Astrid, and Nazima Shaheen. 2008. "Weakest Link in the Textile Chain: Pakistani Cotton Pickers' Bitter Harvest." *Indian Journal of Labour Economics* 51 (4): 619–30.

Simpson, Isaac. 2016. "Vexit: Venice Beach Wants to Leave Los Angeles." *Curbed: Los Angeles*, August 18. https://la.curbed.com/2016/8/18/12528616/venice-secession-los -angeles-vexit.

Singh, Nikhil Pal. 2004. *Black Is a Country: Race and the Unfinished Struggle for Democracy.* Cambridge, MA: Harvard University Press.

Slate, John Dickerson. 2014. "Opposition to Obama Is All Republicans Have." *Salt Lake Tribune*, October 29. www.sltrib.com/opinion/1757287–155/obama-percent -republican-republicans-gop-party.

Small, Christopher. 1998. *Music of the Common Tongue: Survival and Celebration in African American Music.* Middletown, CT: Wesleyan University Press.

Smith, Ben, and Maggie Haberman. 2010. "Pols Turn on Labor Unions." *Politico*, June 6. www.politico.com/story/2010/06/pols-turn-on-labor-unions-038183.

Smith, J. B. 2015. "'Waco Horror' at 100: Why Jesse Washington's Lynching Still Matters." *Waco Tribune-Herald*, May 15. www.wacotrib.com/news/special/waco

-horror-at-why-jesse-washington-s-lynching-still-matters/article_1e2e0e86-dc1f
-5442-bc35-9c2debad14c7.html.

Smith, Neil. 1996. *The New Urban Frontier: Gentrification and the Revanchist City.*
London: Routledge.

Smucker, Tom. 2012. "Boring and Horrifying Whiteness: The Rise and Fall of Reaganism
as Prefigured by the Career Arcs of the Carpenters, Lawrence Welk, and the Beach
Boys in 1973–74." In *Pop When the World Falls Apart: Music in the Shadow of Doubt*,
edited by Eric Weisbard, 47–61. Durham, NC: Duke University Press.

Snorton, C. Riley. 2014. *Nobody Is Supposed to Know: Black Sexuality on the Down Low.*
Minneapolis: University of Minnesota Press.

Somerville, Siobhan B. 2000. *Queering the Color Line: Race and the Invention of Homo-
sexuality in American Culture.* Durham, NC: Duke University Press.

Southern Poverty Law Center. n.d. "Hate Map." Last modified February 17, 2016. www
.splcenter.org/hate-map.

Squires, Catherine T. 2012. "Coloring in the Bubble: Perspectives from Black-Oriented
Media on the (Latest) Economic Disaster." *American Quarterly* 64 (3): 543–70.

Squires, Catherine T. 2014. *The Post-racial Mystique: Media and Race in the Twenty-First
Century.* New York: NYU Press.

Stein, Louisa Ellen. 2015. *Millennial Fandom: Television Audiences in the Transmedia Age.*
Iowa City: University of Iowa Press.

Steinberg, Leigh. 2014. "LeBron Transcends Superstar Athletic Profile." *Daily Pilot*
(Orange County, CA), July 12.

Steinberg, Stephen. 1995. *Turning Back: The Retreat from Racial Justice in American
Thought and Policy.* Boston: Beacon.

Stinson, Scott. 2010. "Sultry Miami Gets Final Rose in LeBachelor." *National Post*, July 9.

Stoever, Jennifer Lynn. 2016. *The Sonic Color-Line.* New York: NYU Press.

Stoever-Ackerman, Jennifer. 2010. "Splicing the Sonic Color Line: Tony Schwartz Re-
mixes Postwar *Nueva York*." *Social Text* 28 (1): 59–85.

Sullivan, Denise. 2011. *Keep On Pushing: Black Power Music from Blues to Hip-Hop.*
Chicago: Chicago Review Press.

"Survey Finds Support for Veil Ban." 2006. *BBC News*, November 29. http://news.bbc.co
.uk/2/hi/uk_news/6194032.stm.

Syed, M. 2009. "Infashion: Young at Milan." *Dawn News*, October 11. http://archives
.dawn.com/archives/45361.

Taibbi, Matt. 2015. "The Republicans Are Officially the Party of White Paranoia." *Rolling
Stone*, September 4. www.rollingstone.com/politics/news/the-gop-is-now-officially
-the-party-of-dumb-white-people-20150904.

"Taliban Defied by Pakistani Models." 2009. *Telegraph*, November 7. www.telegraph.co
.uk/news/worldnews/asia/pakistan/6520470/Taliban-defied-by-Pakistani-models
.html.

Tallbear, Kim. 2013. *Native American DNA: Tribal Belonging and the False Promise of Genetic Science.* Minneapolis: University of Minnesota Press.

Tannenbaum, Rob, and Craig Marks. 2011. *I Want My MTV: The Uncensored Story of the
Music Video Revolution.* New York: Penguin.

Taussig, Michael. 2010. *What Color Is the Sacred?* Chicago: University of Chicago Press.

Taylor, Jessica. 2011. "The Meteoric Rise of Allen West." *National Journal*, February 12. www.nationaljournal.com/s/172764/meteoric-rise-allen-west.

Taylor, Kirstine. 2015. "Untimely Subjects: White Trash and the Making of Racial Innocence in the Postwar South." *American Quarterly* 67 (1): 55–79.

Taylor, Paul C. 1997. "Funky White Boys and Honorary Soul Sisters." *Michigan Quarterly Review* 36 (2): 320–36.

Taylor, Paul C. 2007. "Post-black, Old Black." *African American Review* 41 (4): 625–40.

Taylor, Paul C. 2014. "Taking Postracialism Seriously: From Movement Mythology to Racial Formation." *Du Bois Review* 11 (1): 9–25.

Thomas, Deborah A., and Kamari Maxine Clarke. 2006. "Introduction: Globalization and the Transformation of Race." In *Globalization and Race: Transformations in the Cultural Production of Blackness*, edited by Kamari Maxine Clarke and Deborah A. Thomas, 1–36. Durham, NC: Duke University Press.

Thompson, M. S., and V. M. Keith. 2001. "The Blacker the Berry: Gender, Skin Tone, Self-Esteem and Self-Efficacy." *Gender and Society* 15 (3): 336–57.

Thornberg, Christopher, Robert Kleinhenz, and Rafael De Anda. 2016. "USC Lusk Center for Real Estate Casden Real Estate Economics Forecast 2016 Multifamily Report." Accessed November 2, 2017. https://lusk.usc.edu/sites/default/files/attachments/2016-Multifamily-Forecast-Report.pdf.

Tompkins, Kyla Wazana. 2012. *Racial Indigestion: Eating Bodies in the 19th Century*. New York: NYU Press.

Tongson, Karen. 2011. *Relocations: Queer Suburban Imaginaries*. New York: NYU Press.

Tongson, Karen. 2015. "Empty Orchestra: The Karaoke Standard and Pop Celebrity." *Public Culture* 27 (1): 85–108.

Tu, Thuy Linh Nguyen. 2010. *The Beautiful Generation: Asian Americans and the Cultural Economy of Fashion*. Durham, NC: Duke University Press.

Tuvel, Rebecca. 2017. "In Defense of Transracialism." *Hypatia* 32 (2): 263–78.

US Census Bureau. n.d. *Census of Population and Housing*. Accessed October 5, 2016. www.census.gov/prod/www/decennial.html.

US Department of Health and Human Services. 2011. *Disparities in Healthcare Quality among Racial and Ethnic Minority Groups: Selected Findings from the AHRQ 2010 NHQR and NHDR*. Agency for Healthcare Research and Quality: Rockville, MD. www.ahrq.gov/qual/nhqrdr10/nhqrdrminority10.htm.

US General Accounting Office. 2016. *K–12 Education: Better Use of Information Could Help Agencies Identify Disparities and Address Racial Discrimination*. GAO-16-345, April. Washington, DC: Government Accountability Office.

Vats, Anjali. 2014. "Racechange Is the New Black: Racial Accessorizing and Racial Tourism in High Fashion as Constraints on Rhetorical Agency." *Communication, Culture and Critique* 7:112–35.

Villarejo, Amy. 2003. *Lesbian Rule: Cultural Criticism and the Value of Desire*. Durham, NC: Duke University Press.

Virani, F. 2015. "Business of Fashion: Baby Steps from Ramp to Retail." *Dawn News*, April 8. www.dawn.com/news/1174493.

Wagner, Kurt. n.d. "Marc Andreessen Offends India Defending Facebook's Free Basics. (Yes, the Country.)—Recode." Accessed August 19, 2017. www.recode.net/2016/2/9 /11587726/marc-andreessen-offends-india-defending-facebooks-free-basics-yes-the.

Wald, Gayle. 2007. *Shout, Sister, Shout! The Untold Story of Rock-and-Roll Trailblazer Sister Rosetta Tharpe*. New York: Beacon Press.

Walker, Hannah, and Dylan Bennett, 2015. "The Whiteness of Wisconsin's Wages: Racial Geography and the Defeat of Public Sector Labor Unions in Wisconsin." *New Political Science* 37 (2): 181–203.

Walker, R. 2003. "Whassup, Barbie? Marketers Are Embracing the Idea of a 'Post-racial' America." *Boston Globe*, January, 12, D1.

Wallace-Wells, Benjamin. 2006. "Is America Too Racist for Barack? Too Sexist for Hillary?" *Washington Post*, November 12, B1.

Walters, Suzanna Danuta. 2001. *All the Rage: The Story of Gay Visibility in America*. Chicago: University of Chicago Press.

Ward, Brian. 1998. *Just My Soul Responding: Rhythm and Blues, Black Consciousness, and Race Relations*. Berkeley: University of California Press.

Ward, Jason Morgan. 2016. *Hanging Bridge: Racial Violence and America's Civil Rights Century*. New York: Oxford University Press.

Warner, Kristen J. 2015. *The Cultural Politics of Colorblind TV Casting*. New York: Routledge.

"Washington: Glenn Beck Wants Ted Cruz's 'Velvet Hand' in Control When America Descends into Martial Law." 2015. *US Official News*, May 6. www.lexisnexis.com /hottopics/lnacademic.

"Washington: Ted Cruz Tries to Justify Trump Endorsement to a Furious Glenn Beck." 2016. *US Official News*, September 26. www.lexisnexis.com/hottopics /lnacademic.

Webster, J. G., 2014. *The Marketplace of Attention: How Audiences Take Shape in a Digital Age*. Cambridge, MA: MIT Press.

Weems, Robert. 1998. *Desegregating the Dollar: African American Consumerism in the Twentieth Century*. New York: NYU Press.

West, Allen. 2011. Remarks to the Conservative Political Action Conference. February 12. www.c-span.org/video/?298003-8/representative-allen-west-remarks&start =800.

White House, Office of the First Lady. 2015. "Remarks by the First Lady at Martin Luther King Jr. Preparatory High School Commencement Address." June 9. www .whitehouse.gov/the-press-office/2015/06/09/remarks-first-lady-martin-luther-king -jr-preparatory-high-school-commenc.

Wilbon, Michael. 2010. "Exit Strategy Leaves Much to Ponder." *Washington Post*, July 10.

Williams, Alec. 2017. "Prozac Nation Is Now the United States of Xanax." *New York Times*, June 10.

Williams, Linda. 2004. "Melancholy Melodrama: Almadóvarian Grief and Lost Homosexual Attachments." *Journal of Spanish Cultural Studies* 5 (3): 273–86.

Williams, Patricia. 1989. "The Obliging Shell: An Informal Essay on Formal Equal Opportunity." *Michigan Law Review* 87 (8): 2128–51.

Williams, Pharrell. 2012. *Pharrell: Places and Spaces I've Been*. New York: Rizzoli.

Williams, Raymond. 1977. *Marxism and Literature*. New York: Oxford University Press.

Williamson, Kevin D. 2014. "The White Ghetto." *National Review*, January 9. www
.nationalreview.com/article/367903/white-ghetto-kevin-d-williamso.

Williamson, Kevin D. 2016. "The Father-Fuhrer: Chaos in the Family, Chaos in the
State." *National Review*, March 28. www.nationalreview.com/nrd/articles/432569
/father-f-hrer.

Wilson, Bobby. 2000. *Race and Place in Birmingham: The Civil Rights and Neighborhood
Movements*. Lanham, MD: Rowman and Littlefield.

Wilson, Carl. 2007. *Let's Talk about Love: A Journey to the End of Taste*. New York:
Continuum.

Wilson, Eric. 2013. "Fashion's Blind Spot." *New York Times*, August 8, E1. www.nytimes
.com/2013/08/08/fashion/fashions-blind-spot.html.

Wilson Gilmore, Ruth. 2007. *Golden Gulag: Prisons, Surplus, Crisis, and Opposition in
Globalizing California*. Berkeley: University of California Press.

Winant, Howard. 2002. *The World Is a Ghetto: Race and Democracy since World War II*.
New York: Basic Books.

Wise, Mike. 2010. "Having His Fun but Losing His Legacy." *Washington Post*, July 9.

Wise, Mike. 2011. "Race Could Hijack NBA Talks." *Washington Post*, October 22.

Wise, Mike. 2012. "Manchild Approaches the Promised Land." *New York Times*,
December 5.

Wissinger, Elizabeth. 2011. "Managing the Semiotics of Skin Tone: Race and Aesthetic
Labor in the Fashion Modeling Industry." *Economic and Industrial Democracy* 33 (1):
125–43.

"With President Obama's Birth Certificate, Klansman Trump Reminds Blacks They Will
Never Be American." 2011. YouTube, posted by Baratunde Thurston, April 27. www
.youtube.com/watch?v=vX5ueEKsSWc.

Wolfers, Justin. 2015. "Why the New Research on Mobility Matters: An Economist's
View." *New York Times*, May 4. www.nytimes.com/2015/05/05/upshot/why-the
-new-research-on-mobility-matters-an-economists-view.html?rref=upshot&abt
=0002&abg=1.

Wolfers, Justin, David Leonhardt, and Kevin Quealy. 2015. "1.5 Million Missing Black
Men." *New York Times*, April 20. www.nytimes.com/interactive/2015/04/20/upshot
/missing-black-men.html?emc=edit_au_20150420&nl=afternoonupdate&nlid
=1420294&abt=0002&abg=1.

Wong, Julia Carrie. 2016. "How the Tech Industry Is Exploiting Black Lives Matter."
Guardian, July 12. www.theguardian.com/us-news/2016/jul/12/black-lives-matter
-marc-benioff-facebook-twitter-uber.

Wood, Robert W. 2015. "Pharrell Williams, Robin Thicke Lose $7.4M Verdict for
Marvin Gaye Song Theft—Before Taxes." *Forbes*, March 11. www.forbes.com/sites
/robertwood/2015/03/11/pharrell-williams-robin-thicke-lose-7-4m-verdict-for
-marvin-gaye-song-theft-before-taxes/.

Woods, Clyde. 2009. "Les Miserables of New Orleans: Trap Economics and the Asset
Stripping Blues, Part 1." *American Quarterly* 61 (3): 769–96.

Wright, Michelle. 2015. *The Physics of Blackness*. Minneapolis: University of Minnesota Press.

Yin, Alice. 2017. "Education by the Numbers." *New York Times Magazine*, September 8. www.nytimes.com/2017/09/08/magazine/education-by-the-numbers.html?em_pos=medium&emc=edit_ma_20170908&nl=magazine&nl_art=4&nlid=52544459&ref=headline&te=1&_r=0.

Young, Cynthia A., and Min Hyoung Song. 2014. "Forum Introduction: Whiteness Redux or Redefined?" *American Quarterly* 66 (4): 1071–76.

Young, Robb. 2015. "Fashion Weeks Wage Global Talent Wars." *Business of Fashion*, March 8. www.businessoffashion.com/articles/intelligence/fashion-weeks-wage-global-talent-wars.

Yúdice, George. 2003. *The Expediency of Culture: Uses of Culture in the Global Era*. Durham, NC: Duke University Press.

Zaitchik, Alexander. 2010. *Common Nonsense: Glenn Beck and the Triumph of Ignorance*. Hoboken, NJ: Wiley.

Zirin, Dave. 2015. "Apartheid Games: Baltimore, Urban America, and Camden Yards." *The Nation*, April 28. www.thenation.com/article/apartheid-games-baltimore-urban-america-and-camden-yards/.

Zirin, Dave. 2016. "Kevin Durant and the Discomfort with Player Power." *The Nation*, July 5. www.thenation.com/article/kevin-durant-and-the-discomfort-with-player-power/.

Zook, Krystal B. 1999. *Color by Fox: The Fox Network and the Revolution in Black Television*. New York: Oxford University Press.

Contributors

INNA ARZUMANOVA is Assistant Professor of Media Studies at the University of San Francisco. Her research examines racial and gender performativity and aesthetics within popular culture, global media, and cultural industries.

SARAH BANET-WEISER is Professor in the Department of Media and Communications at the London School of Economics and Political Science. She is the author of several books, including *Authentic™: The Politics of Ambivalence in a Brand Culture* (2012) and *Empowered: Popular Feminism and Popular Misogyny* (Duke University Press, 2018).

AYMAR JEAN CHRISTIAN is Assistant Professor at Northwestern University and a Fellow at the Peabody Media Center. His first book, *Open TV: Innovation beyond Hollywood and the Rise of Web Television* (2018), charts the rise of indie production online. His work on television has been published in numerous journals, including the *International Journal of Communication, Cinema Journal,* and *Continuum.*

KEVIN FELLEZS holds a joint appointment in the Department of Music and the Institute for Research in African American Studies at Columbia University.

RODERICK A. FERGUSON is Professor in the Department of African American Studies and the Gender and Women's Studies Program at the University of Illinois, Chicago. He is the author of *The Reorder of Things: The University and Its Pedagogies of Minority Difference* (2012).

HERMAN GRAY is a former radio producer and jazz announcer whose interest in media, culture, and politics is wide-ranging. Gray is Professor of Sociology at the University of California, Santa Cruz, where he teaches courses in media and television studies, cultural theory and politics, and Black cultural studies. Gray's research is on the role of television, media, and culture in organizing, sustaining, and challenging racial projects.

EVA C. HAGEMAN is a University of Maryland President's Postdoctoral Fellow in Women's Studies. Upon completion of the fellowship she will become an Assistant Professor of American Studies and Women's Studies at the University of Maryland, College Park. She received her PhD from New York University in American Studies with a joint Certificate in Culture and Media through Anthropology and Cinema Studies. Her manuscript "'Relatable Meets Remarkable': Crafting Race in the Reality Television Industry" examines reality television and the central role it plays in shaping articulations of race in the twenty-first century. She has directed two documentaries, *Legendary* (2010) and *You, as Seen on TV* (2011).

DANIEL MARTINEZ HOSANG is Associate Professor of American Studies and Ethnicity, Race and Migration at Yale University and the author of *Racial Propositions: Ballot Initiatives and the Making of Postwar California* (2010).

VICTORIA E. JOHNSON is Associate Professor of Film and Media Studies and African American Studies at the University of California, Irvine. She is the author of *Heartland TV: Prime Time Television and the Struggle for U.S. Identity* (2008), which was awarded the Society for Cinema and Media Studies Katherine Singer Kovacs Book Award in 2009, and *Sports Television* (2018). She is coeditor (with Travis Vogan) of the Studies in Sports Media series at the University of Illinois Press.

JOSEPH LOWNDES is Associate Professor of Political Science at the University of Oregon. He researches and writes on right-wing politics, race, populism, and US political development.

ROOPALI MUKHERJEE is Associate Professor of Media Studies at the City University of New York/Queens College. She is the author of *The Racial Order of Things: Cultural Imaginaries of the Post-soul Era* (2006) and coeditor of *Commodity Activism: Cultural Resistance in Neoliberal Times* (2012).

SAFIYA UMOJA NOBLE is Assistant Professor in the Departments of Information and African American Studies at the University of California, Los Angeles. Her monograph, *Algorithms of Oppression: How Search Engines Reinforce Racism*, examines racist and sexist bias in digital platforms. She is coeditor of two additional books: *The Intersectional Internet: Race, Sex, Culture and Class Online* (2016) and *Emotions, Technology and Design* (2016).

RADHIKA PARAMESWARAN is Herman B. Wells Endowed Professor in the Media School at Indiana University, Bloomington. Her research interests are feminist cultural studies, globalization and media, India, and postcolonial studies.

SARAH T. ROBERTS is Assistant Professor in the Department of Information Studies, University of California, Los Angeles. She is an expert on content moderation, digital labor, and internet culture and its impacts on society.

CATHERINE R. SQUIRES is Professor and Director of Graduate Studies in the Department of Communication Studies at the University of Minnesota, Twin Cities. She is the author of *Dispatches from the Color Line* (2007), *African Americans and the Media* (2009), and *The Post-racial Mystique* (2014).

BRANDI THOMPSON SUMMERS is Assistant Professor of African American Studies at Virginia Commonwealth University. Her forthcoming book, *Black in Place: The Spatial Aesthetics of Race in a Post-chocolate City*, explores the ways that blackness structures efforts to raise capital and develop land in Washington, DC.

KAREN TONGSON is Associate Professor of English, Gender Studies, and American Studies and Ethnicity at the University of Southern California, and the author of *Relocations: Queer Suburban Imaginaries* (2011). She has a forthcoming book titled *Why*

Karen Carpenter Matters, and has two books in progress: *Empty Orchestra: Karaoke in Our Time* and *Normal Television: Critical Essays on Queer Spectatorship after the "New Normalcy."* Tongson discusses pop culture, the arts, and entertainment on the weekly Pop Rocket Podcast, hosted by Guy Branum.

CYNTHIA A. YOUNG is Department Head of African American Studies and Associate Professor of African American Studies and English at the Pennsylvania State University. She is the author of *Soul Power: Culture, Radicalism and the Making of a U.S. Third World Left* (2006) and is working on a manuscript tentatively titled "Culture Wars–Terror Wars: Race, Popular Culture and the Civil Rights Legacy after 9/11."

Index

arranged marriage, 64

art, 181, 184, 201–2, 211–12, 215–16, 218–19, 223, 254, 278; British, 248–49; Islamic, 277–78

Artforum (magazine), 218

Associated Press, 58

Atlantic, The (magazine), 109

Au, W. James, 125

audition, 137

Austen, Jane, 214

authenticity, 181, 200, 203, 213, 219, 223–25, 234–35, 253

autonomy, 40

Avedon, Richard, 254

Azwer, Nida, 276

Baartman, Saartjie, 247

Bad Girls Club (TV series), 223

Baker, Dean, 226

Bakhtin, Mikhail, 71

Bakke, Allan, 41

Baldwin, James, 42

Baldwin Hills, 125

Bale, Tim, 271

Banet-Weiser, Sarah, 159, 174, 180, 188, 203, 223

Bannon, Steve, 111

Barreto, Matt, 90–92

Battla, Sonya, 272

Battle of Algiers, The (film), 282n10

Beck, Glenn, 53, 86–87, 96–112

Beinart, Peter, 109

Bell Curve, The (Herrnstein and Murray), 46

Berlant, Lauren, 161

Berlet, Chip, 43

Beyg, Rizwan, 276

Beyoncé, 255

Bhabha, Homi K., 262

Bhutto, Benazir, 269

Billionaire Boys Club (clothing line), 187

birther movement, 104

Birth of a Nation (film), 219

black achievement, 188

black criminality, 31

black excellence, 220

blackface, 252–56, 259, 261

black femininity, 247

Black History Month, 53

"Black Issue, A" (*Vogue Italia*), 246

Black Lives Matter, 50, 103, 105, 109, 126, 195

blackness, 11–12, 41, 49, 52–53, 67, 101, 163, 202, 205–6, 219, 230–31, 245–63; as aesthetic, 230–31, 245, 248, 256; performance of, 262

Black Panther (film), 285–86

Black Panther Party, 30, 76

Black Power, 79, 81–82

black presidency, 2, 30, 32, 52, 67–68, 88–91, 94, 101, 186, 190, 195

Black Robe Regiment (BRR), 104

black sexuality, 205, 216–17, 230

black Twitter, 207

Blaze (radio program), 111

blindness, 138–51. *See also* color blindness

Blow, Charles, 104

blues, 138, 141–42, 147–48

Boina, Maida Gregori, 250

Bond, Justin Vivian, 212

Bonilla-Silva, Eduardo, 7, 25, 92, 261

Booker, Cory, 53

Border Security, Economic Opportunity, and Immigration Modernization Act of 2013, 93

border wall, 54, 106

Bourdieu, Pierre, 62, 70, 165, 190

bourgeois revolution, 79

Boyd, Todd, 154–55

Boys and Girls Clubs, 170

Brady, Tom, 154

branding, 10, 17, 132, 162–63, 169, 203, 205, 207, 223–25, 261

Breaking Bad (TV series), 207, 215

Brexit, 54

British Fashion Council, 266

Bronner Brothers, 257

Brooks, Daphne, 141

Brown, Jerry, 43

Brown, Michael, 186–87
Brown, Sherrod, 167
Bundy, Ammon, 105
Bundy, Cliven, 105
Bureau of Land Management, 105
Burger King, 73, 259
burqa, 280
Bush, George W., 50, 88, 97, 106
Business of Fashion (magazine), 271
Buy and Sell, 228
Buy Me (TV series), 228
Byrd, James, 96

Calvin Klein, 249
Cameron, Jibz, 212
Campbell, Naomi, 254
capital, 39, 41, 44, 72–85, 159, 201, 203, 217–18, 223–25, 230, 234, 266, 268; creative, 237–38; cultural, 62; finance, 155, 164; gendered, 169, 175; global, 228, 282; limits of, 200; venture, 117–19
capitalism, 27, 40, 55, 76, 123, 161, 201, 218, 230; black, 78–82; late, 159, 166, 257; liberal, 73–75, 84–85; racial, 9, 11–15, 20, 26, 77–78
Carson, Ben, 51, 105
caste, 59, 62, 69–71
Castile, Philando, 126, 127
Chamuel, Michelle, 150
Chao, Maureen, 57
character development, 213–14
Chicago Tribune, 83
Chicanx, 106
Cho, Sumi, 74, 114
Chowkwanyun, Merlin, 39
Christie, Chris, 43
Christopher Street TV, 213
Chump ChangeS (web series), 209
citizenship, 61, 92–93, 139, 168, 256, 268; creative, 271, 273–74 (*see also* creative citizenship); global, 278–81; normative, 28; silly, 61, 69; symbolic, 268
civilization, 73, 81–82; clashes of, 279; European, 77; Western, 51

civil rights, 28–32, 41, 45, 49, 50, 52–53, 73, 82, 85–87, 94–96, 99–105, 111–14, 117; activism, 194; movement, 8, 50, 82, 114, 194
Clarke, Kamari Maxine, 70
class: conflict, 39; dominant relations, 39; warfare, 50
Clear Channel, 96, 97
Cleveland, 156–77
Cleveland: Gateway District, 163
Cleveland Cavaliers, 157, 163–74
Cleveland Clothing Company, 162
Cleveland Hustles (TV series), 174
climate change, 20, 179, 195
Clinton, Bill, 52
Clinton, Hillary, 108, 110
Cloud, Dana, 279
CMEA Capital, 117
CNBC, 174
Coates, Norma, 181
Coca-Cola, 73, 82–85
Cochran, Johnnie, 96
codes, 24, 26
cognitive elite, 46
collective bargaining, 43
collective struggle, 128
colonialism, 62, 122–23, 128, 189, 277, 285–86
colonialist logic, 230
color blindness, 6–10, 24, 114–15, 118–19, 122, 194; discourses of, 6–9, 31, 78, 186, 188. *See also* diversity; multiculturalism
colorism, 57–71; commodity, 60, 66, 71
comedy, 57–68, 121–22, 187. *See also* parody; satire
Coming Apart: The State of White America 1960–2010 (Murray), 46
Comme des Garçons (fashion company), 187
Communist Manifesto, The (Marx and Engels), 79, 85
community, 124–25, 148, 156–58, 160–68, 170–71, 173, 175–76, 196n11, 214–15; of artists, 213, 218–19; black, 48, 202, 210; imagined, 98–99; national, 91; political, 86; virtual, 59

Harlow, Barbara, 273

Harper's Bazaar (magazine), 254

Hartley, John, 61, 210

Hartman, Saidiya, 25, 27

Harvey, David, 224

"Haute Mess" (magazine spread), 245–63

Haves and the Have-Nots, The (TV series), 199

Hay, James, 169

headscarves, 264

hegemony, 70, 278, 281; of whiteness, 58

Herrnstein, Richard, 46

heterogeneity, 266; aesthetic, 274–76

heteronormativity, 120, 199–200, 231

Hicks, Marie, 116

Hidden Potential (TV series), 227

hijab, 264, 275, 279, 281–82

Hiles, Heather, 119

Hindustan Lever, 61

hip-hop, 180; culture, 256

hiring: bias, 115; equal opportunity mandates, 114

Hirschfeld Davis, Julie, 198n18

Hitler, Adolf, 104, 110

Holder, Eric, 197n16

Hollinger, David, 186

Hollywood Diversity Report, 120

Holman Jones, Stacy, 152

Holy Family, The (Marx and Engels), 85

home, 225, 242; valorization, 232–33, 237–38, 242

Home and Garden Television (HGTV), 221–43

homeownership, 227, 238, 243

Homer, 141

Home Town (TV series), 229, 239–40, 243

homogeneity, 224, 234–35, 239–41

Hong, Grace Kyungwon, 270, 282

hooks, bell, 258

hope, 283–86

hot comb, 232

hotghettomess.com, 256

Hottentot Venus (Saartjie Baartman), 247

House Hunters (TV series), 227, 229

House of Cards (TV series), 206

housing market: bubble, 226–27; racialization of, 243

housing speculation, 228–31, 234, 238, 244

How to Get Away With Murder, 199, 207, 208

Hugo, Chad, 181

Humara TV, 64

Hunt, Darnell, 120, 209

Hunter, Alberta, 143

Hussayn, Fahad, 272, 287, 281

hybridity, 258

hyperblackness, 245

hyperbole, 110

hypervisibility, 205–6, 216, 248

i am OTHER (brand), 183

Ibrar, Madiha, 275

iD (magazine), 253

identification, 148–50

identity, 137, 139, 141, 143, 147, 150, 152, 183, 218; categories, 10–11; collective, 80; national, 139; politics, 13; racial 13, 16; social, 161; white, 87–88, 92–94, 100

ideology, 161, 194; capitalist, 84; colorblind, 119, 223; consumer, 227, 237; folk, 39; libertarian, 92, 113; postracial, 74, 114, 223; white supremacist, 197n16 (*see also* white: supremacy)

If I Was Your Girl (web series), 208

"I Have a Dream Day," 52

Ikea, 234

Iman, Chanel, 252

immigration, 28, 93, 102, 106

imperialism, 122, 286

Inaaya (fashion brand), 271

Income Property (TV series), 228

Independent, The (newspaper), 253

India, 57–59

indie dramas, 209–13. *See also* serial dramas; web TV

indigenous genocide, 286

Indigo Girls, 148

individualism, 80, 155, 170, 185, 196n11

individuality, 85, 180, 183–84

industry, 164, 171, 207; beauty, 58; fashion, 16, 132, 245–56, 265–81; knowledge, 20; music, 182, 201, 213; skin-lightening, 70; technology, 114–15, 119–20; television, 205, 210, 215, 222; textile, 268–71

information and technology workers, 113

information flow, 128

Instagram, 214

Institute for Research and Education on Human Rights, 93

International Day of Happiness, 194

International Fashion Showcase, 266

intersectional: identities, 183, 204–5; logics, 137; specificity, 17, 133, 200

Interview (magazine), 255

intimate public, 161

invisibility, 205–6, 245

irony, 191–92

Islam, 107, 279

Islamic: extremism, 51, 111; fashion, 264–65, 274–75, 277–82

Islamophobia, 87–88, 90, 96, 105–8

Ivy League, 119

Jablonski, Constance, 255

Jackson, Jesse, 52, 96, 99, 100, 103

Jackson, John, 70

Jackson, Michael, 220

James, LeBron, 154–77

Jefferson, Thomas, 139

Jeffries, Hasan Kwame, 285

Jenkins, Lee, 173

Jezebel (website), 263

Jhally, Sut, 161

Jim Crow, 55, 80, 101, 105

Jindal, Bobby, 51

Johnson, E. P., 206

Johnson, Lyndon, 47

Jones, Jacqueline, 39

Jones, Van, 100, 103

Joplin, Janis, 148–49

Jordan, Michael, 158, 176

Jordan, Vernon, 52

Julia (TV series), 208

Kapor, Mitch, 120

Kapor Center for Social Impact, 120

Kapor Klein, Freada, 120

Karachi, Pakistan, 264–65

Kasich, John, 43

Keeling, Kara, 25, 27, 200, 207, 220

Keene, David, 51

Keith, V. M., 62

Kelley, Robin D. G., 77

Kentucky, 47

Kessler, Sarah, 151n2

Khan, Khizr and Ghazala, 106

Khan, Shahrukh, 69

Khan, Zarmina, 275

Kharkongor, Nick, 65

King, Alveda, 103

King, Martin Luther, Jr., 30, 86–88, 95–99, 109, 111, 285

Klein, Steven, 253–54

knowledge, 24

Knowles, Beyoncé. *See* Beyoncé

Knowles, Tina, 255

Koestenbaum, Wayne, 137, 147, 152n10

Kohan, Jenji, 208

Kuku, Diepiriye, 68

Kuti, Fela, 255

labor, 9, 20, 27, 43–45, 77, 87, 116, 118–19, 121–22, 164–65, 218; aesthetic, 282; discursive, 15, 19; gendered, 270–74; ideological, 40, 53; of race, 37–40; political, 42, 45; raced 155; slave, 76–77; valued categories of, 41

laborers, 239–41

Lahore, Pakistan, 265, 271, 287

Lakhani, Misha, 274

La Raza Lawyers of San Diego, 106

LaVoy, January, 212

LAWeb Fest, 211

Layard, Richard, 182

Lean In (Sandberg), 117

race: commodification of, 261; neutrality, 248; as a social construction, 40
racecraft, 39
racial: antagonism, 38; boundaries, 225; difference, 74; disavowal, 29, 30, 35; invisibility, 188; justice, 41; markers, 259–60; performances, 260; subjectivity, 270; subordination, 37
Racial Backlash movement, 114
racialization, 55, 70, 141–44, 223, 229, 243, 274
racialized: embodiments, 230–31; narratives, 158; subjects, 41, 44, 55, 272; violence, 186, 240–41 (*see also* violence: police; violence: racialized; violence: state)
racism: antiblack, 2, 12, 45, 91–92, 94, 96–100, 105; color-blind, 6–10, 16, 92, 131; institutionalized, 189; structural, 38, 189
racist police, 55. *See also* violence: police
Rainbow Coalition, 52
"Rallies for America," 97
Rana, Nosheen, 275
R&B, 143, 182
Rankine, Claudia, 285
Ray, Amy, 148
reactionary: politics, 56; white identity, 88, 96, 100 (*see also* identity: white; white: supremacy)
Reagan, Ronald, 111
real estate, 221–34, 238–42
Real Housewives (TV series), 223
reality television, 16, 132–33, 168–69, 172, 221–23, 242–44
Recode (website), 119
recognition, 150
Reconstruction, 50
Rector, Ricky Ray, 52
redistribution, 44–45, 73, 75
redlining, 228
Reed, Adolph, 39
regressive modernization, 258
Rehab Addict (TV series), 232–34, 241–43

Rehman, Maliha, 271, 282
Renn, Crystal, 263
renovation, 238–39
representation, 151; aesthetic, 139–40; gay, 200; queer, 200; tools of, 139
representational strategies, 240
republicanism, 138
Republican National Committee, 112
Republican Party, 49–51
residual ideals, 163–65
resistance, 59, 71, 74, 123, 126–27, 193
resolve, 283–86
respectability politics, 256
Resurrection Boulevard (TV series), 207
revitalization, 229, 232–33, 237, 241
Rice, Condoleezza, 50, 53
Richeson, Jennifer, 89
right-wing: conservatism, 86; fascism, 116; media, 86–112; politics, 17, 33–34, 90, 95–96, 112; populism, 43
Rizwanullah, 275
Roberts, Frank Leon, 213
Robinson, Cedric, 27, 33, 77
Rocha, Coco, 246
rock (music), 181
Rock, Chris, 257
Roediger, David, 78
Rolling Stone (magazine), 185, 194
Rose, Charlie, 107
Rose, Tricia, 141
Rosen, Ellen Israel, 270, 282
Rosensweig, Daniel, 163
Rossing, Jonathan P., 70
Rubin, Donald L., 152
Rubio, Marco, 51, 105
RuPaul's Drag Race (TV series), 212
Rust Belt, 165, 171, 176
Ruttenburg, Nancy, 139
Ryan, Paul, 106

Saai, 278
Samosa TV, 66
Sandberg, Sheryl, 117
Sanders, Bernie, 108, 109

street art, 223
Strickland, Ted, 167
Strong, Danny, 199
Su, Bernie, 214
subjecthood: production of, 272–73
subjectification: capitalist modes of, 66
subjection, 35; of the body, 26
subjectivity: bourgeois, 85; unified, 142
subjects: alienated, 179; dependent, 43; political, 40; racialized, 41, 44, 55, 270, 272; visual, 247
subprime loans, 228
Sun Ra, 195
Super Bowl, 167
surplus, 41–42, 266
surveillance, 28, 128, 136, 198n18, 216, 256
Survivor's Remorse (TV series), 199, 207, 208
symbolic capital, 224
symbolic citizenship, 268
symbolic imaginary, 268

talent, 235
Taliban, 272
Talley, André Leon, 267
Tamilian ethnic group, 57–59
taste: standards of, 225
Taylor, Paul C., 179, 186, 197n12
Tea Party, 50–51, 87, 89, 109
Tea Party Express, 90
Tea Party Nation, 90
Tea Party Patriots, 90
TechCrunch (website), 115
technolibertarian: ideology, 113; postracial project, 127. *See also* postracialism: technolibertarian
technology, 24, 26, 235; biogenetic, 34–35; digital, 25, 32–33; elites, 113–29; of power, 26, 31; of race, 11
Telecom Regulatory Authority, 123
Telenor Fashion Pakistan Week, 265, 269, 271, 276
television, 10, 15, 121, 131, 135–53, 199–219, 221–44; address, 172; broadcast,

199–206; codes, 148; commercials, 61–64; drama; genres; legacy; narratives; reality. *See also* genres: television; legacy TV; narratives: television; reality television; serial dramas
temporality, 25, 26
terrorism, 88–89, 97, 106, 271, 279
textile manufacturing, 268–71
Thakur, Varun, 68
Thicke, Robin, 191
third world, 57–58
This Old House (TV series), 232, 234
Thomas, Deborah A., 70
Thompson, M. S., 62
Thurston, Baratunde, 92, 112
Times of Bullshit, The (satirical website), 67
tolerance, 235; liberal, 72; racial, 25; of sexuality, 99
torch songs, 147
traditionalism, 275–77
transnational: capital, 165, 282; circulation, 264; corporations, 123
Transparent (TV series), 203
Trump, Donald, 29, 49, 54, 90, 105–6, 108, 125
Trumpism, 51, 112
Trump University, 106
truth, 160–62, 165, 173. *See also* authenticity
Tu, Thuy Linh Nguyen, 282
Tumblr, 214
2016 presidential election, 23
Twin Peaks (TV series), 207
Twitter, 214. *See also* black Twitter

UK Telegraph (newspaper), 272
Unicorn Booty (blog), 150
union busting, 222
unions, 43–45
United Kingdom, 54
United Nations Foundation, 194
universalism, 78
University of California, 41
Unsellables, The (TV series), 228
urbanization, 247

U.S. English, 95
US exceptionalism, 50

V (magazine), 254
Vats, Anjali, 255
veil, 264, 278, 279
Venice (Los Angeles neighborhood), 124
Vice (magazine), 265, 275
victimhood, 89, 100
Video Game High School (comedy series), 203
Vietnam War, 29
View Park, Los Angeles, 125
Viktor and Rolf (fashion company), 252, 263n2
Villarejo, Amy, 151
Vimeo, 208, 209
violence, 77, 193, 209; police, 23, 51, 188–89, 240; racialized, 186, 241; state, 3, 5, 13, 56, 99, 103; structural, 88; vigilante, 55
Virani, Faiza, 265
visibility, 138, 273; black, 188; controlled, 251; of difference, 250–51; gay, 200 (*see also* hypervisibility); global, 264–82; lesbian, 150–51; racial, 263
vision: as a technology of power, 245
visual discourse, 245
visual technology, 247
Vlogbrothers, 214
vocal: expression, 142; identification, 137; passing, 143; performance, 211; racialization, 141–44, 146–48; recognition, 136
vocality, 138
vocalization, 136–62; racialized, 138; transgender, 137
Vogue, 254
Vogue Italia, 246
Vogue Japan, 263
voice: disembodied, 151
Voice, The (reality TV series), 132, 135–51
voter suppression, 23
voting rights, 41
vox populi, 140

Waco Horror, 241
Wadhwa, Vivek, 115
Walker, Scott, 42
Walking Dead, The (TV series), 203
war on terror, 88. *See also* terrorism; violence: state
Warhol, Robyn, 214
Warner, Kristen, 203, 208
Warner Bros., 177
Wash, Howard, 241
Washington Post, 108, 109
Wazana Tompkins, Kyla, 253
We Are From L.A., 185
web TV, 200, 203, 205. *See also* new media; streaming media
welfare system, 52
Werbowy, Daria, 255
West, Allen, 50–51
West, Cornel, 186
West Wing (TV series), 207
WFLA-970, 96
white: backlash, 30; 93; normativity, 114; poverty, 92; rage, 54; supremacy, 25, 86, 99, 111–12, 208
white dispossession, 87
whiteness, 28, 41, 43, 51, 87, 94, 248, 256; as property, 48
white privilege, 7, 44, 48–49, 70, 89, 94–95, 248
Whitman, Walt, 138
Williams, Linda, 152, 214
Williams, Patricia, 250
Williams, Pharrell, 178–98
Williams, Raymond, 81
Williams, Serena, 247
Williamson, Kevin, 47, 91
Wilson, Eric, 249
Winant, Howard, 38
Winehouse, Amy, 141
Winfrey, Oprah, 246
Wintour, Anna, 267
Wire, The (TV series), 208
Wired (magazine), 125
Wisconsin, 42–43

Wissinger, Elizabeth, 282
Witch's Flight, The (Keeling), 207
World Trade Center, 88
World War I, 286
Wynter, Sylvia, 286

Xeeshan, Ali, 276, 278
xenophobia, 33, 112
XM satellite radio, 96

Y Combinator (YC), 120
YouTube, 51, 127, 194, 201, 203, 208, 214
Yúdice, George, 242

Zillow, 228
Zionism, 100
Zirin, Dave, 157, 176
Zuckerberg, Mark, 120